P9-DJV-147

Places Lost and Found

Places Lost and Found

Travel Essays from
the *Hudson Review*

Edited by
Ronald Koury

With an Introduction by
Tess Lewis

Syracuse University Press

Copyright © 2021 by Syracuse University Press
Syracuse, New York 13244-5290

All Rights Reserved

First Edition 2021
21 22 23 24 25 26   6 5 4 3 2 1

∞ The paper used in this publication meets the minimum requirements of the American
National Standard for Information Sciences—Permanence of Paper for Printed Library
Materials, ANSI Z39.48-1992.

For a listing of books published and distributed by Syracuse University Press,
visit https://press.syr.edu.

ISBN: 978-0-8156-3691-5 (hardcover)
      978-0-8156-1123-3 (paperback)
      978-0-8156-5503-9 (e-book)

Library of Congress Control Number: 2020937571

Manufactured in the United States of America

To Jane Bishop and Paula Volsky,
my ideal travel companions

Photograph by Jane Bishop

Ronald Koury, a graduate of Columbia College with a degree in English, joined the *Hudson Review* in 1981 and has been its managing editor since 1985. He has been a speechwriter for the delegation of the Permanent Mission of the Kingdom of Bhutan to the United Nations. He is the editor of another Syracuse University Press book: *Literary Awakenings: Personal Essays from the* Hudson Review (2017). He lives in New York.

Contents

Illustrations

Preface

RONALD KOURY

PAUL FUSSELL WROTE, "I am assuming that travel is now impossible and that tourism is all we have left." He also quoted Frederic Harrison approvingly: "We go abroad but we travel no longer." This book is a refutation—a whole series of refutations, in fact—of this absolutist claim. Travel, even if endangered, *is* still possible, and there are many who have a spirit of adventure and share that in their testimonies.

Not limited to travel essays, this book is about *place*, the built environment as well as the natural one, war and its aftermath, history/the past and its many meanings, the endurance of culture/civilization, resilience—all published in the *Hudson Review*. The book's trajectory, from war and revolution—Joseph Bennett's "A Cambodian Diary," 1971—to the experience of exile—A. E. Stallings's "Letter from Athens," 2018—takes in many tragedies of history. The opera house in Dresden, however, is a sign of hope. Destroyed in World War II, it was faithfully re-created in 1985, as an exact replica of the 1878 version. It is therefore a place at once "lost" and "found."

I had always wanted to do a project with Tess Lewis, so when she wrote the introduction and advised me on crucial aspects of the book, it was the fulfilment of a dream. She really "got it," and she has my eternal gratitude.

So many others deserve credit for making this book a reality. Special thanks to my colleagues at the *Hudson Review*, first of all Zach Wood, who did the lion's share of our in-house work, and who kept us on schedule. His professionalism made all the difference. Heartfelt gratitude, as always, to Paula Deitz, mentor and friend, whose advice and guidance were decisive. My appreciation to Eileen Talone, a master proofreader and fact-checker, the best there is. Thanks also to our outstanding interns Adam Young, Victoria Laboz, and Katherine V. Seger.

The experts at Syracuse University Press were a joy to work with. Foremost thanks to Deborah Manion, acquisitions editor, whose enthusiasm is an inspiration; she is the ideal editor. Thanks also to Mary Doyle; Mona Hamlin; Lynn Wilcox, whose cover design is so extraordinary; Kay Steinmetz, as always, with her high standards as editorial and production manager; Lisa Kuerbis; Kelly Balenske; Nora Luey; Meghan Cafarelli; and Victoria Lane. Last but not least, Marcia Hough's astute work as copyeditor saved me from many an embarrassment.

In a book of this nature, the photographs are a major asset. My warm thanks to Lars Kehrel, who provided the cover photo of the Semper Opera in Dresden, to Peter Aaron, for his stunning photos of Syria (sites which may no longer exist), to Susan Cohen, an old friend, who provided the exquisite photos of the gardens of Kyoto, to Nadina Christopoulou and Adrianne Kalfopoulou for their moving photos of the refugees in Athens, and to Jenny Erpenbeck for her charming elementary school class photo in East Berlin.

Deepest appreciation to Michael A. Boyd for his generosity in supporting this anthology.

Last but not least, my thanks to the essayists. May their work long endure!

Introduction

TESS LEWIS

"NO PLACE IS A PLACE until things that have happened in it are remembered in history, ballads, yarns, legends, or monuments," Wallace Stegner wrote in his 1988 essay "The Sense of Place." The essay, too, can play an instrumental role in defining both particular places and the idea of place. At its best, the essay is a flexible form, capacious and capricious, intensely personal and wide-ranging, able to focus on the immediate and the over-arching at the same time. It can enlist the gamut of elements that comprise the quality of attention necessary to apprehend and define a place: facts and imagination, memory and desire, experience and observation, historical record and subjectivity, speculation and study.

In the essays collected here, selected from six decades of the *Hudson Review*'s collective memory, the contributors train lenses with varied focal points on an array of places, some of them deeply layered with history and meaning (Kyoto, Phnom-Penh); others relatively unformed (America through Tocqueville's eyes, Alaska); some have disappeared (the Damascus and Aleppo of old, divided Berlin); others are all too familiar (the Mall of America). Reading this collection is much like looking through a kaleidoscope and seeing the tiles of memory, imagination, history, politics, and surprise shift and shift again, forming ever new patterns.

Ours is a transient species, both chronologically and geographically, yet the relative brevity of an individual life and the succession of generations held up as emblematic—X, Y, Z, then what?—can easily obscure this fact. The illusion that the world is as we know it is a seductive one. But sooner or later the march of history, whether one believes it straight or cyclical, confronts us with the hard fact that permanence is an exception, a state of affairs that has been tragically illustrated by the renewed flood tides of migration in our own decade. These essays play on the tension between durability and flux and remind us of the world's variety, variability, and complexity as well as the characteristics and experiences our planet's far-flung inhabitants have in common.

Reflecting on diversion in his *Pensées*, Blaise Pascal noted "There is one cause for all of man's unhappiness, which is that he does not know how to stay quietly in his room." Of course, a room can be a universe as Xavier de Maistre or, rather less happily, the hapless Oblomov have shown. But few are granted such a wealth or dearth of inner resources, and readers of this anthology will find themselves grateful for glimpses over the shoulders of these intrepid writers. In the epigraph, "Iran, Twenty Years Ago" (now forty), Dick Davis muses on the fact that what remains to him most vividly from his eight years in Iran and his visits to the fabled cities of Esfahan, Kashan, or Hamadan and the poets' towns of Shiraz and Nayshapour, are empty afternoons in dusty backstreets, "[A]s if that no epiphany, precisely, / Were the epiphany." This revelatory non-epiphany, however, is only possible against the backdrop of the bustling streets and crowded mosques. Davis quotes Hafez: "[To] know you must have gone along that way," and so it is that Davis knows and convinces us that those sunlit hours changed his life even if he does not precisely express how.

It is a delight and an education to "go along the way" with these *Hudson Review* writers even when the actual, geographic way leaves something to be desired. In his essay, "Making It Uglier to the Airport," Guy Davenport traces the corrosion of American cities as communities and the obsolescence of the pedestrian under the relentless pressure for return on capital, political venality, carelessness, and the plague of traffic. His observation that the "automobile is an insect that eats cities, and its parking lots are gangrene," has only become more fitting in the forty years since he wrote this essay. Still, he reflects that "the inner life of cities—voices, children, baths, meals—has not undergone any substantial change since Jericho, the oldest city still inhabited." What has changed, quite dramatically in some places, are the public lives and the strategies for navigating urban environments. The historical idea of the city as "the only known unit of civilization" is waning as modern cities grow, evolve, metastasize. Cities are increasingly becoming symbols of transience and adaptability.

"Acceleration in culture is demonic, and there ought to be periodic recesses to look back and reclaim elements that were ditched along the way," Davenport aptly warns. In one such recess, Robert S. Clark recounts a 1985 trip to Dresden in search both of that city's fabled musical and artistic past and for a glimpse of its grim present behind the Iron Curtain. Indeed, he finds more than a few traces of the fabled "Florence on the Elbe," yet he remains aware of the terrible price paid over the centuries. "Could ground so seared by battle, so stained by the blood of wars and revolutions and wanton killing for the pleasure of killing, where families slaughtered their own for carrying the wrong party card, and where a repressive foreign power now stations an army in part to guarantee that it will not happen again—could such ground succor those few human products that at least partially redeem it?" Clark asks and responds with "a tentative yes."

Some places have been able to resist or adapt to acceleration in culture. In "The Gardens of Kyoto in Summer," Charles W. Millard finds that the nuanced and highly formal aesthetics of garden design in Japan are not only an overwhelming source of beauty, but a point of stillness within the constant flux in nature and culture. He describes the structural and visual complexity of a number of gardens and persuasively argues that Japan's gardens "are the premier esthetic expression of traditional Japanese art" and "a concrete expression of what is most profound in the spirit and philosophy of Japan."

When Christian N. Desrosiers wrote his "Letter from Indonesia," eight years after the tsunami of 2004, he described a nation bearing visible scars from political and natural destruction and a society on edge from incursions by an al-Qaeda affiliate. An enormous freighter dragged four miles inland by the water becomes a grave marker for the families in the four houses crushed beneath it and "both a memorial to the past and an ominous suggestion for the future." In Desrosiers's eyes, it captures a split in the nation's psyche: "There had been no warning then; would there be one next time? This kind of memory mingled with fear was part of the psychology of the place." Will this tension spur or suffocate the evolution of the traditional arts as a central part of Indonesians' daily cultural life? One longs for more essays on this particular place.

This collection also offers a binocular view of Haiti in "Miroir Danjere," Madison Smartt Bell's incisive and expansive exploration of the Haitian cultural and music scenes complete with a brush with *vaudou* in the mid-nineties, and in Herbert Gold's account of his visit to Port-au-Prince a year after the 2010 earthquake, "Tremblement de Terre! The Gods Turned Their Faces Away." On a visit to Haiti to meet the politically outspoken "mizik rasin" (roots music) band Boukman Eksperyans, Bell enters the "hall of mirrors of the Haitian sense of time" and becomes more attuned to the strong presence of multiple pasts in present-day Haiti, the shifting and overlapping forces that come from its history of slavery, revolution, liberation, its years as a pariah state, and its blend of African, European, and indigenous religions. The Haitian identity is often inscrutable to foreigners, who frequently come to help or exploit with ideas cemented in place. Bell, however, manages to shed his "*I* full of anxious personal intention and become merely *one* who was sitting cross-legged on the floor." This openness and vulnerability leads him to insights into the country to which many foreign visitors are blind. He astutely observes that in Haiti, as in many other places in the developing world, it is "hard to forget that the First World can destroy a culture more thoroughly with money and good intentions than with knives and guns. Our great weakness in the First World, and particularly in the States, is that whenever we look in a mirror we always assume we are seeing ourselves." Gold is another devotee of Haiti who used to express his long fascination with the country by calling it "a tragedy you can dance to." But after the earthquake in January 2010, he finds such irony toward Haiti's place in the world is no longer possible. On a visit to Port-au-Prince six months after the earthquake, Gold was moved nearly to despair: "Suffering has shaken this brave people, with all their wit, talent, and charm into a darkness almost impossible to measure." He describes Port-au-Prince as "a crushed ant heap city, stepped on by the gods in their childish indifference to human pain." And yet, Gold's essay on devastation is not solely devastating. His six-decade engagement with Haiti makes him alert to the "shards of charm" and glimmers of hope that remain: children playing an ardent game of soccer in a space cleared of rubble, UNESCO's eagerly awaited libraries in the tent encampments, a dance school offering everything from hip-hop to classical ballet.

The demonic has accelerated in some places to a nearly incomprehensible pace. In parts of our world foreign powers are still supporting repressive regimes bent on destruction or playing cat and mouse with other geopolitical heavies. Indeed, a recent BBC report called Damascus a "Garden of Eden turned Hell," and Brooke Allen's 2010 "Letter from Damascus" is heartbreaking in its descriptions of her encounter with a vibrant, cultured society that bore no resemblance to the idea she had formed of Syria from reports in the mainstream media. The citizens of this culture have now been decimated or exiled, and the cultural treasures in Damascus and Aleppo Allen describes have been obliterated, no doubt beyond recovery.

In early 2016, the poet A. E. Stallings, a resident of Athens, agreed to run a poetry workshop for the Melissa Network for Migrant Women. At first, the participants were primarily economic migrants, among them an Albanian poet famous in her own country and Filipino women supporting families left behind by cleaning houses in Greece. The workshop soon expanded to include refugees, most of them from Syria and Afghanistan. Stallings began with "list poems," since "anybody can make a list; lists don't require syntax or grammar, yet tend to tell a narrative." These list poems offered the economic migrants as well as the refugees a feeling of being heard and fostered an emergent self-confidence. Stallings notes that quite a few things that surfaced in the list poems were forbidden under the Taliban, and the workshop became a source of reclamation. Donated cosmetics, as Stallings has written elsewhere, are important "humanizing elements in lives brutalized by problems of everyday living." For these women, lipstick or nail polish is "not a luxury or an oppressive necessity, it is subversive, a kind of liberation," a symbolic step closer to the Europe they are desperate to reach.

In her "Logbook," Stallings chronicles the arrivals of ships in port every week, every two days, every day, sometimes twice a day—the *Mykonos* with 688 refugees onboard, the *Ariadne* with 1,800, the *Blue Star Patmos* with 1,277, the *Blue Star 1* with 1,355, the *Ariadne* with 1,900, in February 2016, the *Diagoras* with 691 and five months later, the *Diagoras* again with an unknown number of refugees onboard—the Homeric Catalogue tolls incessantly. Arriving in a relentless flood, these exhausted travelers, desperate and destitute, disoriented and often dejected, maintain what glimmers of hope and normalcy they can even as Europe's borders begin to slam shut. Still, the sense of mortification begins to toll as inexorably as the names of ships bearing human cargo: the mortification of being a teenager and a refugee reduced to accepting handouts of exceedingly ugly or ill-fitting clothes, the mortification of parents unable to feed their children or themselves, the mortification felt by a young child accidentally damaging another child's drawing of his lost home, Stallings's own sense of mortification at not being able to do more to alleviate the suffering and at repeatedly causing unintentional offense. Emotions, too, define a place.

As a counterbalance to the centrifugal essays mentioned, we have a number of centripetal ones in this collection. These essays embark on voyages of discovery and recovery. Travel does, indeed, broaden the mind. But it can also sharpen it and make one more attuned to one's inner life and private self. The narrator of Ralph Ellison's *Invisible Man* says, "if you don't know where you are, you probably don't know who you are." An intent gaze outward reflects inward.

For years, in an almost daily ritual, Antonio Muñoz Molina, a Spaniard turned New Yorker, would run along a stretch of the path that extends from

Battery Park City to the George Washington Bridge. He had always assumed that he saw the river, but only when an injury slowed him to a walking pace did he begin truly to see it. But seeing—observing closely and carefully—is only part of the process. Perception, he explains in "The Lighthouse at the End of the Hudson," is not just physiological. "Seeing a bird or a tree and not knowing its name is not really seeing it." We also perceive the world through language or, as in his case, through several languages. And each language is a different filter for perception and apprehension. Muñoz Molina's walks become epistemological adventures, an education not just in what he sees before him, but how he sees it. Learning the Lenape name for the Hudson River, *Muhheakantuck* or "river that flows in two directions," alters the way he sees and experiences the river. "I didn't see the river before me but the abstract image of a river . . . It took walking there and transiently exiting the hermetic bottle of my obsessions to see that sometimes the river's stream goes backwards, pushed by sea currents." He becomes attuned to the history of the river as well as to its ever-changing present identities. The new quality of attention he brings to his surroundings—his urge "to see everything, to hear everything, to pay attention to everything"—makes him as receptive to the creations of the artist of the Hudson, a mysterious and reclusive sculptor of driftwood, as to the trash washed up on the river shore amidst the natural flotsam and jetsam. One afternoon he is so intently focused on the way the oblique light from the sun makes a piece of beam look exactly like a whale's head that he draws the attention of a passerby, who asks him what he is looking at. When he points out "its round eye almost under its hump, its lower jaw narrow and hanging," she gives a reply that could serve as the motto of this collection: "You can see some strange things when you look through somebody else's eyes."

Otherness is the central elusive, but inescapable trope in C. S. Giscombe's "Ontario Towns." Over the twenty years he lived in Upstate New York, Giscombe was drawn every summer by "the great colorless blankness of the map" of northern Ontario, and he would set out on his bicycle for the coast of Labrador. In part, he wanted to be moving through the wilderness, heading ever farther away from landscape he knew. In part, he was searching for traces of his great-uncle, one of the first and very few black men in the Ontario Northland. Through the long, arduous hours on his bicycle, he cannot shake the feeling that something unacknowledged is at stake. "Why," he asks himself, "was I always running to Canada when I had some time, crossing that border to touch the big otherness? Why does it feel so good to be alive with all thoughts of home intact so far from home itself?"

Giscombe's repeated journeys north are spatial dislocations of a journey inward. He comes to realize that he is retracing his family's progress from "south up this way,"

> indeed, it's an African-American archetype—culture occurs in land-scape—and here I am, the first generation born admittedly bourgeois across the Ohio River, still having the impulse, *north!*, though it's metaphor-ized into something other than the sane set of reasons-for-migration that belonged to those who went earlier.

There is no hermetic seal between our inner and outer landscapes. "[T]he landscape changes, and the changes make their demands, revise the experi-ence." Whatever our impulses, strengths, or weaknesses, our landscapes can be windows into ourselves.

There are intimate landscapes, too, that can be powerfully revealing. The Blue Grotto Bar and Grill on Lenox Avenue in Harlem was a semi-secret cave of camaraderie and indulgence the young Jacqueline W. Brown shared with her father. It was his escape from a fraught marriage and a per-vasive sense of failure, a place he could show off his young daughter to the "regulars." As much as she disapproved, Brown's mother did not explicitly forbid her husband from taking Jacqueline to the Blue Grotto. The Grotto and their shared sense of collaboration and complicity became an emo-tional center for Brown, an unstable but powerful grounding from which she could observe and learn from the adult world through a child's eyes, eyes which saw much more than she knew at the time.

At the opposite extreme, a few of these essays encompass vast land-scapes, looking out, like Wallace Stevens's anecdotal jar, over "the slovenly wilderness," which then sprawls around, "no longer wild." Clear as the jar on the hill, they offer a prism through which to apprehend a place and, while their authors try to avoid imposing preconceptions, they are none-theless subject to the observer effect. Alexis de Tocqueville's letters from America to his family in the early 1830s describe a New York City with not "a dome, a steeple or a large edifice in sight," that is nonetheless "a boil of physical and intellectual activity." Then a deputy royal prosecutor, Tocque-ville had journeyed to the United States to study American prisons for the purpose of prison reform in France. He is a sponge, as fascinated by the small-town life of Newport and the bustle of the somewhat larger cities as he is by the vast expanses of wilderness—from a church steeple he sees "trees as far as the eyes can reach swaying in the wind like waves of the sea"—and the impact of humans upon it and upon each other. Although everything he sees in this new land "bespeaks newness," he is clear-eyed enough to recognize the human stain spreading through slavery and the treatment of the Native Americans. "Just imagine," Tocqueville writes his dear Mama, "what queer byways the human mind can take when left to its own compass!" In "The Guiana Connection," John P. Sisk looks back from a vantage of more than four decades at his wartime assignment to British Guiana, where "the fabulousness of plain reality conspires against the effort to distinguish fable and history." He interweaves memories of his own "Guiana odyssey" with those of Sir Walter Ralegh in 1595, Evelyn Waugh in 1932, and the Reverend Jim Jones, "first and last messiah of The People's Temple, and an expert in bogus connections" in 1963 and again in 1976 accompanied by "his band of doomed utopians." Sisk engagingly traces ways in which searches for the "Shining, the Many Watered, the Bright Feathered City" in the mind and on the ground can end up in Hell on earth. Queer byways, indeed.

No one approaches a place, familiar or new, a blank slate. Memory and imagination, one's own experiences and the experiences of others inevitably, irresistibly define the places we inhabit and those we visit or merely dream of visiting. Some places brim with individual and shared memories, others are periodically wiped clean. Berlin is a particularly poignant palimpsest, a site of wars and horrors, of failed utopian aspirations and dreams of countercultural chic. Jenny Erpenbeck recalls her ordinary childhood in "ugly, purportedly gray" East Berlin in "Homesick for Sadness: A Childhood in Incompletion." She mourns the erasure of a landscape and a society in which she felt at home. "Seen from the outside, there may well have been something exotic about our Socialist reality, but we ourselves saw our lives as neither a wonder nor a horror—life was just ordinary life, and in this ordinariness we felt at home." She has a vivid memory of the ruins that surrounded her as a child. Whether the result of war or the "absurdities of city planning" due to the Wall, these ruins formed "landscapes in the middle of the city" that offered freedom and a lesson that could be learned "only by existing in this city and living this life—that the things you could grasp were not all there was." Indeed, the empty, ruined lots of East Berlin were places for questions, not answers, and became a powerful nurturer of her imaginative life.

> For me as a child, an empty space did not bear witness to a lack; instead it was a place that had either been abandoned or declared off-limits by the grown-ups and therefore, in my imagination, belonged entirely to me.

The ruins of the former East Berlin have been consumed by the city's appetite for developable property in prime locations. Erpenbeck is acutely aware that her memories of the GDR and East Berlin will disappear with her, and that before long others will walk over the same ground and remember a completely different city. But the process of reminiscing and testing memories against one's surroundings is an essential part of knowing ourselves, the world, and our place in it. "It takes you an entire lifetime to make sense of your own life. Layer after layer, knowledge piles up atop the past, making it look again and again like a brand-new past you have lived through without actually knowing it."

This brings us back to Stegner's observation on how a sense of place is formed through the accumulation of associations, how a place does not become a place until successive generations have been born, lived, and died in it, until natives and newcomers have come into contact with it and shaped it. "Some are born in their place, some find it, some realize after long searching that the place they left is the one they have been searching for. But whatever their relation to it, it is made a place only by slow accrual, like a coral reef." A place acquires a specific human gravity over time through experience, yes, but observation and description are just as crucial. The experiences and observations relayed in these essays, of which this introduction gives only a taste, form a diverse and intriguing coral reef that invites the reader to dip in and linger, to drift and plunge deeply, and return to land with a sharper sense of place.

Places Lost and Found

Iran, Twenty Years Ago

DICK DAVIS

1994

Each summer, working there, I'd set off for
The fabled cities—Esfahan, Kashan,
Or Hamadan, where Hephaestion died,
The poets' towns—Shiraz and Nayshapour,
Or sites now hardly more than villages
Lapped by the desert, Na'in or Ardestan . . .

Their names now mean a dusty backstreet somewhere
Empty and silent in the sunlight's glare,
A narrow way between the high mud walls—
The worn wood of the doors recessed in them
A talisman to conjure and withhold
The life and lives I never touched or knew.
Sometimes I'd hear a voice, a radio,
But mostly there was silence and my shadow
Until a turn would bring me back to people,
Thoroughfares and shops . . .

                    Why is it this that stays,
Those empty afternoons that never led
To anything but seemed their own reward
And are more vivid in my memory
Than mosques, bazaars, companionship, and all
The myriad details of an eight year sojourn;
As if that no epiphany, precisely,
Were the epiphany? As Hafez has it,

To know you must have gone along that way;
I know they changed my life forever but
I know too that I could not tell myself
—Much less another—what it was I saw,
Or learnt, or brought back from those sunlit hours.

Autumn 1998

A Cambodian Diary

JOSEPH BENNETT

AUGUST 1969

Approached from either side, the country is an oasis of quiet and contentment in the midst of an America-wracked area. To the west is the harsh cacophony of Bangkok with its screaming tires, its traffic jams, its blaring Miami hotels, its hordes of restless GIs on leave, surging the pavement, renting cars—Bangkok a vast jukebox, gimcrack plaster temples, miles of whores—military vehicles everywhere, the consciousness of American power cresting higher and higher, in a total aimlessness, seeking some vast combustion . . . the planes streaking overhead . . .

From this exercise in the dynamics of waste and the havoc of sensibility, the destruction of composure, of analysis, of stance, the unbalancing of poise—the Pentagon relaxing in Las Vegas, the astronauts on holiday . . . to drop down from the skies in a peaceful little airliner marked "Royal Air Cambodge," and to drop into that "royaume," is to awaken in green fields, beside murmuring brooks, from a nightmare, and to be told and to be comforted that it was all a dream, that it wasn't true; there can't be a Bangkok, there is no America; America is still tree-shaded, the first automobiles, perhaps, being tested on rural roads in Ohio—

To have an artist for a ruler is a novel experience for a nation, even a small one—we are familiar with Nero's histrionics, with Churchill's easel, with Eisenhower's palette; are aware that Hitler was once a sign painter—Mao a female impersonator on the classical stage—of all these Nero alone had ambitions of professional status, wept over his accomplishments—the others, a means of relaxation, or an earlier method of making a living—

His Highness Prince Norodom Sihanouk, uniting in his person the royal lines of Sisowath and Norodom, claiming descent from the Khmer

3

kings who fled from Angkor to escape the Siamese incursions of the fif-teenth century, the two royal families settling in the plain of the Mekong and then finally, prodded by the French, by this little stupa on a hillock by a bend where the Tonle Sap is joined to the all-flooding Mekong—hoping that history will ignore them—

The Siamese to the west the traditional enemy, gnawing, devouring, pushed in turn by the demonic Burmese warlords; to the east, the Chinese in their Annamese form, less disturbing, more debilitated—the royal fam-ilies, all descended from King Ang-Duong, were taken up and made much of by the French, who, using Siam as a neutral stretch of ground for their struggle with the British colonial power, in 1907 wrested the western part of the Khmer territories from the Siamese at the conference table.

This was ostentatiously restored to the Sisowaths and the Norodoms; and since it contained the ancient Khmer capital of Angkor, once again, after five hundred years, the Khmers had a consciousness of national and dynastic identity.

Sihanouk had an excellent education and returned to Cambodia a dev-otee of the beaux-arts.

His portrait greeted you in the small, relaxed airport buildings; there was an intimacy among the staff, a familial relationship—quiet, calm, happy, and effortless—papers were meant to be stamped, not pored over or puzzled out—the important thing was the smile—no American military were allowed in the country, no representative, or employee of American government, there was no embassy or legation—all believed in serenity, in a tenor of life, no struggle—a well-regulated kingdom.

From the secluded, sylvan, inactive (no American airlines) airport, a miniature bus set out alone on the lonely road.

Automobiles seemed to have been abolished; there were bicycles and carts, a few lorries; the trees arched overhead, leaves rustled—where were the clogged superhighways leading to the Bangkok airport? There seemed to be one or two factories, inactive, deserted, entrepots of brick and lime, and then, inside the town, broad Haussmann avenues, broken into four, sometimes six, paths for vehicles through the interconnecting parallel courses of trees.

The mound, with its stupa and plaque commemorating the return of Angkor to the Norodoms and Sisowaths, rose modestly from a great circle of verdure and trees at the end of one of these placid, trafficless promenades; an occasional cycle-carriage, a single horse-cart punctuated the view. The flowers rustled.

The royal families own a few Peugeots; there are a few more for the government; the Chinese (here Vietnamese) who own the shops and control trade do not own cars; they dwell, as Chinese do throughout the southeast, in the center of the bazaars, above their godowns and shops. They will hire a cycle-carriage, for a short distance, a shade carefully drawn above their heads, their soft and sensitive skins. It is not that Prince Sihanouk officially discourages cars; it is just that there aren't any of them; there is no reason for them; employees of the American government, no matter how innocuous their function, are prohibited from entering the country.

Note that the diplomats refrain from using their own vehicles, except for official functions. All respect the Prince's desire to keep his manicured garden capital free of exhaust gases and the snarl of the internal combustion engine; he wants the flowers to grow, the children to breathe. Vespas and motorbikes are his special dislike, sources of pollution and racket, immense harm in small packages, reminders of that Japan he found so disturbing on his sole visit. Composure is everything. No one is hurried. Can this be a dictatorship?

Japanese goods are not flaunted. Japanese transistors do not blare out rock music and news; there are no glitter-yarn shirts. There is not even any press. Once a week a French-language bulletin gives snippets of information from the world outside; many of these are encomiastic references to Peking or to that lovable, sweet-tempered, sugar-coated, toothsome sweetheart-of-the-masses, the former female impersonator of the Chinese classical theater, Mao Tse-tung, who has one of the tree-lined Champs-Élysées French avenues named after him: Rue de Mao Tse-tung.

Thus filtered out, the world recedes; what is happening in Cambodia? Prospects for the rice harvest, new outrages: another downed American plane on the Cambodian side of the border. There is the schedule of the dance rehearsals and recitals for the week at the Palace, where his mother the Queen (a Sisowath) resides. He is only a Prince. There are the plans of his niece, the prima ballerina of the Royal Ballet, for the next full-moon performances at Angkor. The Prince can occasionally be seen, rushing in his Peugeot, to the new multi-unit hotel he is building by the Quatre-Bras of the rivers, each individual unit in traditional gilded Cambodian, peaked temple-roof style. There will of course be no Muzak in the hotel; one or two musicians, traditionally garbed, will be on hand with padded sticks to strike odd tones from a set of gongs duplicating those in his mother's palace.

No Western radio music is allowed: the sole radio station for the country strikes these same gongs at all times of day, interspersed with temptress-voiced singsongs of ancient Cambodian folk tales couched in the phraseology of the former Khmer court, kings strutting on high terraces of Angkor temples; and the soft, effortless music that accompanies the universal village steps of the Ram Vong, where the couples circle, shuffling, but never touch.

There is no news, not even of Mao Tse-tung, who is expected to be contented with his Avenue and behave as a properly propitiated demon. The Prince, whose mother's father preceded him as King, wants nothing discordant. He supervises the gilding of each temple-peaked point on the roofs of his hotel. He did not build his beautiful capital to be corroded and soiled by the fumes of the internal combustion engine, its umbrella-shielded orange monks to be stricken at their meditations and their strolling by its crackle. The Chinese embassy, prudently, grateful for its Mao-avenue, walks or uses cycle-carriages; the Chinese have no individual cars.

There are few jails in Cambodia, laid to the fact that the French built no schools; thus the Khmers did not learn enough to want something enough (a motor, a radio) to steal it; it is a rice-exporting country, thus everyone has more than enough to eat; the Chinese (Vietnamese) do all the storekeeping (how degrading, how tedious, impossible to keep standing at it) chores, what is there to buy (no Japanese watches are allowed in), therefore why steal money from the Chinese (no Khmers have money) since they have nothing in their stores for you to buy with the money? A few kerosene lamps, and stoves, textiles from France—

Banned is the Seiko, the thick, heavy day-and-date automatic watch; banned also is the instruction of the Japanese martial arts: no karate, no judo. The youngsters grow up knowing only a little Thai-style kickboxing. There are no firearms—the so-called army, productive of generals of the Sisowath and Norodom families, can scarcely get a bullet inside its guns. Unofficially the dictator prefers the "troops"—a gang of harmless, wandering peasants—to exercise with blanks.

Sometimes prisoners forget to leave jail, form an attachment to the cook; or jailers forget to watch them, leaving the door open. They wander out to their families, have another baby, wander back at mealtimes.

Gauloises are preferred, but American cigarettes trickle in through the borders. A whole village will suddenly sport GI green gear, sturdy new expensive clothing, captured by the Viet Cong or pried loose from PX stores. In the center of the riverbank monumental avenue, a pile of crashed American plane-fuselage junk, and tank-junk, and artillery-junk, growing daily, makes an impressive sight for the Chinese embassy to comment upon and write to Mao about; Cambodia suffering under the heel of the American oppressor.

Mao is his problem, Sihanouk is after all a monarch; Mao was not very sympathetic to the survivors of the Ch'ing dynasty; its senior member, the last of the Manchus, washes floors in Shanghai and makes public confessions; the family of Bao Dai, "Empereur d'Annam," are proscribed as enemies of the revolution. Sihanouk waves his Gauloises. He wears excellently tailored suits.

Each year the Queen comes to life with the Reversal of the Waters. This is when Mother has her moment. Kept in storage the rest of the time (someone, alive and real, has to be used for living in the palace), smiling at dance recitals, encouraging all her great-nieces to take up ballet, she seems to have been made into the Spirit of the Mekong. During the rainy season, the south-flooding Mekong thrusts its waters northward up into the channel of the Tonle Sap, swelling its lake to triple the normal size. Regulated by the full moon at the end of October and the beginning of November, the Mekong, when the Queen speaks to it, bobbling on Her Floating House, reverses itself and begins to flow southward again, back down the Tonle Sap, in its normal direction. The waters have subsided, the rains have ended. The Quatre-Bras, where this hydraulic drama takes place, is before her palace, and she is annually hoisted out on her great gilt throne and placed on Her Floating House, to remain there until the water is duly returning.

Her portrait is everywhere, cross-ankled on that gilded throne. Can one imagine Stalin's mother, or Hitler's, or Franco's, in every tobacco shop, smiling, and once a year in charge of the local equivalent of May Day?

Prince Sihanouk's wife is an actress; the film festival, organized by Sihanouk and with himself on the panel of judges, has awarded the prize to films produced and directed by His Highness and starring his Princess Monique, in each year of its two-year existence.

There are the "auberges royales," architectural (and heavily traditionalist) caprices of his younger days; an attempt has been made to make them into hotels. One, at Siem Reap, is Rockefeller Center modern in feeling, with rooms modeled on that of an airport of the 1930s; the Marine Air Terminal at La Guardia gives an idea of what was in mind. On the treeless heights of Bokor, 3,200 feet above the sea, is a hewn-stone, rustic, iron grillwork villa, a tropical ski lodge two thousand miles from the nearest snow. No one ever seems to have stayed there, and now the traveler is forced to sleep in a few grisly rooms above a lugubrious casino where the Chinese shopkeepers of Phnom-Penh eat greasy Chinese food and play at dice and roulette. But at Kep (charming, French colonial, reminiscent of a Biscay summer resort) the bungalows use as their restaurant a fine, open, airy colonnaded pavilion, in

Beaux-Arts style, perfectly suited to the view, terrain landscaped all the way to the sea.

Bungalows, bungalows, bungalows—before his obsession with individual, gilded, Cambodian peaked-roof temples for tourists, the Prince felt they should have bungalows, not individual (except at Kep) but connected, highly utilitarian, heavily plumbed, disturbingly and thrashingly air-conditioned. When he realized that he had a gold mine at Angkor (accompanying the pale, fragile nun, renouncer of the world, tragedy-afflicted Mrs. Onassis), he decided he could make them pay for his personal taste as well; they would sleep on Cambodian temple-styled beds if he so wished. There was no reason too why tourists should not enjoy Sihanouk-made films; one of these was shown every night at Angkor just before the Prince's niece began her ballet across the way; another was of the ballet itself.

The Phnom-Penh museum is room after room of carefully labeled sculptures; detailed monographs of each section of the collection come off the press. Nobly housed in a red palace in purest peaked-roof style, the museum is allowed no electricity; all must be seen naturally. There are no guards, no watchers, no latrines; a lone typewriter clicks sporadically in some research office far off to the side. Like the Cairo museum (untouched for political reasons), the Phnom-Penh museum shows what can be done to instruct the seeker after knowledge when there are no glamorously high-paid theatrical, narcissistic personalities constantly shaking it up, issuing ear-sets, suppressing detailed historical labelings, and keeping the bulk of the collections in the basement so that the selected items can be mounted singly as if for open-air elephant-assisted performances of grand opera. The curator actually did spend his time adding items to the collection and lining them up side by side; he never had a "happening" in his museum; there is not even a toilet, much less a tearoom.

The minibus threading the vast, empty avenues, with its eye on the spire of the stupa, ducked in among the trees; an Australian or two got out; we were at the hotel, a heavy, outflung construction of French colonial days, at one time very stately quarters for senior French military officers. Here a shallow, warm swimming pool was set down in the back with several couples of sophisticated Parisian young moderns, slipping back and forth between argots; they were not tourists, they had no interest in archaeology. Plop! one dives into the pool, nearly breaking his nose on the bottom, which is five feet at most; the others cheer derisively. They are always there during the hot hours.

The sun slants down over the Phnom; the trees rustle, the flowers spar-kle—one glides down the vast avenue, as down the arcades of a forest, noiseless, around the darkening mound with its stupa, admiring the bright terra-cottas with which the French commemorated the return of Angkor to the Norodoms and Sisowaths—one can climb that stupa of the Phnom, through a side garden, and then descend the eastern approach, with its Angkor naga serpents carved in stone on the rails, and on past an ornate, embowered royal building to the riverfront. There is a vast bridge, too far to the north to be of use to anyone, leading nowhere, another monument to the Prince, built with the hopeful funds of some friendly, rich power.

There is the Independence Monument, one of the *meru* towers of Ang-kor Wat placed atop the Arc de Triomphe, on Norodom Sihanouk Avenue, next to the Norodom Sihanouk museum; this last filled exclusively with gifts made to the Chief of State, stamp collections, autographed photos.

But the greatest monument to the Prince's diplomacy was Sihanoukville, with its highway, built with $35,000,000 in American funds. The Cardamom chain cuts off Phnom-Penh, a river port, from the sea. Sihanoukville pro-vided an artificial harbor, capable of unloading four modest-sized freight-ers at once. The first freighters to berth at the port were not US, but Mao Chinese. As soon as he had the key to the port in his pocket, the ungrate-ful Prince expelled the American Ambassador, closed the Embassy, and in effect diverted the port and its 135-mile highway to the purpose of supplying the Viet Cong with arms. The four small ships were always unloading there, brimful of tanks and guns, while others waited their turn offshore. The flags tended to be British, though the supplies came from Canton and Shanghai and Odessa; another problem for the beleaguered Washingtonians.

How did Sihanouk survive? His problem was Mao: as helpless a plaything in Mao's paws as Hong Kong or Macao, he had to prove the usefulness of his independence to the ex-theatrical transvestite. What was the point of tying up divisions of Hanoi troops to hold the country down (the Khmers hate the Annamese-Vietnamese almost as much as they hate the Siamese) when the grateful and obliging Prince would get the port built at US expense and keep it free and open for the flood of supplies to reach the Viet Cong effort-lessly and safely? As the Prince pointed out in Peking and Hanoi, if they took over his country, the Americans would quickly bomb into uselessness the vulnerable artificial port, open on a flat peninsula, and the deeply rock-cut highway. The compromise was arrived at: the supplies flowed through the port and the highway to the east to the Viet Cong; and the rest of the country remained free, adoring their Samdech for so cleverly preserving them. For their part, the Viet Cong remained strictly within the boundaries of the territory assigned them in the east and did not engage in political activity.

Wise also, the Prince, in not creating an army, merely a few thousand stumbling, well-fed peasants to provide an excuse for distributing generalships to the royal houses. Had he established a military force, Mao would have moved, for the possibility of its use by the Americans would then become a factor. By this means, a miraculous set of external political circumstances acted to confirm the already non-militant nature of the Khmers and make their country one as if shaded by an orange parasol from the destructive turmoil and violence of the American satellites to the west and east. Thus not even karate or judo. Thus the pile of American military junk, constantly being added to, on the riverbank boulevard. Especially favored were the tailpieces of American planes, with resplendently repainted USAF markings, and helicopter rotor vanes, khaki-green. This was to convince the nodding and approving, hand-rubbing and contented Mao diplomats that all was well, that the dutiful Khmers were seizing the naughty American war-folk who strayed over.

As well, the happy Khmers were preserved from contact with non-uniformed employees of the US Government, saved from having a US Embassy gassing away its motor fumes and portentous bumptious pettifoggery, its Congressmen and libraries, its photos of astronauts, its masters of the democratic style of social greeting. Mao would have become suspicious and closed in. Not even an agriculture expert, a public health official, or a cultural lecturer could get past the barrier. The Khmer tradition was enforced and purified by the shadow of Mao and Hanoi. French, too, remained the language.

The whores, lovely slit-skirt Chinese (never Khmer) butterflies, featuring black silk and skins whitened with powder, long black hair, confined themselves discreetly to the ambience of the Café de Paris and the Venise—they were luxury whores, tinkling in their French, and witty and gentle and regulated. They were not allowed to have drinks; they did not appear on the streets, swaying blaring transistor radios (Bangkok, Saigon); they were visible only at night. A lower echelon, equally well regulated, fluttered to nest in the evening in the two floating restaurants on the river, much favored by the Australian do-gooders and helpers, who were unused to such simplicity and refinement. Arrangements were subtle, discreet, and sufficiently clandestine; nothing could be noticed. A smile, the departure of a couple to a villa distant, dimly lit among trees.

The Australians on these aid-to-Cambodia (dams, health, electricity, seeds) missions were overwhelmed; most had never seen Europe; most had been married young to mates selected for health, strength, and good character. They began to disguise the dates of their home leaves; the place to spend one's home leave was in a villa; none of these charming creatures would think of being exposed to the glaring public entranceway of the hotel, though there were bungalows—

The hotel, in its bulk, featuring large and solid suites that had been the quarters of the military French, had in all twenty flimsy, jerry-built bungalows thickly massed flank-to-flank in the area of that warm pool, with its expensive and uninspired restaurant (the sophisticated Parisians used it only for breakfast and sandwiches). I learned which of the two exits (east-west) was the most private, which bungalows had the best furniture, which the most rooms. Night-butterflies could occasionally be seen, faces muffled and veiled, only the white skin, or a jewel in the hair, or a flower visible.

These lovely creatures disdained any Australian who drank, who smoked, or who raised his voice. Quickly the Australians learned to emulate the young poolside sophisticated Parisians, and at night the twittering of the lovely spidery creatures in and out of all twenty bungalows was as natural and delightful a sight as the nocturnal egress of night-flying birds from their daytime homes inside the vast four-faced ruins of Angkor. They would not enter automobiles, whether to arrive or leave, too public—the noise of motors, the glare of lights, the clack of doors—the noise of the starter. The carriages waited in files, silently. These ladies were skilled and took pride in their professional accomplishments, insisted upon high health standards; the portrait of our Samdech which each bungalow contained over its dresser looked down on extraordinary scenes when successful, middle-aged high-income Australian officials became debutants in acts so far unknown in the temperate Antipodes.

The carriage glides along the riverbank, and it is sunset. Where in other Asian countries most government employees are set at desks, to confound and confuse, here the bureaucrats seem to have been liberated at their various salary levels, so that all can become gardeners—literally, it is true, the Government offices (my constant one: Ministère de Sécurité Nationale) are almost understaffed. The royal families are supposed to become generals, not bureaucrats. So this vast sea of flowers undulates along the riverbank after one leaves the *Port des Bateaux*—there is a "Port de Phnom-Penh": it handles goods coming down the Mekong from Kratie and the north and river steamers.

The long and graceful lines of the Queen's moderately sized palace rise up in the dark; people are walking in small groups along the river; there is not a motor in sight to the south or the north along this huge planted esplanade. . . .

But there is a Chinese (Vietnamese) population as well—all those shops are owned and manned; the retail, the wholesale trade of the country is in their hands. To satisfy them, well out of the Queen's angle of view to the south, the Casino pulsates with light, surrounded by food stalls. Inside the same Chinese faces pore over the crushingly lighted gambling tables as in Bangkok and Saigon, Singapore and Hong Kong; this is the only recreation the Chinese allows himself, a holiday of the abacus, an amusement based on calculation; never sports or physical exercise. Their lusts are short and sharp, like the opening and clicking of a shutter camera, behind their lensed glasses, and they are lusts of money, briefly revealed. No Khmer faces (broad foreheads, wide cheekbones) are in the Casino—the Khmers are too poor; they are mainly dancers and flute players, gong ringers; they don't like bright lights, only faint single flame lamps flickering out of doors reflect their faces, listening to soft dissonances. The Chinese inside the Casino move like automatons, greeting, calculating each other, spotlessly clean; with clothing carefully pressed and creased; no dust on their shoes, for they will not walk, even more than a hundred feet outside their shops.

In Phnom-Penh as the river turns black the wind seems to push you forward; the horns of the Queen's prang-roofed palace now stand out against the dry stars; star-fields appear. A Chinese temple near the foot of the monumental bridge goes bang-out with explosions and rockets, crackers and sparklers; the staid merchants alight from their carriages; ignite their incense sticks; rotate their wheels; revere their ancestors. The temple yard mills with Khmer poor, ragged and bright; there seems no reason not to go around the river parks all night. Next day in the town there are sidewalk cafes everywhere; with the round tables of Paris; tea, coffee, the pressed citron, in the busiest quarters, by the markets; one watches the life; there is great sweetness in the air.

A long Peugeot station wagon, with the customary eleven passengers, lumbers beside the Tonle Sap River for the five hours' run to Siem Reap; one eats dried lotus heads at the ferry; none of the villages on the route have been disturbed or harmed. Crossing at last a carved stone snake-balustraded bridge built by the monarch of the Bayon and Angkor Thom, one enters the Angkor country. The whirr of the Prince's air conditioners grips one in its deep freeze; the bungalows are utilitarian luxury and situated in the high silk-cotton trees. A dining room clatters with the voices of all Europe, seen from the outside.

I stumble out in the dark. There are no lights across the road. There is a wide, vast, endless moat. A raised causeway leads across it. This is very long. Then there are difficult steps up onto a stone porch.

On the other side, through the stone porch, one stumbles downward. All light from the road has been cut off by the great closed length of the porch. I blunder ahead. An endless causeway leads on and on, snakes wriggling in stone as balustrades to either side; occasionally, seven heads, arranged fan-shaped, arise to ornament it. Dim small buildings, like islands, rise up from the empty lakes to either side. Far off, high up, is a tiny light, flickering, yellowish in the darkness. Stars punctuate.

A corner of the red rising moon stares out from the shoulder of the black hill ahead. I am walking down the full distance of the causeway, and the moon moves out further and further to the right; it is free of the hilltop and strong, vastly distant. I fall under the shadow of a long high portico stretching to either side. I am up against some steps, hard and high, uneven and treacherous. Under the portico, small courts to either side, smudged with starlight, heavily galleried with stone. Up and up. Another court, squeezed together, short, obliterated by the huge mass overhanging it, small raised buildings to either side.

The final stairs hit your nose, colossal, meant for a race of gods.

With the four other high ghostly towers at the corners of the topmost court, the central tower overhangs the earth like a celestial plane. It is a surface bearing the gods, and their servants, the kings, above all that level of unlighted, intersected rice fields.

The courts at the top begin to form shadows in the moonlight. The cusps ascending the towers begin to take form. In the rice fields the heads of sheaves rise and stir. The sandstone, deeply carved, resists the moonlight. The core of this monument is sand, held in, incompressible, by stone embankments and blocks. If the sand spreads out at the base, the roofs, the cloud city, will collapse.

Now down the long descending galleries and steps, the passages, the stairs meant for giants. The public was barred; the rice cultivators worshipping the kings above. The Khmer deities spoke in elevated tones, addressing each other across vast stages, referring in elaborate circumlocutions only to the most dry and uplifting subjects: narrations of their ancestry from the gods; of the assistance of Krishna in battle; of their hurling axes, their chariots, their horses, their fire processions. On these platforms, amid such elocutions, they moved beneath ceremonial parasols, held by highly placed priestly relatives.

It was a short trip, swayed over by long-handled, bending fans, from temple to wooden palace and palace to temple again.

The delicate, airy light buildings of their residence were set up on piles, among the cool, high trees, surrounding ornamental lakes, tiered with water plants and fish carven in stone.

The moon is rising outside. It leads away, along the long pool, the shape of Angkor Wat across the water receding huge and hollow with gray detail, defined in the glare. It leads along the road into the forest. There is a high mound, touched by moonlight, to the left.

Across an immense moat, huge solid walls rise, endless in the distance. It is Angkor Thom, an enormous, moon-struck city. The moon seems to have heat, beating down on this empty metropolis, this cubic jungle fortress.

The great gate looms; above its corbel the front face is crowned with a high, receding tower. The east and west faces appear in sharp profile of nose and eyes and lips. The Bodhisattva of the current cycle, Avalokiteshvara, extends the protection of his gaze. His faces are everywhere the same; the faces too of the broad-browed, flat-cheeked Khmer peasants of the region. Elephants feed on stone lotuses on each side of the gate, their sculptured trunks dipping low to sway over this celestial fodder.

The long central roadway leads forward, inside the walls, under the archway of the high trees.

The grayishness, the whitishness ahead takes on a slight blur, a slight complication; there is a subtle darkness within the whiteness. It is a low mass, rising above the trees, with a tower or cone, all whitish-gray, scarcely distinguishable in the white haze which drowns all contours.

Dimly the faces begin to appear, lower down. The building is long, with a central tower; the smaller towers sprout with faces seeing in all four directions. It is Avalokiteshvara, guarding the city, at its heart. Axes radiate to the four walls and the five gates.

This cathedral of protection is tied to the human; the preservative, the paternal, are sought by this Buddhist monument. These gentle faces of death offer recourse, soundlessly from their stone lips. Annulling reassurances, deadening of pain; a vast, multiple, gray-stone anesthesis.

A mile to the east, at the gate of the dead, the same faces stare out. Those who go out of the city carried on pairs of shoulders are reassured, as they are burnt in the jungle; their smoke arising as the scent of perfume to the blank lips. To lose identity beneath the devouring horizontal gaze.

Here at the Bayon we are at the heart of the realm of the weeping king, Jayavarman, and his ameliorating four-faced god; it is very late, almost at the end of empire. In the reliefs below, the King destroys the fleets and armies of the Chams; but above, the stone faces of Avalokiteshvara proclaim: it is vain, it is vain.

On the moon-viewing platforms one wanders at the base of the face-studded thick spires. Black lichens cover plump noses, thick lips, staring out smiling into a jungle which steams with moonlight. The trees, with dry, immobile leaves, rise high around the clearing. One looks out at the bright, foaming jungle, listening for the call of a bird, which does not come. The cold black stone lips rise, waiting to be kissed, in the flashing sky.

Jayavarman, who made this, sits softly in the Phnom-Penh museum, late Egyptian, smiling, Saite, of the period of the delta invasions. His platform was not meant for day viewing. The trees crackle, soundlessly, in the light; their hazy density, million-leaved, shimmers like dry snow.

Returning, one sees Angkor Wat arise from its sea, black, blocking out the sky. The superhuman dimension crushes, of this Hindu archaeological skyscraper. Angkor Wat never wholly returned to the jungle; monks kept coming, bringing Buddha statues. The peasants went to its summit in times of peril.

In the Phnom-Penh museum, the statue of Lokeshvara, that looked out from the Gate of the Dead to the smoke of the burning places, concentrates inward, savoring the thoughts of polarized divinity. Along with the statue of Jayavarman, these carvings were taken erect, square-shouldered, through the moonlit jungle, on a journey over roads and lakes, to sit in the wooden, prang-roofed palace, in a quiet, somnolent city of slow vehicles and wide parks. The statues, accustomed to gaze over the jungle, over those wisps of smoke, dominate the museum, burgeoning with suppressed moonlight; their silence becomes overpowering.

Back at the foot of Angkor Wat, troubled by the gigantesque, the tiny lights of the Prince's bungalows twinkle. In a few hours I am back out again, in the trees, prepared for heat. The pedals and chain of my bicycle creak; the trees are monotonous, the road vibrates with heat. At last, the road swings to the left, past ruined towers of brick, and I approach the sheet of water of Sras Srang, terraced and lion-surmounted, serpent-railed.

A woman sits across the road from the long side of the lake, selling food and tea; behind her stretching back from the road is a group of houses. They are wooden, raised on stilts, covered with palm thatch; sleeping mats of coco-nut straw; two wooden chairs, the best of which is permanently occupied by the mother of the food vendor, corpulent, nodding, inarticulate. Cooking is done on the ground below; sanitation is among the trees. The grandmother is house owner and owner of their small strip of rice field. The grandfather and father are dead; the house is a matriarchy; the work of the rice field is done by a grown grandson and the mother and sisters; this is the heart of the dry season; there is no work to do.

I want to shift from the Prince's bungalows with their clatter of languages. The Japanese guests wear kimonos and bathe, interminably, in their rooms. They are not popular, in spite of their heavy expenditure and full use of every rentable auxiliary, their constant requirement for guides. The occupation was harshly severe, and since the Japanese were committed to their Thai allies, the Khmers were identified as an inferior, subject race. The Japanese, before Pearl Harbor, in March 1941, awarded the western part of Cambodia to their Siamese allies; and in 1942, all of Laos; the Siamese, who had been driven out in 1907, once again occupied Angkor. In 1907, the Khmers tore down the citadel which the Siamese built in the center of Siem Reap with stones taken from the staircases of the Phnom Bakheng, a ninth-century temple; in 1941 they saw the Siamese return in full concert with their Japanese allies. Following this, the Japanese awarded Thailand the four northern states of Malaysia and the two eastern Shan states of Burma.

Japan is no longer the Thai military ally; instead, Thailand has the United States in its place; together, the two partners work at the grand design of pacifying Indo-China. Cambodia, squeezed between the twin American outposts of Bangkok and Saigon, sees the Japanese and the Thais, who raped it in World War II, now the favored pets of American power; it sees the Japanese returning, not as warlords to set them at forced labor in construction gangs in the death-jungles of West Thailand (the Burma railway) and Tongking (the Red River above Hanoi), but as luxurious lords of creation who live in the fine hotels surrounded by expensive appliances and treated with deference by the swarms of servitors of the tourist industry.

Of all the Asian national groups, only the Thais were able to profit from the full favor and protection of their Japanese allies, followed by heavy subsidization from America. Switching away from Japan just in time in 1945; since 1952, convincing Washington that the Korean problem was being duplicated in Hanoi, they have made Thailand the funnel for pouring untold quantities of money into the Indo-China pacification. The corrupt and heavy-handed military dictatorship in Thailand is skilled in only one accomplishment: extracting money from its frightened, gargantuan, lavish, and helpless ally in Washington. Individual fortunes among the generals, in Switzerland, vary from twenty to a hundred million dollars. When games of dominoes are mentioned, it is Bangkok that is meant that might fall.

At Sras Srang the family of Oeur Sam Bath shelters me. Excursions spring up: to the great lake, with its fishponds and stilt villages; to the vastness of the northern jungle; to a pool from which arises an immense lotus of stone and a flying horse to whom cling those it saves; this is Avalokiteshvara. Sunsets are followed by dinner in Siem Reap as the moon gets older and more feeble; the Apsara restaurant turns out to be the place where the good cooking is; small, an exterior blackboard, and giant winged cockroaches, like bullets, which roar directly into your mouth and eyes, falling on your plate. I return to the great monuments later at night; then it becomes necessary to view them in starlight, and a new, more delicate effervescence is detected.

More and more I come to live in the ruins, watching the change of light, becoming a troglodyte. At Ta Prohm the four faces have umbrellas . . . of trees sprouting above their heads; slender tendrils of vines attach themselves with tiny adhesive feelers, shooting across lintels and sticking there; then digging in deeper and deeper, etching their lines through the stone balustrades of the windows, wearing themselves through the noses and chins and tiara-headdresses of Apsara maidens. Stones are lifted and cracked off their bases; the green gloom turns to black. Then to walk back without a cycle to my stilt-house from the fading, inking, undersea labyrinth, along a road shared by a shepherd of thin brown ducks (controlled by a long slender wand, with a rag at its end, held by an infant of five)—to walk beside the water-sheet, gazed at by tall-forelegged lions, of Sras Srang—to eat rice at the roadside stand—not to go into the leisurely, Frenchified rhythm of dances and restaurant at Siem Reap—this is to find the even level of peasant life.

Then to sit by the lions of Sras Srang and watch the stars press their light on that slowly shrinking basin, the grandeur of the day forgotten, the gods put to sleep without a moon, gazing alone into their jungle through the veil of vines and branches—

A return to Phnom-Penh; an exploration of the west bank of the river. Even though it is the dry season, the Mekong is full and miles wide. In the villages, the idleness of the dry season; the only motor sound is an occasional chug as an antiquated, dwarfed river steamer struggles up the giant flow of the Mekong . . . time stops, the trees grow. The population is thinly scattered, even here so close to the capital; Phnom-Penh sits easily in this hinterland;

there is no harsh change between city and country; the green of the forests and the rice fields becomes the green of the parks and the gardens. . . .

❧

Approached from the other side, it seems that this country is enfolded in a crystal mountain, far apart from the convulsions and unnatural tremors, like a pool of slowly boiling volcanic mud, of its neighbor to the east. In the central avenue before the Parliament, the National Assembly, rises the newly erected symbol of Saigon: two immense, roughly clad cement soldiers, full of reinforcing iron, an expression of delight on their features; helmets askew, their shoulders twist and the bodies strain their haunches above monstrous squat legs to thrust an imaginary bayonet into the entrails of thin air; the whole is a movie-palace come-on for the exhibition of a sadistic film.

All these America-created, America-obsessed cities, Tokyo, Seoul, Taipei, Bangkok, Saigon, have in common a smog that strangles and burns the lungs, product of the exhaustion of so many motors into a naturally damp, sluggish atmosphere, sitting inland in bowls where air can scarcely arrive. In Taipei, Seoul, and Saigon the filth piles up among the flashing new motors, crawling atop each other's backs, newly imported from Japan; sewage or water supply is scarcely a consideration. At the trail's end lie Las Vegas and Miami, where they all want to go when they die, living off money piled up in Switzerland.

One longs for the austerity of a Marx or an Engels, even of a Lenin; one realizes why Marx and Engels have lost; everywhere the peoples move toward electronically amplified sound, join in the giant rhythm of the motors, of speed, of elevators, the wild spurt of the demons which are exclusively Western, and for which the principles of the Revolution, and its blood, are meaningless. The communal, sharing, austere balancing of society seems ridiculous and strangling; the deferring of individual aims to a mass purpose, intolerable. In India at the temples of Puri and Konarak I am surrounded by a crowd of young Russians; they want to know about Japan, about its department stores, its escalators, its hairdressers; its motors and Hondas and Yamahas and tape recorders, its video screens and electronic doors. Because of my nationality, I am an ambassador of Las Vegas and Miami, the capitals of the future. The children have been let out of the libraries, sterile with political theory, and the factories, heavy with production of machine tools, let away from the gaze of the portraits of Lenin, to a kaleidoscope of neon and flesh and movement that must be at random, without purpose, the exhaustion of the day. There are no more enemies; there are no more classes; there is one more day. One admires the purposefulness and the focusing upon aims of the revolutionary leaders. Now, stranded by history, they are Easter Island heads above the treeless grass, their black granite heads and monumental beards (the only heritage they have left the young) are as effective a world force today as say, the teachings of Matthew Arnold or Thomas Carlyle.

Their greatness lay not in their teachings, which are probably as much rubbish as Las Vegas and Miami proclaim them to be, but in their ability to hypnotize whole populations, however briefly, into the illusion that there is such a thing as communal purpose and a justification for the organization of society. Like the experiment of Cromwell and the Roundheads, the interlude between cutting off the head of the king and the Restoration of the monarchy was very brief. The Puritanism of the great revolutionary leaders has not survived their death; Mao's hysterical and irrational gyration is motivated by his realization that he is an anachronism, an Easter Island head left stranded by the tide. The Bible and the Handbook of Kapital alike have been forgotten.

The extraordinary thing was that, like the monsters and the miracles of the Old Testament, the text of Marx could be believed at all, so contrary is it to human nature, so demanding, so disciplining, meant for a society of martyrs and ascetics. That a doctrine of such superhuman austerity could be accepted as the formal article of belief for a large section of the world's population is one of the riddles of history, like the jihads of the Muslims, the Crusades, the diaspora of the Israelites, all examples of the power of the Book. The rise and fall of the book of Marx is another example of the power of faith to cause, for short periods of time, the masses to act contrary to their natures, their expectations, their comforts, and their amusements. The next generation finds itself deceived. That Las Vegas was to be the alternative to *Das Kapital* Marx could never have dreamed; too Puritanical and too obsessed; Sodom and Gomorrah he was aware of, but that problem had been solved, in another system. Their triumph over the theories of this bearded prophet was as the triumph of the golden calf; the people of Israel turned back to the worship of idols.

The cement statue is the focus of Saigon; whores, pimps, petty criminals, and swindlers swarm about it by day and night. The hard-faced whores on platform plastic slippers eye those lower-echelon beneficiaries of Washington's largesse who are not able to get away to Bangkok, or who have just come back. All this revenue is being drained upwards, to higher receptacles; the intake is enriching those already in power. Even for an evening the higher military will fly to Bangkok; this Saigon is not Las Vegas, merely a gate into the hall of judgment of the dead.

The whores weigh the hearts and find them worth nothing; street after street resound with the thud of artillery barrages after dark. By a river jammed with barges and steel ships one can sit, threading the barbed wire, and watch the police and the helmeted military crash by, in jeeps and armed cars, and snarling motorcycles. An explosion in the distance. Tinkling of glass; no one moves. American is spoken everywhere. A hotel on the waterfront announces with banners a congress of Buddhist monks from the Buddhist countries: Ceylon, Thailand, Laos, Burma (none from Cambodia). Orange- and yellow-robed shaven heads pass by in the lobby, umbrellas folded, by the registration desk. I find one who can speak Sinhalese from the Siamese seminary in Kandy. His expenses have been paid by the US Government, with the Vietnamese Government as the paying agent; it is a cultural front for the breaking-down military machine. They waited in Bangkok, putting up at the Wats, for an idle civilian transport. They are warned not to stray from their watchful protectors, lest they be bombed, maimed, or robbed. They look on, fragile, terrified, thinking of their rice bowls in their various jungles, as lost and as high-stemmed as storks on a lake of boiling pitch.

Another hotel, advertised as the largest, the most cubical, modern, stands somewhat away from the center, on a patrolled avenue, listless Chinese at the reception. It turns out to be the temporary haven where low-ranking GIs take their whores; thus the low rates are geared to a brief occupancy. It is like a lost prison compound, or the Federal fort on the Dry Tortugas of the Florida Keys—row after row of plastered brick cells, doors slamming, cracked washbasins being banged to encourage the dribbling of faucets; the whores are blank-faced; the GIs are sullen; it is all very expensive; there is no pleasure, only mechanical relief in a process like urination; the Chinese, scrutable, rest on their chairs in the reception below, counting their receipts; their sons man the paying windows; all eyes gleaming with money, intent on the hard green currency.

The lights go off, then on; there is a dull, huge thud in the distance; two GIs relieved of their bladder pressures and their purses decide to fight; they bang briefly in one of the lower corridors of the huge hexagon but give it up; their echoes resound for a while. Their hands drop to their sides, they stand in the corridors, blank, having nowhere else to go; there is the dull clatter, and shifting, in the rooms. All wait for the tolling of some bell which will release them from present misery, but the roofs press down, squeezing the air. The senior Chinese, wisp-bearded in a jacket of braided and raised black silk, sits on his throne like Minos, describing with his tail the number of circles each must descend; they ascend to the proper ring; each enters his cell. There is no screaming. The whores are expert, lifeless. Medical stations lie in a lower circle. Whores who hope to feed (there are no dining places) with their bladder partners wait outside, while burning chemicals are applied to the animals' parts. Killing is easier than this, and more joyous, the statue with the upraised blade proclaims. The Parliament sits there like a travesty, as if discussions, dispute, voting, proposals, had any meaning. Generals pass, with slit-eyed faces, stiff, bespectacled, in staff cars, guarded. It is hard to tell which side they are on; of course they are on "our" side, but tomorrow, or tonight they may be on the other side, if it profits. They calculate the odds, their minds, like those of their Bangkok confreres, on Switzerland.

At night, above the second most expensive hotel, the roof, formerly a pleasure resort, is just high enough to cut off the view of the statue. It is not raining, merely threatening; around the brown-glowing horizon, which must reach rice fields somewhere, electric and military flashes fan up; the dull boom goes on; there must be a war near at hand. One sleeps by this rhythm, everything double-locked and padlocked. In the marble lobby of the office building facing the statue, a tout offers to change twenty dollars at double the official rate; the wad of notes stuffed with worthless denominations is pushed into the palm; the light goes out; the men flee, grasping the $20 bill. The brown light of day outside in the smog is a different type of night; the traffic grates; motors of all sizes spit and snap and dissolve the atmosphere; the eyes and lungs burn; one longs for night to fall, real night, not this false, sweating, wavering light, drawn from somewhere deep in the pavement; the sky drops down forever.

The long avenues have the remains of trees, tall giants whose leaves are without juice or greenness, dying from fumes, the Champs-Élysées, planted by the French. Trees ringed with barbed wire; military traffic, military police pass by. In the remains of a public park are a museum, a botanical garden, a zoo, discredited and deteriorating; the few remaining animals cough in the carbon gases muffling the city. There must be rice fields, peasants, somewhere. In this asphalted area, heaving and cracking atop a lake of pitch, the vehicles crawl back and forth, mechanized, aimless, bumping against each other, and against the barrier limits which force them back, crowding their backs up on one another. A girl in an airline office, a girl in a bank, have been sheltered; how do they get from their homes to work? Small boys attempt to get their hands in one's pockets. The way back, on the military pavement, leads past the American Embassy. Like a child's castle of the knights of old it stands behind the high walls turreted at each corner; above the gates, barbicans bristling with machine guns, ever-swiveling, a GI calls out "Hi," smiling. A staff car with the eagle insignia enters. All snap to attention. Inside stands an anxious, rather prim building. Here is the true Parliament. Lesser embassies and legations are trivial, unguarded; the Australian one, tree-shaded, open to all, is run by two girls.

Newly arriving at the Saigon airport, the mere opening of the door and placing of the descent steps introduces chaos into the antiseptic mass-convenience atmosphere of the cabin. We file out into a sky buzzing with giant airlift; there is vast confusion, howling, at the entrance wickets. No one can change a check; everyone has black market notes. There is no transport; the lone rentable car approaches, scenting carrion. The hotel, a money-devouring machine, is in league with the rentable car. On the top floor of the hotel some senior US businessmen dine or have breakfast. The thudding continues.

To visit Cambodia one must have an exit permit. Another struggle with a taxi. The passport office swarms with desperate people who, until they arrived there, thought they had enough money to get out of the country. I am the only tourist. The hours pass; the closing bell is about to sound. The eyes are burning through to the pocketbooks of the suppliants. The clerks are decorative and obstructive, dreaming of their own air tickets; their function is to funnel the majority of the money away from the applicants before the squeeze is applied. The higher office waits until only the rind is left, exhausted and penniless, scarcely able to board the plane. But I do not require an escape ticket; merely an exit permit to Cambodia.

I return next day. The passport is lost. If one lives there, and knows the methods, it can all be done by a telephone call, a discreet messenger. They look at me to see what I will offer. I know the answer to this; it is that fortified building, that fairy-tale child's castle, in the center of town, with the US flag on top of it. The inner-office apologizes. The passport appears. It is the only US passport in the office.

But why would anyone want to go to Cambodia, an enemy country? No Vietnamese, no employees of the US Government are allowed in. It has been many weeks since they were asked for an exit permit to Cambodia. Why do you want to go? What is your plan? What is your work? Why do you not want to go to Bangkok?

But I am in no hurry. I have no schedule. I have fallen down another notch in the hotel scale. When they see that I can wait, when I point out that I can actually go to Bangkok, like everyone else, the passport is handed back. I have not had to pay. The stamp is in it. But they still cannot understand why I do not want to go to Bangkok; that is where they want to go; that is where everyone wants to go. What is Cambodia, just more rice fields, without any mortar fire.

Returning to the second-best hotel to eat, I see that it has features; an inner court, with tent awnings, remains of a French-trained staff; carved wooden beams and tinted glass. In cinemas one sits with hands in pockets; fingers are extracting money everywhere: money to get out, money to eat, money to build a bar for the Americans and the whores. The more beautiful, the whiter the woman's face, the more erect her carriage, the more ruthless her nature; they have a gift for business. They are sharp and clutching; these are businesswomen; they are desperate.

No one can sleep; the women fill up with barbiturates; wake up again, and watch their bars and restaurants and taxi-fleets. The brown and scaling wart throbs and throbs; it cannot stop heaving and moving and breathing in its fumes; it will not sleep ever but watches and waits. The Americans will not lose, they are counting on that; they have their money on it; else there would be no shops or bars or whore-operators; the money would then all be in Switzerland.

But it earns such high returns here; just a little more, just a little more time, while it can earn, only part being siphoned off; besides, the American Presidents are both on their side. When a rocket comes in, near the center, no one hears it until the heavy crash; there is a hole in the pavement; gutted trucks and buildings. Badly guided, coming from a distance, they don't seem to hit anything important. Viet Cong creep in and bomb a city street, kill a policeman, a few whores, try to get a general. The Catholics, French-educated, French-protected, are the ruling class; their prudence is to have half their money outside the country; the earning half, inside, gives them their local living, and its profits are drained abroad. Taxes, by a series of stratagems, hit mainly the poor. When the shops and the bars and the whores close their shutters, that will be the time to leave; for they will all know when the Viet Cong is coming, when the corpse has been devoured to the bones. And the regime of Hanoi is one of austerity. No dance of death. No profits. Fade out into the rice fields. Get aboard a junk, if you can't get into one of those last airplanes. But if your destination is indeed Switzerland, you will have no trouble getting a luxury seat.

Saigon booms, under Nixon. For a while, in 1968, when Johnson lost his nerve, it was ready to cash in. Now it knows that it will stay, as long as there is a dome on the Potomac. Abandonment of Saigon or Bangkok would be as unthinkable as abandonment of Las Vegas or Miami; the latter provide recreation; the former provide a purpose which gives each administration a focus for its energies and its worries, gives it a raison d'être. Here Old Glory waves with a defiant thrust, and beats its helicopter rotor vanes, screaming and coursing over jungle and paddies; there *is* an American power; it is valid, it is virile, it is enterprising.

The American intention, that the world shall be free, goes out in the military air traffic over Saigon. Our hopes are centrist and executive and ameliorative. To say that thus and so-and-so can put a stop to Saigon, can be elected and cut out and cauterize, is to ignore the moralistic basis of American power, that white-gowned girl going down the steps of the White House, while her Texas or California daddy beams, to be married to a young lawyer, a young soldier, or businessman. It is fashionable to say that Kennedy was a hero and Johnson a villain, but both were steps in the process. The man swiveling in front of that Executive desk in that Executive office is the heir of all the instinct, the momentum and the rhythms that make the American past mythic and make it necessary for that myth to be projected into the future; as impossible for a McCarthy to put a halt to Saigon as, say, for Truman to have put a halt to World War II. The Presidential seed is full of white-clad daughters, and it is these whom we are protecting in Saigon, by subsidizing the whores. The guns boom on, but they are purifying. The American suburbs, where Presidents live, the hippies who parade in the doomed cities and are objects of curiosity, are being cleansed and protected while they are cleansed.

There are rock singers in Saigon; the blast of electronic amplification proclaims the triumph of the West, not its decline; Mao and Ho and Marx would have us do without these things; thus they are the losers; they have miscalculated the future. The girl going down the White House steps knows what the future is, it is freedom, it is Las Vegas. All the books, and all the dialectic, all the little red volumes of *Thoughts*, all the useful, durable, padded-cotton blue uniforms are not equal to the blast of the electronic guitar or the growing of hair long over the shoulders. The heroic mortar and rocket fire, the grenades of the teams of the heroes of the Revolution, stepping out of political posters, bear the date of 1917 or 1935; they are no match for the chance of owning a Honda or having a transistor radio, rock-blaring, of your own. The wild, Western, corrupted avant-garde wears the beards of Marx, but the revolutionaries are expected by their regimes to be clean-shaven; they must be totalitarians, living austere lives, adhering to military disciplines; they must be Puritans.

There is an airport bus for passengers departing from Saigon. One gets to a central point in the city; then it lumbers toward the airport, passing the barriers. The desk at the hotel is enraged that I have found this out. At the airport I move in a file of US military and civilian workers.

In the waiting bar, a Bangkok-bound, recreation-aiming civilian worker tells the usual tale of huge salary, barbiturates and alcohol, the dwindling of sexual energy. All is lost, he says, in Saigon; it is a matter of months before the Viet Cong take over the city, the higher officials have prepared cushions for themselves (brothers in Hanoi, transmission of war plans) with the Viet Cong, or have planes warmed up ready for exit. But there are still guns sounding at the airport as we leave. American power is pounding away, as real as the assembly lines of the River Rouge or the blast furnaces of the Alleghenies. Washington is not giving up. The Dome is gleaming. It is only money, and there is plenty of that.

Now we lift off, and the thick brown coating of this last circle in the city of Dis fades into a jumble and a blur, not to be seen again until we encounter Minos at the gates of the underworld. It will be familiar to us, when we see that the black-coated judge has a wisp-bearded Chinese face, for we have been here before. And just as each GI takes his appointed cell in his appointed ring of that Dry Tortugas Fort Jefferson hostelry of the damned, to spend his virility into the rubber sac of a softly urinating Chinese whore, we will take our final places, without appeal. But why devise this on earth, before our time? The rotor vanes of the helicopters are like the wings of the lazy, slowly rotating monsters which hover over the pits and fires, and flaming bogs, and hot quicksands of Doré's hell; pterodactyls, these dinosaurian birds come not to lift us higher and higher into the empyrean where the President's daughter, a white-clad Beatrice, awaits, but into a hospital full of flasks of plasma, flowing through the gravity tubes, where a course of drugs unhinges the mind and undoes the brain.

We will not be dropped by US power back into Phnom-Penh or the flowers or the temple ruins, for we are warned against going there; the Prince is evil, and his is an enchanted garden designed to pervert and numb our sense of what is right, corrupt our sense of mission, so that we will never become worthy of the girl. She must be won by blood and suffering, by the vanes of slowly rotating pterodactyls above bogs and burning lakes, not by sniffing blossoms and sipping wines, savoring moonlight on barges propelled by an evil Prince, who would seduce her while she sleeps. The hero must be covered with blood; he must, in part, look like that concrete statue in front of the Saigon Parliament.

But I, having seen and met and talked with Minos before my time, prefer to browse on the poisoned flowers of the Prince, eschewing my chance to raise my sweat-stained helmet and, putting down my bayonet, to awaken with my bloodstained lips the sleeping Beauty. It is in another forest, that of Angkor, I would wander, and by another castle, that of Avalokiteshvara, that I would dream, my life away if possible.

And so I drop to earth, rescued, not by rotor vanes or a pterodactyl, but by a simple transport. And I come to the small airport, and its small buildings, and gentle, idling, courteous, helpful people. The nightmare has ended. The Beauty, unawakened, goes on to be married. I have not awakened her, and it is she, like her spouse, who walks in a trance. For I have awakened, and it is the Prince who is real, and they who are false. How can they let him exist? How can Phnom-Penh, forbidden to any American personnel, civil or military, be allowed to bloom and flourish between the Dis of Saigon, the Acheron of Bangkok?

It is monsoon time, and down at the Prince's port, reached through the US-financed highway, the wind and rain soak the sand continuously. I walk along the white strand, among the trees of the jungle. From the hill of the town bazaars I watch the British-flag freighters, four at a time, unloading war supplies bought in the world markets, for the Viet Cong, with which to attack unawakened Beauty on the very day of her White House wedding. Can this be allowed to continue? Will not someone press a button, black or red, on a giant, shining mahogany desk below the great eagle insignia? But another four freighters, and another and another, lie waiting. The railway, the highway, are fully utilized, speeding war supplies to the Viet Cong. The ornamental pile of downed US military aircraft grows on the avenue beside the river in Phnom-Penh; fuselage tails brightly numbered are in greatest demand; downed pterodactyls with their giant rotors.

Phnom-Penh is much dryer than the port; its rhythm goes on in the showers. Angkor is beginning to be wet. The great lake is filling. The villages leading down to it along the Siem Reap River are idyllic. Pigs, ducks, and chickens; babies appearing, fat, at every door, every year; the population blends with the paddies and the canals; there is a great rice surplus. We dance at night; I watch sunsets from the three main Phnoms (hills).

The peasants haunt the green underneath the trees, like slender surprised Avalokiteshvaras. Many die young, especially the men; there is not much effort made to preserve life. There is the hospital, free clinics, all that, at Siem Reap, which is a provincial capital. The peasants are not greatly concerned about longevity. Procreation is not a world-shaking event, merely a routine occurrence. The sex act is not of great importance. Dancing is greatly enjoyed.

Mostly these people are contemplative. They know, and have learned, for many years, how to pass the time. They walk and sit and look. Descendants of the last artisans and caretakers left to guard the cities, they belong to the ruins; know where to find individual stones far out in the tangle. They don't want to sell the stones. The flying horse of Avalokiteshvara raises the merchants, trapped by vampires on a desert island, high above the demons; its wings, pieced together, beat from a stone lotus in a dried pool, slowly filling as the rains begin.

Delicate small ruins, of earlier, discriminating dynasties, lie far out, with roseate, pillaged sculptures. In the wet season, all is softer, blurred. Sras Srang mills about, impervious to the slowly increasing rain. The cart sludges along the wet ruts; the bullocks have been feeding. We move in a private cloud of rain, passing the misty trees and streams. The odor of the animals, straining at the shafts, is pungent and piercing; a compound of digested grass, and stomach linings, and saliva, dripping mouths; intestines and bowel. As they strain harder, their aroma becomes all-powerful, the perfume and fuel of our moving cloud.

Because the light is failing, the cart halts at the village of Pradak, and the animals are turned to feeding. Beyond the village lie ruins, of Bantéay Samré. They know every stone, leaping ahead. We stumble across moats, up steps, into galleries and halls. Through carved balusters inner courts are seen; we go deeper into the ruin; here coconut oil lights up in a shell.

Above, the gods and demons appear, pulling at the serpent which churns Vishnu's sea of milk; the liquor of immortality streams down the walls. Inside the shrine, the square-browed, flat-cheeked, flat-nosed broad faces look out, perfectly composed, ready to stay till dawn. A carved naga serpent, with upraised heads, winds around the galleries outside, its mouths washed with rain.

They do not move. Here flesh, brown-yellow, immortalizes as stone. I have heavy breathing, vibrate and twist and quiver. Their only movement is that of the pupils of the whites of their eyes which must alter direction to take in my eccentricities.

We are awaiting the Bodhisattva of the current cycle, perhaps as a flying horse, perhaps as a woman with four arms, the naked doctrine itself;

perhaps as a being with four faces. We await release from the current cycle, through the agency of these divine beings.

Back to Phnom-Penh, then up the Mekong, past Kompong Cham, to Kratie, on the steamer. I go with a Chinese (Vietnamese), not a merchant; the family live in Kratie; they are peasants. Here is nothing but rice and rubber; temple after temple; Avalokiteshvara, slender-headed, in yellow plaster, with ten heads, in three tiers, four, four, and two, overseeing the world from the gates. His wife is a Khmer: we go down the opposite direction, south toward the coast, to Kampot Province, on the railway that brings up munitions for the Viet Cong from the Prince's port.

Here in the village I meet not so much the wife but the all-important "Sa mère Yen," who owns the stilt-house and the strip of paddy field. All the men are dead, only Chhea Kan, the Vietnamese-Chinese peasant from Kratie, is available to help the women in the paddy field at the working times. He is delicate and shy. He drops everything at Phnom-Penh, where he earns money in the port, when it is time for planting, Sa mère Yen making the decision.

Why did the women select such a slender, refined worker (headaches, dizziness, stomachaches) for their paddy field? An attack of everything combined assails him next morning in the rain. Sa mère applies the universal remedy (even for fractured limbs)—silver coins are rubbed and rubbed, painfully, into the area of the afflicted spot, until raw angry weals, exactly round, exactly the shape of the coins, appear, and begin, gratifyingly, to throb with pain.

At least partially redeemed, Kan sets out for the fields, admonished by the stern Sa mère; he may have been saved by his marriage to a Khmer, by the fact he was not a merchant; he may have been driven back into Vietnam with the mass; his body may have floated down the Mekong with thousands of Phnom-Penh Chinese when the button was pressed in Washington. I feel that this must be a requiem for Kan; too fragile and sickly and delicate a creature for the responsibilities even to Sa mère and the paddy field; ill at ease in Phnom-Penh and not aware or informed enough to get out of that river port, focus of the town, in the dry season when he was normally on the barge. They swept down the steps at the port, cutting down the Chinese concessionaires, for which I cannot blame the Khmers. But a pogrom of race claims the innocent as well as the guilty, and I wonder if Sa mère Yen is back again at the undignified (for one of her august age) task of working her own paddy field.

Conversely, there can be no question that the Oeur Sam Bath family has survived at Sras Srang; the villagers live inside the temple of Angkor Wat, and the Viet Cong keep them supplied with rice. Naturally they must worship their Prince (they did that anyway), and unnaturally they must let their mouths water over the enticing prospect of Mao Tse-tung; like any American hippie, a portrait of Ho Chi Minh (this last, one of the Khmer-hated Annamites, successors of the Chams of the water-battles on their reliefs) must adorn their living space in the galleries, but it is a service they perform, adoring or at least tolerating this icon, in return for rice—even today they lead you at once to the reliefs showing the victories of the Khmers over the Chams on the Lake; though they hate the Siamese more, their memory is long, and the Chams are as real, the Annamites are Chams—

The Viet Cong has recruited the peasants of the Angkor villages who are of military age to join their forces, so Croi-Oeur himself is now prowling the jungle, knife and rifle in hand, ready to massacre brother and cousin Khmers from Siem Reap, only three miles to the south, and heavily intermarried, who have been recruited into the American forces. The line between the Viet Cong and the US-supported forces lies exactly halfway between Siem Reap and Angkor Wat, where the family is now living. Croi-Oeur, at Angkor Wat, is learning the martial arts as practiced by the Viet Cong in Hanoi; his cousins Posoman and Khou-Chea, who lived in Siem Reap and were my friends, are learning those practiced by the USA in distant Saigon.

Both sides, north and south of that line one and a half miles from Angkor Wat, are running training camps to instruct peasants how to kill, since each accuses the other of doing so—"pre-dawn rifle training in Angkor Wat." And of necessity, how to kill each other, since each other is the enemy. Croi-Oeur is learning bayoneting and eviscerating, and Posoman and Khou-Chea, children of his mother's sister, are learning rifle-shooting and grenade-tossing. On alternate days they shift classes. It is too much to say that perhaps they have the same instructors, adepts who slip back and forth between the lines to garner fees. But if the instructors are Chinese, I would say it is not impossible.

If they are the best instructors, if the supply of field-trainers is limited, why should they not change uniforms each day and go back and forth (so easy for countrymen in this jungle), teaching Croi-Oeur how to hurl grenades at Posoman and Khou-Chea one day, and Posoman and Khou-Chea how to bayonet Croi-Oeur the following day? The important thing is to teach killing, as quickly and efficiently as possible, to peasants who have never had a punch in the nose before. Both Hanoi and Washington would have it so. To Ho Chi Minh's successors in Hanoi, Croi-Oeur's cousins are ideologically inferior; they can be butchered. To Johnson's successors in Washington, Croi-Oeur is a communist; he is shooting for the Viet Cong; one more vermin to be gotten rid of. For all the world must be free; Marine generals can relax in Bangkok, it is a free country; Saigon itself is more for the recreation of enlisted men. . . .

Get the cement up and get it carved. Phnom-Penh, according to its generals, lacks the inspiration of a martial spirit. Siem Reap may plead in vain for a statue of Avalokiteshvara. Perhaps it will get a replica of the Saigon Statue, reduced in size for its tiny population. Perhaps a Las Vegas entertainment celebrity, such as are provided to Saigon, may come through.

What was there in Johnson that caused him to hold off? What caused him to refrain from taking the obvious step in those dark days of February 1968, when the defeat of his policies faced him with the necessity of abdication? He did not clutch at this last straw, as the generals would have had him do. It was so easy: cut off the port, shut off the supplies, make the Viet Cong divert troops to confront the Khmers. The chance of success was there, and Texans like to succeed. Johnson refused to destroy this fragile, lotus-eating, defenseless, incapable nation, with an army made up only of generals from royal families, an army of epaulets and medals and dummy rifles, ivory-handled ceremonial pistols. There was the chance of gazing down on the record as final victor of an insoluble war.

Now that we know how easy it was to seize Cambodia, Johnson's refusal to comply is perplexing. The drowning man did not clutch at the lotus blossom. He preferred to sink himself and let the lotus float for a while in the jungle pool, below the walls of Angkor, with the winged horse rising and succoring from amid the pink and blue blossoms.

Avalokiteshvara had a friend in LBJ; or, in theologically more accurate terms, LBJ was pulled up on the back of that horse from the desert island of the vampires, eager to suck at his jugular; he fell under the protection of the all-seeing, four-sided gaze.

Thus the bodhisattva, all-powerful in the current cycle, who renounced his own divinity to suffer in our midst, had a facet in the Presidential forehead; LBJ acted in accordance with the wishes of the god; for a while longer the maidens danced on the terraces of Angkor.

Autumn 1971

Making It Uglier to the Airport

GUY DAVENPORT

EVERY BUILDING in the United States is an offense to invested capital. It occupies space which, as greed acknowledges no limits, can be better utilized. This depressing fact can be thought of as a kind of disease of the American city for which the only specific is law, and, to make a wild gesture toward common sense, aesthetics. One might as well say that multiple sclerosis can be cured with cough drops.

In Chicago six years ago they tore down Adler and Sullivan's Old Stock Exchange, a perfectly useful building. That it was bone and blood of Chicago history, that it was an architectural landmark, that its ornamentation was beautiful and irreplaceable were arguments that could not save it. Money has no ears, no eyes, no respect; it is all gut, mouth, and ass. The Heller International Building went up in its place, a glass cracker-box forty-three stories high. Its mortgage payments are $400,000 every first of the month: interest—*interest*, money which bankers earn by tightening their shoelaces, yawning, and testing teakwood surfaces for dust—on a $48,300,000 loan. The building cost $51,000,000, and is up for grabs, as the speculators can't hold onto it. This time nobody cares if, as they shall, they tear it down and put up something more "economically viable," as they say.

Heaps of New York are being torn down because what's left over after property taxes isn't quite what our greedy hearts would like to take to our investment broker. Between the banker and the tax collector, life can be very hell. But then, they built the cities in the first place. One of the greatest of architects built snowmen for the Medici children (a use of Michelangelo we would have expected of J. Pierpont Morgan sooner than Lorenzo the Magnificent); all architects are now sculptors in ice.

Ada Louise Huxtable, who writes about architecture and city planning for the *New York Times*, has collected up a batch of her terse essays on buildings going up and coming down, on design, and practically anything else that her lively eye hits on.[1] Her comments are all arrows of the chase, released when the aim seemed good, and with some fine hits. Like all such writing, you can feel the pressure of the deadline on her attention. She turns up many problems (the war, apparently to the death, between city design and real-estate adventurers; the coherence of American cityscape; the preservation of landmarks; the tension between contemporaneity and tradition) that I would like to have seen her expand and explore.

While I was reading her essays, I happened to run across Manfredo Tafuri's *Architecture and Utopia: Design and Capitalist Development*, which I saw in the MIT catalog when I was ordering Dolores Hayden's fine survey of American utopian communities.[2] Tafuri traces the decay and disorder of cities to the rise of commercial centers during the industrial revolution, causing cities to enter a paranoia of identity. His little book is worth reading—worth studying with care—but it gleams and blinds with too much Marxist intellect for me to pretend to discuss it here. The one idea that I want to take from it is that what we call a city bears little resemblance to the historical city or to cities outside the United States. Yet our cities still sit on top of a living archeological base that used to be a city in the old sense. The automobile and the truck have shaved the yards to mere margins in the quiet residential sections, the streets have become freeways all over every city and town. Automobile exhaust, equal in volume daily to that of the Atlantic Ocean, has replaced breathable air. The automobile is an insect that eats cities, and its parking lots are a gangrene.

The simple fact is that cities in America came into being not as the historical city did, for mutual protection and to be the home of a specific family of people, but as commercial ports. That is, their model was the kind of prosperous city Defoe describes in the first inventory the mercantile class made of itself, his *Tour Thro' the Whole Island of Great Britain*. All important elements were in walking distance of each other; *nearness* defined the city. If it grew large, each neighborhood (as in Paris and London today) remained a conglomerate of components within easy reach.

1. Ada Louise Huxtable, *Kicked a Building Lately?* (New York: Quadrangle/The New York Times Book Co., 1976).

2. Manfredo Tafuri, trans. from the Italian by Barbara Luigia La Penta, *Architecture and Utopia: Design and Capitalist Development* (Cambridge: The MIT Press, 1979). Dolores Hayden, *Seven American Utopias: The Architecture of Communitarian Socialism, 1790–1975* (Cambridge: The MIT Press, 1979).

Within the last twenty years the automobile has gradually canceled this definition of the city as a community. And the smaller the city, the larger the inconvenience has grown. When I moved to Lexington, Kentucky, fifteen years ago, I could walk to three supermarkets in my neighborhood, to the post office, and to the mayor's house, which happened to be around the corner. All three markets have moved miles away, to the beltline; God knows where they have put the post office. I have been there but once since they moved it. It took me an hour to get there, and an hour to get back. It is technically in the next county, and is near no habitation of any citizen. Only some desolate warehouses does it have for company. This happened when Nixon and his government of scoundrels, liars, and sneaks had us *scrotum in mano*, and I assumed that sheer hatefulness snatched the post office from downtown and put it out in the horse pastures.

The post office, in any case, was only good for buying stamps at. When I tried to renew my passport there a few years ago, a passport kept functional for thirty years, I was told that if I couldn't show a driver's license, I couldn't renew my passport. (I will not spin out the Gogolian scene that ensued, though it featured my being told that I didn't deserve to live in this country, my pointing out that I could scarcely leave it without a passport, and on around in circles that left the art of Gogol for that of Ionesco, until I got the State Department on the phone, and had my new passport, together with an apology, in three days.) The point of the anecdote is that the pedestrian is officially a second-rate citizen and definitely an obsolete species.

Where the mayor moved to I do not know. The neighborhood is now zoned for business. Henry Clay's townhouse, part of the neighborhood, sits in a tarred-over parking lot.[3]

I had not realized before reading Dolores Hayden's *Seven American Utopias* that the Civil War marked the end of utopian experimentation in American communities. We now know how very much of modern design derives from Shaker clarity and integrity, and how useful, if only as models to modify or tolerate, the Owenite, Fourierist, Moravian, and other eccentric societies were.

Acceleration in culture is demonic, and there ought to be periodic recesses to look back and reclaim elements that were ditched along the way.

---

3. There is an excellent essay on the kinds of cities bequeathed us by history as paradigms, in *Salmagundi* No. 24 (Fall 1973), "The City under Attack" by George Steiner. This is a rich essay, with long historical perspectives. He shows us that much of what we take to be peculiarly modern ills are in fact very old, and that our double tradition, Classical and Judeo-Christian, gives us two distinct ideas of what a city is.

To read Dolores Hayden is to see how much we elbowed aside, or smothered, or deliberately obliterated. Fourier's phalanx seems to be a congenial mode of life that might have forestalled our present alienation of the young, the old, and the lonely. Shaker respect for materials is certainly the corrective we need for our present norm of tacky shoddiness, for mushroom proliferation. Shaker morals wouldn't be amiss either.

Backward surveys can also turn up some astonishing forks in the road. Alison Sky and Michelle Stone have compiled what amounts to a treasury of American designs, from cities to individual buildings, that never made it from the blueprint into actuality.[4] One purpose of this book was to assess our architectural legacy—designs, for instance, that might still be realized. There is a postmortem career awaiting Frank Lloyd Wright; all great architects are ahead of their times. Sadly, many of these plans have been chucked into the wastebasket. An architect's firm is a business, not an archive. Not even so distinguished a figure as Frederick Law Olmsted was spared this kind of careless destruction. A vigorous society might well build Thomas Jefferson's President's House, if only in Disneyland, where, in effect, Jacques J. B. Benedict's Summer Capitol for President Woodrow Wilson (projected for Mt. Falcon, Colorado) already stands—it looks like an Arthur Rackham drawing for Mad Ludwig of Bavaria. Many of these rejected designs are lugubrious and hilarious: a robber-baron New Versailles for Manhasset Bay, Long Island, that would have been the biggest building in the world, something that Hitler and Albert Speer might have drooled over; art-book cathedrals recapitulating the whole span of the Gothic in Europe, beacons taller than Everest, Babylonian banks, war memorials that would have trivialized the Pyramids, linear towns with highways for halls, space islands, underground metropolises, a New Harmony phalanx that looks like a Victorian penitentiary crossbred with Flash Gordon's spacecraft port. And yet these designs are full of attractive and charming ideas: a Manhattan with separate thoroughfares for pedestrians and traffic, garden cities, beautiful vistas that would have made Chicago as handsome as Paris, and buildings that ought to have existed for the fun of it, William McKinley Xanadus, palaces, follies—outrageous flowers for the granite forest.

The depressing obliteration of communities can sometimes be as thorough as Noah's Flood. New Burlington, Ohio, a town between Dayton and

---

4. Alison Sky and Michelle Stone, *Unbuilt America: Forgotten Architecture in the United States from Thomas Jefferson to the Space Age* (New York: McGraw-Hill, 1976).

Cincinnati, is now at the bottom of a lake created, as it often seems, to keep the Army Corps of Engineers busy. Before New Burlington went under, an extraordinarily sensitive writer, John Baskin, talked with the old-timers and recorded their memories. The resulting book is poignant and, if you're in a reflective mood or of a pessimistic turn, heartbreaking.[5] The obituary of an entire town has the aura of doom all over it. The only horror of death is in waiting for it, and here was a community that knew its doom: not of life, but of so much of it that the difference perhaps is not accountable. The terror of Hektor's death was that, moments before his heart tasted Akhilles's blade, he had to run past places where he had played as a boy. John Baskin carefully avoids dramatics in this book. His business was to hear the past. In the process, however, it dawned on him that American life has changed. What's different is that whereas just a few years ago we all had something to do, now we don't.

It is tempting to believe that New Burlington, Ohio, was built before the Civil War (partly by Methodists, partly by Quakers) by people for whom skill and hard work was as natural a fact as breathing, and that it went underwater because a society had emerged that is neurotic with idleness and pointlessness. (The Red River Gorge in Kentucky was saved from flooding by the Corps of Engineers because when our governor asked the Corps *why* they wanted to obliterate so much natural beauty, they could not give an answer.)

It is good to know, on the other hand, that a small community can fight and can win against the restless greed of investment capital and botchers of all breeds. A nameless town in California has so far held out over a sudden influx of developers and do-gooders working together. The do-gooders noticed the town when it was gunked up by an oil spill (halt and give some time to the ironies that crisscross here). During the cleanup it was noticed that the community had an inadequate sewer system. This attracted the money boys from a water company, who convinced the state that vast sums must be spent to get everybody onto a flushing toilet. This alerted the osmagogue bankers, who alerted the real-estate gang. As long as this community—half retired folk, largely hermits, half young utopians who had fled the city—was to be modernized, so thought the developers, let's pop in resort hotels, Burger Kings, miniature golf, redwood-shingle condominiums, and let's see these old geezers and hippies clear the hell out.

5. John Baskin, *New Burlington: The Life and Death of an American Village* (New York: W. W. Norton & Co., 1976).

The struggle and triumph of this community (not named, for its own protection) is presented in a thoroughly good book.[6] Orville Schell, who has written well and humanely about Chinese communes, shows how a community that is eccentric, almost centerless, and even casual, can knit together and drive away the bulldozer, sanitary engineer, and real-estate shark. He presents his problem in a paragraph that it would be brutal to paraphrase:

> A town which is a community is a delicate organism. As yet, it has virtually no legal means at its disposal by which to protect itself from those who choose to search it out. Unlike an individual, it cannot sue for invasion of privacy. It cannot effectively determine how many people can live in it. It cannot even decide for itself the number of visitors with which it feels comfortable. The roads are there; anyone may travel on them. A commercial establishment is free to advertise the town's name and its desirable attributes in the hopes of attracting people to it in order to make money. If the people who call that town home find the influx of people, cars, and money unsettling, they have little recourse.

If those words were attributed to a New England Conservative complaining about Italian immigrants, or to Robert Moses complaining about the influx of Puerto Ricans, they would outrage Liberal ears. Paradoxically they illustrate how accurately we must understand a writer's point of view. "Organism" is the word to hold onto. Schell's words are true, and astutely stated. The nature of the organism determines what kind of turbulence it can tolerate.

Poland survived the Second World War better than my hometown in South Carolina. Main Street has rotted into a wasteland. Gracious old homes came down to make way for used-car lots, tacky little finance companies, and drive-in hamburger pavilions. The seven ancient oaks that stood around the house where Thomas Wolfe's sister lived fell to the power saw, and the house itself, deporched, hokied up with neon and Coca-Cola signs, was islanded in a desolation of tar paving and converted into an eatery called, with that genius of the destroyer for taunting, The Seven Oaks. Some two miles of magnolia shade became a glare of festooned light bulbs, and all the used-car dealers are named Shug and Bubber, a semiology I am not equipped to explore. The ugliness of it all is visual migraine. And yet a

6. Orville Schell, with photographs by Ilka Hartmann, *The Town That Fought to Save Itself* (New York: Pantheon Books, 1976).

mayor and his councilmen let it happen. The American politician may be a psychological type, like the kleptomaniac, peeping Tom, or exhibitionist. He is the only professional who may apply for a job and present as his credentials the blatant and unashamed fact that he has none. (Lincoln Steffens was surprised to discover that city management throughout Europe requires a college degree.) But the explanation of why our cities are being uglified is not to be found wholly in political venality, capitalistic exploitation, greed, and carelessness, or any one force.

The history of a city ought to disclose how it came to be what it is. John and LaRee Caughey have put together a composite "history" of that monster metropolis Los Angeles.[7] The apology for the word *history* is because the book is an anthology of short passages from over a hundred writers. The method seems appropriate for a sprawling subject, the locale of such contrasts (Hollywood and Watts, UCLA and Sunset Boulevard). I suspect the book is of greatest interest to Angelenos themselves, though it is a marvelous book to read around in. It makes the tacit assumption that no American city of such size can be got between the pages of a book. The word *history* is wonderfully tricky when applied to a city. One can write the history of England better than the history of London. In another sense, the history of Los Angeles can be written sometime in the next century, but not now.

A more thorough and integral history of a city is Roger Sale's of Seattle.[8] This is a model of how city histories should be written. Seattle is a perfect example of the American city in that it was not an accidental pooling of settlers in its beginning, but a deliberate act by stalwart citizens who had come to found a city. The university, the neighborhoods, the businesses, the bank, practically all the elements were decided on as the first buildings went up. We think of the westward expansion as so many pioneers clearing the wilderness for *farms*; that's mythology—they were colonists who had the plans of cities in their heads, the first since Greeks and Romans set out from *mother cities* (*metropolites*) to reproduce examples of the model they came from.

Professor Sale, a highly skilled and spirited writer, gives us each epoch of Seattle's history in fine detail. He knows that cities are really so many people and inserts full biographies throughout. He gives a lucid account of the city's economic and sociological history; he knows its institutions and

7. John Caughey and LaRee Caughey, *Los Angeles: Biography of a City* (Berkeley: University of California Press, 1976).

8. Roger Sale, *Seattle, Past to Present* (Seattle: University of Washington Press, 1905).

newspapers. Most importantly, he knows the city's lapses and false steps; not a syllable of chauvinism or whitewashing mars these pages. The book is therefore vigorous in its honesty and in the range of its considerations; it is as good on labor leaders (Dave Beck) as on intellectuals (Vernon Parrington). It is a speculative book that can discuss the benefit of good high schools and parks and can explain how the American labor movement, which by rights ought to have emerged as leftist and radical (as the Seattle friend of Mao, Anna Louise Strong, urged), became rightist and conservative.

A city's history can be done in finer and finer detail. You can zone off a decade, as Michael Lesy has done with the twenties in Louisville, or study neighborhoods family by family, as Roslyn Banish has done with a London and a Chicago neighborhood, or trace a single family through six generations.[9] Lesy, who began his method of composite history with *Wisconsin Death Trip*, repeats that work with Louisville in Prohibition times. Using photographs from the commercial firm of Caulfield and Shook, police and insane-asylum records, he constructs, with what seems to me like morbidity and gratuitous cynicism, a sustained surrealistic picture of the period. His point, of course, is that's the way they chose to see themselves—Masons in all their gaudy trappings, blacks at lodge banquets, society folk looking superior, T-Model wrecks, prehistoric Gulf stations, promotion photos by go-getter salesmen. A lot of the surrealism is, I'm afraid, mere psychological tone. Similar photographs of the 1860s we would perceive as History. These things come in phases: today's junk is tomorrow's antique, etc., but the process has some subtle quality one can't pin down. Lesy makes the age seem indecent; I grew up in it and don't remember it that way at all. The present moment is far tackier (he would probably agree), and it is true, as he claims, that newspapers speak in a tongue all their own. And all documents in a neutral voice (police recorder, case histories from the asylum) tell us more about the institution keeping such files than about the subject. It is Lesy's hope that raw documents speak for themselves and that captionless photographs are powerfully meaningful. I have my doubts. The method seems to me to be a bit cocky and fraudulent. The truth of a period cannot be summoned by a few eloquent photographs and a batch of newspaper clippings. It is the equivalent of trying to understand the Second World War from newsreels alone.

9. Michael Lesy, *Real Life: Louisville in the Twenties* (New York: Pantheon Books, 1976). Roslyn Banish, *City Families: Chicago and London* (New York: Pantheon Books, 1976). Dorothy Gallagher, *Hannah's Daughters: Six Generations of an American Family: 1876–1976* (New York: Thomas Y. Crowell Co., 1976).

Roslyn Banish supplements her photographs of London and Chicago families with responsible statistics and with commentaries by the subjects themselves. She also allowed the subjects to choose their setting (almost invariably the best-looking room, as they thought) and pose. Ms. Banish is a canny photographer, giving us in splendid light just enough detail to complete the portraits (a coat-hanger inexplicably in a living room, a dime-store Gainsborough over a policeman's mantel), and an even cannier sociologist to have conceived and carried out her project. She has made a book from which one learns about people in a particular and piquant way without any violation of their privacy, without condescension, and with gentleness toward their vulnerability. There is more respect for human beings in these photographs than I have ever seen a photographer achieve. One falls in love with the eighty-year-old Alice Williams in the first photograph (love birds, electric heater, paper flowers) and remains in awe of the dignity of these homefolks right up to a smiling Irish Chicago police sergeant in the last. I liked Douglas Humphreys (butler, Buckingham Palace), who looks like the Hon. Gally Threepwood in Wodehouse, part of whose interview recalls a buffet supper for heads of state after Churchill's funeral: "I was entertaining myself a few moments with Mr. Khrushchev. Oh yes, now he had two bodyguards and an interpreter with him. I took off his greatcoat and I felt the eyes of those burly guards. I hung his greatcoat up and I said to the interpreter, 'Just tell your two men to relax. I'm on duty on the occasion of Her Majesty's Royal Household.' And I added, 'One day I should like to pay a visit to your country, sir.' He . . . actually shook hands." One feels that Humphreys was *comforting* Comrade K., and not even Trollope could have thought of such a wonderful moment.

Dorothy Gallagher's *Hannah's Daughters* is an oral history, taken down in a series of interviews, of six generations of a Washington family of Dutch descent, members of all of them being alive in August 1973, a chain of daughters reaching from the 97-year-old Hannah to her two-year-old great-great-great granddaughter. The hundred photographs illustrating the narratives progress from tintype to Polaroid. The text has the interest of good talk and covers a great deal of American history in very American voices (". . . everybody was kissing everybody. It was really something. That was V-E Day. It was absolutely wild. I didn't think there were that many people"). Gertrude Stein would have liked this book, and even tried to write it, the wrong way round, in *The Making of Americans.* Family history has traditionally been a woman's preserve. And what a distance there is from "They'd kill a hog and I'd get the fat cleaned off the hog intestines to make lard. I was quick at that" to "Even if Tony had an affair, if it was a quickie affair, I'm sure we'd still be together. If it was a long one, I'm sure we'd get a divorce."

The inner life of the city—voices, children, baths, meals—has not undergone any substantial change since Jericho, the oldest city still inhabited. When Odysseus was finally united with Penelope, they talked all night in a cozy bed, under sheepskin covers. Children and the old are the same the world over. Only public lives are different: the automobile and airplane have made us nomads again. The city seems to be obsolete, a sense of community evaporates in all this mobility and stir. As persuasion is impotent in so distracted a world, and as our legislators seem to be mere pawns of lobbies, their hands hourly open to bribes, we must stoically wait out whatever awful hiatus there is to be between the technological destruction of the only known unit of civilization, the city, and its logical and natural reinvention, however that is to come about. Meanwhile, as a voice says in Zukofsky's "A-18,"

>   . . . all
> their world's done to change the world is
> to make it more ugly to the airport.

Summer 1977

On a Greek Holiday

ALICE BLOOM

ONCE OR SO A SUMMER we do an ordinary—which is to say frantic, standardized, and expensive—American thing with the children. At 5:30 on a weeknight we hit the supermarket, then Sears for something dull but crucial like a mattress pad and a supply of vacuum cleaner bags, then supper at the Burger King or its equivalent, and then the early movie at the mall. By the end of the evening we're all, children especially, a bit wan with the strain of being caught up smiling in this family commercial, and we're relieved when it's over. Last night was this summer's night, and after the double cheeseburgers with bacon and the chicken-fat mocha malts, we go on to Cinema 1-2-3-4 and pay $3.50 apiece for four children to re-see *E.T.*, and, for the sake of the scenery of blue, white, and ocher which the ads claim it "glorifies," we go into this summer's older-adolescent mild-porn film, shot in Greece, called *Summer Lovers*.

Like most fantasies, this movie has more action and less description than occur in actual life, but aside from this quibble, I enjoyed it immensely, all of it, not only because we were just there, in Greece, in the blue, white, and ocher a few weeks ago, but also because I had never seen a movie of this kind before. I was not allowed to attend this sort of movie or indeed seldom allowed to attend any movie at all in the summers of my own early adolescent years, on the grounds that one caught polio at the movies, and from wearing what we then called "tennis shoes," and from swimming in public pools. Therefore I, and many of my best friends, were deprived of the three fatal elements that continue to make up the persistent teen dream: love without adults, proper and sufficient gear, and the unlimited public pool.

Since the time when I longed for them, love, gear, and the public pool have been considerably fleshed out, both in life and in the movies.

Summer Lovers is a reliable example because although it has a modern application—three young lovers instead of the classical two—it remains otherwise true to the ancient pattern, sometimes painted on Greek urns, in fact, in which Spring/Youth/Fertility prevails at last against Old Man/Winter/Authority/Society/Parent with his heavy, arbitrary, laughable rules, foolish old-fashioned iron grip, long-gone beauty, and his one foot in the long-deserved grave.

The public pool of dreams today is far beyond the Malibu beach parties which was the extent of what we, my friends and I, in our one-piece pink-checked gingham suits with ruffles on the derriere and flowered swimming caps to match, could possibly, back in the 1950s in the simmering, flat, corny Midwest, imagine. According to *Summer Lovers* the public pool is now the radiant, crowded, nude beaches of Greece. And the fantasy of love without adults, which to our minds was double-dating at the drive-in, is now having your parents give you and your boyfriend a several-hundred-dollar-a-week sea-view apartment for two months on the island of Santorini for a graduation present rather than, say, a demure Bulova with two tiny diamonds and a card that begins "We're proud of you today." According to this movie, teen gear, to be proper and sufficient these days, must include a Rolex, a Nikon, a leather case of lenses, a complete darkroom (in the apartment on the island), enough changes of American playclothes to sink a freighter, running shoes in every color and number of stripe, a Martin guitar, a bright orange Citroën "Pony," a hardback copy of *Nice Girls Do* on the bedside table, and a nice second girl you can pick out with your expensive binoculars from your terrace who is sitting with her binoculars on her terrace picking you out from across the way until, that is, this silent but potent flirtation ends and she packs up her gear (portable stereo system, library of art books, clothes) and moves in with you—Nice Girl Number One, and Boy. And love without adults is a suddenly blissful, innocent, uncomplicated, defiantly pastoral threesome; and permanent (for the summer, hence the title) fun: at the discos, the souvlaki stands, the cafés, the shops, on the nude beaches, and on the water bed.

About five or ten minutes into the film, before this second girl turns up, and after such bits of dialogue as "Gee, it's like a dream, Michael," and, "Well, sure, freedom means you'll get hurt now and then," and, "My mother is so uptight she didn't even want us to live together," it's clear there's not much to be milked from the plot of a mere twosome. Their situation involves so little struggle—shall we take the Citroën or the bus to the beach, which beach?—that they are nearly Jamesian in their untroubled purity, their freedom from life's coarser issues of survival. Not that this frees them for talk and feeling and talk about feeling. Presented to us as, apparently, congenitally unable to converse, they do the next obvious thing: they enlarge the cast. If two is fun, three will be more so, so the plot of the movie is this: will three work out? Of course it will, this is 1982, so this hardly keeps us on the edge of our Cinema 4 seats, but it does allow for the camera to keep turning.

The action of binocular gazing back and forth then goes about as far as it can sustain itself, so Boy is suddenly made to meet Girl Two, accidentally, on the way to the (nude) beach. Girl One is out, alone, with her Nikon, photographing the natives engaged in genre activities such as mending fishing nets or sitting in the sun, smiling. Girl Two and Boy haven't formally met; that is, they don't yet know each other's first names, but he spots her walking toward the bus, he brakes and abandons the orange "Pony," and he joins her on the jam-packed trip to the beach.

There are only about two exchanges during the bus ride. He says, "I had the car. Why didn't you let me drive you? Why did you want to take the bus?" To which she replies, "I like people." Here, and elsewhere throughout the movie, it's the camera that provides the eloquence, if not to say the content, and at this point the camera is speaking from two vantage points: one at belly button level, shooting into the public busload of bouncing, eager, stand-up flesh on its way to the sun and sand, can't wait, and the other angle on intensely close-up faces of Boy and Girl Two, all eyes and lips. No more dialogue from them, as I recall, until they and their fellow (no Greeks, though) bus riders have disembarked, run onto the beach past the wooden, hand-lettered sign that states: "Absolutely forbidden to Camping or the Nakedness," and stripped, and arranged themselves, like old village women stretching out laundry, onto the oven-hot pebbles.

After a long shot of the now simmering, ecstatic beach scene, camera fastens on Girl Two's face. She's flat on her back, saying nothing, looking rather prissy in fact, eyes closed, seriously sunbathing. Then camera on his face, saying nothing, but eyes open, glittering, staring down at her, and looking as full of uncomprehending wonder as if he had just discovered fire. The shot is so close we can see, reflected in his pupils, the individual beads of sun oil on her naked brown skin. At last he says, "What do you do all day?" And the camera shifts to the level of the sand alongside her bare stomach, shooting up at her face. She replies, eyes suddenly open, and hostile, suspicious: "Why do you ask such a question like this?" (She's French, it turns out later, so her syntax is a little stilted.) "I want to get to know you, that's all," he says, abashed. "Well, the first thing to know about me is that I don't like personal questions," she answers and recloses her eyes and slightly flares her nostrils, a signal that she, anyway, is back to the serious, if not to say superior, business of what we came to the beach for—sunbathing, not these questions.

Like Tiresias, only the camera knows. Boy doesn't know, and he ponders this reprimand, one can tell by his now-clouded eyes. And audience doesn't know: we're left with the old-fashioned difficulty of making art make sense, and we're trying to resolve the apparent contradiction between the grunted proprieties of the sparse, stiff dialogue, their two, blurred, very private faces in the background, and the foreground shot of her nipples which fill the front of the screen like a moonscape.

Heavily clad in our sopping gingham suits we lay, my friends and I, eyes closed against the sting of chlorine, by the side of the concrete pool dug out of the cornfields and, tired of graceless flirtations with pimply, wet, large-footed boys, fantasized about "personal questions" someday, and someday, nakedness too, probably. Now, stark naked, the camera explains this repeatedly, nameless to each other (our parents all knew each other on Main Street, and at church), these new teens fantasize, it seems, about graceless flirtations, about ordinary yucking it up, the titillation of binocular gazing, a little hot pebble put down the back of your suit by some dumb boy, coy sparring talk as antiquated as swordplay. To us, nakedness would be, if and when it happened, full of awful significance, not at all in the Greek idea of the natural electric body under a democratic sun. We were scrupulously careful not to be caught by each other, girls, in the showers after gym, even that much was mortifying, one just instinctively didn't do it, not even in underwear, a momentary bad dream taken from that large dream of ultimate mortification, naked on the street downtown, in English class, at a dance.

And nakedness meant sexy, sex, pure and simple, with an unmet special someone someday in private. I don't believe that I, we, even thought it could be otherwise; certainly we never thought of public nakedness as possible or desirable, or in terms of health, mental or physical, or in terms of liberation, or as a statement, or politics, or as the opposite of being uptight, or as natural, because we didn't even have that vocabulary, or, indeed, any vocabulary that limned for us our "rights." Things grated, but we never thought, never talked of what our "rights" might be, against parents or friends' parents or teachers or deans or housemothers or the general public of adults, required courses, music lessons, skirts, required hats on Sunday, much less of our "rights" in connection with our own ideas and bodies with which we were, anyway, uniformly disgruntled. We didn't know anybody who went anywhere for a graduation present, and about what our parents paid for was summer camp or vacations in the family car, with them. Plots, though, we had, plenty of plots.

The movie doesn't tell why Girl Two prissily uncovers her body but resents "personal questions." She does a respectable thing with her "day," she even has a snappy khaki safari outfit to do it in, and her own Rolex. She's an archaeologist, employed on a dig, and she does things every day like find perfectly intact vases with paintings on them of the Minotaur in the Labyrinth, and it's not immediately clear why she couldn't just say that. But as the movie reels on, it does become clear that the three main characters (everyone else is employed as scenery) assiduously, punctiliously avoid what one might think was actually a rather benign, polite, even public sort of question, such as "What is your last name?" or, "Where are you from?" or, "And what sort of work do you do?" None of the three has a criminal record, none is on the lam, yet such questions, the dialogue grudgingly explains now and then, would be a kind of unthinkable violation of privacy, an intimacy that might ruin the happiness of three in a bed. Knowing last names might lead to complications, a possibility at which they shudder and which is as potentially mortifying to them as were the old nightmares of nakedness in public for us. Complications, we would have died for; and our plots were dreamed in order to have, in the future, as many complications as possible.

The Midwest, planted in rows of towns and zinnias and soybeans and railroad tracks straight into the horizon, with a life so thinly and recently there, so shallow it seems as though the dry wind will knock the cemetery stones right over, is the steppes of America, and if one is born there, one is born into a mild sense of exile from a real place. Everything else, all that feels as though it would be thick and delicate—towers, small lights, wet anonymous streets, old parks with secrets, passing conversations, gardens with aged lilacs, austere sensitive rooms where verse is written, a bouquet of crowds, lives, ages, questions, odd clothes, languages, stories, plots—seems impossibly, inhumanly in the future, and when I finally reached an age of action, all other places were news.

The idea of other places was derived from literature, and when I got there, Chicago was via Frank Norris, and New York by way of almost any Thomas Wolfe sentence, and New England sprung pristine from the tall, washed foreheads of Hawthorne, Melville, and Sarah Orne Jewett. This latter image was a pure but lasting association, drawn from literary photographs in which the foreheads of Midwestern writers wear a perpetual scowl, as though they had continually to watch out for abuses from mayors and Methodists, but the foreheads of New England writers are lonely coastlines from which the tide of thought has just receded. The first images of Greece, along these impressionable lines, were through pencils stamped with Venus de Milo, then through the words "Ionic," "Doric," and "Corinthian" in spelling contests, then from a field trip with the Latin Club to see Judith Anderson play *Medea*; then, finally, before actually getting there, through Aristotle and Henry Miller, through Freud, Sophocles, Edith Hamilton, Moses Hadas, Isadora Duncan, Gerald and Lawrence Durrell, Kazantzakis, George Seferis, Cavafy, Sappho, Heraclitus, and a lifetime of pictures: blue, white, and ocher.

All these were lovers and not salesmen. They only inadvertently described me, and what I longed for. Their passion was for a land. For the reason of this kind of introduction, I suppose, I am unable to "go on a vacation." To borrow the parlance of travel ads, I don't go to "get away," I go to get into. In addition to following their love—lovers of place being such a trustworthy sort, an enviable sort—one travels not to enjoy oneself, or to repeat oneself, or to cosset oneself, or—past a certain age—to find oneself, but to find the distinctly other. That other, that is there, and is loved. The only interesting question on a trip for me is—what sustains life elsewhere? How deep does it go? Can one see it? This hope, this anticipation, is forcibly blocked. Henry Miller, in 193—, stood in Epidaurus, alone, in a "weird solitude," and felt the "great heart of the world beat." We stand at Epidaurus with several thousand others, some of whom are being called "my chickens" by their tour guide who calls herself "your mother hen," whose counterpart, this time at Delphi, explains several times that what is being looked at is the "belly button of the world, okay? The Greeks thought, this is the belly button of the world, okay?" "These stones all look alike to me," someone grumbles. There is no help for it; we're there with guidebooks ourselves; but this fact—tourism is big business—and others throw us back, unwilling, into contemplation of our own dull home-soul, our dull bodily comforts, our own dull dwindling purse, our own dull resentments; because the other—in this case, Greece— is either rapidly disappearing or else, self-protective, is retreating so far it is disappeared. You can get there, but you can't get at it.

For instance, a study of travel posters and brochures, which in the process of setting dates and buying tickets always precedes a trip, shows us, by projection into these pictured, toothy, tourist bodies, having some gorgeous piece of ingestion: the yellow beach, the mossy blue ruin, a dinner table laden with food and red wine of the region, dancing, skiing, golfing, shopping, waving to roadside natives as our rented car sails by, as though we only go to play, as though all we do here at home is work, as though, for two or four weeks abroad, we seek regression.

Also in the posters, but as part of the landscape, there are the natives—whether Spanish, Greek, Irish, etc.—costumed as attractions, performing in bouzouki or bagpipe bands, or doing some picturesque and nonindustrial piece of work such as fishing, weaving, selling colorful cheap goods in open-air markets, herding sheep or goats. The journey promised by the posters and brochures is a trip into everyone's imaginary past: one's own, drained of the normal childhood content of fear, death, space, hurt, abandonment, perplexity, and so forth, now presented as the salesmen think we think it should have been: one in which we only ate, slept, and played in the eternal sun under the doting care of benevolent elders.

And we are shown the benevolent elders, the imaginary natives who also, for a handsome fee, exist now, in the present of the trip we are about to take. ("Take" is probably a more telling verb here than we think.) They exist in a past where they are pictured having grown cheerfully old and wise doing only harmless, enjoyable, preindustrial, clean, self-employed, open-air work, in pink crinkled cheeks, merry eyes, and wonderful quaint clothes, with baskets, nets, toy-shaped boats, flower boxes, cottages, sheep crooks, country roads, whitewashed walls, tea shop signs, and other paraphernalia of the pastoral wish. I have never seen a travel poster showing natives of the country enjoying their own food or beaches or ski jumps or hotel balconies; nor have I ever seen a travel poster showing the natives working the night shift in the Citroën factory, either.

The natives in the posters (are they Swiss, Mexican, Chilean, Turkish models?) are happy parent figures, or character dolls, and their faces, like the faces of the good parents we are supposed to have dreamed, show them pleased with their own lot, busy but not too busy with a job that they obviously like, content with each other, and warmly indulgent of our need to play, to be fed good, clean food on time, and to be tucked into a nice bed at the end of our little day. They are the childhood people that also existed in early grammar school readers, and nowhere else: adults in your hood, in the identifiable costumes of their humble tasks, transitional-object people, smiling milkman, friendly aproned store owner in his small friendly store, happy mailman happy to bring your happy mail, happy mommy, icons who make up a six-year-old's school-enforced dream town, who enjoy doing their nonindustrial, unmysterious tasks: mail, milk, red apple, cookie, just for you, so you can learn to decipher: See, Jip, see.

A travel remark I have always savored came from someone surprised in love for a place, just returned from a month in the Far East (no longer tagged "the mysterious," I've noticed), and who was explaining this trip at a party. She said, "I just loved Japan. It was so authentic and Oriental." Few people would go quite so naked as that, but the charm of her feelings seemed just right. Perhaps she had expected Tokyo to be more or less a larger version of the Japanese Shop in the Tokyo Airport. It is somewhat surprising that she found it to be anything much more.

One of the hushed-tone moral superiority stories, the aren't-we-advanced stories told by those lucky enough to travel in Soviet Russia, has to do with that government's iron management of the trip. There are people who can't be met, buildings that can't be entered, upper story windows that can't be photographed, streets that can't be strolled, districts that can't be crossed, cities in which it is impossible to spend the night, and so on. However, our notions of who we are and what comforts we demand and what conditions we'll endure, plus any country's understandably garbled versions of who we are, what we want, and what we'll pay for, are far more rigid than the strictures of any politburo because such strictures don't say "This is you, this is what you must want," but "This is what you can't, under any circumstances, do." That, though it inhibits movement, and no doubt in some cases prevents a gathering of or understanding of some crucial or desired bit of information, has at least the large virtue of defining the tourist as potentially dangerous. What we meet most of the time, here and abroad, is a definition of ourselves as harmless, spoiled babies, of low endurance and little information, minimal curiosity, frozen in infancy, frozen in longing, terrified for our next square meal and clean bed, and whose only potential danger is that we might refuse to be separated from our money.

Suppose, for a moment, that tourism—the largest "industry" in Greece (it employs, even more than shipping, the most people)—were also the largest industry in America. Not just in Manhattan or Washington, DC, or Disneyland or Disneyworld or at the Grand Canyon or Niagara Falls, but in every motel, hotel, restaurant, in every McDonald's and Colonel Sanders and Howard Johnson's and Mom & Pop's, in every bar and neighborhood hangout, truck stop, gas station, pharmacy, department store, museum, church, historical site, battleground, in every taxi, bus, subway, train, plane, in every public building, in post offices and banks and public bathrooms, on every street in every city, town, village, and hamlet from West Jonesport, Maine, to

Centralia, Illinois, to Parachute, Colorado, and every stop in between and beyond, just as it is in Greece: tourists.

Suppose that every other business establishment across the country therefore found it in their best interest to become a souvenir shop, selling cheap, mass-produced "gifts" for the tourists to take back home that, back home, would announce that they had visited America. What images would we mass produce for them? Millions of little bronzed Liberty Bells? Tepees? St. Louis Arches? Streetcars named "Desire"? Statues of Babe Ruth? of Liberty? of Daniel Boone? In Greece we saw miniature bottles of ouzo encased in tiny plastic replicas of the temple of Athena Nike. Could we do something so clever, and immediately recognizable, with miniatures of bourbon? Encase them in tiny plastic Washington Monuments? Lincoln Memorials? Would we feel misrepresented?

Third, suppose that a sizable portion of these tourists wanting gifts, toilets, rooms, baths, meals, dollars, film, drinks, stamps, directions, are Greek; or else, let us suppose that we assumed, that whether actually Greek or not, wherever they come from they speak Greek as a second language. Assume, therefore, that our map and traffic and road signs, postings of instruction and information, advertisements, timetables, directions—"stop," "go," "hot," "cold," "men," "women," "open," "closed," "yes," "no"—to name a few rudiments of life, plus all the menus in all those sandwich counters, truck stops, fast-food outlets, lunchrooms, and so forth, had to be in Greek as well as in English. We have never been, so far, an occupied country, whether by forces enemy or not. Undoubtedly, if we were, as an ongoing fact of our "in-season" summer months, we Americans, having to offer our multitudinous wares in Greek, would come up with items as hilarious as those we collected from the English side of Greek menus: baygon and egs. Xamberger steake. Veat. Orange juise. Rost beef. Shrimp carry. Potoes. Spaggeti. Morcoroni. And our favorite, Fried Smooth Hound. (This turned out to be a harmless local fish, much to the disappointment of our children, born surrealists.)

Suppose that we had to post Bar Harbor, Plum Island, Chincoteague, Key West, Bay St. Louis, Galveston, Big Sur, and Seattle beaches with "No Nakedness Allowed" signs, but that the Greeks and other tourists, freed from the cocoons of air-conditioned tour buses, armed with sun oil in every degree of protection, rushed beachwards past the signs and stripped to their altogether, anyway? Would our police sit quietly in the shade and drink with other men and turn, literally, their khaki-clad rumps to the beach, as did the Greek police?

And food. Suppose we had to contrive to feed them, these hungry hordes? They will come here, as we go there, entrenched in their habits and encumbered with fears of being cheated, fears of indigestion, of recurrent allergies, of breaking their diets, of catching American trots, of being poisoned by our water, fattened by our grease and starch, put off by our feeding schedules, sickened by something weird or local. Suppose we decided, out of some semi-conscious, unorganized, but national canniness, that what these tourists really want is our cobbled version of their national foods. Whom will we please: the English who want their teas at four, or the Italians who want supper at nine at night? Or both? And what will we cook and serve, and how will we spell it?

Or suppose they want to eat "American" food. What tastes like us? What flavors contain our typicality, our history, our heroes, our dirt, our speeches, our poets, our battles, our national shames? The hot dog? Corn on the cob? I have eaten, barring picnics and occasional abstention, probably about 130 meals in Greece. And Greek food, I feel somewhat qualified to say, contains their history, and tastes of sorrow and triumph, of olive oil and blood, in about equal amounts. It is the most astounding and the most boring food that I, an eater, have ever eaten.

Greek food is tragic. Why? Because each bite is a chomp into history, our history. Why? Because this lunch—small fish, cheese, olives, wine, bread—exactly this lunch, and tomorrow's lunch—fish, cheese, olives, wine, bread—has been eaten since the time of the glory that will someday be called Greece, the glory that existed for a moment, the glory that Greece was, and the glory that mankind—for Greece is that, not Greek, but mankind—might yet be. Each bite is archaeological, into fine layers of millennia: fish, oil, cheese, wine, bread—in the partaking we join, on the back of the tongue, Amazon forces and single crazy saints, mythical men who married their mythical mothers, and men, and mothers, who today and tomorrow only dream of it.

One uses a big word like "timeless" with caution, if at all. But there is nothing timely about two things in Greece; therefore it is not rhetorical to claim that, in Greece, the quality of the heat of the sun on the skin and the quality of the food in the mouth are perhaps as close as we can come to the taste of "timelessness." Along with the oldest human question—how can we make God happy?—this sun and this food are among the most ancient sensations recorded.

Under this summer sun every meal, beginning with breakfast, is eaten in 100 degrees of heat and hotter—115, 120—by afternoon. The meal, any one of them, is composed of food that grows best in this climate and yet is entirely unsuited to it as daily refreshment. No one could possibly, certainly not a tourist, need this oil-soaked food for fuel in mid-July. It tastes and feels, though, like fuel: heavy, shiny, slow-moving food, purple, brown, red: tomatoes, eggplants, fish, lamb, olives, black wine, blinding white cheese, much bread. We eat this three times a day; three times a day the tourists eat it and the Greeks eat it. Everyone seems to look forward to the next meal, and all around our table, where we eat again with relish, are others eating with relish, sometimes even with a look of reprieve and relief. And there is no escape from it. Who would risk whatever "shrimp carry" might be? There is no ordering something else—a salad of lettuce for a change, or a thin chicken sandwich. There is nothing but this food with its taste and texture of ancient days, of old crimes, forbidden loves, of something tinny and resigned, something of both gluttony and renunciation.

In addition to being a tragic cuisine, a sacramental cuisine, it is also practical, cheap, crude, and uninventive. The raw materials are without equal: eggplants hang with the burnish of Dutch interiors; the fish still flap as they are headed oil-wards; the lamb chop's mother befouls the yard next to your table; fruit so perfect, so total, that the scent of a single peach in a paper bag perfumes the whole room overnight and brings tears of love of God to the eyes. On a walk into the hills, meadows of thyme and mint and basil are idly crushed under heel. What happens to all this in the pot is a miracle of transformation, of negligence or brutality, or possibly, stubborn evidence of some otherwise lost political knowledge of what draws out the best, most noble, and most beautiful in the masses.

For the food is destroyed, each meal, in the process from vine or net or garden to violent table. Its facts are these: it has always been eaten thus, with the exception of the late-coming tomato. It is—lamb, eggplant, olive, fish, white cheese—even now, perfectly indigenous. It is plain cooking. It is cooked for hours, all day; oil is poured on without restraint, discretion, or mercy. Every morsel is the same temperature and consistency by the time it reaches the palate. In a profound way, it is stupid food, overfeeding the flesh while tasting as though one should renounce the flesh forever.

We did not, to be fair, eat in a single Greek home. However, we were careful to eat where the Greeks ate, and the Greeks eat out—in family groups, starched, ironed, slicked-down heads, whited summer shoes, strictly disciplined children; or in tense, dark groups of greedy, hasty men; which is how, as families or as men, the Greeks travel through the day. From the second-story, open-air, Greek-family-filled restaurant where we ate most of our meals while on the island, we could, if we had a table near the edge, throw our bread scraps, if we had any left over, straight down into the blue-green sea for the melon- and dove-colored fish to mouth; and we could watch the evening sky turn from the day's bleached-out white to a pale English blue, then to lime-green streaked with apricot, and finally, with the fall of night, to a grape-purple that rose, in that instant, up from the sea.

Without the heat on the skin, without the food in the mouth, there is no hope of understanding the poetry of Greece. I am not talking of the possibility of reading it in the original, but of understanding the poetry in translation, in English, or French, or whatever one normally speaks and reads. Seferis, Sikelianos, Pappas, Yannis Ritsos, Odysseus Elytis: whatever their differences, all write poems of homesickness, of celebration, of sorrow for the land, of the comradeliness of the common denominators of war, occupation, loss, burned-out villages, lost youth, old simplicity, brotherhood, and always—the longing for the sea, for the sun, and for the grace of shared food: bread, wine, cheese, olives. A line from the poem "Lost Incorruptibility," by Pandelis Prevelakis, for instance—"The sun of Greece no longer bakes / on my lips the bread of poetry"—is not a thought, in any language, but the rendering of an absolute physical sensation; but also, not one that is universal: he means Greek sun, that bread, and no other. After feeling the two, the sun and the bread, for only 130 meals, no other is ever strong enough again.

Nor, without that exhausting strength, is there any hope of understanding the sinuous, tearful, hectic music which plays—or rather, which is played—on the island's several public jukeboxes, at top volume, not during the day, but all night until close to dawn, when it stops so abruptly, the silence wakes you up, as though the real function of the music, through the black night, was to act as an insistent, imploring, coaxing prayer, ensuring the sun's return. If, and when, it does, we will eat again.

Day after stupefying day, for our weeks on the island, we drown ourselves in the heat of the beaches. These public beaches—two or three of them—are intermittently bitten into the rocks and woods encircling the island. To get to them, since there are few roads, one must catch one of the daily taxi boats, converted fishing boats now fitted up with wooden benches and gay awnings, which bob and toot and whistle in the town's main harbor early each morning. The half-hour ride costs less than a dollar, and the boat putts its polyglot cargo round to St. Patros or further, to the Paradise Beach, and unloads us. The captain ties it up, turns off the motor, and then he retires for the heat of the day to the shade of the seaside café. There he eats, and drinks, and talks with Greek men—stray police, other boat captains and crew, the sweating, white-aproned cook, and occasional delivery men who roar up on mopeds laden with cases of mineral water or eggplants for the café. Five or six hours later, the captain reboards his boat, blows its horn, starts up his motor, and the sun-soaked tourists drag back on to return to the main town, to its hotels, shops, and restaurants.

Ten years ago, when we were also on this island for several weeks, everything was very nearly the same. The same waiters, the same shops, the same striped shirts and wool bags fading against sunny walls, the same elaborate gray leather English prams, filled with lacy pillows, canned tomatoes, and enthroned, one beruffled, olive-eyed Greek baby. The same village simpleton employed with his broom in a dozen small establishments, wearing his Hell's Angel's T-shirt. But, this trip, aside from the bakery, which had been fixed up and painted a fresh green, there was one large change. Ten years ago, though they may have been scantily clad, no woman appeared on any of the public beaches without a top to her suit. Now, ten years later, except for the Greek women who remain most emphatically suited, nearly every woman on the beach, of whatever age, has bare breasts, and in some coves, bare everything. "Mom," said one of our boys the first day embarking from the beach taxi, thirty hours from the chill proprieties of Logan Airport and our own northern beaches where, for all but a few days of the year, you need a wool sweater, "Mom, that lady over there doesn't have on a whole suit."

We had not expected this, I don't know why we didn't, but so she doesn't, and, at once clear, neither does anyone else. This is not at all a normal moment. It is a startling moment. More so if one has no thought of doing it oneself. It is the sort of outlandish but limited experience about which you have immediately to ask: how do I feel? Much less, what do our eleven- and fifteen-year-olds feel? These breasts aren't just lying down either, they're up and moving, hundreds of more or less matched pairs.

The first thing you have to do is arrange your face and hope that the children will have the decency to do the same. They don't of course, they can't, and for two or three days of this, they do the worst: point and giggle and hit each other and stroll slowly, staring. Finally they seem to get used to it, or tire of it, at least they say so, and they return to playing with snorkels and whining for food.

The second thing you have to do, now that the obviously untraumatized boys have their faces recomposed and are back to lunch and swimming, is to work on your mind. You try to make this scene rhyme with its advance publicity: this is beautiful, and free, and healthy, and what's more, to go as naked as you please is *everyone's right*, and if you are such a pig that you find it either sexually exciting or morally offensive, then *that is your problem.*

Third, wishing ever, at first, to be rational, modern, and especially broad-minded, you try to compose in yourself the most difficult piece of the publicity: one is not supposed to think about this at all. Naturally, one is not supposed to look or stare or say something or in any way notice or react, certainly not sexually nor prudishly, but more difficult: one is not, if one is really modern, supposed to *think* about this. What's current bad behavior, what's truly shocking, is to think it is worth thinking about. It's natural, it's normal, two attributes which go without saying and which preclude thought. If you think about it, there's something wrong with you. Bare breasts on the beach, here and there bare genitals, should be as normal, as everyday, as are the empty faded packs of Marlboros, the abandoned bottles, the tattered oily paperbacks of *Airport* and *Princess Daisy*, and the squeezed-out tubes of Nivea Soleil. Breasts are simply something else on the beach, and you, brother and sister of the flesh, had better bloody well think so, too.

A spine of wooded, uninhabited hills, small mountains really, forms the imposing center of the island from end to end. On each side of this furry spine, the dry land falls abruptly to the sea. Every few miles, a bald stripe appears: the fire line, cut straight up through the trees, with the purpose of containing forest fires, too wide a bare space for sparks to jump. The Greek men sit under the fig trees, their backs to the beach. Their own women move in a weight of clothes, in the protection of their own cumbersome shade. The tourist men lie on the beach mats, clothed in their tiny suits, reading *Airport* or *Princess Daisy*, or adjusting the knobs on multi-wave radios. Sometimes they empty tubes of Nivea onto themselves or onto the breasts and bellies and backs of their women. Otherwise, they occupy themselves; they don't stare; they don't giggle; they are not playful, either, and their faces have an expression of somewhat lofty, gentle unconcern. They gaze out to sea as though they are thinking about business; perhaps they are. They seem careworn, forlorn, and not much warmed. And they behave like quiet eunuchs, especially so when they methodically and without feeling do the servicing of radio knobs, dig in their shorts for wads of money, and rub on the oil. A fire line has to cut through them. Otherwise, they'd become the missing piece of the beach: satyrs, noon gods, cavorting, slathering Pans.

Because they are not, because they are so diminished, they have the powerful effect of turning the woman from bare-breasted Artemis into slave.

That's the fourth beach thought. The men must have to work so hard not to notice, to be liberal and free-minded and nonchauvinistic, that their effort transforms the nakedness of the women into costuming, as conscious and stagey as Halloween crone or shepherdess. To go naked, after all, is to dress up as an infant, as a victim, or as a slave. This seems inescapable. There is no escaping history by untying a string, and for too long in the art and tribal lore of cold, northern, imperial places, nudity is established as peril. Escaping, the slave must first find garments to cover his shame, to hide and protect his true menial, owned state. These breasts on the beach, though brazen, are not proud. This unfortunate effect, created first by the studied, peaceful neutrality of all the men, is compounded by the difficulty of getting up and down the beach. These are not sandy beaches. It is a cruel walk, burning hot and sharp and stony. The women can't stride; shod, a proud free stride is difficult. Barefooted, barebreasted, it is impossible; they pick and mince, curse and stumble, their hands fly up stiffly to keep balance. They walk as though their breasts should be on trays. They move with such joyless, servile effort it seems as though they have been forced to go naked, as sign, as chattel, as someone else's visible symbol of power, acted out through drudgery, hard simple chores, and pitiless exposure. Their eunuchs, though sweet and free from lust, are powerless to alter the women's essential degradation of having to do as the master wills; and he, whoever he is, wills nakedness, even in these hard conditions.

You have to turn away from it. The general impudence and coldness of things is too sorrowful, and is perhaps the result of defiance. For how does one handle a position of defiance, of dare? By acting cold. And defiance is also inescapable. No one can go naked in a country whose native inhabitants are clothed without having to arrange an attitude. Blithe Spirit, thou cannot pull off. Nor relax, naked in public, because a front must be kept up against the clothed. And it must be, in Greece, of extreme mental difficulty to label and hence dismiss the old, funny, cackling, self-satisfied Greek women, puddling in the warm shallows, embalmed in their dark skirted bathing suits, big beach hats, baskets of food and wine and blankets, as uptight Puritans. They're having too good a time for that to stick. You would have to work too hard to escape their mirthful eye, and too hard to catch the eye of the waiter who will not look at you at all. And it is difficult to imagine what effort must go into the regendering of the patient escorts, temporary eunuchs on polite holiday.

Hence there is, at last, the last thought: light without warmth, provocation without sympathy, a cold, blue glare, like cans of burning Sterno. It sinks into you, this sadness, from the quarter mile of bodies lying exhausted with their feet toward the sea, like a blow to the bone, a hard slug in the pit, and leaves behind the utter coldness, the terrifying, unimportant, empty arrest that follows an unexpected slap. Cover the breasts, and the face is free. Uncover the breasts, and the face must perforce become a policeman.

Two women are walking toward us, at noon, across the nearly deserted rocks. Most of the other swimmers and sunbathers are up in the café, eating lunch under the fig trees, the grapevine. These two women are not together, they walk several feet apart, and they do not look at each other. One is tall and blond, dressed in a flowered bikini and clogs, a tourist, English or American or Scandinavian or German. The other woman, a Greek, is carrying a basket, walking quickly, and gives the impression of being on a neighborhood errand. She is probably from one of the small old farms—sheep, olive trees, hens, gardens, goats—that border this stretch of sea and climb a little way into the pine and cypress woods.

Both are smoking, and both walk upright. Beyond that, there is so little similarity they could belong to different planets, eras, species, sexes. The tourist looks young, the Greek looks old; actually, she looks as old as a village well, and the blond looks like a drawn-out infant, but there could be as little as five or ten years difference between them.

The Greek woman is short and heavy, waistless, and is wearing a black dress, a black scarf pulled low around her eyes, a black sweater, thick black stockings, black shoes. She is stupendously there, black but for the walnut of her face, in the white sun, against the white space. She looks, at once, as if she could do everything she's ever done, anything needed, and also at once, she gives off an emanation of humor, powers, secrets, determinations, acts. She is moving straight ahead, like a moving church, a black peaked roof, a hot black hat, a dark tent, like a doom, a government, a force for good and evil, an ultimatum, a determined animal. She probably can't read, or write; she may never in her life have left this island; but she is beautiful, she could crush you, love you, mend you, deliver you of child or calf or lamb or illusion, bleed a pig, spear a fish, wring a supper's neck, till a field, coax an egg into life. Her sex is like a votive lamp flickering in a black, airless room. As she comes closer, she begins to crochet—that's what's in her basket, balls of cotton string and thick white lace coming off the hook and her brown fingers.

The blond tourist, struggling along the hot pebbles in her clogs, is coming back to her beach mat and friends. She looks as though she couldn't dress a doll without having a fit of sulks and throwing it down in a tantrum.

It may not be the case, of course. She is on holiday, on this Greek island, which fact means both money and time. She is no doubt capable, well-meaning, and by the standards and expectations of most of the world's people, well-educated and very rich and very comfortable. She can undoubtedly read and write, most blond people can, and has, wherever she comes from, a vote, a voice, a degree of some kind, a job, a career perhaps, money certainly, opinions, friends, health, talents, habits, central heating, living relatives, personalized checks, a return ticket, a summer wardrobe, the usual bits and clamor we all, tourists, have. But presence, she has not. Nor authority, nor immediacy, nor joy for the eye, nor a look of adding to the world, not of strength nor humor nor excitement. Nearly naked, pretty, without discernible blemish, blond, tall, tan, firm, the product of red meat and whole milk, vitamins, orange juice, women's suffrage, freedom of religion, child labor laws, compulsory education, the anxious, dancing, lifelong attendance of uncounted numbers of furrow-browed adults, parents, teachers, pediatricians, orthodontists, counselors, hairdressers, diet and health and career and exercise and fashion consultants, still, she is not much to look at. She looks wonderful, but your eye, your heart, all in you that wants to look out on the substance of the people of the day, doesn't care, isn't interested long, is, in fact, diminished a little.

She could be anything—a professor of Romance Languages at a major university, a clerk in a Jermyn Street shop, a flight attendant, a Stockholm lawyer, but nothing shows of that life or luck or work or history, not world, not pain or freedom or sufficiency. What you think of, what her person walking toward you in the fierce noon light forces you to think of, after the momentary, automatic envy of her perfections, is that she looks as though she's never had enough—goods or rights or attention or half-decent days. Whether she is or not, she looks unutterably dissatisfied and peevish. And yet, in order to be here on this blue white beach on this July day, unless you are chasing your own stray goat across the rocks, requires a position of luxury, mobility, and privilege common to us but beyond any imagining of the Greek woman who walks here too with a basket of string and her hot, rusty clothes but who, however, and not at all paradoxically, exudes a deep, sustained bass note of slumbering, solid contentment.

Insofar as ignorance always makes a space, romance rushes in to people it. With so little fact at hand about either of these lives, fact which might make things plain and profound as only fact can do, there is little but romance, theories, guesswork, and yet, it seems, this accidental conjunction of women in the sun, considered, says it is not a matter of the one, the blond, being discontent in spite of much and the other, the farm woman in black, being smugly, perhaps ignorantly content with little. That theory is too much the stuff of individual virtue, and of fairy tales: grateful peasant, happy with scraps and rags, and querulous, bitchy princess, untried, suffering every pea, pursued by frogs, awaiting a magic deliverance. Because in literal, daily fact, the Greek woman has more than the tourist, and the tourist, wherever she comes from and despite her list of equipment and privileges, is also, in literal daily fact, deprived. To see this as a possible deciphering of this scene means to stop thinking of the good life strictly in terms of goods, services, and various rights, and think instead, insofar as we can, of other, almost muted because so nearly lost to us, needs of life.

Beyond seeing that she has two arms, two good legs, a tanned skin, blond hair, and friends, I know nothing about this particular tourist. Beyond knowing that she has two arms, two good legs, a face that could stop or move an army, and a black dress, and can crochet lace, I know nothing about this particular peasant woman. I don't even know, it's only a clumsy guess, that "peasant" should be the qualifying adjective. I can only talk about these women as they appeared, almost a mirage in the shimmer of beach heat, almost icons, for a moment and walked past; and as they are on an island where I, too, have spent a notch of time. Whatever the Greek woman, and her kind, has enjoyed or missed, has suffered or lost in war, under dictatorship, under occupation, from men, in poverty or plenty, I don't know. The other woman, I won't describe, won't further guess at, for she is familiar to us; she is us.

I don't know in what order of importance, should that order exist or be articulable, the Greek woman would place what occurs on the visible street of her life. For that is all I do see, all that we can see, and it wrings the heart, that visible street. For one thing, in most places, the street is not yet given over to the demands of the motor. The Greek is still a citizen, and a large part of his day is given to whatever life goes on in public, and that life takes place on the street. Much of what we do in private, in isolation, in small personally chosen groups—eating, drinking, talking, staring into space— is, in Greece, done on the impersonal, random street. This habit of daily gathering, which is done for no particular reason, that is, there is no special occasion, lends to every day and night the feel of mild, but lively festival.

Second, among the other visible things that "underdeveloped" means, it means that—due either to a generous wisdom that has survived, or else funding that is not yet available—there is not enough money for the fit to invent shelters for the unfit. For whatever reasons, the Greek woman still lives in a culture where this has not yet happened. That is, not only are the streets used by and for people, but all sorts of people are on them, still privileged to their piece of the sun, the common bread, the work, the gossip, the ongoing parade. Our children are pitying and amazed. After several days on these streets they assume that in Greece there are more fat and slow and old, more crippled and maimed, more feeble of mind and body, more blind and begging, more, in general, outcast folks than we, Americans, have. They are especially amazed at how *old* people get to be in Greece. Being young and American, and not living in New York, the only city we have that approximates the fullness and variety of a village, they assume this is evidence of extreme longevity on the one hand, and evidence of extreme bad health on the other. It was as hard to explain about American nursing homes and other asylums and institutions as it was to explain about public nudity, how archaeologists find hidden ruins, and other questions that came up on the trip.

A "developed" country is seldom mysterious but always mystifying. Where do things come from and where do they go? Life can be looked at, but not often comprehended in any of its ordinary particulars: food, shelter, work, money, producing and buying and selling. The Greek woman on the beach, again for many reasons, does still live in a world that, in those particulars—food, shelter, work, product, etc.—is comprehensible. Outside the few urban, industrial areas in Greece, it is still possible to build and conduct life without the benefit of technicians, specialists, explainers, bureaucrats, middlemen, and other modern experts. This means that there is possible an understanding of, a connection with, and a lack of technological mystification to many of the elements, objects, and products commonly lived with in any day. A typical Greek house is so simple and cunning that it could be built, or destroyed, by almost anyone. This may mean less convenience, but it also means more comprehension. For the ordinary person, there is relatively little of the multiform, continual, hardly-much-thought-about incomprehensibility of daily things—where does this lamb chop come from? where does this wash water go?—that most people in developed countries live with, or manage to ignore, every day. Therefore, for this Greek woman on the beach and her kind, there is another mind possible, one which sees, and understands, and in most instances can control many details; and a mind in which, therefore, many mysteries can grow a deeper root.

Food, to take another example, is eaten in season, and most of it is locally grown, harvested or butchered, processed, sold, and consumed. There is no particular moral virtue in this fact, but this fact does signify the possibility of a sharper, more acute (it sees, it has to see and comprehend more details), and more satisfied intelligence. Having money means being able to buy the end product; therefore, money replaces the need for intricate knowledge of processes; therefore, money replaces knowledge. The understanding of a glass of water or wine, a melon, an onion, or a fried fish, from inception to end, does mean living with a different kind of mind than the one which results from having merely bought and consumed the wine or fish or onion at the end. In that sense, therefore, it is possible that the unhappy peevishness and dissatisfaction on the face of the pretty tourist comes in part from a life of being left out of knowledge of the intricate details of the complete cycle of any single thing she is able to consume.

Including the country of Greece.

There is a new world everywhere now that money will buy. It is a world without a nation, though it exists as an overlay of life, something on the order of the computer, in almost any country of the globe. It is an international accommodation, and wherever it exists—whether in Madrid, London, Istanbul, Athens, Cleveland—it resembles a large airport lounge. In this way, the new world specially constructed everywhere for tourists is something like the thousands of Greek churches, as alike as eggs, and no matter what their size all modeled on the single great discovered design of Constantine's Hagia Sophia.

Inside this international accommodation is allowed only so much of any specific country as lends itself as background, decor, and trinkets. In this sense, the travel posters are an accurate portrayal of exactly how little can happen on a well-engineered trip: scenery and "gifts." Because most of the world is still what would be termed "poor," the more money you can spend, nearly any place, the more you are removed from the rich, complex life of that place. It is possible to buy everything that puts an average American life—taps that mix hot and cold, flush toilets, heating and cooling systems, menus in English—on top of any other existing world. It is possible to pay for every familiar security and comfort and, as the posters show, still have been *there* having it. At the end of the trip, you can say that you were there.

However, the extent to which one buys familiarity, in most of the world today, is also the extent to which one will not see, smell, taste, feel, or in any way be subjected to, enlightened by, or entered by that piece of the world and its people. The world's people are not blind to this fear of the unfamiliar and uncomfortable, nor insensitive to the dollars that will be paid to ward it off. In the winter months, when life returns to normal, the friendly Greek "waiters" resume their lives as masons, carpenters, builders, mechanics, schoolteachers, and so forth, a fact unknown to or overlooked by many tourists who assume, for example, that many unfinished buildings, seen languishing in the summer season, are due to neglect, laziness, disinterest, or what have you.

We all assume, and usually safely, that the more money you have the more you can buy. In travel, however, the opposite is true. The less money you spend, the less money you have to spend, perhaps, the more your chances of getting a whiff, now and then, of what another place is like. There are the ideals: walking a country, living there, learning its language. Short of that, those conditions which most of us cannot meet, one can try spending as little as possible: class D hotels, public transportation, street meals. And then one must try to be as brave and patient and good-humored and healthy as possible because, without a doubt, the less money you spend the closer you come to partaking of very annoying, confusing, exhausting, foreign, debilitating, sometimes outrageous discomfort.

For instance, the two things one would most want to avoid in Greece in the summer are the intense heat and the unworldly, unimaginable, unforeseeable amount of din. Pandemonium is, after all, a Greek idea, but in actual life, it is hardly confined to the hour of noon. Silence is a vacuum into which, like proverbial nature, a single Greek will rush with a pure love of noise. Two Greeks together produce more noise than 200 of any other Western nation. Greeks love above all else the human voice, raised in any emotion; next to that they love their actions with objects. One Greek with any object—a string of beads, a two-cylinder engine, preferably one on the eternal blink, a rug to beat, a single child to mind, a chair to be moved—will fill all time and space with his operation; it will be the Platonic scrape of metal chair leg on stone street; it will be the one explanation to last for all eternity why the child should not torture the cat in the garden. A generalization: Greeks love horns, bells, animal cries, arguments, dented fenders, lengthy explanations, soccer games, small motors, pots and pans, cases of empty bottles, vehicles without mufflers, cups against saucers, fireworks, political songs, metal awnings, loudspeakers, musical instruments, grandmothers, the Orthodox liturgy, traffic jams, the sound of breaking glass, and Mercedes taxi cabs that tootle "Mary Had a Little Lamb."

A further generalization: the above generalization is one that only *not* spending money will buy. That is, you have to be in a class F room, in a hotel on the harbor, one flight above a taverna frequented by fishermen, 120 degrees in the room, no screens, mosquito coils burning in the unmoving air through the night, and through the night—a donkey in heat tethered in the walled garden below your shuttered, only shuttered, window. In other words, it's quiet, and cool, at the Hilton; and there are, God and international capitalism be thanked, no donkeys.

And the Greeks love what the human hand can do. The Greek woman on the beach, crocheting the heavy lace, lives in an atmosphere created in part by the exceptional amount of touching that goes on, both of other people, children especially, and of all objects. It is a visible world burnished, rounded by the human hand, and foot, and the intimate, mysterious, warmed contours that come only from the brush of years of hands, petting and shaping, hands speaking. Surfaces are so much handled it's as though they now move out from themselves toward the caress of the hand. There are few hard edges, mathematical edges, even in the cities where, from the top of the Acropolis, for instance, Athens at its gentle foot is a smooth, rounded, whitewashed spread of infinite village. Things, hundreds of things furthermore, are the size that human hands can do. Living elsewhere, waiting, knowing all one's life that the great monuments of grandeur yet exist for us only in Greece, and then going to Greece, what surprise to find all habitations, whether of old god or new man, so small, so sensible, so pious, so mysteriously scaled. When the hot tourist grumbles, "These stones all look alike to me," he's absolutely right. And therein is some meaning to reach for.

The Greeks gave us our patterns. They invented the patterns for us. Surely such patterns—of logic, of love, of invocation—exist elsewhere in the world, but these are still ours, these, our organizations of emphatic, comprehensible meaning. These the patterns that have penetrated our bones; we resonate with them, even in ruins, like struck gongs. Despite having had one of the worst histories of the last ten, or hundred, or any number of years, something in Greece has survived, lives on still, is still all right, still blessed; something has not gone down or been lost. It lives on in these remarkable faces. The invisible worm does not yet live here. Sometimes what has survived feels like a sense of humor that comes of a self-love so forthright, rich, grave, curious, so gentle, that it survives all terror, upheaval, and excess. Sometimes it feels like a chosen poverty of goods and a ceremonial elaboration of daily events that consciously refuse the intervention of metal, calculation, efficiency, ideologies, speed, abstraction. It feels like Henry Miller's assertion that God has not yet turned his back on Greece; and it feels like the sum of the gifts that Aristotle says endow the happy man. It feels as though Greece has yet managed to escape the tyranny of the merely fit. It feels as though life on the visible street still corresponds to the totality of the old human lot: the tragic, the comic, the lame, the fat, the halt, the silly, the invented, the play-acted, the smallest needs, the infinite variations of the exceptional and human.

Drama, one of the patterns that has come down to us, began as propitiation of the gods, and asked, "Was this it? Is this right?" Whatever it is that yet survives the worm here, it keeps that question alive, that question, and love enough for everything to have its say, its sun, love for the intelligence of touch, for the immediacy of ancient gossip, and for the incarnate knowledge that life is short, and we are all of it.

Autumn 1983

The British in India

C. B. COX

MANCHESTER, SEPTEMBER 1984—A few years ago my wife and I visited India for the first time. At the Oberoi Hotel in Delhi we found ourselves at lunch in the company of a group of Anglo-Indians. Thirty years after India became independent, they were revisiting their old homes.

At a table near us sat a typical upper-class English lady in a flowery silk dress and straw hat. When she needed some more butter for her bread, she turned toward a middle-aged Indian waiter and in a loud voice shouted "Boy!"

My wife and I cringed. It was as if we had walked straight into Forster's *A Passage to India* and were being confronted by Mrs. Turton.

After this incident I was surprised to find how many Indians recall British rule with nostalgia. I've now visited India to teach for the British Council on three occasions, and I've always been treated with great courtesy and generosity. At Simla a couple of years ago an old army sergeant, very polite and proper, stopped me in the street and harangued me for fifteen minutes with his reminiscences. The Indians don't want us back again, of course, and they're proud of their independence, but, now so many years have passed, they recall the virtues of British administration as well as the snobbery and intolerance.

An assistant registrar at my university once worked for the Indian Civil Service. He told me that it was a rule that if he received a gift from an Indian, he must in courtesy accept, but within 24 hours he must return a present of similar value. It's this kind of honesty which Indians recall with so much admiration.

The British too are rediscovering and reassessing their role during the great days of Empire. After the enormous success of Richard Attenborough's

Gandhi, the film of Ruth Prawer Jhabvala's *Heat and Dust* has been drawing large audiences. And then this last winter the whole country has been switching on television to watch Granada TV's brilliant *The Jewel in the Crown,*[1] an adaptation in 14 episodes of Paul Scott's *Raj Quartet.* When this comes to American homes this autumn it is likely to be as successful as *Brideshead Revisited.* At dinner parties in Britain everyone has been discussing the latest episode, and the conversation inevitably involves revaluation of the British Raj. I've heard more talk about India during the last year than in the previous twenty.

In common with many recent English visitors to India, I wasn't happy with Attenborough's presentation of Gandhi. Ben Kingsley's acting, of course, was beyond praise, and the film was wonderfully dramatic, but I felt Gandhi was treated too sympathetically, almost at times with sentimental reverence.

When the film was running in London, Salman Rushdie published in the *Times* a strongly worded attack. This inevitably provoked a hurt reply from Attenborough and a lively correspondence. Rushdie thought that the film did not do justice to Jinnah, the Muslim leader who became the first governor general of Pakistan, and that Gandhi's policies were in some degree responsible for the deaths of the two million people slain in the riots and massacres after Partition in 1947.

Mrs. Gandhi's recent problems with the Sikhs and the killings of the extremists in the Golden Temple of Amritsar have reminded the world of the fanatical religious conflicts with which the British in their time contended. I've always felt some sympathy for Ronnie Heaslop in *A Passage to India,* who is conscientious and honest in his work as a magistrate. After he's been successful in preventing bloodshed between Mohammedans and Hindus during preparations for a religious procession, his self-satisfaction is mocked. Forster undervalues the Anglo-Indian sense of duty and the integrity of the British administration.

As an outsider I feel I've no right to adjudicate between rights and wrongs when Hindus and Muslims come into conflict. The poverty of India is deeply depressing, and involved with religious practices. As you leave the Grand Hotel in Calcutta, after a sumptuous meal, you are jostled by starving beggars and mothers with emaciated babies in their arms. If you give them

---

1. *The Jewel in the Crown* was aired by PBS beginning December 16, 1984, through March 17, 1985.

a rupee, you're likely to draw a crowd, and it may be difficult to escape. You push your way through the outstretched hands and depart in your taxi. If you have a conscience, you can make a donation to Mother Teresa's home for children before you catch your plane back to the West.

In Calcutta's fetid atmosphere it's not easy to believe any political solution to poverty exists. As Forster himself said, things aren't so jolly easy.

It is this sense of complexity which Granada's epic film of *The Jewel in the Crown* captures so brilliantly. Ronald Merrick (played by Tim Pigott-Smith), who tortures Hari Kumar, his Indian rival for the love of Daphne Manners, might have fitted into Forster's *A Passage to India*; and Judy Parfitt as Mildred Layton splendidly portrays English arrogance. But the scene is so varied, so rich compared with Forster's limited canvas.

Peggy Ashcroft's acting rivals that of Ben Kingsley. Her portrayal of Barbie Batchelor, the old missionary teacher, is a great triumph. Barbie's old friend, Edwina Crane, hurt during the riots, commits suicide by burning herself to death in her garden shed. My one major criticism of the film is that it returns too often, presumably in search of continuity, to such symbolic scenes. In the novel Miss Crane courageously chooses to teach poor Indian children. On her first visit to a school she is nervous and ashamed of her supposed English superiority. She experiences a sudden moment of insight:

> And it came to Miss Crane then that the only excuse she or anyone of her kind had to be there, alone, sitting on a chair, holding a nosegay, being sung to, the object of awe of uninstructed children, was if they sat there conscious of a duty to promote the cause of human dignity and happiness. And then she was no longer really ashamed of her dress, or deeply afraid of the schoolhouse or the smell of burning cowpats.

Peggy Ashcroft's performance creates many moments that realize Paul Scott's sense of the dignity that resides even in the most ordinary of people.

The novels depend on complicated flashbacks. Sir Denis Forman, Chairman of Granada Television and the enthusiast who set the whole project in motion, decided that television needed a chronological narrative, broken down into sequences each of which would form a one-hour episode. A roll of wall paper was chopped into segments about one yard square, pinned around the walls of a room, and then on each was written down the outline of scenes for each episode. After walking some miles around the gallery, shifting pieces and deliberating, he decided it could be done. The result is a magnificent achievement.

A huge problem was that the love story between Hari Kumar and Daphne Manners ends with her death in childbirth after the third episode. How could interest be maintained? The story of Sara Layton takes over, played by Geraldine James who was Mirabehn, daughter of an English admiral and a dedicated follower of the Indian leader in Attenborough's *Gandhi*. Miss James's extraordinarily attractive personality holds together the rest of the sequence.

The photography dwells on Indian landscapes, Simla, Kashmir, Mysore, and Udaipur, with delicacy and love. *The Jewel in the Crown* is worth watching for this alone. It's easy to understand why so many Anglo-Indians were charmed for life by these vistas.

At a celebration lunch in Manchester, my wife sat next to Christopher Morahan, the producer. He explained to her that in many scenes the outside locations are in India and the interiors in Granada's Manchester studios. In the opening sequences the outside of the MacGregor House was filmed in Mysore, but the interior was created in Manchester. When an actor arrived for a party, he stepped out of his car in India and then walked through the front door in Lancashire. A ball bounced by a child in India was caught in England by Charles Dance, playing Sergeant Perron.

I sat next to Sir Denis Forman. As he holds Paul Scott in such high esteem, I didn't like to tell him I think his straightforward narrative sequences a great improvement on the novel.

The film begins with the riots of 1942, and the rape in the Bibighar Gardens, shot in a disused Lancashire quarry. It ends with the massacres of 1947. The last sequence includes the horrific killing of Muslim men, women, and children in the carriages of an ambushed train. Morahan decided it would be tactless to stage this butchery in India, where memory of those savage times is still fresh, and so the scene was re-created in a disused station at Quainton in Buckinghamshire.

The film explores the difficult conflict of interests between Hindu and Muslim, British and Indian; but its great distinction is that, as Paul Scott would have wished, it promotes the cause of human dignity and happiness. I shall never forget the acting of Peggy Ashcroft as Barbie, Fabia Drake as Mabel Layton, and Susan Wooldridge as Daphne Manners. As soon as Granada arranges a British repeat, I shall watch it all again.

Autumn 1984

The Gardens of Kyoto
in Summer

CHARLES W. MILLARD

For M. B. W., hid in death's dateless night.

A CONVINCING ARGUMENT can be made that gardens, particularly those of Kyoto, are the premier esthetic expression of traditional Japanese art. They, at least as much as painting, sculpture, and other media, are the products of great creative talents and embody the strength and sensitivity characteristic not only of the best Japanese art, but of all great art. Kyoto's preeminence in the field no doubt arises from its having been the Imperial capital and a center of Buddhist power (almost all the finest gardens are attached to temples) for almost a thousand years. In particular, the city benefitted from the presence of a series of major artists during what were the late Medieval and Renaissance periods in the West.

The medium of the gardens—vegetation—and the subtlety with which it is managed in Kyoto demand that any consideration of them be qualified by the season in which they are experienced. Since they are green in summer, scarlet with maples in autumn, white with snow in winter, and pink with cherry blossoms in spring—not to mention the coloristic contributions of azaleas, chrysanthemums, and dozens of other species of flowers—the gardens can be fully understood only by being observed for not less than a year. The present consideration is limited to their appearance during late August and early September.

Among the first surprises of Kyoto's gardens for a Westerner is the realization that they are meant less to be walked through than to be contemplated from specific and removed vantage points. The precisely delimited dry garden at Ryōan-ji, for example, cannot be entered and is viewable from only one side, while more elaborate compositions, such as that at Katsura, are embellished with pavilions intended as belvederes. Although there are vistas and hidden effects that reveal themselves only as one moves through Japanese gardens, as in the secret world visible through a cleft in the azaleas at Shisen-dō, the presence of more than one person in most gardens seriously alters their scale. This is so in part because they are meant to be seen not merely from the shelter of buildings, but sitting down. Thus, their scale is usually calculated to be intimate in the foreground and to increase with distance. There is, moreover, the simple fact that people in the twentieth century are taller and broader than those by and for whom the gardens were designed. In any case, the gardens were not originally public and were to be experienced only by the few people who lived in the adjacent buildings. The abstractness of the ideas underlying Japanese gardens places them at considerable remove not only from English gardens, which are intended both to be pleasing to the eye (the more so when inhabited by animals) and to be roamed through, but from such formal French gardens as those of Vaux-le-Vicomte. Although the latter extend before one's eyes like a tapestry, their patterns and the regularity of their broad paths are conceived to tempt one out through the ground-level doors that give onto them to stroll from parterre to parterre.

Given that the gardens of Kyoto are intended to be wandered through with the eye, like a Chinese scroll, rather than with the feet, it comes as no surprise to discover that the best of them were designed by painters. Like paintings, the gardens, whether looked at or walked through, are meant to be contemplated, to be part of a continuing and reciprocal relationship with the beholder. And as in paintings, the points of view from which they are seen are rigorously controlled. The buildings that mostly provide these points of view become integral parts of the experience of the garden, and the famous natural quality of Japanese architecture arises in part from this spiritual interdependency. This is not infrequently expressed in the forms and features of the structures themselves. One of the teahouse pavilions in the grounds at Katsura, for example, is supported by posts made of untrimmed sapling trunks. These occur at the periphery of the building, at some remove from the tatami-matted floor on which one sits. As one looks at the garden, it is unclear whether the particular post one sees at any given moment is a manmade structural element or the trunk of a tree just beyond the eaves. This ambiguity ties building and garden together, while the trunk's powerful vertical, cut off by the eaves, provides a *repoussoir* against which the garden is seen. The effect is very much like certain devices adopted by Impressionism from Japanese painting. It is enhanced by the presence of a pine tree not far from the pavilion, which mediates between the abstracted trunk and the expanse of landscape beyond by being nearby like the former but a complete tree like those in the latter. The garden is thereby pictorialized to an extent unknown in the West. A different but related effect is achieved at Shisen-dō by the great tree that rises at the right of the garden as one views it from the house, the branches of which spread horizontally across the view just below the eaves. One is reminded of nothing so much as the framing foreground tree of which Cézanne was so fond in his views of Mont Sainte-Victoire.

The buildings from which Kyoto's gardens are contemplated function much like the frames of Western paintings. Their openings, whether carefully shaped windows or opened shōji, inevitably embrace a particular view. It is part of the genius of the garden's designers that they were able to make every such view satisfactory, allowing for constant, even slight, changes of position within the building. Their art is, thus, related not only to painting but to sculpture as well and takes the beholder's movement into account. The adaptability of this scheme is strikingly illustrated at Shisen-dō, where the shōji have been removed. What would originally have read as a sequence of vignettes of the garden separated by open shōji now appears as a continuous panorama. It is no less satisfactory on that account.

Perhaps the most telling example of the subtle calculation that makes Japanese gardens as a whole, and every element within them, coherent from any point of view is a pine composition at Ginkaku-ji. Two trees flanking the path into the garden, one substantially smaller than the other, are clipped so as to form a visual unit. Seen from any angle except immediately between them, it is virtually impossible to perceive these pines as other than a single entity, even when one knows they are distinct. Such devices accentuate the fact that *nothing* in a Japanese garden is unplanned. Every shape, placement, and color, and almost every sound and movement, is calculated by the artist, even to the vegetation on the hillsides that occasionally form backdrops against which more manicured nature is presented. The full effect of such gardens depends, therefore, on the continuous and perfect maintenance that assures that bushes and trees will always be trimmed to the shapes intended for them, flowers always blooming where their colors are most effective, etc.

The materials available to the Japanese garden designer seem to be numberless. They begin with the interior spaces of the house, temple, or pavilion from which the garden is to be viewed, which may be either given or created by another. These broad, tranquilizing, and largely uninhabited spaces, defined by sliding screens and shōji, open one into the other in a sequence that ends only with a final view into the garden. Not infrequently, such vistas are diagonal, giving added complexity and variety to the experience. Outside, the designer is able to shape less restrained spaces, placing trees and bushes not in linear sequence but so that they call to one another across the total composition. He can use a complete range of greens, from almost white to almost black, inflected in late summer with the grays of rocks and water, the cold white of gravel and dressed stone, the creamy white of water lilies, the rusty red of pine trunks, and the gold and yellow of carp. He has an almost limitless variety of scale, from moss to massive trees, and of shape, from the compactness of clipped azaleas to the indistinctness of billowy bamboo. There is an infinity of textures available to him—the velvety softness of moss, the discrete precision of maple leaves, the featheriness of bamboo, the shiny smoothness of lily pads, and the rough bark of pines with the spiky punctuation of their needles. Moreover there is sound, created by wind in the trees, by the splashing and dripping of water, or by such manmade devices as the bamboo pipe that periodically falls against a rock, embellishing what is otherwise still and soft with its dry, hollow thud. There is also the movement that creates the sound, such as the waving of the trees and the running, dripping, and splashing of water, or is divorced from it, as in the lazy swimming of carp. Insofar as possible, such movement is carefully controlled; witness the waterfall at Nanzen-in, in which water is made to splatter from a rock as if it were the wildest form of flung-ink calligraphy.

Perhaps the most sympathetic of the green gardens in Kyoto is that of Shisen-dō, a Zen samurai's retreat. Modest in size, as is any Japanese garden when compared with the achievements of a Le Nôtre, it is extraordinarily reposeful in effect. It is on two levels, of which only the upper is visible from the house. Framed by a large tree, and distanced slightly from the building by fine raked gravel, its most obvious feature is a series of compactly clipped, rounded azaleas. A small stone pagoda arising from among these bushes works one of those miracles of scale at which the Japanese are so adept by suggesting that the bushes are a range of mountains in which a real structure is set, as at Kiomizu. As one descends to the lower level, most effectively seen from a teahouse placed there for the purpose, the garden becomes less obviously controlled. A rivulet issues from under the azaleas into a pond in which grow lilies and grasses, and as one proceeds farther, the garden ends in an apparently wild hillside. In one sense, each portion of the garden is independent of the other, and the area visible from the house (or that visible from the teahouse) is entirely satisfactory on its own. But taken together each part completes the other, enriching the esthetic experience in such a way that, having explored the whole, one cannot imagine one without the other. Each subsequent experience of part of the garden is inevitably enhanced by one's memory of the remainder. A similar effect is achieved in a more inte-grated manner at the Imperial villa of Katsura, which is graced with a gar-den of somewhat the same character as that at Shisen-dō, conceived on a less intimate scale. Within the grounds are four teahouses, one for each season, each with a different view calculated to concentrate not only the experience of the tea ceremony, but the time of year at which it takes place and, conse-quently, one's enjoyment of the garden. The autumn teahouse, for example, has views in two directions. One of these encompasses the pond visible from all the pavilions, most movingly seen by moonlight. The other looks onto a hillside of maples, which would be brilliant in the fall.

The most surprising garden in Kyoto, and in many ways the finest, com-bines the planted water garden typical of Shisen-dō and Katsura with the intellectuality of a Zen dry garden. Designed by Sōami, it is the garden of Ginkaku-ji, the never-completed silver pavilion, a masterpiece of subtlety, delicacy, and austerity. It is entered down a long path bordered with man-icured hedges some fifteen feet high. A line apparently parallel with the ground is clipped into each hedge about halfway to its top, and it takes con-siderable concentration or repeated experience of the allée to realize that as one enters either the line rises slightly or the ground descends. One is, thus, imperceptibly led from the quotidian world into an environment of a differ-ent scale and nature. After passing through a handsome small gravel garden with trees (the present path of entry is probably not that originally intended), one is immediately confronted with what is surely the most remarkable and cerebral phenomenon to be found in any garden in the world. A large sand garden extends from the main temple building almost to the lakeside pavil-ion and consists of nothing more than a truncated cone some eight feet high and a large flat-topped, free-form area, banked up about eighteen inches from the ground, the top of which is alternately smooth and raked in broad bands. These two sand constructions confront each other, the garden of which they are part, and the beholder with what can only be described as an absoluteness that defies accommodation. Attempts to identify the cone as Fuji and the flat extent as the China Sea are feeble at best. They are efforts to explain something that not only resists explanation but refuses to make the slightest concession to feeling or ratiocination, something that seems

Shisen-dō: View from verandah. Photo credit: Susan Cohen.

Ryōan-ji: The dry garden. Photo credit: Susan Cohen.

to be trying to break through to some underlying and unitary level of consciousness at which it and its beholder will be simultaneously distinct and
identical. Beyond this remarkable construction stretches one of the most
benign and subtly thought out gardens in Kyoto. In part a cultivated garden
with a pond, in part a wild garden with a waterfall, and in part a serene moss
garden, it is graced with the harmonious silver pavilion. Not only is this
structure more reticent and delicate in proportion than the golden pavilion
that inspired it (Kinkaku-ji), but had it been silver-leafed as intended, its
effect would have enhanced, and been enhanced by, the green garden in
which it is set. It would have had a lunar reticence in striking contrast to the
opulent gold of Kinkaku-ji and, indeed, both it and the sand garden would
have been most effective by moonlight. Taken as a whole, Ginkaku-ji is a
manmade universe of unusual complexity, power, and reticence, and among
the greatest esthetic accomplishments in Japan.

The different types of garden confronted so starkly at Ginkaku-ji are
developed separately, or subtly combined, elsewhere in Kyoto. At Ryōan-ji,
the dry garden by itself is brought to a pinnacle of perfection. Here, in a
roughly tennis court-shaped space surrounded on three sides by a wall and
on the fourth by a temple, white gravel and fifteen stones have been used to
create a composition that has been described as islands in a sea or mountain
peaks above the clouds. Like Ginkaku-ji, however, although less austerely,
Ryōan-ji demands acceptance rather than explication. The gravel is raked
around the worn and cratered stones, and in long striations elsewhere. The
whole is so exposed that from photographs and descriptions one expects a
barren and puritanically cold effect. Nothing could be further from reality. Without being in any way baroque, the result is tremendously rich. The
richness results from the texture and coloristic variation of the gravel, the
unevenness of the ground over which it is placed, the pattern and finesse of
the raking, the character of the stones and sensitivity of their relationships,
and the behavior of the daylight, which not only inflects the gravel but casts
shadows into the garden from the trees beyond its wall. It is, thus, a garden
devoid of vegetation that is immutable and constantly in flux. Its immutability would indeed be barren without the flux, while the effect of flux would
be imperceptible without the immutability. In synthesizing what is kept separate at Ginkaku-ji, it achieves an external harmony that frees the beholder
from himself being the agent of harmony.

At the Kokedera of Saihō-ji, precisely the opposite means are used. A garden with over 100 varieties of moss, its gently undulating emerald carpet is
inflected by the trunks of artfully placed trees, which rise up some distance

before their branches flower. The result is a sort of outdoor building, one of the few Kyoto gardens that needs primarily to be walked through. Since it is almost entirely a composition in green, the Kokedera is not only a garden of particular harmony but is the quintessential summer garden. The filtering of the sunlight through the trees, unlike the dappling of Ryōan-ji, emphasizes its unworldly reticence. This effect is enhanced by the garden's indefinite scale, partly a result of the absence of emphatic forms. If austerity, however rich, characterizes Ryōan-ji, the Kokedera is an oasis of gentleness. After a late summer rain and under a fitful sun, it is an experience of yielding calm and profound coherence. The extreme economy of its means results in its also being a synthesis of apparent opposites, bringing together those strains that were separated at Ginkaku-ji, but in a manner diametrically opposed to that of Ryōan-ji. Here one is immediately aware of spiritual intensity and mechanical complexity resulting in an effect of straightforward simplicity. This reconciliation of opposites not only makes the Kokedera, like most of Kyoto's gardens, a concrete expression of what is most profound in the spirit and philosophy of Japan, but identifies it as a phenomenon of the highest esthetic order.

Summer 1985

Scenes from Nicaragua

PAUL MOORE JR.

WE SAT IN A HOT, DARKENED ROOM. A young officer was reciting the history of the Sandinista revolution from a document in front of him. His eyes were clear, his face young. He spoke with nervous authority. On the bench across from us sat four solemn-faced soldiers: two of them young, sporting bright Sears & Roebuck–style T-shirts, the other two grizzled and wrinkled in fatigues and beret with their firearms across their knees. The older ones were called Isidoro and Francisco. Francisco Moreno had participated in the first battle of the Sandinista revolution here at Pancosan. After our conversation, we went to see the museum commemorating the event—a wooden shack on the site of the battle in which eighteen Sandinistas were attacked by two hundred Somocistas and the house surrounded. The Sandinistas lost several of their men, and the rest escaped to a nearby mountain. It was akin in my mind to visiting Lexington and Concord guided by Paul Revere. Inside the museum were pictures of the original eighteen, one of whom bore the sobriquet of "The Tiger from the Mountains." They told us a bit about the fighting, which particularly interested me because of my own background in the Marine Corps as a rifle platoon leader during World War II. Tactics do not seem to have changed much in the last forty years. When asked who the Contras were, they replied that the most tragic thing is that most of them are campesinos, too ignorant to understand the issues at stake but led to fight against their brothers by cynical former members of Somoza's guard. As I looked into the faces of these soldiers and listened to them recount tales of the raggedy guerilla warfare going on nearby, I did not feel that the United States was threatened.

The foreman at La Fundadora, a coffee plantation, could not wait to show us the way they process the coffee and to boast of the thousands of sacks harvested this year. With some glee he pointed out Somoza's house where he stayed when he was still the owner of this plantation. It wasn't very grand, I admit; yet our friend said, with some passion, that in the old days none of the campesinos were allowed to go up the street toward the house.

An evening conversation, two or three days later, gave an insight into the urban areas. We met with Christian Base Community leaders in Barrio 14 de Septiembre in Managua. Two middle-aged men, Julio and Carlos, described how they built the Christian communities—one of them was the oldest in the country. They said the communities could not exist in parishes where the priest opposed them, but that essentially they were a lay movement. Their leaders were trained to instruct couples for marriage, to give catechism and to perform other Christian services, and were also involved in the neighborhood organizations of their districts. I asked about the separation of Church and State. Carlos said, "I don't quite understand. We act as Christian individuals in the neighborhood organization. And it is so different when you have a revolutionary government. You can have access to authorities and suggest change. You do not have to be separate in order to be critical. You do not have to criticize from a distance." We sat on Julio's porch; the street outside was dirt. He and a large family live inside, and I could see them peering out; nice-looking kids, full of smiles. Julio continued to describe the Base Communities. "They bring the words of Jesus to us to show us how to act about our own problems in our community." Carlos joined in, "We are working to get a school now."

I spent an hour and a half with the Foreign Minister, Miguel D'Escoto Brockmann, one morning. The Foreign Ministry is a handsome, modest one-story building built around a central garden. On the walls of the Foreign Minister's office were two striking Nicaraguan paintings: one an abstract canvas of cogged wheels, the other an impressionistic painting of a group of campesinos. Miguel D'Escoto is a Maryknoll father, soft-spoken, earnest, ingenuous. He has a nice open face, good eyes. He pulled up his chair to talk to me in a more intimate fashion. I'd met him before but never had a chance to have a long discussion with him, and after a few minutes I felt as if I had known him for many years. We had much in common as fellow clergy and as people concerned with social justice issues. He spoke quite easily of his faith and of his politics. He spoke of hope. "Hope? Yes. The best thing to happen in a long time," he began—his eyes lit up, and he tapped my knee as if to emphasize the urgency of this development—"is that the Heads of State of every Central American country will meet in May. We want to establish a Central American Parliament, regularize the meetings of Foreign Ministers and Vice Presidents, and have occasional summit meetings of Heads of State. And we really *want* to meet. The new President of Costa Rica suggested it. It is becoming clear to us all, whatever our politics, that this is a North/South struggle, not an East/West struggle, and that we must stick together."

We spoke about many things, but chiefly about the difficulty of communication—the distortions, the untruths, the myths with which the citizens of the United States are showered. As we finished our conversation, I suggested we pray together. Kneeling, he asked for my blessing and gave me his.

The night before we left, my son George, who lives in Managua with his wife, Alice, gave us a party. Most of the people present were artists, priests, nuns, and journalists, and I picked up a good deal from conversations with them. One of the most shocking things I heard was from a Roman Catholic sister, an American, who had been in Nicaragua for many years. A week before Easter she had been down at the coast and had been told of Contra atrocities. She told of a convent they set fire to in the middle of the night two weeks before. She told of a delegate of the Word (a Catholic lay worker) who was murdered on Good Friday and horribly mutilated, having been castrated and had his eyes taken out. She said the Contras had no use for the Church, that none of them went to Mass the Sunday she was there. She spoke of her affection for the people and particularly for the community of Miskito women whose convent had been burned down, one of whom, with four small children, had barely escaped with her life that night. For the man who was assassinated on Good Friday, they held a Mass of the Resurrection on Easter. It was filled with joy at his witness and love for his people. When his body was found, the cross he had always worn had disappeared. The sister said that was like Jesus; on Easter Day he, too, had lost his cross.

Summer 1986

Letter from Dresden

ROBERT S. CLARK

ORDINARILY I am far too great a snob to sign up for an organized tour to any part of the world. But I went to Dresden and Leipzig as part of one early in 1985 for three reasons. It is the 300th anniversary of the birth of Johann Sebastian Bach, and I felt an urgent need to touch the stones of the Thomaskirche in Leipzig, where he served as cantor for the most productive years of his life. Too, Dresden was holding a season-long celebration of the reopening of its gem of an opera house, designed in the mid-nineteenth century by Gottfried Semper and destroyed on the evenings of February 13–14, 1945, as three waves of bombers, the first two British and the last American, annihilated Dresden's treasurable medieval core and killed 135,000 people. Finally, and perhaps most compelling, I wanted a quick and easy way to get another glance behind the Iron Curtain. A trip just a year before had yielded tantalizing glimpses of life in Bulgaria, Roumania, and Hungary, and I found myself (and still do) in the grip of a slightly obsessive curiosity.

It goes back even further, really. Dresden had haunted me ever since I learned the story of the bombings. The triple blow, dropping about 3,000 tons of bombs, including more than 650,000 incendiaries, on the city, kindled the most savage firestorm of the war, worse than similar conflagrations in Berlin, Tokyo, Hiroshima, or Nagasaki. The pretense was that Dresden was an important Wehrmacht communications center and the fulcrum for troop movements to the besieged eastern front, where the Russians were advancing daily through Poland, East Prussia, and Silesia. But the truth was that Dresden—like Nagasaki—was of slight military significance, and the Allies probably knew it.

As early as 1942, the British Air Ministry, prodded by Churchill, had made the bombing of German population centers a priority second only to

The Semper Opera House. Photo credit: Lars Kehrel.

the destruction of oil storage and synthetic fuel production facilities, with the aim of breaking the German will and hastening the war's end. Though American SHAEF officials tacitly agreed, the British feared the American government would never accept the change as official policy, and it was never proclaimed as such. But as the air war moved into its late stages in the opening months of 1945, the change was the foundation of a series of attacks on the German capital and other eastern cities such as Magdeburg, Halle, Chemnitz, Leipzig, and finally Dresden.

One story has it that the Russians, meeting with the Allies at Yalta, specifically requested that Dresden be added to the target list. Soviet officials have denied that since the war. It seems indisputable, however, that part of the rationale for the bombings was to impress the Soviet leaders with a show of Allied air strength. Relations between the Eastern and Western powers were strained or worse: British pilots involved in the raids were warned that if they strayed beyond the eastern front, which lay at that time along the Oder and Neisse rivers, and had to ditch, Russian soldiers might shoot them on sight. Some Westerners wondered whether the fierce Russian sweep would stop short of the Atlantic's waters. So British and American commanders wanted to demonstrate that the expense of blood and treasure on the western front had not sapped their ability to deliver devastating blows elsewhere.

Dresden was virtually undefended. Because it had so little importance to the war effort, the Nazi high command had not assigned it antiaircraft guns, and the few night fighters in the vicinity were immobilized during the raids by surprise and communications failures. But though the city had neither the concentration of German troops massed to move east, nor the Gestapo headquarters, nor the poison gas plant that the British bomber crews were told were their targets in their preparatory briefings, its population of 630,000 was swollen to something between 1,200,000 and 1,400,000 by refugees.

They had come in farm carts and wagons and on foot from the Pomeranian and Silesian marches, fleeing the Red Army, which was visiting atrocities on the German-speaking population in retaliation for what the German army had meted out in its drive toward Stalingrad years earlier. On the first night of the raids, thousands of these refugees were huddled in Dresden's Central Railway Station and the surrounding squares, and perished there. The city, lulled into complacency by its apparent insignificance as a military target, had also neglected its civil defense readiness—though any degree of preparedness would have been of little avail against the magnitude of the firestorm that ensued.

Word of the horrors of the bombing and its aftermath spread quickly through both combatant and noncombatant countries. A firsthand account by a Swiss resident in Dresden during the attacks appeared in a Swiss newspaper in March, telling in graphic detail of the heaps of mutilated and charred corpses in the city's streets and parks, the mass burials, the devastation of the Old City's historic buildings and churches, and the stench of death and decay everywhere. But even before, both London and Washington were on the receiving end of shocked inquiries and demands for an explanation. The propaganda potency of the incident quickly became apparent to all sides. The Goebbels office, hyperactive even with the Reich collapsing all around it, made use of Dresden in broadcasts and leaflets. Estimates of the dead making the rounds in Berlin, at first between 180,000 and 220,000, were soon revised downward to 120,000–150,000. The Soviets obliquely used the matter in a different way. Dresden was occupied by the Red Army on May 8, 1945, the day of the German surrender. Hanns Voigt, the director of the Missing Persons Bureau's Division of the Deceased, reported in writing to the Soviet commanders his own conservative estimate that the raids had killed 135,000. The Russians, apparently informed that belittling the Allies' might was the order of the day, "calmly struck off the first digit," in Voigt's words.

So, it appears, came about the "official" figure of Dresden's casualties. Thirty-five thousand was the count we saw in the abundance of references to "the barbaric destruction by Anglo-American bombers" on plaques, on signs, in guidebooks, and in a variety of commemorative literature in this fortieth anniversary year. The catastrophe has obviously not outworn its propaganda value—not by a long shot. But there are signs of reconciliation. Our guide told us that a British bomber pilot who had participated had been on hand for the ceremonies in February on the anniversary of the raids, and—in a gesture she said elicited tears from almost everyone present—laid a wreath on the ruins of the city's most famous architectural landmark, the Frauenkirche, now a memorial to the war dead.

The gruesome story had at least one happier sequel. The city's collections of fine, plastic, and decorative arts have been legendary for at least a couple of centuries. The paintings, prints, drawings, and sculpture housed in the Zwinger Museum, and the "Green Vault" treasures, works of porcelain, gold, silver, ivory, precious stones, marble, enamels, coral, ebony, and the like housed in the Albertinum—together with the architectural splendor of the museums themselves—had earned Dresden the sobriquet "Elbflorenz," "Florence on the Elbe." When Allied bombardment of German cities first began, the artworks and treasures were taken from the galleries and museums to nearby fortresses, chalk mines and sandstone mines for safekeeping. Miraculously, most survived, but the paintings in particular— works of Rubens, Titian, Raphael, and Canaletto among them, along with German and French masters of the eighteenth and nineteenth centuries— were damaged by cold and dampness.

One of the first acts of the Soviet occupying forces was to send in a trained team to oversee handling and transport of the art. The works were shipped to Moscow and Leningrad,[1] where they were restored and sequestered, and in 1956 the Soviet government returned them all to Dresden. For once, his immersion in proletarian sloganeering notwithstanding, the Westerner had to concede the aptness of the rhetoric contained in a plaque on the Albertinum's wall: "The rescue of Dresden's art treasures by the Soviet army is an outstanding act of socialist humanism, an event of historical greatness. The people of the Soviet Union deserve our thanks for all time."

---

1. Saint Petersburg.

Now, Titian is Titian, but even granting that the painting galleries are first class, no one would go to Dresden for them alone. The "Green Vault" collection, on the other hand, would warrant the journey: the goblets, vessels, cases, jewelry, weapons, basins, plates, decorative figures, sculptures, carvings, and religious objects add up to an experience that cannot be approached anywhere else. Those who saw the selection sent to the Metropolitan Museum of Art in New York (and to a few other American cities as well, I think) some years back will know what I mean. And what did not travel is more awe-inspiring than what did.

In the sixteenth and seventeenth centuries, mining in the Erzgebirge ("Ore-mountains") to Dresden's southwest made its rulers some of the wealthiest in Europe, and a series of sovereigns of the Wettin clan, Electors of Saxony and Kings of Poland, while neglecting none of the licentious and indulgent behavior of other minor European royalty, amassed art on a grand scale. Much of it came from craftsmen attached to the court, in particular from the patronage of Augustus the Second (1670–1733), called the Strong for his fabled stamina in a variety of exertions. (One of his numerous illegitimate children was Maurice de Saxe, marshal of France in Louis XV's reign.) The architect Pöppelmann, who created the Zwinger galleries, the sculptor Permoser, the porcelainist Kändler, and the goldsmith Dinglinger are hardly names to reckon with in standard art history texts. But what these artisans fashioned for the Wettin court illustrates the phenomenon of ostentation creating the conditions for expansiveness of artistic invention. The means, precious ores, stones, and materials, seem inconsequential next to the grace, richness, and imagination of the combinations and permutations.

Take just one example—for me the most extraordinary of the 1,500 or so works, half of the "Green Vault" collection, on view while I was there. It is Dinglinger's masterpiece, a panoramic scene called *Grand Mogul Aurungzebe Holds Court in Great State at Delhi on His Birthday* (1701–8). On a field of partially gilded silver measuring some four and a half feet across by four feet deep, numerous miniature figures, in gold decorated with multicolored enamels, are arrayed on several levels, ascending to the central figure of the lavishly robed emperor seated on a cushion on his royal dais, sheltered by an elaborate embossed gold and silver canopy decorated with enamels and precious stones. The lesser princes come with their households and their domestic animals—elephants, horses, dogs—to bring gifts, borne in ornamented trunks, and to pay homage. Caravans enter from each side to join others already spread before the mogul. The multiplicity of human and animal figures, in various attitudes of strain and repose, is staggering: some grovel before the mogul, some stand reverently or attentively by, some—farther away—are lifting, carrying, holding parasols or banners, attending to the horses or elephants; some, well away from the center, link their arms behind them or lean indolently on a balustrade that defines the forward edge of the activity, staring into space and ignoring the hubbub. None is as big as your thumb, yet each is an exquisitely rendered depiction of a human action or mood. You could gaze at this scene day and night for a week and not exhaust the life it so vividly represents. The opportunity to stand mesmerized before it was alone worth the fare to Dresden.

Though the music, as it turned out, was not on that plane, Semper's extravagant neoclassical opera house approached it. Built in 1841, it was destroyed by fire once before, in 1869, and subsequently reconstructed. But in 1945 only the outside walls were left standing. Dresden would not let them be pulled down, and seven years after the war's end studies began on restoration. Early on, the decision was made to rebuild and redecorate it to Semper's specifications, altering them only to accommodate side stages, modern stage machinery, and so on. (An analogous decision guided restoration of the Zwinger.) So the auditorium's circular shape, the four balconies of the interior and its decoration, and the sumptuous marble columns and stucco walls, arches and ceilings of the vestibule, foyers, and corridors, painted with mythological and pastoral scenes, rosettes and swags and *putti*, are now much as the house's first patrons saw them.

The programs celebrating the theater's reopening included Strauss's *Der Rosenkavalier* and Weber's *Der Freischütz*, both of which had their world premieres there. The fine Dresden Staatskapelle provided sturdy orchestral underpinning for both, supported by the clear and somewhat bright acoustics. Joachim Herz, stage director for both works as well, fashioned effective and idiomatic productions for the most part. Only in the Wolf's Glen scene of *Freischütz* did he succumb to the temptation to sermonize, with an effort to link the spirits Samiel summons up with the dead of February 1945. Among the singers, the veteran Theo Adam strolled through the role of Baron Ochs, which never seemed fully to engage him either vocally or dramatically (but Harold Rosenthal, reporting on the performance of opening week, heaped praise on him). Two others were outstanding: Reiner Goldberg sang *Freischütz*'s Max with strong, plangent tone and a sense of style that justified the enthusiastic word of mouth that has reached me, and a young mezzo-soprano named Ute Walther turned in a first-class Octavian in *Rosenkavalier*.

Of course, there was Bach: our party heard two performances. One, a chamber concert by the Staatskapelle led by Friedrich Goldmann, consisted of the Fourth Brandenburg Concerto and Fourth Suite, an arrangement for orchestra by Goldmann of fourteen canons on the first eight bass notes of the *Goldberg Variations* aria, and an original work by Goldmann, all splendidly played. The second, Bach's *St. John Passion*, performed in Leipzig's Nikolaikirche by the choir and orchestra of the Thomaskirche and their leader Herbert Pommer, was disappointing. The choir sang well, but the soloists—with the exception of the estimable Peter Schreier—and the conducting were undistinguished. Yet this was Bach at the source, and for austere music that will never be counted among "Bach's greatest hits," the Nikolaikirche was filled to capacity by an audience whose tongues included at least English, French, and Spanish in addition to German.

I had come for the music only in the sense that I came to East Germany for the reassurance that these little stretches of ground reaching away from the Elbe's banks, where so much that has beguiled me—a citizen of a nation and a culture so remote—over a lifetime was first created, could still nourish those creations. Could ground so seared by battle, so stained by the blood of wars and revolutions and wanton killing for the pleasure of killing, where families slaughtered their own for carrying the wrong party card, and where a repressive foreign power now stations an army in part to guarantee that it will not happen again—could such ground still succor those few human products that at least partially redeem it? The answer is a tentative yes.

Of course there is tension between the East German state's orthodoxies of the moment and its role as custodian of artifacts that sprang from the alien roots of privilege and religious belief. I sampled one official guidebook of the early seventies and found this treatment of the architectural monuments of Dresden: "For centuries the brilliant and ostentatious royal court of the Saxon sovereigns swallowed the vast fortunes earned by the people. Glory was gained by Pöppelmann, Permoser and Chiaveri, who were the creators of the world-renowned baroque buildings, yet the numerous builders whose craftsmanship contributed so much to Dresden's worldwide fame as the 'Florence on the Elbe' were nameless." The implicit quarrel is not over the monuments' value, but only over who deserves credit for them.

Today East Germany seems to be shaking off some of its postwar malaise and stagnation. Because of its unique political dualism, it had been ground hard under the Soviet boot. The road we traveled from Berlin to Dresden, the equivalent of a West German *Autobahn* but of an outmoded ridged kind of construction and in poor repair, passes through flat tableland with little visual interest, and nothing but road signs and an occasional distant smoke-stack spewing vapors to relieve the monotony. As the visitor's first view of the country, it was dismaying, and more so because every overpass on the way bore a proletarian slogan: "Bless and thank all diligence that strengthens our socialism." "Our indestructible brotherhood with the Soviet Union—the source of our strength." "Attentive, thoughtful, disciplined—I am with you." It was enough to make you long for billboards.

But eventually what I saw and heard dispelled these first impressions. A sign of the times is that, in Dresden, Leipzig, Halle, and many other places, construction and reconstruction are abundantly evident: new factories, new apartment buildings, and restorations of, for example, Dresden's formerly scorned late-nineteenth-century bourgeois quarter on the riverbank to the city's southeast. Why now? Because, our Dresden guide told us in candor, "the Russians are only just letting us do it."

Our hotel in Dresden was a mark of the change: no Helmsley Palace (thank God), but comfortable, fresh, and graced with a few amenities that new Western hotels seem to have forgotten—my windows, looking out on the Elbe, *opened*, and from either the side or the top depending on how much fresh air I wanted. The Hotel Bellevue, like Leipzig's Hotel Merkur, was built for the East Germans by Mitsubishi, another sign of the times: the minibar was by Sanyo and the TV set a Sharp. Since, like other spurs to tourism, the hotel's principal objective in the socialist scheme of things is to increase the take of Western hard currencies, its restaurants and shops are for hotel guests only and nominally closed to local people. But they come into the shops anyway and purchase goods with smuggled West German marks.

On a Sunday, on the promenade of the handsome shop-lined Street of Liberation in Dresden Neustadt, fathers carried smiling young children on their shoulders, women pushed pristine baby carriages, and a few young people sported punk-rock clothes and haircuts. The shops had plenty of goods, from housewares and furniture to books, cosmetics, and clothing of simple but good fabric and cut. In both Dresden and Leipzig I saw such capitalist extravagances as furs and jewelry on sale, but at very high prices. I saw only one line, and not outside a food market: people waited to get into the ice cream parlor at the corner of the square on the Street of Liberation. Everyone pulls for the Dresden Dynamos, the local soccer team, and on a warm day during our stay schoolboys gathered on the wide lawns fronting the banks of the Elbe to practice for the big time. I have heard of no riots among East German soccer fans.

A few days later, I was in the Frankfurt airport, watching customers sheepishly enter and leave "Dr. Mullers Sex Shop," jostling and being jostled at a souvenir stand and the beer and wurst bar, waiting to board a jumbo jet with more than 500 other footloose Westerners. (Our guide had spoken wistfully of her hope that one day she could visit Paris.) And a few hours thereafter I was in New York, waiting for a train out of Grand Central, passing the time at the Trattoria bar and comparing New York's cacophony of enticements, its siren song in a hundred keys at once, with the subdued hum of the city on the Elbe. Whatever its hidden terrors and privations, East German life seemed free of the anxiety and narcissism that power the daily existence of so many Americans. Or was that only an illusion? After all, I got just a glimpse. But, once again, what a tantalizing glimpse.

Winter 1986

The Guiana Connection

JOHN P. SISK

THE CONTEXT of E. M. Forster's famous "Only connect!" in *Howards End* leaves some readers with the impression that the strenuous job of making vital connections among what would otherwise be disparate fragments is entirely up to them. Fortunately, as Forster himself no doubt knew, some of the most interesting connections are the serendipitous consequences of being in a certain place at a certain time. In my case, if it had not been for a wartime assignment to British Guiana (the last place in the world I would have chosen), Sir Walter Ralegh,[1] Evelyn Waugh, and the Reverend Jim Jones would have remained forever disconnected fragments.

In 1595, the first of three incarcerations in the Tower of London behind him, Sir Walter Ralegh sailed to and explored the northeast coast of South America. He spent most of his time in what we now call Venezuela, but that does not keep his subsequent bestseller, *The Discovery of the Large, Rich and Beautiful Empire of Guiana*, from being a proper beginning point for anyone's experience of the Guianas. Evelyn Waugh discovered Guiana during a three-month period beginning in late 1932 and got from the experience two books, *Ninety-Two Days* (an account of his travels through British Guiana into northern Brazil) and the brilliant novel (now a brilliant movie), *A Handful of Dust*. Being an Oxford-educated Englishman, he would have known that Ralegh, himself an Oxonian, had preceded him. However, it is not likely that Reverend Jim Jones, first and last messiah of The Peoples Temple, and

---

1. In this essay all quotations from Ralegh's *Discovery of Guiana* are from the 1596 edition, as republished now in the Hakluyt series. I have followed the English spelling of Sir Walter's name since it appears to be the one he preferred.

an expert in bogus connections, had Ralegh in mind when he first saw British Guiana in 1963 or when he returned there thirteen years later with his band of doomed utopians.

My own discovery of Guiana came between Waugh and Jones at a time when Ralegh was not much on my mind, and Waugh himself, no longer a man-at-arms, was safely back in England. In the summer of 1945, on orders from the Caribbean Division of the Air Transport Command, I flew from Miami to Atkinson Field in British Guiana (now Guyana) with the expectation that I would function as Special Service Officer. It was immediately apparent that I was not needed. To make matters worse, I was quartered with a newly arrived Protestant chaplain who was trying to live with his own irrelevance: the Catholic chaplain, everybody's favorite, had cornered the religious market. In the meantime, he had picked up some kind of fungus that had spread to his back, which it was my duty to anoint with salve each night before he went to bed. Under these circumstances I was often as bored as Ralegh was during his first days in the Brick Tower, where he was denied not only Queen's favor but a sight of the traffic on the Thames River.

My release came while the chaplain's fungus was still in full flower: I agreed to take on a weekly radio program to be aired Sunday afternoons at Georgetown in the interest of solidifying relations with our allies, the British, whose empire had not yet begun to disintegrate. So I rode the riverboat twenty-five miles downstream to Georgetown, seeing for the first time the great and muddy Demerara, established myself at the Park Hotel (destined thirty years later to be the in-town headquarters for Jim Jones's Peoples Temple), and made my arrangements with what I took to be the only radio station in town. For the next two months I spent two or three days each weekend discovering Guiana in ways that would have been impossible if I had remained at Atkinson Field—which, like most American air bases on foreign soil, was organized to make possible the constant rediscovery of home.

The discovery of Guiana entailed the rediscovery of Waugh's *A Handful of Dust*. When the novel's central figure, Tony Last, disembarked at Georgetown, "The custom sheds were heavy with the reek of sugar and loud with the buzzing of bees," exactly as they were for me. At this point not only had Tony's marriage collapsed, but his vision of a "whole Gothic world had come to grief." Like a Renaissance explorer, he had come to Guiana in search of the "Shining, the Many Watered, the Bright Feathered" City, a transfiguration of his ancestral Hetton, the discovery of which would be the compensation for all other losses. In search of that City, and led by the eccentric Dr. Messinger, he went arduously up the Demerara and on south into Brazil, where he found not the Shining City but the village of the illiterate half-caste James Todd (played superbly in the movie by Sir Alec Guinness), to whom he spent the rest of his life reading Dickens.

Ralegh too had gone in search of a City, Manoa, in the kingdom called Eldorado, which, he wrote, "for the greatnes, for the riches, and for the excellent seate, it farre exceedeth any of the world." After coming back from his first voyage relatively empty-handed, he did not give up on his dream of the Golden City. Sentenced to the Bloody Tower for treason (he went to the trial puffing his pipe), he continued to publicize Guiana. After thirteen years, the king by then being sufficiently hard up to be tempted by visions of New World gold, the Shepherd of the Ocean (as he called himself) was freed for his second and disastrous voyage, from which he returned to the chopping block.

The radio program was a primitive affair. Most of the time I played popular American music which I interrupted with disk jockey chatter and a three- or four-minute disquisition on some aspect of the Air Transport Command's contribution to the war effort. The station manager said the response was good, which was easy enough to say since my only serious competition was the afternoon cricket match. Usually I took the night boat back to the base, lounging on deck with a good Havana cigar as we throbbed into that immense heart of darkness. Sometimes candlelight from a native hut winked through the riverside foliage, or cast a Halloween glow on the water if the hut had been stilted up on the bank, and the candlelight combined with the tropical stars to intensify the dark. It was easy to believe then, as it was widely believed on the base, that there was voodoo in the jungle, orgiastic rituals presided over by garishly costumed priestesses of the powers of darkness. It was the perfect setting for the atheistic and necromancing School of Night to which Ralegh was suspected of belonging. At such times it was easy to understand too how Ralegh could believe that in Guiana there were Amazons, "cruell and bloodthirsty" women, as well as men whose eyes were in their shoulders and whose mouths were in the middle of their breasts.

Nevertheless, it was a pleasant trip unless it rained, which in Guiana country as Ralegh had learned, it might at any moment ("the raines came downe in terrible showers" so that one's only shirt "was thoroughly washt on his body for the most part ten times in one day"). Coming downstream in daylight I found the jungle shoreline endlessly fascinating, especially when it was tormented by the sudden rain squalls, and was never inclined to spend the time reading. Years later when Waugh's diaries became available,

I noted that there were times when the jungle wildness was less than fascinating to him—times when he preferred to lie in his hammock reading Thomas Aquinas or Shakespeare's *Titus Andronicus*. But by then the jungle had become an all too intimate reality for him, whereas I knew it only from a safe distance. Ralegh, a great reader, had a chest of books with him, but what he read out of it I don't know. It's hard to imagine him not taking along the first three books of Edmund Spenser's *Faerie Queene*, especially since the available edition contained not only his own beautiful commendatory sonnet, but the famous letter to the "Right noble, and Valorous, Sir Walter Raleigh," in which the "dark conceit" of the poem was spelled out. However, there are sections in it, particularly in Canto XII of Book II where in the Bower of Bliss gold is a symbol of deceptive sensual display, that are not likely to give comfort to a man in search of a Golden City.

The Demerara is tidal, like Ralegh's Orinoco, and when the boat had to buck the tide, the twenty-five-mile trip could take three hours. Learning that an amphibious courier plane sometimes made the trip, I looked up the pilot, an engaging youngster, and arranged to fly with him the next Saturday morning. Thus I was able to discover Guiana from a new perspective, one that made it all too apparent that no one in his right mind would expect to find a fabulous Golden City in it. But when Jim Jones brought his Peoples Temple to Guiana, he was not, as Ralegh and Tony Last were, in search of a City. He would himself build a City, and it would resist the assaults of time, including the inevitable nuclear holocaust. Against his voodoo powers his entranced followers, having been Cityless too long and for the most part, like Tony Last, secular to begin with, would have had no defense. Like secular people everywhere, they would have lost the habit of religion without losing the appetite for it, so that a false prophet could come among them like a fox into a henhouse. That Ralegh had not lost the habit of religion, in spite of all the dark rumors about his unorthodoxy, is apparent enough in his *History of the World*—the masterwork which, as was the case with his friend Spenser's *The Faerie Queene*, he left incomplete.

No one could have been less secular or less distracted by visions of a Shining and Bright Feathered City than the Catholic chaplain, whom I got to know well after the fungus-ridden Protestant chaplain had been invalided back to the States. On Sundays he managed to say mass in French, Dutch, and British Guiana, so that it was one o'clock in the afternoon before he had his first meal of the day. He was actively concerned with the welfare of natives who worked on the base, and he had taken under his wing a leper colony on the Essequibo River. About his own discovery of Guiana he could have said what Waugh said about his excursion from Georgetown to Brazil and back: "It makes no claim to being a spiritual odyssey." The chaplain could not afford the luxury of a spiritual odyssey in search of a visionary City: there was too much to be done to keep that part of the earthly city to which he was committed from becoming thoroughly disconnected. Withal, he was a merciful realist who knew better in that fungus-nurturing humidity than to give a sermon that lasted more than two minutes. Jones, the mad charismatic who, like Hitler, had the burden of a whole world on his shoulders, could get his congregation up in the middle of the night and ramble on for hours.

Certainly the jungle, whether seen from aloft or at ground level, was a blank check one could fill out in terms of one's dearest apprehensions. Some said there were cannibals in it. Once as Officer of the Day, in fact, I had an encounter with what I at first took to be a cannibal. The Sergeant of the Guard and I were returning by jeep at daybreak after having inspected a radio checkpoint about five miles into the jungle. Suddenly, as we jolted along the twisting cart path, a bronzed and virtually naked man was in front of us, imperiously holding up his hand. The sergeant braked to a stop, pulling his forty-five out of his holster and laying it on his lap as he did so. The cannibal, looking menacing enough with his bad teeth and tangled hair, asked us politely if we would wait a minute. Twenty yards behind him a fellow cannibal with a handful of bananas was climbing down from a tree. Would we like to have them for a shilling? His well-modulated British English suggested that he might have been schooled and decannibalized by the nuns at Georgetown. I gave him two shillings, and we drove on eating the gorgeous tree-ripened bananas.

To judge from available reports, the category of cannibal is a spacious one. In fact, not all cannibals have been people-eaters. In his *Discovery of Guiana*, Ralegh speaks of "a nation of inhumaine Canibals" who would "for 3 or 4 hatchets sell the sonnes and daughters of their owne brethren and sisters," but he never says that they ate anybody. In Montaigne's well-known essay "Of Cannibals," we learn that the cannibals of Brazil had a society that put civilized Europe to shame. Indeed, it was not far short of the standard set by those denizens of the Golden Age about whom Don Quixote tells the respectful but bored goatherds shortly after his encounter with the brave Biscayan. Montaigne's cannibals—who make an appearance in Shakespeare's *The Tempest*, by way of John Florio's translation, when Gonzalo describes his ideal commonwealth—believed in the immortality of the soul, respected their priests and prophets, were brave in war and affectionate in marriage.

They wouldn't have felt too out of place in the Garden of Eden, about which Ralegh writes at great length in his *History of the World*. If they did occasionally eat a captured enemy, it was only after they had treated him well and fed him "every sort of delicacy." Clearly, Waugh's Tony Last would have been more comfortable with them than with the Dickens fanatic, James Todd. To them, and no doubt to Montaigne as well, the people of Jonestown would have been barbarians. It is pleasant to think that my banana cannibal might have descended from them.

Georgetown was nobody's idea of the Shining City, but it had its own attractions, few of which Waugh had time to observe in his two short visits. Canals ran down the pleasantly wide streets, originally laid out by the Dutch; St. George's Cathedral was then the second highest wooden building in the world, and the city itself was much admired for its well-preserved and stilted wooden structures; the Georgetown Cricket Club could boast of the finest cricket grounds in the tropics, and when the match was over spectators could repair to their favorite nightclubs convinced that they would hear the best calypso music in the Caribbean; high tea at the hotel Sunday afternoon (one learned to ignore the weevils that had been baked into the bread) was the prandial event of the week; and there in the "Land of the Six Peoples" it was pleasant to get the same British English from a black cab driver or an East Indian hotel clerk that one got from the Jesuits at Sunday mass.

In order to compose my mind before the radio program, I sometimes visited the Botanical Gardens, as famous in Guiana land as Central Park is in America and a good deal safer to stroll in. Sea cows (manatees) lived in its small lake, and for two shillings I could get a native boy to whistle one up from the bottom. Its bovine head would emerge unbelievably from the muddy water; I could pet its slimy nose while the boy fed it a handful of marsh grass. Ralegh too had seen a sea cow, a great fish "as big as a wine pipe," and learned that it was "most excellent and holsome meate." I was told that on an island in the middle of the lake there were alligators whose habit was to eat the young egrets that hatched there. I saw the egrets but not the alligators. Ralegh, however, had seen "thousands of those vglie serpents" and even saw one devour "a Negro, a very proper young fellow."

Ralegh, who among many other things was a gardener, would have loved the Botanical Gardens. On his well-farmed estate in Ireland (where he and Edmund Spenser sometimes read their poems to one another), he planted potatoes and yellow wallflowers he had imported from the Azores. During his long second incarceration in the Bloody Tower, he was allowed to keep a garden in which he grew herbs. His lengthy treatment of the Garden of

Eden in his *History of the World* is no doubt a reflection of his horticultural bent. He was fascinated with the depiction of Alcinous's garden in Book VII of *The Odyssey* and was convinced that Eden had been Homer's grand model. Surely he would have been delighted with the great hydroponic garden (one of the first in the world) which the US Army had built at Atkinson Field. He would have realized that such an artificially accelerated garden was a controlled exploitation of those cannibal-like forces of the jungle against which the army engineers at Atkinson as well as the pathetic doomsday people in Jonestown had to do endless battle.

For Ralegh, universal man that he was, gardening and pharmacy were hard to separate. In the Tower he made pills, a tonic of strawberries, and a "Great Cordial," also known as his "Balsam of Guiana"—a smorgasbord mixture of ingredients that included spirits of wine, hart's horn, mint, gentian, sugar, and sassafras. This witches' brew was not only recommended by Queen Anne of Austria, but was internationally famous. Ralegh had some of it sent to his protégé, the dying Prince Henry, but it arrived too late to save him. Don Quixote too claimed to have a "balsam of Fierabras" so powerful that it could instantly repair a broken body, but since it existed only as a recipe in his head, it was of no use to him after he had lost part of his ear in the battle with the Biscayan.

Montaigne's cannibals favored a less mystical concoction—a drink made from roots, claret in color, "not at all heady, but wholesome to the stomach." The drink Tony Last was given by the Pie-wie natives when he and James Todd dropped in on one of their celebrations was so heady that it knocked him out for two days, during which time he missed the visitors who would have been his last chance to return to civilization. Far less potent, though widely acclaimed throughout the Caribbean in my time, was Limacol, a lotion compounded mainly of lime juice and alcohol. When applied to face or head, especially after a hard night, it had a wonderfully bracing effect, and when taken internally, as a friend told me, was a quick but not lasting cure for constipation. But nothing could compare for sheer potency and permanency of effect with that other Balsam of Guiana (strawberry Flavor Aid laced with cyanide and tranquilizers) which the Reverend Jim Jones, that frightful Man of La Mancha, administered to more than 900 members of his Temple to speed their departure from his Infernal City.

In September I was elevated to Troop Commander, and the radio program had to be abandoned. I missed my weekly trip to Georgetown, perhaps not as much as Ralegh missed Guiana after his first trip, but still I missed it. Before long I was recalled to division headquarters at West Palm Beach, where I spent a comfortable winter and saw much of that American Bower of Bliss, Palm Beach, which, unlike Waugh's London, was then recovering grandly from the austerities of the war. Perhaps Ralegh, his experience in the Bloody Tower having tempered the utopian enthusiasms that had marked his Guiana adventure, would have identified Palm Beach as one of those "vicious countries" about which he writes in his *History of the World*: in them "nature being liberal to all without labour, necessity imposing no industry or travel, idleness bringeth no other fruits than vain thoughts and licentious pleasures."

Back in civilian life I repeated Ralegh's experience; having discovered Guiana, my attention had become programmed, and I kept rediscovering it, often in the most unlikely places. Political developments caught my eyes even when their treatment by the media indicated that the world generally considered them of little moment. Thus I saw British Guiana cease to be a crown colony and, after an interval of civic unrest as the East Indians under Cheddi Jagan contended with the Africans under Forbes Burnham, become the Cooperative Republic of Guyana. Then there were the inevitable major and minor atrocities, aimed as usual at a greater unity, that made small headlines or caught international attention when they took more dramatic form—when, for instance, a Jesuit priest was stabbed to death while photographing an anti-government rally. It was a native of Guyana, Leakh Narayan Bhoge, who, working as a double agent for the FBI, helped to ensnare the Soviet spy, Zakharov. A few years ago, when a Canadian mining company went public with its plans to cooperate with the government of Guyana in the development of its potentially rich gold mines, the Canadian government expressed concern about the country's poor record on human rights.

No doubt the prospect of Guiana gold was as attractive to Cheddi Jagan or Forbes Burnham as in Ralegh's day it had been to Queen Elizabeth of England or Philip II of Spain. The country was as hard up as one might expect a largely managed economy to be. In my day a Guianese dollar (a document as flamboyantly colored as a tropical bird) was worth eighty-five cents American, but I gather from a travel book that now an American dollar will get you from ten to twenty Guyana dollars, depending on where you go shopping for your money. The same book warns against walking out alone at night in Georgetown, whether for fear of cruising Amazons or hungry cannibals it does not say. In my day the worst I had to fear was a not too insistent prostitute or a youngster wanting a stick of gum. I like to imagine that one of those youngsters was Cheddi Jagan himself, the East Indian dentist who later became Prime Minister and was even pictured on the front page of the

New York Times as he conferred in the White House with President John F. Kennedy. Kennedy would have had reason to be wary of Jagan, who apparently had dreams of building his own Marx-inspired City in which all things would connect. But the picture is especially interesting given the fact that the young president was himself the inspiration for a dream of Camelot that quickly proved to be as much an idol of the mind as Manoa was for Ralegh.

News of Waugh's sudden death on Easter Sunday in 1966 was another and sad connection with my Demerara days, but for sheer drama no connection could compete with the mass suicide at Jonestown in November of 1978. The latter was much on my mind the following spring as I pursued Ralegh to the Bloody Tower of London. On Pentecost Sunday I saw where he lived during the thirteen years of his second incarceration, and where with the assistance of many others, including Ben Jonson, he wrote his *History of the World*. There was room for his family and servants, and friends could visit him. He had with him a chest of books and papers; he had easy access to his garden and to a terrace with a view of the Thames where he could take his exercise. He had his numerous projects to keep him busy, including experiments with ways of distilling fresh water from sea water and preserving meat for sea voyages. He dispensed his pills and his Balsam of Guiana and cured his own tobacco. Some believed that he had plenty of time left over to plot and scheme: King James, for instance, suspected that he was involved in the Gunpowder Plot. He complained of the cold and damp and suffered from various ailments, but surely there were many at Jonestown who would gladly have changed places with him, and surely there were moments during his second trip to Guiana when he yearned for the relative security and comfort of his Tower apartment.

Nevertheless, like the famous lions that were caged elsewhere in the Tower, his thrusting spirit was in chains. He was out of favor with the king, reprieved but legally guilty and under sentence of death, and the future was dark. In fact, it had looked so dark while he was waiting trial for treason that he attempted suicide. He had to live with the thought that the results of his first voyage had fallen far short of his and others' expectations and that some even refused to believe that he had gone on the voyage—had hidden out in Cornwall because he was "too easeful and sensuall to undertake a iorney of so great travel." There must have been times when he remembered the "digression touching our mortality" in his *History*, in which he had written of the seventh and last age of man that it is a time when "with many sighs, groans, and sad thoughts" we come by a crooked way "to the house of death, whose doors lie open at all hours, and to all persons."

He had to live too with the knowledge that many who did not doubt that he had discovered Guiana had doubts about the veracity of his report. Too much of it sounded like a fairy story: Amazons meeting with men in an annual springtime party in order to conceive and continue their race; men with heads beneath their shoulders; men living in trees and oysters growing in trees; a hundred-ten-year-old man who walked twenty-eight miles a day; a City of Gold. A Gresham's law of discovery was working against him: by the end of the sixteenth century there were too many fabulous stories about fabulous places. Evelyn Waugh, returning from Guiana in the blasé twentieth century, had the same experience, if on a reduced scale. He had brought home a crate of stuffed baby alligators as gifts for children, but the recipients were unimpressed. One youngster thought his alligator was a rabbit; a girl named hers "Evelyn" and tore it to pieces.

Montaigne in "Of Cannibals" claims to have gotten his information from "a plain ignorant fellow," who was "therefore more likely to tell the truth" without exaggerating it to make a better story. This, of course, did not keep Montaigne from using the plain fellow's report in order to enhance his own story of the paradoxical superiority of cannibal culture to the culture of Western Europe. Ralegh, of course, was neither plain nor ignorant, but he was looking for a City, and the fabulousness of the objective helped to determine his standard of credibility. Deep in the Guiana jungle, where it was believed that both men and oysters could be found in trees, the story that somewhere in the jungle one man was forced to spend his life reading to another would be as credible as the story of a tribe that had committed suicide at the behest of a charismatic leader. Thus the fabulousness of plain reality conspires against the effort to distinguish between fable and history. My own encounter with the banana cannibal, who loomed up so fabulously before me in the daybreaking jungle, made it easier for me to believe thirty-three years later that the mass suicide at Jonestown had really happened.

When Waugh refused to claim that his own discovery of Guiana had been a spiritual odyssey, he was in effect saying that he was in a position to write the kind of trustworthy history that Montaigne preferred. It meant also that he was biased for St. Augustine's distinction between the City of God and the City of Man and skeptical of all attempts to confuse the two. Ralegh was closer to this position when he wrote his *History* than he had been in the days of his first Guiana odyssey, but to Jim Jones the distinction must always have been meaningless. When, trapped in the fable of his paranoia, he got to the point of claiming that he was the reincarnation of Christ and Lenin, he was trying to build a City that would have invalidated Augustine by transcending history altogether. Here we can see how inevitable was the Soviet claim that the CIA had murdered the people of Jonestown to keep them from emigrating to the USSR: as if the Soviets, those builders of a secular City of God, could honestly imagine no other destination for them.

Nevertheless, there was ample American precedent for Jones's effort. When his lawyer, Charles Garry, called Jonestown "A jewel that the whole world should see," he was echoing, whether he knew it or not, the famous words of Puritan John Winthrop: "For we must consider that we will be as a City upon a Hill. The eyes of all people are upon us . . ." The ringing words occur in the sermon "A Model of Christian Charity," which Winthrop, the first governor of Massachusetts Bay Colony, preached somewhere in the middle of the Atlantic Ocean as his ship, the *Arabella*, headed for the heroic enterprise of City building in that New World that Ralegh had done so much to publicize.

But there would be trials and tribulations aplenty in the discovery of that New World and the attempt to build a Shining City in it. "The Wilderness through which we are passing to the Promised Land," Cotton Mather would write later, "is all over fill'd with Fiery flying serpents." It was an experience that Ralegh had had more than once in Guiana, perhaps never more memorably than on that day when, boating through "the most beautifull cuntrie that euer mine eies beheld . . . the Deere came downe feeding by the waters side, as if they had beene vsed to a keepers call." Yet two sentences later in that Edenic setting the very proper young Negro goes for a swim and is devoured by an alligator.

One may wonder how often later—back in the Bloody Tower then and writing his *History* so that mortality would have been much on his mind— Ralegh remembered that dramatic proof that Paradise was, as Augustine believed, forever denied to the City of Man. Waugh with his Augustinian bias would have been prepared to expect the alligator, and certainly the comic artist in him would have relished the reversal of expectations. Indeed, such a reversal is at the heart of *A Handful of Dust* as Tony Last's search for the secular City of his dreams ends up, contrary to anything Montaigne might have led him to expect, in a secular hell. He was no more prepared for Cotton Mather's fiery flying serpents than the beguiled utopians of Jonestown were. The recognition of this fact is what causes him to say in the delirium of the fever that finally yields to James Todd's jungle medicine: "I will tell you what I have learned in the forest, where time is different. There is no City."

There is reason to believe that if Ralegh had lived to write an account of his second discovery of Guiana, he would have expressed the same conclusion. Things had not connected. He had lost his son Wat in the disastrous encounter with the hated Spanish, who all along had represented a threat to his cause next to whom Amazons, cannibals, and hungry alligators were minor annoyances. "My braynes are broken," he wrote to his loyal and thoroughly admirable wife as he headed for home for the Bloody Tower expecting the worst. He was taken on a cold October morning to the Old Palace yard of Westminster to be executed. On the way he was given a cup of sack wine. One can imagine that under the circumstances he would have preferred some of his own Balsam of Guiana.

Before he served up the lethal cocktail to his congregation, Jim Jones announced that "It is time to die with dignity." Ralegh in any event died with all the dignity one would have expected from a man who was, as the antiquary John Aubrey later wrote, "one of the gallantest worthies that ever England bred." Addressing the assembled multitude from the scaffold, he spoke with moving eloquence for a good half hour, wanting like the dying Hamlet to have his cause reported aright to the unsatisfied, but seeing no Horatio who would do it for him. Among other things he confessed to "being a great sinner of a long time and in many kinds, my whole course a course of vanity, a seafaring man, a soldier and a courtier."

Afterwards he knelt on the gown that the executioner had spread for him and prayed. Then he put his head on the block, but the headsman still hesitated, so that Ralegh, hovering on the brink of his last discovery, was forced to cry: "Strike, man, strike!" His head came off at the second blow of the ax.

Spring 1990

Ontario Towns

C. S. GISCOMBE

1. September 1988

Up early in my room in the Kaladar Hotel & important to stop departure preparations for however long it took to note in my journal that "I feel the landscape making subtle demands on me." I'd broken down in a misty rain in Kaladar the day before—a flange had cracked on the hub of the bicycle's rear wheel, a thing not supposed to happen—and had had to thumb 60 miles to the nearest cycle shop and then 60 miles back with a new wheel arriving finally again in Kaladar in deep fog: it was by then 6, and I couldn't see where I was going anyway, so I bought a room for $12 Canadian. I'd left the bike in one of the unused service bays at Neueport Services, a combination lunch counter/gas station/cheese shop run by an extended family from India: husband and wife, brothers-in-law, pregnant young women, teenage children. They'd been sweet to me, letting me leave my stuff there, saying that if I returned late and found that station closed, I should knock on the door of their house up the road, walking me out into the mist so I could see it and know it for when I came back, pointing at it. Kaladar is a crossroads and little else: Neueport Services and the hotel across the street from it together are the business district. The patriarch of the family was a man a bit older than I, mid-forties, and he walked and walked around, he was always in motion: checking, worrying. He insisted on helping me put the bike back together upon my return (meaning it took twice as long as it should have) and politely inquired, after I'd got off his pay phone with my wife, if everything was OK at home, sounding nervously pleased when I said yes, relieved almost. For me? I'd come out of nowhere on a bicycle: I don't know what he thought was at stake.

I was heading, most immediately, for North Bay. My father, when he was growing up in Birmingham, had a cousin pen pal there up until World War II, and so I wanted to see the very far-off place that the family had extended to when my grandfather's brother had gone from the family home in Buff Bay, Jamaica, BWI, to North Bay and lived there, God knows why, while my grandfather had landed in Birmingham, USA, and schemed without success to get himself out to the West Coast. The family at Neueport Services then was like mine: people of color from near the equator here among the great outcroppings of rock, mosses, ripple-less still lakes choked with lily pads, coniferous trees looming through the pale, pale mist, all the *northern* things, all their "subtle demands." Across Route 41 the Kaladar Hotel was a ramshackle building, it smelled bad—musty and something worse than musty as well—and so seemed appropriately *of* the place. It had a harshly lit little dining room on the first floor, and I ordered a roast beef sandwich, tough and jagged little strips of meat on quartered white toast. Back upstairs I drew some water to take my nightly anti-asthma pill, gulped it and then spat as much as I could out—it was so awful, fetid tasting. "This is nowhere but I'm alive at the bone," I wrote, appropriating *alive at the bone* from Ondaatje's Billy the Kid book, "in this perfect little room," and then went to sleep for seven hours, leaving Kaladar at 8 a.m. in bright sunshine, waving to the people at Neueport, pleased to be back in the saddle.

At stake? Later that day my new odometer turned over onto 1,000 miles, which pleased me further because I couldn't remember what all the instructions-for-use had said and hadn't known if the little machine would *flip* over onto 1000.0 and not simply and suddenly read 000.0. Plus it was a fine day to be out banging across the Canadian Shield: the atypical early start, shining sun, good lunch—by the time 1,000 miles was drawing nigh—at a hoity-toity Swiss restaurant I'd found in the crotch of an otherwise nondescript fork in the road, and the easy, continual thrill of traveling through at that moment the kind of country I like best: rolling hills to muscle over without dropping down more than one or two sprockets. Singing "John Henry," singing "Rally 'Round the Flag" (which is—if one can forget this moment's popular stupidity about how bad it is to burn one—actually quite moving, the lines in particular "All of us are poor, boys, / but none of us are slaves"), singing "Truckin'," "Erie Canal," and "Hesitation Blues," singing "Midnight Special" about going to North Bay and how, once there, you better walk right. It was long day 5, and it came in, at sunset, at 90.08 miles.

(At stake? I'd started in front of my house in Ithaca, New York, milepost 0, intending to bicycle via North Bay into the Arctic Watershed—where the rivers flow north into Hudson's Bay—and then get the train home. Out over and back across an interesting geographic border. I try to do a week or ten-day bike trip twice a year: the belly drops off, muscles thicken, the asthma vanishes, and I return home with a clear head. When my daughter turns 14 in eleven years, we'll start in Vancouver and bicycle to Alaska, though I'll be almost 50. Then what'll I do?)

I camped that night at Lake Dore, in a pay-place, and got the more typical late start the next day, cruising into Pembroke at 11:30: industrial, long, low shank of a town on the Ottawa River. I crossed Route 17, the next road I'd planned to follow, on the approach, the outskirts, and was dismayed to find its shoulders made of sand and the 2-lane itself choked with fast traffic. Sand's quite impossible to bike in (the wheels sink), and the degree of traffic suggested that even if I stayed at the most extreme edge of the pavement, I'd still have a fair chance of getting smacked within the first hour. That far north in Ontario the number of roads declines dramatically: this one was the only way out of Pembroke in the direction I wanted to go. Bad news, too much to deal with, so I drifted into Pembroke proper, where suddenly it was noon: a lot of women who looked like secretaries were in the streets with bag lunches, walking up the hill from river-level downtown—going where?—still in their summer dresses (it was only September, so only the nights were cold), one very dark black man among them walking stiffly in a three-piece suit. West Indian? No, African, I thought, as he didn't meet my eyes, looking through me instead, haughty. I realized there at high noon in Pembroke that I should have taken the other road, the one that cuts west through Algonquin Park; I'd passed it many miles previous: backtracking then, taking the extra day, was how it would have to be. But right then I was hungry, and my every piece of clothing—except a pair of long khaki pants—reeked of sweat and road, so I did a laundry and ate some lunch, and while my clothes were in the dryer, on an impulse, I found a phone and called VIA, and there was indeed a train to North Bay, and it left Pembroke in 35 minutes. I was there though my socks were still damp, and the conductor lifted the bike into the baggage car. I dropped down into a coach seat, and the big extravagantly tattooed child sitting across the aisle tossed me a can of warm Budweiser from an apparently bottomless stash. Leaving Pembroke.

The train went out along the Ottawa and crossed Route 17 now and again, the sandy shoulder visibly continuing. Ugly little towns, but the deciduous trees were just starting to go over to colors. What route would my grandfather's brother—whose name I didn't even know as I was sitting there in the coach trying to think about him, we're that kind of shutmouthed family—have taken to get to North Bay? This one, from Montreal or Ottawa or, more likely, the Ontario Northland Railway, the straight shot north from Toronto? I also didn't know why my grandfather had wanted to go from Birmingham out west—I can certainly imagine good reasons for any black person to want to leave the American South of the '20s, the '30s, the '40s, the '50s, but I don't *know*, it was never discussed, and he's been dead now near thirty years. A certain impenetrability lies at the heart of things, the ball of (what?) family tendencies I can see in my father, the aloneness centralized, the deliberate silent space around the human part of it. I can see it in myself. The train lurched and squeaked past a beaver lake: ferns, marsh grasses, larches. The big child across the aisle was from Nova Scotia and was going out to work the forests up in northern BC. "Fucking fourteen dollars an hour," he said, "and that's just to start, eh?" I saw a porcupine moving along beside us in that slow-motion way they have and then fell asleep in my seat. An hour later we came to North Bay.

Which I'd always heard described as a hole, a ragged frontier slum town, the heart of nowhere, or its *edge*. It *wasn't* lovely—too much traffic for the narrow streets and particularly devoid of trees—but it was no particular slum, and the people I met were on the surface anyway more conscious, more alert (meaning alive) than people one tends to butt up against in towns in, say, Upstate New York. Maybe the landscape demanded it of them. No Giscombes, though, in the phone book there in the station waiting room, not that I would have called. At stake? What would I have said? I didn't know where I could camp thereabouts, and neither did the station agent, so she directed me instead to the Ontario Provincial Police station, she and I joking companionably over her directions so much that I got lost in the process itself and found myself on a street full of blankfaced postwar houses. I hailed a girl who was walking by—about 12, the breasts bouncing free under her tunic having more to do with fat than with adolescence— asking her if she knew the way to the OPP, and she stared at me then finally exhaled Holy shit! and called another girl slightly older, who came running from a house and didn't know either but who called a third girl assuring me that she—the third girl, Joyce I think—knew where *everything* in town was. Joyce came bopping across the street in her high-tops, one blue and one pink, and deck pants pulled tight over her skinny self. She was pale as the other two girls, but her skin's definition was different, supple where theirs was rough and with a deep glow to it: that and her hair and especially the line of her jaw told me—though it didn't consciously (or *verbally*) register 'til hours later when I was describing her in my journal—that she had a few

African ancestors. Her pals told her how I wanted to go to the OPP station, and so she directed me, with elaborate gestures and succinct qualifications (first explaining to the others, e.g., that she would direct me though, in a stage whisper, "We do not know *why* he wishes to see the police, nor shall we inquire"), and gave me advice for cycling through North Bay. She was casually encyclopedic about the layout of her town, and her words and phrasings were measured: descriptions of the unimportant tossed off, *ways* of proceeding through certain intersections stressed. Fourteen and held in esteem by her friends, a leader of those white girls, the power of language singing within her, singing out from her. "Hey," she'd called after I'd thanked her and was drifting down toward the end of her street, "it was good meeting you," the salute to the social, to the incident itself, from a very mature child. More? I wondered the next day did she know she was black? And I wondered later still, 2 days and a hundred miles up the road it stopped me, at the chance of her being a relative.

In the morning I headed out of town stopping first at a sewing supply shop to buy a needle and thread to sew the button back onto one of my two pairs of shorts. The lady insisted on not charging me and gave me the official Tourism Ministry map of northern Ontario. "We'd not want you to think," she said, "that the only thing going on in Ontario is Toronto." She opened it up to help me find the road I'd be taking, and there was the great colorless blankness of the map: vast, vast, vast Ontario with rivers running through it, symbols for OPP outposts and tiny airports, lakes, hardly any roads anywhere, more rivers, a huge profoundly, blankly white map—it covered the counter and draped over, North Bay at its bottom—of largely unbroken space.

And it was that space I made for, leaving North Bay that morning in weak sunlight that faded into hours of drizzle and more mist, heading farther and farther north, sharing the less traveled of the 2 roads north with, mostly, little convoys of lumber trucks, cruising for two days along the Ottawa, crossing into Quebec—at a strange lumber town with imported-from-Italy antique fountains at every intersection—and drifting up alongside the east shore of Lake Timiskaming, seeing Ontario (the lake's the border) through breaks in the fog and rain. The subtle demands of traveling in rain. To be moving through that—through bear, wolf, and moose country, though I saw none of those animals—was what I'd come for, to be alive and taking myself farther north, farther away from landscape I knew. I'd wanted to be moving and, at the same time, up close against the big space—rocks, exotic mosses, big skeins of wires coming down in cuts through the trees from remote hydro projects, animals, trees and more trees beyond those—stretching away from the edge of my body all the way to the coast of Labrador.

But early the next day it began raining again, and I realized I wasn't going to make it into the watershed—I was missing my wife and my daughter, and I was tired, I'd gotten 500 miles (not counting the little skip on the train), much of which was in rain and had had it—so I cut west, up over the top of the lake back into Ontario, and came to New Liskeard a bit before sunset. I'd picked up a schedule in North Bay, so I knew there was a midnight train I could catch there down to Toronto. Coming into New Liskeard—which is a lovely town built on terraces up from Lake Timiskaming or up rather from an estuary of that lake—I was glad to pass a movie theater showing a film I'd not seen and figured I could stand seeing, *A Fish Called Wanda*, a Monty Python vehicle. I found the Ontario Northland station and left my panniers there, put on the pair of long khaki pants and came back to the theater for my night out on the town: it was strange suddenly to be sitting back in a movie eating popcorn and drinking a Coke alone among strangers laughing together with them at John Cleese and Jamie Lee Curtis. I'd not cared much for the Python "quest" movies, but this was funny, or it seemed so in particular to me that night. And it was strange being entertained in public at an entertainment palace after nights of sleeping out (and one night in a gnomish hotel), strange to pay to be distracted, the distraction oddly more pleasant for my seeing it for what it was.

After the movie, I had a surprisingly decent Chinese dinner then wandered back to the station. It was a cool night, cloudy as it had been all day, a breeze blowing in off Lake Timiskaming. 70 or 80 miles I guess short of the watershed. At stake? The Arctic Watershed is a ragged line on a few specialized maps, a fact of drainage; perhaps there would have been a sign. But it was—or would have been—an extremity, a new physical state to muscle *knowingly* into: body, mind, geography. (But here I was only as far as New Liskeard instead, having had a good dinner, having enjoyed myself at a film, having coincided with an artistic black child in surprising North Bay, having cycled 70, 80, and 90 miles a day for day after day, and now waiting for the southbound feeling OK. I was alive and, more, corporeal—feeling good and strong to be even this far north—and consciously deferring the big gratification. A long freight train came by—incredibly bright constellation of three headlights on the first engine, two of which were down low at either end of the base of the triangle, *the better to see you with*—picking up speed, and the stationmaster and I were standing there in the wind it made on the platform watching it, car after car after car until the shapes blurred: I don't know what was in his mind, but I was thinking of living a long life of this.) At stake? Why was I always running to Canada when I had some time, crossing that border to touch the big otherness? Why does it feel so good to be alive with all thoughts of home intact so far from home itself?

I woke up once during the longish stop in North Bay and then slept all the way until we slowed for the Toronto 'burbs: Saabs and BMWs jammed into the commuter station parking lots, it being mid-morning, so all the lawyers and bankers and what-have-you had already been at their desks a good two hours. And more or less suddenly the city itself was visible, one of the major ones of the Western world: publishing, theater, commerce, immigrants from all over the world, a thousand posh things to do at night. But still, above the tracks where it would be visible to the commuters on their trains that also used this route in, was a huge billboard advertising hiking boots, good old-fashioned Vibram-soled waffle stampers to live in all day whilst tromping across the muskeg, through exotic mosses, along the marges of those still lakes, *that* sense of the world saluted at the marge of sophisticated Toronto. All that space behind me, I thought, that I'd gone off into and come back out of, and I'd not even got to the place where the rivers flow north or the place beyond there where the roads stop (or the place beyond even that where the Ontario Northland tracks stop). This, I thought—though I recognized the presumption a few days later—living *with* all that space, this was what it meant to be Canadian.

2. June 1989

I glided down the hill into Kaladar, and there was Neueport Services, doing a brisk trade in the heat, cars lined up at the pumps for that Shell gasoline. This time it was only the end of my second day—I'd gotten a lift from Ithaca to near Watertown, New York—and it being only 6 and one of the longest days of the year, I was thinking of going farther, pressing on to the provincial park 12 miles up the road. But it was hot, and I was tired, and they remembered me when I went in to buy a bottle of apple juice. The man *I* remembered as being patriarch was absent, and one of the younger guys—who perhaps had always really been in charge? the other having been only patriarchal?—took me around to show me how they'd expanded the business since I'd been there the previous September: the under-one-roof complex now included a package store and a novelty shop, the sort of place where one buys funny bumper stickers. I was pleased that they were doing well and said so as I felt my body beginning to acknowledge road-weariness, as the miles caught up with me as they say, as the Kaladar Hotel squatting—again—across Rte. 41 started to look good.

This was a different kind of trip, a bit more frantic, that much more directed. I'd broken one of my rules for bike traveling—*all trips* must *start at home*—and taken a lift for the first 150 miles with my friend David Warren to Lake Bonaparte, at the northwestern edge of the Adirondacks: this meant I could head straight west and actually be—via 2 ferries—in Canada, the big otherness, by the end of Day 1. What was at stake: After living 20 years in Upstate New York, I'd had a pre–middle age surge of ambition and taken a faculty job at Illinois State University in Normal, Illinois, in the Corn Belt, far from everywhere in the world I'd gotten familiar with. This was—as I explained to 2 cyclists from Toronto whom I met on the first of the two ferries to Kingston—my farewell tour of the East. *It was good of you,* said the woman as we cycled across Wolfe Island to the second ferry, *to take your farewell tour in Canada.* I camped with them that night in Kingston: her name was Jackie, and she was tough and arrogant and smart and awkwardly sweet. I don't recall the man's name: there was tension between them, their end probably as lovers (or the awkward *beginnings* of their being lovers). At stake? I wanted to get back to North Bay and spend a day or so checking out the Giscombes there—what public history or notation I could find—and then get myself quickly back to Ithaca to recommence packing for the move west. North Bay's a long, long way from central Illinois: this was just about the last chance to get up there, even this casually.

Leaving Kingston the next morning, Sunday, in hot hazy sunlight and pressing on north through Napanee and then up into the woods and lakes, I got to Kaladar, the end of Day 2. I steeled myself and went on into the Kaladar Hotel, finding the lobby different: it didn't smell bad, the moldy stacks of magazines were gone, and there was a large etching propped on one of the couches (which were new) of a black man playing a flute. No one around, though, except in the dining room, which had also been refurbished. The waiter took me back through hallways, and there, in a tiny office, was one of the new owners.

The hotel itself, she said, wasn't ready yet, they were still fixing up the place having just bought it in April. But I persisted until she agreed to let me have my old room, with its spray-painted #1 on the door, just for the evening "since you stayed here before and know what the rooms are like"; she filled out a lodging card for me, taking care to cross out the name of the former proprietor, Beulah Tricky. In the dining room, her husband, the cook, shook my hand and told me to sit anywhere. She was white, he was black, both somewhere past 50 and from a town nearby. Their names— Donna and Andy Anderson—were listed on the hotel's ad on the Chamber of Commerce paper placemat in among the car dealerships and fishing camps, "Open Under New Management." I ordered a bottle of Labatt's and the day's special, liver & onions, using the beer glass to prop open my copy of Eugene Genovese's book about the slaves, *Roll, Jordan, Roll*: I'd be teaching a course in African-American Lit in a few weeks, and I wanted to know as much as I could about context. A fellow at the next table inquired as to what I was reading, and we began talking about recent history, about Salman Rushdie's troubles and what few options the British had in dealing with matters of his protection. Soon we were talking about nations and the nature of power, politics, things that related rather much to Brother Genovese's themes in *Roll, Jordan, Roll*. It was a conversation I'd not expected to be having in the Kaladar Hotel. He was, it turned out, a white (or apparently white) Trinidadian, a bit older than I, who'd just given up on finishing *The Satanic Verses*, having found it tiresome. A young man sitting nearby commenced about how the Rushdie thing was nothing but another insult to the West by the A-rabs, and that the Brits just ought to nuke Iran, but the man from Trinidad and I agreed in gestures and in a couple of words exchanged over the younger man's head that the world is what it is.

The dinner Andy Anderson brought me that evening was one of the best dinners I've ever had, and I didn't even know I was very hungry. Simple food exquisitely prepared: the liver was more tender than I'd imagined it ever would be, more delicately breaded, more beautifully garnished with asparagus and cauliflower and broccoli. Afterwards there was pie and easy talk with him and Donna. They bought up dilapidated places like the Kaladar Hotel had been for years and would run them until the places got successful, and they—Donna and Andy—were bored, at which point they'd move on down the road. They were both older than they looked. Looking at him, listening to him talk in that Canadian lilt (with no recognizable black inflection), I thought naturally of my grandfather's brother but had no project agenda at the moment and didn't think to ask him the questions that have occurred to me since meeting him and since being in North Bay again. I mentioned my great-uncle and how I was going to North Bay to look for family things, seeing if he'd have anything to say about that but didn't press the point when he didn't. Now of course I see it as being a constellation of points: I mean my ignorance of black life in the Ontario bush and frontier towns, my ignorance of the context within the context. I didn't—and still don't—know what's at stake in the bigger pictures: I'd been thinking of my great-uncle's blackness making him anomalous in North Bay, but that's the way my family has always thought of itself: *whatever* the context, we are separate from it. I'd had my hiking boot epiphany on the train the year before about Canadian identity, but that was myself being knee-jerk literary, meaning presumptuous as well as detached from anything specific. I'd not been prepared to meet a native black man in upper Canada who served me an incredible dinner while wearing penny loafers. And besides, in my house at home I'm the cook, for company and the weekdays both, and have been for years—I'm intimate with that whole production including some of the metaphors. Otherness? How are we different, exactly, and how are we similar (exactly)?

Halfway through the next day, I made the turn I should have made the year before and pressed on northwest over the hill roads. One stretch of ten miles was all uphill and under construction: a loose gravel road surface then over which thundered dump trucks (meaning layers and layers of dust in the air). The lads had all the other big yellow machines at play as well (more dust) while bored flag-girls sat on coolers smoking cigarettes, 90° or so: it took an hour and a half to get that 10 miles, but then I came to the hamlet of Palmer Rapids on the Madawaska River and turned there onto a beautifully paved wide-shouldered road that went alongside the river for 10 more, straight and flat, the river hidden beyond a thick line of trees, but its coolness touching the road. I camped that night at Carson Lake Provincial Park eating cold beans for dinner and then dozing off still dressed. Waking at midnight, I stripped and swam out into Carson Lake itself until I got a chill, and the fact of swimming alone at night in a strange lake suddenly struck me as being a bad idea. I'd come that day 85 miles.

Two days later I arrived in North Bay, again by train. I'd intended to cycle all the way and had taken measures to ensure that, but a terrible and persistent headwind—on the day I left Carson Lake—had held me to 7 and 8 mph all the way through big Algonquin Park, and that skewed my schedule just enough to matter, so I spent the last 50 miles of the trip set up in the dining car drinking coffee and watching the landscape slip by. Certainly this was the way my father's uncle had got to North Bay, and this train ride I knew his name—Charles Giscome. I'd got my father talking on the phone about him and my grandfather a few days before I'd left. They "fell out over something," he said, "or, more likely, a lot of somethings" early in the century, and then Charles had dropped the *b* from his name on account of whatever the fights were about. This story I'd heard before, when I was in high school, but my memory from then was that my grandfather's brother had dropped the *e* from the name, making it *Giscomb*. This is folk culture, storytelling. This is the naming act mutating, specificity shifting up and shifting down, the oral tradition.

I set up camp where I'd camped before in North Bay and the next morning went out to the regional museum at the edge of town. It was cramped and ugly but not a bad place at all, and the intense young man in charge found a J. Giscombe—spelled like that—on the list of local men who'd come back alive out of WWII. Johnny, whose name I'd heard before, my father's old pen pal: the obvious—that they'd stopped writing because of Johnny going off to the war—hadn't occurred to me, and I was relieved to discover that he'd not been killed there, that I wasn't present at the site of some 50-year-old tragedy. By the time I quit the museum and was cruising back downtown, it was noon, and the construction crews were breaking for lunch: lots of building was going on, a new subdivision to fight the woods back some—a couple of the fellows were black, we nodded to each other in the sunshine. (Two years before, when I was cycling through Wales, I met another black man walking toward me on the road out of Penrhyndeudraeth. We both slowed, making eye contact, realizing that some sort of exchange, some sort of salute, was called for, Wales being what it is. But all either of us could think to do was discuss the distance from the point where we *did* stop to speak to one another and the town I'd recently passed through: he asked how far it was, I told him. We wished each other well then and continued on our ways. He had a strange accent, a soft and lovely voice, neither West Indian nor one of the sets of intonations I recognize as African.)

I took my lunch at a crowded greasy spoon back downtown on the main drag, sitting at the counter near the window so I could watch the city parade by: not *many* black people, but more of us than I'd figured from my first trip there. After lunch and coffee, I settled down in the library with the big stack of city directories. The earliest one was 1914, and there he was with his name spelled G-I-S-C-O-M-E, Charles Giscome was a chef then, living on Front Street in what seemed to be a largely Italian neighborhood, immigrants like him. Later there was a wife, Lucille, and later still there were children. I made pages and pages of notes on the family's progress, jobs, addresses, then lost the notebook when we moved to Illinois. Typical. But I remember that Charles Giscome's kids took jobs, moved away from home, apparently lost the jobs and moved back. One—Sybil, I think—eventually became a teacher, another ran a realty company. The old man himself, in the '30s, was listed for a while as a "labourer" and then for a year had a tourist camp. And then in 1940 both he and John had been porters, the classic mid-dle-class job for US black men for so many years, porters on the Timiskam-ing & Northern Ontario Railway. But the next year they were all gone, all of them: I stared at the book at the place between the 2 other names, Giscard I think and Givens; and they were gone for the year after that as well, and then there were no more directories until the '50s, and they weren't in any of those either. Suddenly then I was back in the library basement and it was past 3 o'clock, too late really to start checking out anywhere else—city hall, the schools, etc. (When I came across the porter job, I'd called the railroad archive and got nowhere.) I felt tired and hot, as though I'd walked across town several times, and began to think about how I'd spend the rest of the day, the suddenly immense blank time before the 3 a.m. train south.

I fumbled through the library some reading bits in *Certain People*, white Stephen Birmingham's book about the US black middle class and, from the same shelf, some social science essays on the black Canadian community, an entity "prone to fragmentation," or something like that. Leaving the library, I cycled around until I found Front Street, but the numbers were all wrong. Still, I realized that I was in the same neighborhood I'd been in the year before where the black girl had talked so beautifully to me: it made, of course, *sociological* sense, but it pleased me as well on the other levels. But the fragmentation was setting in, the feeling of breathlessness, of a profound and generalized *fade*, meaning severance, meaning the com-ing invisibility: no name in the street in this town or in Ithaca. I must have looked lost: a teenager wearing a Simple Minds T-shirt asked if he could help me find something. I gave him a number, an address, on Front Street beyond the point where the street T'd into another, asking if Front recom-menced somewhere later on, across the RR tracks, say. No, he said, this is it, man, and asked the name of the people I was looking for. I told him, warning that it had been a long time since they'd lived there, let him shake his head *no*. It felt something like good, though, pronouncing the name aloud and correctly into the North Bay streets, into the woods and lakes past the gates to the city. In a spate of the directories from the mid-'30s, the name was spelled, oddly, *with* the b, and I imagined as I sat in the basement of the North Bay library that during those years my great-uncle had been aiming at a reconciliation with my grandfather, the name spelling being *emblematic* of that; but it's such a weird name anyway that you never know how someone's going to pronounce it after seeing it written or, more to the point, write it after hearing it said—maybe whoever put the city book together "corrected" the spelling, based on hearing the name or based on

-combe being a common British name suffix. West Indians recognize *Gis-combe*, though, as West Indian, I don't know how.

As we'd approached the lights of Kingston on the ferry, my 2 companions and I had been talking to some hip people from Toronto. When they found out I was heading for North Bay, they were politely incredulous at the distance I had yet before me and politely baffled at my choice of destination: with their faces they reaffirmed the commonly held attitude toward the place (the edge of nowhere, the northernmost slum), enough so that I could joke with them some—in that mocking way hip people have—about North Bay being the garden spot of the golden north, etc., and then turn a mysterious half-smile on 'em as I turned to gaze Kingston-ward. *I had to leave a little girl*, Belafonte sang, *in Kingston-town*. Other places, even farther, loom: when my daughter Madeline and I bike from Vancouver to Alaska, we'll go through Giscome, British Columbia, named for the nineteenth-century black miner John Robert Giscome. I've been asserting casually for years, mostly in conversation, that his name is an "arguable phonetic spelling" of my own, forging a tie that way between myself and John Robert, between myself and *out there*. And now my thinking is that maybe it could be something beyond the phonetic, a blood connection, a real family *thing* in the insistence on particular spellings (and whatever loyalties that might imply) at the heart or *alongside* however the long heart of a family is figured or construed. The Canadian spelling. I mean I was surprised to find that my grandfather's brother had spelled his name as John Robert had—or as John Robert's was written down. (A Pacific Great Eastern Railroad map I saw once places the "Giscome Portage"; the old Grand Trunk Western map I own places the "Giscombe Portage.") I don't care much for mysteries, they make me irritable. But I do have a thing for the north. This has been the family's progress of course, the movement from south up this way; indeed, it's an African-American archetype—culture occurs in landscape—and here I am, the first generation born admittedly bourgeois across the Ohio River, still having the impulse, *north!*, though it's metaphorized into something other than the sane set of reasons-for-migration that belonged to those who went earlier. But the part of North Bay where I was looking for my great-uncle's addresses does look strikingly like the west end of Bloomington, my current city, the side of town where the poorer people live, the side split and split again by those railroad tracks. The difference of course is that North Bay *is* Canadian, so there's no one big empty street, as there is here as there is in every other US city, no one big empty street named for Dr. King.

The station agent in North Bay remembered me from my having been there before, but I embarrassed and surprised myself by failing to recognize her when I trailed into the depot that night: I'd thought *about* her, recalling that I'd liked her and had wondered, hopefully, whether or not she'd still be there working for them, this last as I sat through the new and dull Batman movie at a theater downtown, killing time, 2 of the many hours before the train. But if she was offended she didn't show it, and why should she be? It's not as though we'd been lovers or even friends. But she is, I realized at some point, the person I know best in that town which is the farthest known edge of this my ragged family.

Three o'clock came, and the depot was filled with people waiting for both the Southbound and the Northbound, which were due to pass each other at North Bay. Four o'clock came, and still neither train had showed. Many of us were out on the platform by then watching for them and telling stories. The station agent came out and joined us after a while: we had all seen the headlight appear, but the train itself had stopped half a mile or so down the track, so we got the light mixed up with other lights down there, streetlights, God knows what else. Soon the sky itself began to lighten, and only then, slowly, did the train ease in. The agent went inside and came out again, with a sleepy crowd behind her, saying, *This is the Northbound.* I looked up and saw the red-light marked tail end of another train backing silently in behind on the same track, a conductor with a walkie-talkie riding the vestibule. When it stopped, ten feet from the Northbound, I got on the coach looking over my shoulder at the woman working both trains with the baggage cart, wondering how long she'd remember me from this time. But then the train started with a soft jerk forward. "Now *he's* gonna have to back out," the conductor said to another passenger, pointing back at the Northbound. The sun was almost in the sky, my last long night in Canada spent where else but in a train station. One needs songs to sing on the road, of the road—music should have come up, some sort of as yet unimagined straining *northern* jazz, an *insistent* strain, say, of straying muted horns, fragmented, breaking. Leaving North Bay.

3. November 1989

Midterm exam in my African-American Lit course, English 165-01, Illinois State University, Fall 1989. I'd assigned 3 take-home essay questions about the books I'd had the students read and, for many, these were the first three essays they'd been called upon to write since they'd left the university's one required Freshman English course. I hadn't known, at the time, that this was the case. But all that's to say that lots of distraught kids called the night before the morning the exam was due telling me that they had no idea what the questions were about, and could I please tell them "what you want." They were being thrown, in part, by my using terms like "discuss" and "evaluate," which they'd, apparently, not encountered much before.

Most of my students in that course were black like me but, for the greatest part, from Chicago, a city I don't know, and from lives I don't know—I was their age 20 years ago and in college in Upstate New York living, more or less by default, with white people and described accurately by those people as a loner: walking all over town by myself, reading books, trying to write. "We're not a reading people," suggested another new black professor here, though he is and I am. And I think that his comment, made over lunch in the quiet, spacious week after our first year at Illinois State had ended, made us both uncomfortable or, more to the point, brought home to us the strain between ourselves and our students. (Of course, my white ISU students don't, as a group, read much of anything either, but that's not the point, or it's a different point.) That night, though, there I was on the phone with the kids—one on one—after speaking so much from my spot in the rough circle I'd had them pull the desks into 3 mornings a week and from which I'd suggested Genovese's Marxism to them and tried to get them to speak about Frederick Douglass or Zora Neale Hurston, about Langston Hughes. I'd suggested to them the presumption I saw in white authors like William Styron and Eudora Welty when those authors dealt in fiction with black characters. But only rarely would one of them come to see me during office hours (though my white creative writing students often came). They were, as a class, very different from the classes of black students I'd had in the years I'd taught part-time at Cornell: a percentage (small but visible) of those students were the children of West Indians who'd gone to New York City instead of Toronto or London or, God knows, North Bay. Immigrants' kids. But on the phone that night with the kids from Chicago, I began to realize how much of what I'd been asking of them—meaning *expecting* of them—they hadn't understood in spite of all the years I'd spent teaching and studying and talking about the act of language, the years spent achieving some success with my own written work. "But all value is assigned, / is brought in," I said in a poem. Once, when I was in Britain for a few weeks with my wife, I'd cycled (while she was at a conference) from London up to Edinburgh; and when we got back to the States, a black friend had suggested that I was "probably the first black person ever to do that," seeing metaphoric implications, I think, regarding England's colonial power, not to mention it being the place where our language—he's also an English professor—came partly from. Assigned value. So I came to realize, during my evening of talk on the telephone, that other things were at stake for my students now, their expectations were other than mine or even what mine had been. But *how* are we different, exactly?

One woman was close, I think, to tears over the question concerning the character development of Janie Crawford in Hurston's *Their Eyes Were Watching God.* I asked her about other novels she'd read, thinking that if we had some book in common, I might be able to get her considering the function of character in *Their Eyes* by talking at some length with her about the characters—how minor ones complement major ones—in that book from long ago. But she hadn't read a novel since sophomore year in high school and couldn't remember what it was she'd read then. I figured I'd better try a different angle.

"How 'bout movies?" I said. Films, books, what the hell's the difference between made things? "You like movies? What movies have you been to recently?"

She paused, then laughed ambiguously and said, "*Batman.*"

And there I was again, out of my kitchen in Bloomington, Illinois, a million miles away from my office at Illinois State, from meetings of the faculty and of the handful of interested students who make up the Black Writers' Forum, off the lone prairie and back in a sweaty line outside a theater in Canada and then inside with the loud crowd, slack-faced and noisy—every fool in North Bay had been there. And I'd *liked* North Bay, I'd felt comfortable and curious both in that raggedy-ass narrow-street town at the edge of deep and romantic space where that beautiful black child had spoken so brilliantly to me (she must have known she was black, I think, as I reconstruct her now in Illinois, in memory: her gestures had that *thing,* or edges of it anyway—maybe she her-supple-self and her language of easy reference, point casually broken/fragmented into inventive variations, vocal dances for a stranger, the *semblance*—the half rime—of relation, maybe this was the northern jazz I'd longed for when I was leaving North Bay). But there in the movie theater that night had been nothing but 42 million dollars of US junk culture shrunk into a 2-hour format, seven or eight hundred white Canadians who were lapping it up, and myself the only black person I saw in the house. Of course even sweet and smart Jackie, the lady with whom I'd sailed into Kingston, had warned me, as we'd loitered at the ferry-slip, that I'd be "in the minority in Ontario," waiting a beat to smile broadly and explain that I'd be in said predicament because I wasn't wearing a Batman T-shirt. Change the joke please, I'd thought, try for a different double-entendre, save yourself. *Batman.* Poor Billy Dee Williams had had to walk around looking baffled through the whole flick, jive-ass in Gotham and this the final evening of my farewell tour of the East. Is this my life? I'd thought unhappily in the theater, my characteristic thought when I realize I'm wasting time, just killing time as though time wasn't committing suicide on its own fast enough. But the landscape changes, and the changes make their demands, revise the experience.

"OK," I said, "we had, say 4 characters: there was Batman himself, Jack Nicholson as the Joker, Kim Basinger as the love interest and, say, Police Commissioner Gordon."

Winter 1991

In Co. Cork

WILLIAM TREVOR

ALL MEMORY is grist to the fiction-writer's mill. The pleasure and the pain experienced by any storyteller's characters, the euphoria of happiness, the ache of grief, must of course be the storyteller's own. It cannot be otherwise, and in that sense all fiction has its autobiographical roots, spreading through—in my case—a provincial world, limited and claustrophobic.

I grew up in what John Betjeman called "the small towns of Ireland"—in my case, Mitchelstown, cut down to size by the towering Galtee Mountains and the Knockmealdowns, Youghal by the sea, Skibbereen lost somewhere in the back of beyond. There were others besides, but to these three in Co. Cork I go back often and look them over. Mitchelstown is still famous for its martyrs and its processed cheese, a squat little town, looking as though someone has sat on it. A good little business town, my father used to say, knowing about such matters.

Youghal, smartly elegant in my memory, is tatty on a wet afternoon. A carful of German tourists crawls along the seafront, the misty beach is empty. Once, people pointed here, and remarked; I listened, and my eaves-droppings told of an afternoon love affair conducted on that brief prome-nade, he a married doctor, she a lady in disgrace. I see them now as I made them in my fascination: she is thin, and dressed in red, laughing, with pale long hair; he is Ronald Colman with a greyer moustache. They smile at one another; defiantly he touches her hand. They are breathtaking in their sin-ning, and all their conversation is beautiful; they are the world's most excit-ing people.

I walk away from their romance, not wanting to tell myself that they were not like that. On the sands where old seaside artists sprinkled garish colors the rain is chilly. Pierrots performed here, and the man and woman who rode the Wall of Death sunned themselves at midday. From the Loreto Convent we trooped down here to run the end-of-term races, Sister Therese in charge. The sands haven't changed, nor have the concrete façades of the holiday boardinghouses, nor the Protestant church with its holes for lepers to peer through. But Horgan's Picture House is not at all as it was. It has two screens now and a different name, and there are sexual fantasies instead of Jack Hulbert in *Round the Washtub*.

In Youghal there was a man who shot himself in a henhouse. Life had been hell for this man, the voices whispered, and the henhouse, quite near the back of our garden, developed an eeriness that the chatter of birds made even more sinister. The henhouse isn't there anymore, but even so as I stand where it was, I shudder and remember other deaths.

Youghal itself died in a way, for yellow furniture vans—Nat Ross of Cork—carted our possessions off, through Cork itself, westward through the town that people call Clonakilty God Help Us, to Skibbereen, at the back of beyond.

Memory focuses here, the images are clearer. Horses and carts in the narrow streets, with milk churns for the creamery. On fair-days farmers with sticks standing by their animals, their shirts clean for the occasion, without collar or tie. A smell of whiskey, and sawdust and stout and dung. Pots of geraniums among chops and ribs in the small windows of butchers' shops. A sun-burnt poster advertising the arrival of Duffy's Circus a year ago.

It was a mile and a half, the journey to school through the town, past Driscoll's sweetshop and Murphy's Medical Hall and Power's drapery, where you could buy oilcloth as well as dresses. In Shannon's grocery there was a man who bred smooth-haired fox terriers. He gave us one once, a strange animal, infatuated by our cat.

In the town's approximate center, where four streets meet, a grey woman still stands, a statue of the Maid of Erin. E. O'Donovan, undertaker, still sells ice cream and chocolate. The brass plate of Redmond O'Regan, solicitor, once awkwardly high, is now below eye level. In the grocers' shops the big-jawed West Cork women buy bread and sausages and tins of plums, but no longer wear the heavy black cloaks that made them seem like figures from another century. They still speak in the same West Cork lisp, a lingering careful voice, never in a hurry. I ask one if she could tell me the way to a house I half remember. "Ah, I could tell you grand," she replies. "It's dead and buried, sir."

The door beside the Methodist church, once green, is purple. The church, small and red-brick, stands behind high iron railings and gates, with gravel in front of it. Beyond the door that used to be green is the dank passage that leads to Miss Willoughby's schoolroom, where first I learnt that the world is not an easygoing place. Miss Willoughby was stern and young, in love with the cashier from the Provincial Bank.

On the gravel in front of the red-brick church I vividly recall Miss Willoughby. Terribly, she appears. Severe and beautiful, she pedals against the wind on her huge black bicycle. "Someone laughed during prayers," she accuses, and you feel at once that it was you, although you know it wasn't. *V. poor* she writes in your headline book when you've done your best to reproduce, four times, perfectly, *Pride goeth before destruction.*

As I stand on the gravel, her evangelical eyes seem again to dart over me without pleasure. Once I took the valves out of the tyres of her bicycle. Once I looked in her answer book.

I am late, I am stupid. I cannot write twenty sentences on A Day in the Life of an Old Shoe. I cannot do simple arithmetic or geography. I am always fighting with Jasper Swanton. I move swiftly on the gravel, out onto the street and into the bar of the Eldon Hotel: in spectral form or otherwise, Miss Willoughby will not be there.

Illusions fall fast in the narrow streets of Skibbereen, as elsewhere they have fallen. Yet for me, once, there was something more enduring, nicest thing of all. Going to Cork it was called, fifty-two miles in the old Renault, thirty miles an hour because my mother wouldn't permit speed. On St. Stephen's Day to the pantomime in the Opera House, and on some other occasion to see the *White Horse Inn*, which my father had heard was good. In Cork my appendix was removed because Cork's surgical skill was second to none. In Cork my tongue was cut to rid me of my incoherent manner of speaking. To Cork, every day of my childhood, I planned to run away.

Twice a year perhaps, on Saturday afternoons, there was going to Cork to the pictures. Clark Gable and Myrna Loy in *Too Hot to Handle*. *Mr. Deeds Goes to Town*. No experience in my whole childhood, and no memory, has remained as deeply etched as these escapes to the paradise that was Cork. Nothing was more lovely or more wondrous than Cork itself, with its magnificent array of cinemas, the Pavilion, the Savoy, the Palace, the Ritz, the Lee, and Hadji Bey's Turkish Delight factory. Tea in the Pavilion or the Savoy, the waitresses with silver-plated teapots and buttered bread and cakes, and other people eating fried eggs with rashers and chipped potatoes at half-past four in the afternoon. The sheer sophistication of the Pavilion or the Savoy could never be adequately conveyed to a friend in Skibbereen who had not had the good fortune to experience it. The Gentlemen's lavatory in the Victoria Hotel had to be seen to be believed, the Munster Arcade left you gasping. For ever and for ever you could sit in the middle stalls of the Pavilion watching Claudette Colbert, or Spencer Tracy as a priest, and the earthquake in San Francisco. And for ever afterwards you could sit while a green-clad waitress carried the silver-plated teapot to you, with cakes and buttered bread. All around you was the clatter of life and of the city, and men of the world conversing, and girls' laughter tinkling. Happiness was everywhere.

Autumn 1991

Veblen and the
Mall of America

LYNDA McDONNELL

WHEN IT'S CROWDED, you drive up the levels of the parking ramp, from California to Hawaii to Arizona, and on to Nevada and Colorado. At the entrance to each level is posted a corresponding symbol: sunglasses for California, pineapple for Hawaii, cactus for Arizona, dice for Nevada, mountains for Colorado. In reality, we have none of these. No endless summer, no tropical sweetness, no desert, no roulette wheels, no cloudy peaks. It is December in Bloomington, Minnesota. The sky is a quilted grey mass, and the world is flat, white, and frozen to the horizon.

But the nation's largest shopping mall, which calls itself the Mall of America, offers refuge from the numbing winter. The ramp has no level named for Nebraska or New Jersey; the associations are all wrong. Neither has it a Minnesota—for Minnesota surrounds us, and we have enough of reality.

Today, I find a space in Arizona, where the red-nosed attendant flaps his arms against the cold, and head into the heated walkway. It is three weeks before Christmas. Along with 100,000 other people this day and more than four million since it opened, I am here to see the latest and by far the biggest in American emporiums. Bars, amusement rides, and 14 movie theaters share a vast roof with 370 stores. We locals recognize the primacy of scale and call it simply the Megamall. In essential ways, every shopping mall is the same. They are cargo ships on seas of angled parking, beckoning us to come, look, eat, buy. The Megamall is not a ship but an armada. No one can walk there, buffered as it is by asphalt and freeways. It is built on the scale of airports and stadiums, intended to have a relationship with the crowd, not the individual.

The titanic mall may be peculiar to this time of endless diversions and few answers for the things that most worry us—rising crime, insecure jobs, a fickle economy. But every age produces its own excess. Nearly a century ago, economist Thorstein Veblen complained about Americans who cared too much for status and too little for "the collective life." In *The Theory of the Leisure Class*, Veblen coined the terms conspicuous consumption and conspicuous waste. He had no trouble finding plenty of both.

As it happens, Veblen grew up as the son of industrious Norwegian immigrants on a farm about an hour's drive south of the Megamall. After decades of neglect, the home and barn built by Veblen's father are being restored. To Veblen's admirers, the sturdy Greek Revival house embodies the values he most respected—altruism ("the parental bent"), craftsmanship ("workmanship"), and critical intelligence ("idle curiosity"). He decried more "predatory" values—pecuniary gain and a form of winning through intimidation which he called "sportsmanship" because of the brute force and affectation he found in many sports.

Definitely not a sports bar or shop-until-you-drop kind of guy. With his clarity of values, he'll be a good counterpoint to my Megamall tour. For here I am, about to enter Macy's, appalled and intrigued, determined to stay aloof, to be an observer, but with credit cards in my pocket. For Christmas, I've asked for some books, a bedside lamp, a pottery bowl. I didn't ask for a leather recliner, an espresso machine, tickets to Negril. But I'd like them all. My desires are doubtless driven by social norms and marketing, as Veblen says. But desire is driven also by cravings of spirit. I want leisure, comfort, the searing beauty of bougainvillea in January.

Hold the psychic prattle, Veblen would say. As he wrote in *Leisure Class*, "The standard of expenditure which commonly guides our efforts is not the average, ordinary expenditure already achieved; it is an ideal of consumption that lies just beyond our reach. Or to reach which requires some strain. The motive is emulation." In other words, my cravings of spirit are merely another dreary violation of the ninth commandment, the injunction against material covetousness.

I enter the mall on the third floor of Macy's, surrounded by families who joke about leaving the car in Nevada and arrange where to meet if someone gets lost. We are in the small-appliance department, the perfect place for a Veblenian critique since most of the electrified gadgets perform jobs once done more simply, by hand. Veblen was no foe of change. He prized technological innovation; he just wanted it to contribute to the common good.

Many appliances have done just that. Once, at a history museum, I saw a photograph from the 1940s of women in hats and dresses gazing admiringly at a wall of shiny electric irons. Plugging in the steam iron is surely a big improvement over shoving hot flatirons across sizzling cotton. Perma-pressed is even better.

This season's headliner appliances, with big displays on the major aisles, are electronic bread makers and heart monitors. Macy's is featuring the Panasonic bread maker, for $349.99, and the Gym Man Talking Heart Rate Monitor, for $99.90. In the photo on the Gym Man's carton, a muscular man climbs mythical steps on a StairMaster, his skin shining, his rib cage hugged by a chunky yellow belt that looks like a cameraman's battery pack. The belt plays music, counts his heartbeat, and measures his elapsed time simultaneously. The bread maker's carton has photos of a white plastic box with many dials and a crested cube of brown bread.

There are clearly more than bread and pulse rates at issue. Veblen would quote John Stuart Mill: "'It is questionable if all the mechanical inventions yet made have lightened the day's toil of any human being'" because—to use Veblen's words now—"as increased industrial efficiency makes it possible to procure the means of livelihood with less labor, the energies of the industrious members of the community are bent to the compassing of a higher result in conspicuous expenditure, rather than slackened to a more comfortable pace."

Veblen had other uses for his industry. To buy the freedom to say what he thought in eleven books on everything from social mores to German imperialism, he kept his wants modest. As a writer, he was never a big seller. As a teacher, he never stayed long enough at one institution to get tenure. So he lived simply and bartered for services. At Stanford, he provided a cottage and food to two students and their father in exchange for work done by the students. They cooked, kept things clean, and took care of Veblen's horses. I doubt that he cared whether the bread was homemade.

There is, of course, something wonderful about making bread the old, slow, manual way. The tough heel of the hand working the dough. The dough filling the pans as it swells with air. The air ripe with the scent of steaming loaves. There is also something wonderful about taking pulses. The summer I was eighteen, I worked as a nurse's aide, taking temperatures and pulses before breakfast. I also had to inquire about patients' bowel movements. How I hated asking. How cheerfully the elderly patients told me, happy for any sign of regularity. When I had recorded their answers, I touched my fingers to their cool, thin wrists and counted, my embarrassment fading against the weary cadence of old hearts.

The electronic bread maker and pulse taker have status appeal—Veblen's "secondary utility as evidence of a relative ability to pay." They have mechanical exactitude. The Panasonic bread will not fail to rise. The Gym Man's pulse never falters. But something has been lost. No one would associate these machines with feeble bodies or the delicate stew of fermentation. They seem to defy the messiness of being human.

John Kenneth Galbraith once wrote that Veblen "did what every thinking man would like to do if he had the time, the tenacity, and the mental endowment. . . . Taking all knowledge for his province, he climbed a mountaintop and surveyed the whole life of mankind."

To read Veblen is to be amazed by his knowledge of obscure tribes, ancient history, British customs, ladies' fashion. What Galbraith called his "polysyllabic profundity" draws from the anthropology, sociology, psychology, technology, and biology he read and learned about at the University of Chicago and Yale. His ideas draw too from a deep well of values. The values of hard work, ingenuity, and sacrifice of self for others were shaped in part by his parents' example. His father was a farmer and skilled carpenter who set the pace for work crews and modified his house and barn constantly to make life easier and work profitable enough to send nine children to college. His mother was midwife and folk doctor to their small village. In Thorstein's accounting of the world around him, everything is measured by its value to "the collective life."

Even here at the Megamall, a place devoted to the satisfaction of private wants, there is recognition of our desire for life in community. Each of the broad aisles that make up the four-floor shopping cube has a street name and an architectural conceit: neon for East Broadway, lattices on North Garden, pushcarts on West Market, wood trim for South Avenue. Camp Snoopy, the amusement park at the Megamall's center, has concrete walkways scored and painted to look like flagstones. It is like Disney's idealized towns—relentlessly clean and cheerful, for visitors only. When meaner streets intrude—as when three young men were shot in Camp Snoopy over the attempted theft of a Starter jacket—few visitors noticed. They thought the gunfire was part of the ambience.

The mall promotes itself as "a place for fun in your life." With the tinsel and clapper of Christmas, fun is flushed and teeming. In the atrium outside Macy's, a young pianist surrounded by poinsettias chases Rachmaninoff up and down the keyboard. The crowd is bigger in the atrium near Bloomingdale's, where a police band in blue trousers and white shirts plays a lively pastiche of Mozart and "Jingle Bells," Beethoven and "Silent Night." I think of other crowds I've joined, crowds that gathered more spontaneously to break the usual rules of public decorum. When the Minnesota Twins won the World Series, sensible citizens shinnied up light poles in delirious pleasure. When Hubert Humphrey died, lines of people who had met him once, twice, or not at all waited on the chilly steps of the State Capitol for their turns to say goodbye. At such times, some fierce emotion or a desire to be part of the common history causes us to click off the TV, step outside, and trespass boundaries between strangers. No one comes to a shopping mall in search of the commonweal. One comes to seek the weal.

But even here, unbidden, connections are sometimes made. To the right of the stage, a blonde girl of eleven or twelve sits in a wheelchair. Her face is narrow and impassive, her eyes deeply set and private, her mouth agape. Behind her stand her parents. The father is a lean, worn man wearing cowboy boots and a brown silk jacket with a dragon stitched in bonfire colors across the back. The mother is soft and round with skin suffused with pink, as if she has just come from a steaming kitchen. As the band plays, she smoothes wisps of her daughter's hair back into a bun. When the child begins to rock, thrusting into the music again, again, the mother brightens like one who sees sunlight after months of rain. She smiles gently and squats beside the unnoticing child to pat her hand. "You like that, don't you?" she says softly. "You like that."

At the intersection of South Avenue and West Market, a clerk stands outside the Disney Store, beckoning. The place is almost impassable, but I push gently in. I make my way slowly to the back, where a scene from *Beauty and the Beast* plays on the big screen. We move like cattle on a worn path, past stacks of *Little Mermaid* placemats, statues of Pinocchio and Cruella de Vil, racks of Aladdin barrettes and Cinderella fashion dolls, Donald Duck hats, and blue Genie watches. Mickey Mouse is everywhere, on ties, brooches, jump ropes, golf balls, toothbrushes that talk. At the back of the store, beneath the big screen, is a sort of throne scene: Mickey and Minnie propped in the center of a huge pile of stuffed animals like ancestors atop a family tree. Scattered around the famous rodents are their anthropomorphic offspring: dwarves and dalmatians, flounder and crickets, skinny pigs and big-eared elephants, pink crustaceans and children who never grow up.

A young woman in a Goofy sweatshirt wanders past. Her boyfriend is close behind her, walking in tandem.

"Buy something," he urges.

"But I don't know what to buy," she moans. "And you don't want any-thing." They turn left, toward the door. The boyfriend's palm is on the small of her back, pushing.

I am taking notes about a lunch box shaped like Mickey's head when a female voice interrupts. "Making a Christmas list?" A clerk stands next to me, peering at my page. It looks like no one's Christmas list, a sprawl of product names and snatches of conversation. She gives up and looks at me. "Looking for anything special?" Like all the clerks in the Disney Store, this one looks like a Mouseketeer without the saucer ears or the full curves that helped Annette Funicello graduate to beach-party films. My clerk is pale, slender, pleasant, with long, wavy brown hair, white socks and sneakers, a pleated skirt, and a cardigan with a blocky M on the left pocket. The cos-tume says Family Entertainment. It says Good, Clean Fun.

I feel sheepish, as if caught spraying graffiti on Cinderella's castle. I turn to a blank page in my notebook and tell her of my nine-year-old nephew with cerebral palsy. She leads me to a rack of plastic tumblers with straws that pop up when the lids are turned. I choose one. Between the double wall of plastic is a scene from *Aladdin* sealed in a film of water. When I shake it, a dozen tiny lanterns float past.

"It'll keep his interest," she promises. "And it won't look like he needs a special cup. Even teenagers like them."

I buy the cup. My nephew will like it. I like it too. But I am embarrassed. The plastic Mickey Mouse bag hanging from my wrist marks the difference between an idealized asceticism, where we take only what is studied and nec-essary and beautiful, and the reality of mass consumption, where we choose what is clever, affordable, and promises some kind of pleasure.

How did Veblen handle Christmas? He didn't say. For all his books, he was intensely private and left few personal papers. Perhaps his resentment of "devout observances" and lack of children allowed him to ignore the whole business. But he too had nieces and nephews. Perhaps he gave only sensible things—underwear and thick socks. He built chairs and a cabin for himself, so perhaps he used his carpentry skills to make clever toys from scraps of wood. Or perhaps, as one who admired innovation, he too would buy a cup suited to a boy with trembling hands.

When my family visited at Thanksgiving, it was the mall's size and variety that impressed them. My father could play miniature golf with my sons. My mother could shop for clothes with my sister. Another sister could take her young son to bounce in the inflated Snoopy or sit on Santa's lap. In the food court, one person could eat hot dogs, another pizza, a third egg foo yung. Another family with yet more far-flung tastes used a cellular phone to keep track of one another.

Today, I brought a sandwich. As I sit on a metal bench and eat it, the gesture seems small and cranky, the sort my tightwad neighbor would indulge. I have not Veblen's stamina for separateness. I keep stumbling from the mountaintop to see what's happening down below.

A crowd has gathered at the benches outside Glamour Shots. They are men and women, mostly older, and a few weary children, staring through a wall of glass at plain women, plump women, women like your neighbor or your sister or your deskmate being transformed into versions of the big-eyed, big-haired, high-colored female, the lounge singer, NFL cheerleader, game-show assistant.

"Our sense of costliness often masquerades under the name of beauty," Veblen wrote. "We readily and for the most part, with utter sincerity, find those things pleasing that are in vogue." He inveighed against the corsets and hoop skirts of his day. By hobbling women and making them merely ornamental, such fashions made them the chattel of men, he pointed out. Fashions have changed. The ornamental emphasis on women has not. Every makeup counter sells larger eyes, fuller lips, higher cheekbones than nature produced. Glamour Shots sells a bigger package, a foxier look preserved on film. "Before to After—only 2 hours," the sign says. I settle on the bench to watch.

On the other side of the glass, three women sit in chairs before huge mirrors framed with light bulbs. They wear black smocks over black tube tops and businesslike expressions. Each has paid $29.95 to be worked over by a stylist wielding curling iron and hair spray, pots of blush and tubes of eyeliner. They will pay more for photos. After her hair is teased and her cheeks rouged, each woman will choose a sequined jacket from a rack, costume jewelry from a chest and disappear into a darkened studio. Right now, on the monitor above our heads, a young woman with short hair and a flashbulb smile mugs in a fur stole, then a sequined dress, then a Twins uniform. Each time the shutter snaps, the moment appears on a second screen, preserved on film. The screen makes private fantasy into public entertainment.

In one chair behind the glass sits a plump woman of about thirty with walnut-colored skin and the straight, glossy hair of a Native American. Her daughter, who is about six and wears her hair in pigtails, squirms on the next chair. The child too wears a black smock and waits her turn at dress-up. The grandmother, a short, round woman with gray hair pulled into a bun, sits on the bench next to me. The child beckons her to the glass and pushes a bobby pin through the crack where two panels meet. The old woman takes it, nodding, understanding that the child will need it later, when the hair spray has lost its force. Perhaps she knows too that the child who waits for curls and sequins and rouged lips needs connection with the plain, the patient, the ordinary.

Another woman, big and young, emerges from the studio with cascades of blonde curls falling to her bare shoulders. In the bright light, she is suddenly shy and holds her hand modestly to her chest. As she and her boyfriend look at proofs and point to the photos they want, she removes the large earrings and rubs her earlobes. The choices made, she puts on her T-shirt and jean jacket, and they return to the mall. In the blue shadow of fluorescent light, she looks garish, like Christmas colors out of season.

As beauty is lure to America's women, sports is to its men. The Megamall offers sports bars, sports videos, sporting goods, and sportswear. There is a mall-walking club and a miniature golf course. Shoppers can buy sneakers with high tops and air cushions and turquoise laces, chocolate wrapped as soccer balls, and chips-and-dip bowls shaped like football helmets. One shop sells baseballs signed by men who played in the stadium that formerly stood on the Megamall site. A Rod Carew goes for $79.95. Many stores have televisions mounted on the wall so that patrons can drink or shop without missing a play.

Veblen was no ivory-tower wimp. One summer, he explored much of Norway by bicycle. But he had the farmboy's rich disdain for pretensions, especially the "rant and swagger and ostensible mystification" he found in sports like football and hunting. Too much fondness for sports "marks an arrested development in man's moral nature," he wrote. How he would goggle at America's Original Sports Bar in the Megamall. You enter as through a vestibule, past a case holding scuffed shoes and soiled jerseys, relics of Famous Players in Big Games. Suddenly, you are in a dark, cavernous room dotted with pools of reverent light. One of them illumines a huge trophy of plastic or Styrofoam, painted matte silver and suspended over the bar like a fetish. Another light reveals two men hunched over a pool table, calculating angles. On the far wall are a dozen vigilant television screens showing football games past or present. One offers a jumble of shoulder pads, buttocks, and turf—the player's view. It is an electronic game that allows one to make a play without risk of torn cartilage or spilled beer. A sign explains: "Virtuality—Experience Illusion Fusion."

Here, by adulation or electronic simulation, we can all be athletes. There is no rant and swagger. Neither is there sign of a collective life. One pale, fat man wearing shorts and a T-shirt sits on the top row of a small bleacher. Alone in the dark, he sips beer and watches athletes collide on a big screen.

On the first floor, there is Santa's house, with walls lacquered red as a candied apple and a winding lane of restless children, waiting their turn at the old man's ear. As I pass by, the blonde child in the wheelchair has her chance. Her chair has been pulled alongside Santa's to face the camera. Her father sits at her feet, trying to coax a smile. But the child has withdrawn deep inside herself and is calmly impassive. Santa's rouged cheeks and her father's words cannot reach her as the music did. I feel for the father, longing for proof of his child's pleasure. And yet I admire the girl who has not learned to fake happiness. Without the capacity to dissemble, she holds out for real pleasure.

Before I leave, I climb to a balcony that overlooks the mall's central atrium. Above is a roof of crimped glass. Below are Camp Snoopy with its whirling rides, potted trees, and towering balloon of Charlie Brown's dog. It is a god's view, or a pigeon's, and it is pleasant. The calliope's shrill music is muted by distance. Silverware clinks agreeably at a nearby restaurant. The carnival colors brighten the winter grayness. The risen air feels warmed and softened by prior use.

Perhaps it is the sticky smell of caramel corn or the arcade's gaudy lights that remind me of the state fair. But no, that's different. That is twelve days in late August and early September when ordinary people's jams and gladiola and green beans share the stage with Dolly Parton and US senators. Because it is fleeting, because each participant has taken great care in the cake she made or the chicken he raised, the ordinary becomes exceptional.

At the Megamall, the fair goes on year-round. It is never closed for the season. It never moves to another town. It is a fixture, a business, not a celebration.

My mind flashes to the scene in *Pinocchio* in which the truant boys take a coach to Pleasure Island. After they have sickened themselves with sweets, exhausted themselves on rides, and broken every window, they turn brutish in form as well as manner. All but Pinocchio are turned into pack mules for the salt mines. He alone escapes by leaping into the sea. But his mulish tail and ears remain until he is redeemed by his own shame and Gepetto's love.

Eksperyans no more than good dance music, with (if you translate the lyrics from Haitian creole) a little politics mixed in. On June 4, the Club Med location a few miles north of Port-au-Prince was reopened for a meeting of the Organization of American States, so again there are foreign swimmers in that beautiful blue water, though it's unlikely that they know they are also drifting in a sea of *vaudou* metaphysics. From Club Med to the Port-au-Prince airport the road has been perfectly repaired (although the reflectors placed on either side have already been stolen), and the roadside has been purged of the beggars and vendors who usually swarm around the airport gates. But if you drive beyond the gates of Club Med and the beach hotels, you enter a completely different world, where the road to Cap Haïtien, in the northern province, has not been adequately repaired since the US Marines left Haiti in the 1920s. The damaged pavement from Saint Marc to Gonaives is almost impassable; it would be better if there were none. And on the way from Cap Haïtien to Fort Liberté on the Dominican border, the road does disappear entirely, along with all other evidence of First World technology, UN presence, or the very existence of white people of any kind.

Parallel universes, *miroir sondé*. The Hotel Oloffson is another kind of mirror, an interface between the foreign presence and the mind-boggling anarchy of Port-au-Prince street life. The younger, hipper journalists and UN fellow travelers stay here, conducting their business in the excellent restaurant or beside the pleasant pool. The Oloffson is Graham Greene's hotel, the scene of his Haitian novel *The Comedians*, but now I am more reminded of *The Quiet American*—perhaps Greene's most powerful statement of the damage to be done by good intentions.

We are waiting for our own connection: Theodore Beaubrun, a.k.a. Lôlô, a member of the group Boukman Eksperyans—waiting, at first, with a considerable degree of First World impatience and frustration. We have several phone numbers, and our French is good, but the people who answer only speak creole—a French-based patois which has been the common language of the Haitian people since slavery time and which is also the language of the Boukman lyrics—the most powerful political songs to appear in world music since Bob Marley. Also, the telephones only work occasionally; yesterday the minister of telephones was deposed. We have an address, but without knowing the back streets, it takes two hours to reach it through the screaming insanity of Port-au-Prince traffic. When we arrive at the Boukman headquarters, a pleasant young man lets us know (through the bars of the iron cage that secures the porch) that none of the Boukman people are presently there. They will be back later . . . indefinitely later. *Plus tard*. It's only later, back at the Oloffson, that I glance at a photo and realize that I have in fact been talking to Hans Dominique, a.k.a. Bois Gris, Lôlô's x-year-old son and one of the Boukman drummers. But it's like that in Haiti: when you look into the mirror, the mirror's also watching you.

In the afternoons it is very hot, heat building to a late afternoon crisis, a sudden drenching thunderstorm that comes around four each afternoon, though not quite regularly enough to set your watch by. We have stopped looking at our watches quite so often. The threads of time are attenuating. We are at the end of the rainy season, and after each evening rain the easing of tension is palpable. When Lôlô does appear at last, we have stopped waiting for him so energetically and are simply there.

Lôlô is not exactly the leader of Boukman Eksperyans because the group does not exactly have a leader, but it would be fair to say that he is Boukman's foreign ambassador, facing the mirror which connects the group with and divides it from the whole world outside Haiti. Today we see him in his aspect as Theodore Beaubrun, whose elegant French might have come from the Sorbonne, and whose style of address makes it easy to imagine him as a Caribbean intellectual emerging into the First World. Theodore Beaubrun has an anthropological perspective on *vaudou* (and his wife, Mimerose, has written a scholarly dissertation on the subject), but his data comes directly from his own experiences. Or perhaps it would be better to say that they are Lôlô's experiences, since in Haiti it is possible and sometimes necessary to have more than one identity, as one may have more than one of the Great *Loa* in one's head.

Boukman Eksperyans takes its name from Boukman, a *vaudou* priest or *houngan* who presided over the meeting at the forest called Bois Caiman, where the slave insurrection of 1791 was planned. That first rising, astonishingly bloody and destructive, began in August 1791; Boukman himself was dead by that October, his head displayed on a stake in the Place d'Armes at Cap Haïtien. Boukman had been a slave in Jamaica before being sold to French-colonized Haiti; some accounts say that he had fought in the American Revolutionary War under Lafayette, as a small but significant number of Haitian slaves had done. Almost nothing else is known of him. Certainly Boukman had the ability to inflame the rebel slaves to a jihad-like fury which allowed them to flood into battle (often possessed by their gods) without fear of rifles or cannon, to overcome better-trained and armed European troops with the sheer force of their numbers and their *loa*-inspired ferocity—but also with horrific loss of life. Boukman's style of leadership got a lot of his own men killed, as it led to his own death in fairly short order. By First

World standards he was not the most effective leader, and so I had always been puzzled by the group's choice of name.

Theodore, however, has an elegant explanation for this peculiarity. In *vaudou* observance, the ceremony at Bois Caiman is fully as important as the birth of Christ. That it invoked the *loa* to aid in the extermination of all the white people in Haiti does not entirely imply peace on earth and good will toward man . . . but for Theodore the bloodthirstiness of the ritual is secondary and what is most important is the unification movement over which Boukman, however briefly, presided, a movement which brought together the slaves from all over the island, most of whom had been born in Africa and spoke the different languages of their tribes. Boukman united all these different slaves with each other and with the communities of runaway slaves called Maroons, who lived in mountain villages known as *lakou*. Before Bois Caiman the Maroons had disliked and distrusted the plantation slaves; some Maroon *lakou* had existed for decades by 1791, and many Maroons had been born free in Haiti. Boukman's tools for the unification were the fusion of different African religions into a *vaudou* which all Haitian blacks could serve together, and also of course the creole language, which made it possible for so many blacks of different origin to commune with each other across the whole of a territory which was just on its way to becoming, in some sense, a nation. All this is the essence of the Boukman experience.

But in speaking to Theodore Beaubrun, I am reminded less of the historical Boukman and more of Toussaint L'Ouverture. It was Toussaint, after Boukman's death, who took the reins of the slave rebellion and turned it into a proper revolution—the only successful slave revolution in history. In 1791 Toussaint was in late middle age and had been for a number of years a trusted overseer on a plantation near Cap Haïtien. Although he had spent all of his life in slavery, he was literate and had read both L'Abbé Raynal and the ancient slave philosopher Epictetus. Born in Haiti, he was more Europeanized than most Haitian slaves; he was a devout Catholic and at the height of his career considered himself to be a citizen of the French Republic. He studied European military methods and adapted them to the natural talents of the rebel slaves, forging an army which successfully repelled several European invasions, including the expedition Napoleon sent from France to restore slavery in Haiti. By the time of this final victory, Toussaint had been betrayed and deported to France, where he soon died. As he embarked on the ship that took him away from Haiti, he turned to his French captors and said, "In overthrowing me, you think you have cut down the tree of liberty, but it will spring back from the roots, for they are numerous and deep."

And Theodore Beaubrun sounds very much like Toussaint when explaining *la musique des racines*, or roots music, the movement of which Boukman Eksperyans is part. *La musique des racines* evolved as a sort of antidote to *compas*, a smiley-faced tourist-pleasing music popular with the Duvalier regime. *La musique des racines* is based on *vaudou* drumming and also on *rara*, a festival music performed in street parades, whose lyrics often seek to make political points. In Haiti, politics and religion are inextricably intertwined, and the power of the political statements in the Boukman lyrics comes from their profound, archetypal religious base (as was also the case with Bob Marley). Since the turn of the nineteenth century, the ruling factions of Haiti have always feared *vaudou* even while practicing it themselves, for *vaudou* (temple to temple and *hounfor* to *hounfor*) is a nationwide network with a marked structural similarity to the cellular architecture of left-wing revolutionary groups, and for two hundred years it has been impossible to eradicate.

Boukman Eksperyans, along with other *racines* musical groups, has the power to bring *vaudou* openly into politics again—to reactivate the energies Boukman tapped in 1791. For that reason the group is feared and hated by the powers behind the coup against Aristide. The whole Boukman entourage came very close to being assassinated en masse at a concert in 1993; they were surrounded by hostile army personnel but protected by other soldiers who took their part. Unfortunately, although the Haitian army no longer exists, both of these factions are still alive and armed, so that the officer who did the most to protect Boukman Eksperyans in 1993 was murdered on the streets of Port-au-Prince four days before our conversation with Theodore Beaubrun. To assassinate someone in Port-au-Prince you shoot from a lightweight motorcycle which can vanish quickly through the stalled bus and car traffic everywhere on the streets . . . but there are a lot of people to kill, and there are many groups who play *la musique des racines*, and the music is heard everywhere. The state of mind of the oligarchs deposed by Aristide's return must resemble that of the French General Leclerc, who reported to Napoleon in 1802 that it was not enough to have deported Toussaint from Haiti because there were at least two thousand chiefs still to be removed, and who later wrote that for the French to regain control of the island it would be necessary to kill all black males above the age of twelve. If to us that seems a long time ago, in the hall of mirrors of the Haitian sense of time, two hundred years can be next to no distance at all.

Now it is once again (though perhaps temporarily) the time of Aristide, of Lavalas, of black power in Haiti—albeit propped up by the UN occupation, the helicopters floundering above the Hotel Oloffson, the rat-patrol Jeeps carrying blue-helmeted troops around the streets of Cap Haïtien. But apart from the UN, everyone on the streets of Port-au-Prince and on the northern roads as far as Fort Liberté looks pure African. The substantial population of mixed-blood people is still here but in hiding, behind the wall of the impressively fortified villas of Pétionville or other similar sanctuaries. *Les gens de couleur*, as they were once known, have always been a significant force in Haitian politics. Before the revolution of 1791 they had much wealth and sometimes owned slaves themselves—if the white colonists had not been so determined to deny them (their own children!) all political rights, the African slave rebellion might have been suppressed. But the white colonial intention toward the mulattos tended instead toward genocide; in prerevolutionary pogroms the whites would, for instance, eviscerate pregnant colored women and display their fetuses on spears. This practice was later adopted by both the blacks and the mulattos for retaliations against the whites. The black/mulatto civil war of 1799 was bitterest of all—known as the War of Knives because the combatants were inspired by their reciprocal hatred to throw down their guns and attack each other with nails and teeth instead. As for today, one has only to remember the face of General Cedras to understand that what Aristide likes to call the struggle of the eggplant and the ginger still plays its part in Haitian politics.

But Boukman Eksperyans is a unity movement. On Saturday nights the group plays at a chic Pétionville club called the Garage, fancifully decorated with old auto parts. The audience here is both multiracial and multinational. *Les gens de couleur* of Pétionville are well-represented, as are UN military and civilian personnel, as are the pure black *vaudouists*, or *serviteurs* as they call themselves, those who serve the *loa*. There are even a couple of reasonably discreet CIA operatives to round out the picture.

The performance does a lot to show why Boukman Eksperyans is winning a broad international popularity, why the band's three CDs sell briskly in markets that have no knowledge of the creole language and little interest in Haitian politics. At the surface level, *la musique des racines* is simply great dance music, based on a fusion of *vaudou* drumming with rock guitar. The drummers, Bois Gris among them, play the *rada batterie*, a set of three skin-headed drums which are extremely sacred and which may themselves sometimes be possessed by spirits. The three drummers create the roots of the band's intricate and rapidly shifting rhythms—far more sensitive and complex than anything found in blues or rock or reggae. The guitar style owes a lot to rock heroes like Hendrix and Santana, although, oddly, it is mostly based on major scales instead of the minor pentatonics of the blues. The guitarists can certainly tear off classic rock solos whenever the spirits suggest it, and this good guitar sound helps account for the group's pop success in the First World. But Boukman Eksperyans is by no means a guitar-driven band. The rhythm function of the guitars is negligible, and the core of the sound, as in traditional *vaudou*, is drums and voice (the women singers, especially, achieve some sweet a cappella effects)—but mostly drums.

I had also had the honor of hearing the drums without guitars, in Cap Haïtien the night before. Cap Haïtien is a very different sort of town than Port-au-Prince; smaller and less hectic; its architecture and its mood retain the aura of the first post-colonial times. Also there is no electricity in Cap Haïtien, or next to none: the two international hotels have generators, as do a few small businesses which don't run them late. The result of this situation is a sort of unofficial curfew. By the time we left the hotel where we had eaten to walk back to the hotel where we were staying, it was darker than the inside of a grave.

Picking our way most delicately through the ink-black streets, we could already hear the drumming, and at the driveway of our hotel we could also hear the voices of *les possedés*. It was the first time I had heard the *loa* speak through a human body, but there was no mistaking the sound. Also the hypnotic power of the drums compelled me, despite the obvious danger; Cap Haïtien neighborhoods are tiny and closely packed, and the corner where the drums came from was one we'd thought unsafe to explore even by daylight.

My companion, reluctant to run toward the drums, returned to the hotel while I squatted down to listen. Gradually I crept up the street, feeling out the invisible surfaces with my feet in case I had to retreat rapidly. There were other people not far from me, but I could not see them. The night was clear, the stars were perfect, and as my eyes began to adjust, I realized the white shirt I was wearing stood out like a beacon.

When I passed through the hotel bar, having changed into a black shirt, I saw a young Haitian painter we'd befriended the night before. That he was willing to escort me turned out to be a very good thing, because the ceremony was not at street level. We entered a small twisting alley which rose almost straight up; because it was also apparently a sort of trash chute, I had to cling to the walls and sometimes drop to my hands and knees, although my guide walked easily erect, with the grace of the resilient little goats that scatter half-wild all through the Haitian countryside. The drum sound coiled through the dark passage and drew me up into itself. Interesting to hear it now without the overlays of guitar and pop production Boukman uses. The sophisticated tonal shading gave the drums the character of human voices, so it was easy enough to forget the players and believe we heard, directly, the voice of the *loa*.

Because of the intractable problem of my skin color, we stayed in the shadows outside the perimeter of the *hounfor*. The arrangement was utterly simple: an area of packed earth with a six-foot-high stake driven into the center; this stake, in *vaudou*, is called the *poteau mitan*—a device for piercing the surface of the mirror that divides the living world from the subaqueous habitat of *Les Morts et Les Mystères*. The intersection of the vertical stake with the horizontal surface of the mirror creates a crossroads—it's the same crossroads that Robert Johnson sang about, and in creole it is called *kalfou*. The Great *Loa*, who form their individual characters from the aggregate spiritual force of all *Les Morts et Les Mystères*, use the *poteau mitan* to pass this *kalfou* and so arrive to take possession of the bodies of the living. But the crossroads is a flexible concept in *vaudou* metaphysics, and can be rotated horizontally to apply to the world of strictly human affairs; thus Boukman Eksperyans' most politically volatile song and album is called *Kalfou Danjere*.

Dangerous Crossroads. What I saw at Cap Haïtien was enough to let me see that the Garage, or part of it, was a *hounfor* too. The club is L-shaped, with the intersection at the stage, and the stage roof incorporates a living tree which serves as the *poteau mitan*. The area directly stage-front became, as the night went on, increasingly the territory of *les serviteurs*, while the multiracial, multinational fraction of the audience tended to cluster on the other leg of the L, close to the bar. Because of the crowding, the easiest passage from one area to the other went through Boukman's dressing room, diagonally, and this became, for me at least, another kind of crossroads.

In Haiti, time is not measured as in the First World; everything is going to happen indefinitely *plus tard*. You adapt to that or go mad with frustration, I suppose. It is no country for impatience of any kind. We had hired a guide to go with us to Cap Haïtien; he could not drive and knew little of geography, but he could ask directions in creole, and his language skill proved invaluable during our various breakdowns. On the northern road there are more potholes than pavement. We changed our first flat with the usual First World sweaty impatience, exacerbated by the discovery, some miles down the road, that our guide had abandoned, somewhere behind us on the ground, the lug nuts that held the spare tire. By the second day, stranded in a village on the northern plain with two tires gone flat simultaneously, our sense of urgency had materially decreased. We had learned from our guide that the road past Gonaives would be both better and worse than the road before, that in creole *icit-la* means both here and there, and that the "*quelques minutes*" required for the repairs could easily evolve into several hours.

For "*quelques minutes*" we provided entertainment for idlers on the town square. A sort of village idiot appeared to incorporate us into his afternoon performance. Around the corner, beside a sacred basin (green with algae and looking prosperous for malaria and typhoid), *vaudou* drumming beat through the heat of the afternoon. As the daily thunderstorm approached, people began tactfully filtering out of the square. The clouds appeared to converge from three directions. Catholic schoolgirls passed us giggling, book satchels gracefully balanced on their heads. Beside the sacred basin, the drumming went on. A boy cantered through the square on a small scrawny pony, his heels not quite dragging the ground. The rain began in a swirl of dust, and we sheltered under the back hatch of the crippled Jeep, without any special impatience or expectation. This was a feeling I recognized from hypnosis, when one sees oneself from both within and without, recognizing one's state, perhaps, but feeling no motive to change it. Let the drums get a little louder, one thought, and perhaps the *loa* will come.

So on Saturday night when Boukman took a break and I slipped into their dressing room, I had in some measure ceased to be an *I* full of anxious personal intention and become merely *one* who was sitting cross-legged on the floor. It didn't matter so much to this one what happened next or how long it would take to transpire. Presently the other Europeans began to leave the room, but when one rose to follow them, one was instead invited to enter a circle of joined hands with all the members of the group.

There was a small mirror in the room, which the women in the group had used to prepare for their act; it must have been a coincidence that my place in the circle faced this mirror, but the sight of a white face was a palpable shock. I closed my eyes to get away from it. I was hideously tense, and my grip was too tight. Perhaps there were other problems in the circle as well. The silence went on for a long time, for some time after I was able to let my hands go slack. Then the band began chanting. On the road north our guide had gradually slipped into creole with us, and by now I understood enough to recognize that they were saying the Lord's Prayer.

Vaudou, as Theodore Beaubrun will gladly explain to you, has been fused with Catholicism to an extent seldom mentioned by the scholars who write books about Haitian religion. Other slave societies also blended African religion with Christianity, but since Haiti has been a pariah state for almost two hundred years, the African strain in *vaudou* is much much stronger than it is, for example, in Puerto Rican Santeria, and it's this near-purity that delights foreign ethnologists. But the daily life of Haiti is devoutly Catholic on one side of the mirror and fervently *vaudouistic* on the other. The visual pageantry of Catholicism has made it easy, since slavery time, for Haitians to look at a sword-bearing image of Saint Jacques and also see their own warrior god, Ogûn. Today, all the buses and tap-tap taxis are elaborately decorated Catholic icons, each crowned with a motto like "Christ Capable," but these icons have their *vaudou* significance too. For a Haitian there is no difficulty in entertaining such paradoxes. It is both here and there, both now and later. There is one who will abandon lug nuts on the ground as being of no further importance once the Jeep can roll again, and there is one who, happening upon these lug nuts later, will recognize their great value—something to be sold to stranded *blancs*—and that both these entities may be contained in the same body is not a contradiction.

Boukman Eksperyans is committed in the making of new fusions. Some of their songs invoke the *loa* and others sing to Jesus. "Sa'm Pedi," a moving, gospel-like lyric from Boukman's latest album, *Libète (Pran Pou Pran'l)* is an ode to the most loving and peaceful of Christian virtues; it speaks of self-surrender to the Christian spirit, and even seems to suggest that the meek will inherit the earth. In Theodore Beaubrun's interpretation, Jesus is not exactly a member of the *vaudou* pantheon but something that surrounds and includes the personified Great *Loa*—an analog, perhaps, to the *vaudou* Oversoul called *Les Morts et Les Mystères*. This surprisingly Zen-like conception of Christ may be reinforced by the New Age meditation circle which Theodore joins on Sundays, together with some other band members and a select few whites who have been doing various good works in Haiti since the days of the Duvaliers. *Vaudou* is a religion constantly in process, capable of adapting itself to local circumstance and able to absorb other forms of observance as easily as China absorbs other races.

There is another fusion at work in tonight's performance; as always there are two sides to the mirror. On the one hand, we have great dance music and all-round quality entertainment for the multinational UN audience, for the world music audience generally. On the other, it's becoming increasingly clear that the performance is itself a *vaudou* ceremony. You can feel this even in the States, listening to Boukman's most thoroughly structured album, *Kalfou Danjere*, which is patterned in the ascending waves of *vaudou* ritual, waves which may carry you into an altered state even if you know nothing about the religion. Tonight's concert begins, like Boukman's latest album and like most *vaudou* ceremonies, with an invocation of Legba. The *vaudou* counterpart of the Greek Hermes, Legba is the *loa* of changes, who controls the crossroads where the worlds of the living are joined; without his assent, no one may pass. With Legba's permission granted, one may invoke the other *loa*, and several of the songs on *Libète (Pran Pou Pran'l)* call different gods: Zaka (an agrarian god of planting and harvests), Simbi Ganga, Malouwe, and the war-god Ogûn. The most politically critical song of the new album, "Jou Malé," summons Ogûn in his most warlike aspect—Ogûn Feraille. And the gods do come. In the more explicitly political songs, it is the *loa* speaking as often as the singers. Lôlô reports, in the classic manner of the *serviteur*, that when he regains his sense of self after a concert, he does not always know what the gods have used his mouth to say.

The ceremonial aspect is reflected in the style of the performance as much as in its content. It's circulatory, instead of in-your-face. Lôlô (definitely Lôlô now) is less rock star than *houngan*, an influence and mediator rather than the godhead itself. Lôlô is sometimes in front of the band and sometimes behind it and sometimes somewhere in between. The center of the performance is not the lead singer, but the *poteau mitan*. In any case, there is no one lead singer, since the women members of the group take lead vocals at least as much as Lôlô, and similarly there is no single lead guitarist. The instruments are passed from hand to hand, as the sacred rattle called the *asson* would pass from one *houngan* to another, during ritual. Audience members circulate onstage among the band as the spirits move them, and as the hour grows late and the drums' intensity builds, some listeners fall into the kicking, jerking, convulsive state that is a crossroads between personal identity and possession by the *loa*. At this point I am standing somewhere on a chair, trying to keep track of things. There's one side of me that wants to obliterate my identity with a nice dive into the swirling *vaudou* mosh pit, but the side that wants to remember what happened later seems to be stronger. When Lôlô salutes me from the stage I answer him with tense raised fists—a mistake, I realize, but only later, when I have lived in Haiti a few hours longer. . . . *quelques minutes.* I have never seen Lôlô make a fist, his hands are always open, moving gracefully as fish. In *vaudou* a *serviteur* will usually have a particular *loa* called the *maît'tête*, or master of the head, who possesses him more often than the others. Lôlô (so I've been told by Theodore Beaubrun) has the war-god Ogûn as his *maît'tête*, which is interesting in view of the band's comparatively pacific mode of presentation, and yet Ogûn, like the other *loa*, has many mirror images, some more violent and some less so. There is horrific latent violence in *vaudou*, and during the

Haitian revolution it swept the island end to end, giving the revolted slaves under the original Boukman's leadership the will to return the atrocities visited on them by their white slavemasters a thousandfold. And Theodore Beaubrun is willing to explain that voodoo does have its savage side, a mood of hate and vengefulness: *Bizango*, the black magic cult of *vaudou*, ruled by sorcerers called *bokor*. Theodore will not discuss it, but it seems apparent to me that the interests of the Ton-Tons Macoutes and more lately the *attachés*—terrorism, control of the night, rape, murder, and zombification—coincide very closely with the interests of *Bizango*. By this reasoning, when Boukman Eksperyans sings "*Ginen pa' Bizango*," ("Ginen is not *Bizango*") the refrain to "*Kalfou Danjere*," the group is taking a very explicit political position as well as a religious one. The inner state of Ginen, which has replaced the old *vaudou* notion of a literal Africa under the sea, is a condition of deep tranquility opposed to the cruelty and violence of *Bizango* . . . yet Ginen too has force to draw on, and Lôlô's *maît'tête* is Ogûn.

At four o'clock in the morning the streets of downtown Port-au-Prince are very desolate—nobody there but us and the police. And yet a visit to Haiti would not be quite complete without spending at least a few seconds looking down the wrong end of a rifle barrel. We are fortunate, however, to be dealing with the new police trainees (though many of these come from the cadre of ex-soldiers, Macoutes, and *attachés*), and once the guns are lowered everything is quite correct. After some discussion (in English this time), we are even able to decline their invitation to accompany them to the station. The fun is not quite over yet, however, for the Hotel Oloffson is in its tactful way a fortress, though luckily not so secure as those in Pétionville, and we are obliged to go over the wall.

I wake next morning with a significant hangover and ears still throbbing with the Boukman drums. It's clear that the rainy season is over now, this minute; the air crackles with a heat which will not be abated. We attempt a Sunday morning stroll through Port-au-Prince, moving like swimmers through the gluey heat. For the first time I understand the old creole proverb, dating from slavery time: *doucement allé loin*, which translates roughly as "the gentlest way goes furthest." A necessary ethic for a slave, perhaps, this line was also one of Toussaint's favorite mottos, but now I feel it is more deeply rooted in the conditions of this country, because if you try to move fast or forcefully in this kind of heat, you will be dead in fifteen minutes. Now I begin to understand the sinuous grace of the women who move through the streets with impossible burdens balanced on their heads, the tenuous persistence of the human cart-hauler dragging a coffin-size block of ice on a two-wheeled truck. Creole itself reflects this principle, requiring fewer, gentler movements of the tongue than French. Now I understand the foolishness of a clenched fist, as in my mind's eye I see Lôlô's open hands. I am no longer well able to distinguish causes from effects, but it seems to me that if we had not understood how *doucement allé loin*, Lôlô would never have appeared to bring us into the *lakou*.

In the *lakou* it was very cool and fresh, as if the sweltering heat of Port-au-Prince had never existed. Eight feet from where we stood in the packed-earth forecourt of a small cabin, a hummingbird spun its invisible wings in the air, beak communing with a blossom. Presently three small girls appeared at our knees and showed with their hands that they wanted to kiss us and for us to kiss them. In the *lakou* one is always greeted with a kiss, even if one is a stranger; one cannot be a stranger there, for no stranger can enter the *lakou*.

The distance from Port-au-Prince to the *lakou* is negligible in miles but enhanced by the fact that the closer you get the more the road becomes a sheer cliff. Lôlô's Jeep tapped out before we reached the top, and we took him and several others, who seemed to be functioning as an informal security team, along in ours. But the last leg of the journey must be made on foot, along a trail no more than shoulders-wide.

The cabins of the *lakou* are arranged along a looping path that goes up and down the mountain slope, describing an ellipse around the central *hounfor*, as dancers circle the *poteau mitan* in *vaudou* rituals, or during Boukman concerts. The dwellers here have found surprisingly rich veins of soil in the rock; there were ripening stalks of bananas and zigzag plantings of corn. The sense of natural abundance was like what we had seen in the fertile mountains above Cap Haïtien. There were chickens too, and pigs. Outside the cities, all Haiti is scattered with livestock, cows and runty pigs and goats which often wear wooden head stalls to keep them from raiding the gardens. But all these animals look thin and enterprising, for the people must eat before the animals do. In the *lakou*, for the first and only time, I saw a big *fat* hog.

Today we had Lôlô, not Theodore; the Sorbonne French was gone, and he spoke to us in a mélange of French and creole and did not speak much in any case. The *lakou* was, that day at least, a place of stillness. When we had made the circuit of the cabins, Lôlô opened the *case des mystères*, a small *ajoupa* made, like the other cabins of the *lakou*, by weaving sticks together and plastering them with mud. Within, the *vévés* of different *loa* were painted on the walls with a turquoise paint that had happened to be there, so that the space within seemed suffused with a cool blue light. Lôlô and the other *serviteurs* performed a simple ceremony, giving drink to the spirits who exist in small clay bottles on the altar.

The *hounfor* itself was a large ellipse of packed dirt along the edge of the sacred pool. A cow had lately been drinking there, but now the waters had stilled. It was astonishingly quiet. In Cap Haïtien the painters like to render the island as one with its reflection in the mirror of the sea, like a planet, like a globe. Regarding the mirror of the sacred pool, we seemed to be inside this sphere, the trees curving up above us and also below; we were embraced, suspended there. One began to feel Ginen, and the sense of peace was so profound that one could hardly bear to leave it.

Leaving the *lakou*, Lôlô spoke a little more, explaining the idea of *la colonne*. This column is the family tree, and the arrangement of the *lakou* is the outward reflection of this inner truth. Within this matrix of relationship, children are the responsibility of the whole village, as in Africa, not just the property of their parents. Indeed, *la colonne* stretches halfway down the mountain to Pétionville, and we made frequent stops for Lôlô to have conversations with his cousins, or if we did not stop, he would flex a hand gently out the window and say hello and goodbye in the same breath with the creole phrase that means "We're here"—*Nou la. Nou la . . .* but for how long? The air is crackling with heat, elections come at the end of the month, and back at the Hotel Oloffson, the staff turn away from a creole broadcast stiff with a tension no rain will relieve. If there is trouble, it may happen in three weeks, and at the airport I am relieved to be leaving Haiti, though in another way one would infinitely prefer to stay.

Four days away from the murder of his ex-officer friend, Lôlô must be aware of his own danger, though he never mentions it. In Haiti they assassinate both priests and *houngans* with a crushing regularity, and up the country there are still plenty of guns in the hands of the *attachés*. Lôlô is protected to some degree by his own precautions, to some degree by his reasonably high profile in the international press, and to some degree by the assassins' fear of making martyrs. It was that fear that kept Napoleon from executing Toussaint two hundred years ago, though Toussaint, who died in a French prison, became a martyr anyway.

It's conceivable that Theodore Beaubrun has some slight vocation for martyrdom, but I believe that Lôlô would see it differently. Certainly Boukman Eksperyans has structured things differently, for it is a group without a leader, and when there is no leader, the leader can't be killed. Also there are many groups besides Boukman Eksperyans. The death of the historical Boukman made no difference to the movement he had forged. As General

Leclerc finally figured out, you give up or else you have to kill them all. In any case, the dead do not depart from Haiti, and Lôlô seems already well versed in the art of living in eternity. Maybe it doesn't matter so much on which side of the mirror he finds himself residing.

Another bloodbath in Haiti remains a lively possibility. The spiking of the Haitian army's sole artillery division is certainly a positive step, a true feather in the cap of the foreign intervention, but the army itself is only disbanded, not destroyed, and the UN effort to retrieve rifles from ex-military personnel seems to have been no more successful than Leclerc's attempt to get the guns back from the rebel slaves who founded Haiti. Without artillery, the next violent power struggle in Haiti, if it does come, will be carried out with small arms and machetes, like the civil war in Rwanda, which in its turn resembles the Haitian War of Knives.

Let us admit, however, that the foreign intervention has done some tangible good in Haiti. For the moment at least it has scotched the worst extremes of terrorism. Without the UN retraining effort and the continued UN presence, our encounter with the police would have been much, much more unpleasant (although I wonder how those officers would have handled a carload of black Haitians). The foreign presence has at least temporarily restored the popular voice of the Haitian people and created forms of democratic process, yet one wonders if First World democracy will ever fit this country, if Haiti does not require something more on the order of the *konbit*, communal work parties rooted in the *lakou*, which Boukman Eksperyans sings about.

Eavesdropping on conversations at the Oloffson, trying to sleep in Graham Greene's old room while listening to chopper blades flogging overhead, it's hard to forget *The Quiet American*. It's hard to forget that the First World can destroy a culture more thoroughly with money and good intentions than with knives and guns. Our great weakness in the First World, and particularly in the States, is that whenever we look in a mirror, we always assume we are seeing ourselves.

Haiti shows that there are some advantages to having been a pariah state for two hundred years. Port-au-Prince is a classic Third World slum, complete with its Cité Soleil where people starve in boxes, enduring famine conditions that resemble Somalia. But outside the cities a self-sustaining agrarian life seems at least marginally viable. Because tourism has been aborted in Haiti, comparatively few Haitians have been turned into beggars and waiters and hustlers and thieves. The archipelagos of discarded plastic that clog the seas around "successful" tourist islands don't exist in Haiti.

Outside Cité Soleil, people don't live in shacks of discarded First World materials, tin and cardboard: they use centuries-old techniques to make houses out of daubed wood and thatch and woven palm leaves; they make most of what they need by hand. In the north, for instance, they still weave indescribably complex donkey saddles out of straw. It's a hard life, and one must not sentimentalize it, but one should also remember that there are worse alternatives. Remember, as Club Med prepares to reopen, that successful tourism in Haiti turned the country into the most appalling prostitution market in the Western Hemisphere and made it a major crossroads in the global spread of AIDS.

In the First World, we are always firmly situated inside our individual selves. In Haiti it's not at all that way. The difference can sometimes be annoying, as when the one who leaves the lug nuts on the ground is not the same one who in some other context would easily recognize their worth. But when it comes to forming communities, it is better *not* to have such a strong sense of one's personal boundaries. Haitians are able to love and care for their children in ways now unimaginable in the First World, where fission has exploded most nuclear families, let alone anything that might once have resembled *la colonne*. A child may wander safely anywhere within the borders of the *lakou* because she enjoys the love and protection of all. Even in small-town America these days, a child alone is simply a target.

Haiti pour les Haïtiens, as angry crowds will sometimes shout outside the US Embassy. There must be some alternative for this country to becoming a cheap-labor market for global corporations, to becoming another Caribbean tourist spectacle. Fish farming, craft exports. Haitians make a sort of pistachio butter that would fly off the shelves of First World gourmet shops. Haitians make the best rum in the world—a five-star bottle compares favorably to Courvoisier or Calvados.

Flying over Haiti, one sees surprising things. I had assumed the country was a dust bowl now. Eighteenth-century reports already speak of overlogging and overfarming and the erosions and floods that resulted. Then there is the population bomb. In slavery time, the people died like flies, from mistreatment and murder and suicide. Mothers would abort or kill their infants—out of love, to send them back to Africa. It was necessary for the slave masters to import twenty thousand slaves a year to maintain a constant work force. But after the revolution the people stopped dying, and I'd assumed that six million Haitians must have eaten up the whole country like a flight of locusts before now.

Not so. In the mountains above Gonaives and the Artibonite there is much erosion, and the peaks are dry and bare. But the mountains above Cap Haïtien are still fertile, as we saw by land. By air we can see clouds blanketing the peaks and know that there must be rich land below them. As we fly deeper over the interior, we see pockets of remarkable fertility. Down there, where there are no roads, there are *lakou* that can only be reached by horse or by foot. Surely there must be places left where you can go up the country with nothing more than a box of matches and a cane knife and not come back for a decade or so. One can imagine that, in the Cibao Mountains along the Dominican border, some rain forest may still survive. The land is wounded but not murdered yet, and the spirit of Ginen is still strong; the Boukman singers know that, but they are not the only ones who know. It is imaginable that after all the Haitian people will not be destroyed. Their roots are planted very deep, and they spring up everywhere.

Winter 1996

Cannibals and Kava

DIANA WEBSTER

Fiji, 1987

In December 1987, my twenty-year-old son Johnny and I were in a boat approaching an island off an island off Fiji. You would perhaps imagine a smallish tropical island with long, sandy beaches, a peaceful bright blue lagoon surrounded by white coral reefs against which the Pacific surf was breaking. You would be right. There was even the wreck of an old steamer poised picturesquely at an angle on one of the coral reefs. You may, if you have read the tourist brochures, also imagine a rather luxurious hotel nestled amongst the palm trees, with discreetly placed cabins for its guests, a large pool, and a smiling, attentive Fijian staff. You would be wrong. As we rounded a promontory, our host in the boat proudly pointed out where we would live—a tin-roofed shack, with corrugated iron sheeting roughly tacked onto the sides, of the kind that was familiar from the TV films of slums outside Rio or Johannesburg. We looked at each other, expressionless—this was not going to be what we had expected.

Not, I may say, that we had expected the luxury hotel, nor had we wanted it. We knew we were going to stay in a real Fijian village. Our guidebook had remarked: "If you are lucky enough to be invited to a Fijian village . . ." And we had been, by a Fijian man called Benny on the ferryboat we had taken to the first island. Most of the people had been seasick on the boat, and so had a cow. A seasick cow is a very sad sight. We had also done the other things that the guidebook had told us to do if so invited: we were both wearing the sarongs, or *sulus*, worn by Fijian men and women, and we were carrying our *sevusevu* or gift to the headman of the village. We had wanted to be generous in our gifts and not take advantage of the hospitality of the Fijians. Benny had helped us choose them; we had quantities of rice, sugar, cigarettes, and other goods, plus also some Fijian tobacco or "Fiji smoke," as Benny called it, which he said would make a good present for his mother, who lived with him.

The Fijian villages we had passed in the bus we had taken across the main island of Fiji to the ferry had all looked clean and well-kept, with attractive thatch-roofed huts. So we were not at all prepared for Benny's village. It was mostly a collection of dilapidated tin huts surrounded by swampy ground, of which Benny's was possibly the poorest. A villager on the first island had laughed when we told him where we were going. He had also informed us that "the mosquito is the spirit of that island." This also was true. However, there we were, committed for several days, because the island possessed no boat of its own, and we had had to arrange to be collected by the boat belonging to a village on another island.

We made our way to Benny's hut. His mother, along with a great many islanders and children, was standing outside to greet us, and we presented our *sevusevu* of "Fiji's smoke" to her, which she eagerly unwrapped. She was carrying a thick stick by her side, which she kept glowing at the end by thrusting it into a fire. It functioned rather in the manner of a car cigarette-lighter, and indeed she was soon lighting up. It didn't take us long to realize that what we had innocently given her was in fact pot, and indeed, thanks to our present, Ma remained totally stoned throughout our stay.

We were then shown into the hut. This was simply one smallish room with an earth floor, a few dirty rush mats thrown over it, and chickens running in and out. There was a small raised box on one side, covered with another dirty rush mat, that served as a single bed, a rag curtain half across it; in one corner were a couple of pots and a spoon or two. There were flies everywhere, as well as tiny mosquitoes—the spirit of the island. The Headman of the village, said Benny, was expecting us up on the hill, where we would have *yanggona*. *Yanggona*, we knew from our guidebook, is the Fijian drink, often also called *kava*: it formed an important part of our *sevusevu*.

Up on the hill we were presented to the *turanga*, the Headman, Seta, accompanied by two or three of the chief men of the village. They were of course dressed in *sulus* and were sitting on rush mats on the floor of another decaying hut, but this was one was grander than Benny's, for it was made of stone. Benny offered our *sevusevu*, which appeared to be graciously received by Seta, and we were told to be seated. We did so, negotiating our *sulus* with difficulty and being careful to keep our naked feet from pointing at other people, which Benny had told us was bad manners. Then the *yanggona* ceremony began.

The kava roots were pounded in a wooden bowl till they were powdery. The powder was then put in a bowl carved like a turtle, and the man making the drink emptied a plastic bucket of water into it. He then took a long length of the roots and used them in the bowl like a strainer, shaking it out of the door with a flicking movement till the liquid had no bits in it. The kava-maker then said a short phrase in Fijian and clapped his hands three times. The kava-server came forward, dipped half a coconut in the bowl and presented it to each person in turn, in strict order of precedence. The Headman was of course first and Johnny was second, as guest of honor (I of course was a woman and only there because of Johnny—women were not usually included in the *yanggona* ceremony). Before each person drank, the drinker clapped his hands once, then drained the bowl at a gulp; afterwards everyone clapped three times and shouted *Matha!* The communal kava coconut went round again—and again—and again. The liquid looked and tasted like dirty sock water, but we had read that in fact it was some kind of drug—a tranquilizer, it was said. It was of course impossible to refuse, and what effect it would have on us we had no idea.

One effect to start with was that the talk got livelier. Seta spoke a little English, as did one or two of his men; Benny spoke English rather well; the rest of the men only spoke Fijian. They of course asked us questions about our country. We had said we were "from Finland," which was strictly true, as that was the country in which we lived. I had often found it useful if I did not know how the fact I was British would be received. No one has anything against Finns. This time it was to rescue us from great problems. We told them about Finland, a country of which they understandably knew nothing. I was carrying some postcards of Helsinki, one of which showed it in the winter snow, with fishing boats in the harbor, surrounded by thick ice. They passed this round, and each gazed at it in wonder for twenty minutes at a time. I wondered what on earth they made of it, for probably some or all of them had never seen ice or snow. Meanwhile, my next-door neighbor on the floor, who spoke some English, explained to me cheerfully that Fijians used to be cannibals and that his grandfather had been one. I had read, in fact, that the last missionary had been eaten in 1887. This was 1987—I hoped they didn't intend to celebrate the centenary.

Meanwhile, the *yanggona* ceremony went on. At some point "the boys" were brought in to entertain us, three boys in their teens with guitars, who sang melodious songs whose main lyrics always seemed to be "Bula . . . bula . . . bula. . . ." Five hours had gone by, hours of sitting with outstretched legs on the floor, hours of the coconut cup. It became obvious that the effect of kava on Seta and several others was far from that of a tranquilizer, as they were getting very drunk indeed, although oddly enough neither Johnny nor I seemed to be feeling any different. Afterwards, we wondered if the effects of kava were cumulative. At this point, Benny suggested that we might eat, and hope rose in us. However, hope was quickly destroyed. "It is I who decide here!" shouted Seta. Then he pointed a finger at me. "*She* stays in my hut tonight!"

I still think that this was one of the worst moments of my life. I had no idea what Seta's motives might be—for all I knew it might be a great compliment, but it was certainly a compliment I had no wish to accept. At the same time, Seta was the all-powerful head of a village from which there was at present no escape. It was Finland that came to our rescue. We explained (through Benny as our interpreter) that in "our country" our customs and religion made it impossible for a son to allow his widowed mother to sleep without him in the room as her protector. This was of course a complete fabrication, but we counted on their knowing absolutely nothing about Finland and its customs. It worked. I was rather angrily dismissed to eat with the women; Johnny, however, was forced to stay.

The women's meal consisted of the bones of a chicken floating in water—the men were later to get the meat. A large number of children gathered round to watch us, amongst whom was a little girl of about five, who screamed with terror when she saw me and had to be carried away. After the meal, the children were given the chicken bones to suck—the killing of a chicken was clearly a feast-day event. Then it was time for bed, for me at any rate, and mercifully in Benny's hut not Seta's. The night was starry as we walked down the hill; sounds of "bula . . . bula . . ." could be heard coming from the hut up above, and I knew the *yanggona* ceremony was still going on.

I was escorted to bed by about twelve women and girls, who stood around waiting to see what I would do. There was nowhere to wash and no water. With such an interested audience, I decided that Finnish women slept in their day clothes at night, and I lay down on the bed. I had been assigned the bed-of-honor—indeed the only bed—which was covered with a rush mat and a very old, dirty pillow. I imagined it must really be Ma's bed, and indeed the pillow smelt strongly of pot. I pulled the mosquito net around me, though I was not optimistic about its efficiency as it was covered with holes. One by one the women filed out—"Goodnight, Diana"—all except for one little girl, who remained to keep me company. I remained sleepless, listening to the faint sounds of guitars and "Bula . . . bula . . ." in the distance and wondered anxiously how Johnny was getting on.

Johnny was not getting on very well. As Seta, the Headman, became more affected by the drink, he became more aggressive. Up to now Johnny had been permitted to drink half a coconut shell of the disgusting liquid as against the Headman's whole one; but now Seta said accusingly, "We are not equal" and insisted that Johnny keep pace with him with a whole shell each time. Johnny, not wanting to antagonize him further, did so. "Ah!" said the men as he drank shell after shell, still fairly unaffected by the drink. "You are a lion!" But this was not enough for Seta. He decided that the gifts we had brought, our *sevusevu*, had not been enough. Johnny must make an apology in front of all the men and promise that he would give a bigger and better *sevusevu* next day—of kava, cigarettes, and "Fiji smoke." Curbing his anger, for he knew our original gift had been generous, Johnny made the apology, promised the *sevusevu*—and was allowed at last to leave and to return to Benny's hut and me. Finally we both fell asleep, Johnny on the floor, along with Benny, his Ma, his daughter—and of course several chickens.

We were awakened by the crowing of roosters and the rattle of pans as Ma prepared breakfast on the small wooden fire in a tin shelter just outside the hut. Ma had a cigar shape of "Fiji smoke" in her mouth as she did so. We sat down on the worn and chicken-stained rush mat. The flies buzzed around our heads and bare arms, and the tiny mosquitoes were still everywhere. Ma had a small bowl of grey water, saved from washing the dishes, into which she dipped a filthy rag. We wiped our hands on the rag and passed it on to the next person, closing our minds firmly to thoughts of hygiene. Breakfast was a bowl of rice and another of lemon tea. The rice was sprinkled with tiny black spots. Some herb, perhaps? Closer inspection revealed that these were small beetles—weevils. We tried to pick out a few, but it was impossible—there was about one weevil to three grains of rice. Again we closed our minds: "Protein," we told ourselves firmly as we swallowed the mixture. A modern restaurant menu would have said that the weevils imparted a pleasant crunchy texture to the rice. The lemon tea was liberally sprinkled with drowned fruit flies, and there was nothing to be done about that either but drink it and them. After breakfast, Benny collected our dollars to buy the extra *sevusevu* for the chief and told us happily that a kava-drinking session was planned for the afternoon and the whole of the night—together, of course, with Seta and company. Silently, we contemplated this unpleasant prospect.

We had of course by now realized that we had possibly done something very foolish. Seta ruled over his village as he might have done 800 years ago, and we were in fact in his power as long as we remained on the island. As far as we could discover, the only tourists who had been there before were a Swiss couple three years ago, who had had their own tent and camped some way away from the village. Nobody of course knew where we were, as we had not thought to tell anyone where we were going, and, since the island owned no seagoing boat, we were stuck there until the one belonging to the neighboring island came back to fetch us—if it did. It would be possible for us to disappear without trace.

Meanwhile, we looked out at the clear, tropical blue waters of the lagoon and the long sandy beach round the island—the idyllic unspoilt setting of one's dreams. We had not up to now had any chance to wash (except for Ma's dirty rag). Could we perhaps, we asked Benny hopefully, go for a swim? Well, yes, said Benny, the islanders did go into the sea, but people did not take their clothes off or use a swimsuit. The idea of entering the water fully clothed and then the salt drying into our skin and clothes again did not appeal. The only other source of clean water was a small tap in the center of the village where the women washed their clothes. However, Benny said he had been on the main island and understood foreigners' ways more than the others. He could take us the next day to a place the other side of the island where we could swim in our swimsuits unobserved; meanwhile, we would go for a walk.

So we walked slowly along the beach amongst black rocks and boulders in animal and human shapes, bending to look at the exotic shells. Benny pointed out to us a huge fragment of baked terra cotta clay: "From one of our old cooking pots," he explained. But he had no need to tell us—its shape was recognizable from every cartoon we had ever seen of cannibals eating a missionary. There had of course been missionaries on these islands, too. Their influence was still strong and obvious, not least in the custom of only being permitted to swim fully clothed; but Benny and his family also said grace and prayed before every meal, as did all the villagers. There was no church on the island: the nearest one was on the larger island farther away; on the Sunday we saw a crowd of churchgoers standing up shoulder to shoulder in a low, flat boat, being slowly paddled across the wide channel between the islands; the sound of hymn-singing drifted across the water.

On the walk, we asked Benny about the village. There were four clans, he said. The Headman's was a hereditary position, and he came from the ambassador or adviser clan. Benny also came from this clan (Seta was his eldest brother), but he was the younger brother of four and, we guessed, occupied a somewhat outcast position, since his hut was on the outskirts of the village and was one of the poorest. We wondered if this was because he had no wife and only a daughter. We gathered he had gained prestige by bringing us as tourists to the island, along with our *sevusevu*. Other clans were the soldier clan and the priest clan—we never discovered what the fourth was. The men tended the plantation, but since they rested in the afternoons and drank kava all night, their work did not seem much of a burden. It was, of course, the women who did most of the work. The women cooked, washed, collected seafood, carried wood for the fires. Occasionally the men had a "fish drive," at which the head of the soldier clan had the right to spear the biggest fish, but the everyday fishing was also done by the women. The women did not drink the kava and did not receive any of the presents from the *sevusevu*, nor were they allowed to walk on the beach. When the men ate, the women brushed the flies away from their faces with rags; when together, the men and women stayed on different sides of the room. Ma, as the mother of the chief, was the only woman allowed to be present at the kava ceremony, although she did not drink but simply smoked her pot.

Lunch was, as all the meals were to be, a variation on the theme of a broth made from an unknown substance, cassava (breadfruit—white, solid, and tasteless), mangoes, and rice, spiced of course with weevils and fruit flies. After lunch we were told everyone rested, so we lay down, hot, sticky, and sleepless in the hut with Benny, Ma, his daughter, and the chickens; then once more we were led up to the kava-drinking hut, and the whole ceremony was repeated. For some reason, however, we were released at ten o'clock in the evening—perhaps the chief found it more fun without us.

The next day was the day fixed for the boat to come and fetch us off the island. In the morning, Benny prayed before breakfast for the weather; I prayed that the boat would come. Benny took us as promised across the island, a long trek barefoot through muddy, swampy jungle, where thick roots tripped us up and the large holes of land crabs were hard to avoid. But we swam. Free in the clear water, we became almost hysterical with the relief of being able to talk to each other and to be unwatched for a short period. Up to now, this had never been possible. Custom clearly dictated that a guest could not be left alone. We were always attended to bed, and then one or more children were left to watch us; even when we reluctantly had to use the only toilet on the island—a broken pedestal in the center of the village surrounded on three sides by corrugated iron—even here a group of children would gather round to attend and watch us.

As we waded through the mud on the trail back to the village, the wind began to pick up. Benny looked at the sky doubtfully. The boat would not come if it was bad weather. However, he said, brightening, it would mean more time for us to drink kava with the chief. We anxiously watched the weather throughout our meal and the hours of rest after it.

We had found the stale air in the hut suffocating and had this time asked if we could rest on the beach. Benny reluctantly agreed—we had realized by this time that any request to be alone was probably impolite. As we lay there with eyes closed, children gradually crept around us: they brushed the flies away from us and fanned my face, then began to sing with natural harmony and grace. A boy beat time with a stick against another stick, and a girl strummed a fan. They thought us sleeping and came closer, pointing out to each other the small brown spots on my arms and examining the soles of my feet. No doubt they were saying: "Look! They have bits that are normal, like us." I felt like Gulliver. Despite these charming children, I strained my ears to catch the noise of a motor. Finally, magically, I heard it in the distance. By this time the sky was darkening and rain threatened. There was no time, thank heaven, for farewell kava. We were hurried into the boat. Once on the sea, the waves grew choppy, and we raced the rain as the light and the color of the sea grew darker. Five minutes before we reached our destination, there was a tropical downpour, and we were soaked to the skin. We did not care—we had got away from the island.

Later, we discussed our experience. Why had this trip been such a nightmare? We knew that the Fijian villagers had treated us as guests. Although our backpacks contained undreamed-of riches for them, such as cameras and watches, nothing was ever taken. All except the chief had been friendly and had done their best for us; the children had been particularly sweet. Of course it could have been a combination of kava and jet lag that made this stay seem like an imprisonment of months, not days; but it was more that the gulf between their world and ours was too great for us to bridge. We had to shut down half our brains to be able to cope and forget the dirt, the food, the flies. The days were endlessly spent in sitting or lying without doing anything to activate one's brain or body. Seven or eight hours of kava drinking each day was a penance of patience. Another penance was never to be alone. Added to the problem of total physical and mental inactivity, there was the frustration of having no power to make any decision. We, who had in our vanity supposed that we could accustom ourselves to anything, were forced to revise our ideas. Travel, they say, broadens the mind; we found that it can also narrow it.

Summer 1999

The Blue Grotto

JACQUELINE W. BROWN

THE ONLY THING BLUE about the Blue Grotto Bar and Grill was its name and the color of the bubbly sign that lit up after dark. Then it cast a pool of shimmery blue waves onto the sidewalk. The poster in the window advertised champagne. It pictured a handsome young man with slicked-down shiny black hair and a glamorous young woman dressed in a formal evening gown. Their bodies were entwined on a chaise longue, and they were sipping champagne from long-stemmed glasses. The sign read "Open the Door and Enter the Thrilling World of Champagne." I never saw any persons resembling the poster couple enter the Blue Grotto. Those who did frequent the bar didn't drink champagne, at least not during the 1930s and early 1940s when Daddy and I went there. Throughout those years requests were for beer, gin, rye whiskey, and, less often, for bourbon. Beer was the only drink of the men who stood outside the Blue Grotto but never entered. They passed the quart bottle around from one hand and mouth to the other as the white foam thickened and the golden brew got shallower with each transfer. The circle of beer drinkers that congregated outside the Blue Grotto was as permanent an exterior fixture as the blue neon sign above their heads. Frayed pants legs and all, their presence in front of the bar gave them a respectability. They were, at least, in proximity to the appropriate place to drink beer, a distinction the other group of drinking men on the corner didn't have.

Daddy first took me to the Blue Grotto when I was two. He picked me up and carried me in his arms as we arrived at the door and put me down once we were inside. When people nearby reminded him that I could walk, Daddy said, "I want everybody to know this little lady is with me." Regardless of where we spent Saturday afternoons, we ended up at the Blue Grotto before we returned home. Daddy wanted the Blue Grotto to be our secret, but when I was three, I pointed out the bar to my mother as we walked past it on Lenox Avenue.

"That's the Blue Grotto," I announced proudly. "Daddy takes me there all the time, and we drink together at the bar." Waving to the group in front that was whistling to attract the attention of two girls, I said, "And that's Grant and Benny and T. C. standing outside. They always ask Daddy for a nickel for more beer for a good time." Sensing I was saying the wrong thing, I added, "But Daddy doesn't give them a nickel. He tells them he's saving it for an ice-cream cone for me. He just tells them that to keep them from bothering him. But it's true, sometimes we do get frozen custards."

My information fueled another argument between my mother and father. I hoped Daddy wouldn't be angry with me for divulging our secret visits to the Blue Grotto. He wasn't.

"You little booger," he giggled. "I know how it is. It just busted out when you remembered how you and me go there together." Daddy and I continued going. To my surprise and bewilderment, my mother didn't mention the Blue Grotto again. I wondered why. Maybe she assumed that once she had made a scene, that was the end of it. Maybe she forgot to bring it up. Maybe she accepted the fact that we'd continue going despite what she thought. Maybe she lost interest. Letting the matter drop and not picking it up again was typical of my mother's "on and off" and "hot and cold" way of reacting to things. What she screamed about one day didn't matter to her the next, or she denied having cared about it in the first place. The more Willie and I tried to make her remember something she had insisted Willie do, like shorten her skirt, the more vehemently she swore she hadn't said anything of the sort. She was so convincing I questioned my own senses. Fortunately, Willie and others who happened to be present recalled her saying and doing what she later denied. I felt safer avoiding my mother and her unpredictable changes. So, I definitely didn't mention the Blue Grotto to her again.

At two, I was attracted to the shiny brass foot rail near the floor. After stepping on it and holding onto the edge of the counter, I glided along the smooth golden rail from one end to the other, pretending I was ice-skating. Daddy lifted me so I could kneel atop the barstool, stretch my neck over the reflection of the bottles of vodkas and Scotches, and look in the mirror behind the bar. My image barely cleared the array of gold, silver, and red labels on the bottles. But I could see Daddy and me, our faces pressed against each other so closely our skin of the same color made us appear joined together. We glowed from the light given off by the frosted ruby shades that covered the tiny bulbs on the ceiling. When Daddy sat me on the counter, the bartender taught me how to slide the drinks from the far end of the bar, where Daddy and I usually sat, to where the customers were seated.

At four, I kept tabs on the number of refills customers received. The bartender appreciated my accuracy, especially when the requests came so fast he had trouble remembering them. I got to know the drinks the "regulars" always ordered, so I put in their orders as soon as they came through the door. The "regulars" were the ones who frequented the Grotto every weekend and looked like they were fixtures, since they sat on the same barstools or at the same tables. Daddy introduced me to the "regulars" every week, as if we were meeting for the first time.

"This here, Jimmy my man, is my little daughter, Jackie. I think I told you about my only child. We go everywhere together. Yes sir, where I go she goes. If she can't go, I don't go."

Time after time I shook hands with each "regular," who always said, "Good day to you, little lady. It sure is good to see you."

Sometimes couples danced in the back of the bar, oblivious to the happenings in the front. Floor space was limited back there, which was why I thought they didn't dance the lindy or boogie. But Daddy said that wasn't the reason they didn't swing out or do fancy footwork. As if enlightening me to a deep, dark mystery at the age of four, he cupped his hand and whispered in my ear:

"You see, they like to dance like that. When they do the slow drag, they don't have to move their feet from the same spot. They just move their bodies up against each other. You see, you gotta understand. Men and women like to hold their bodies close like that. You understand?"

"Is that why he's holding her bottom in his hands, Daddy?"

"That's right, darling."

"Oh I know, like Alice and Uncle Ted are always hugging and kissing."

"That's right."

"Why don't you and Mama hug and kiss?"

"'Cause she don't want to."

During the baseball season, the volume of the radio giving blow-by-blow accounts of the game rose above that of the music in the Blue Grotto. The "regulars," including Daddy, bet on hits, pitches, plays in the infield, catches of long balls, and the outcome of stolen bases. The bets came fast and frantically. Round after round of beers were set up, bought by the loser and devoured in gulps before the next bet was placed. By four I had a commanding knowledge of the game, having learned from Willie as well as from her notebooks of records and statistics. As a result, with me on his lap providing him with advice on how to bet, Daddy rarely had to buy the beers. As the glasses were emptied and slammed on the table, I lined them up and counted them, shouting out "twenty-seven, twenty-eight," while the customers clapped their hands and oohed and aahed.

"You count good for four years old, honey."

"Hey, Dub, can you rent her out so she can help me with my bets uptown?"

Having downed three or four rounds, Daddy's cursing burst forth like booming thunder, exploding over the loudest laughs in the bar. His eyes reddened more brilliantly with each "hot damn" and resembled more the red light bulbs over the counter. Beads of sweat popped out, proliferating on his forehead. Swinging his arms about, as if driving away swarms of attacking mosquitoes, he knocked over glasses, which I very quickly stood back up again in straight lines. I started getting scared when the arm-waving was in full swing because he was letting go of me, little by little. My seat on his lap became shaky, and I could feel myself slipping away from him. I held on around his neck, even though my hands were damp from his sweating. When he asked me how to bet, I pretended I didn't know how the play would turn out or what the best strategy would be. No matter how persistent he was, I withheld my advice.

"Come on, think hard now. You can do it. Is that goddamn pitcher gonna throw a changeup? What the hell is he gonna do?" Daddy was cupping his hand over my ear, which felt like it was catching on fire with each whiff of his hot breath. He thought he was whispering, but every person in the bar easily heard him beseeching me to advise him.

"I don't know anymore, Daddy. Don't bet anymore. Don't drink anymore, Daddy."

From six on, my favorite times at the Blue Grotto were when Daddy and I sat at the bar, sipped our drinks, and talked. The bartender made me a special "cocktail" of club soda, crushed ice, and cherry juice, which closely resembled a whiskey sour, without the whiskey. Most people thought Daddy was too quiet and shy. He went into moods when he didn't talk. But when we were together, especially in the Blue Grotto, he talked a lot. And mostly, I listened.

"I have to tell you this, darling. I'm a man who don't have money. Oh, I got a little, you know, enough to get by, just scrape the bottom, you know, but it's not enough for your Mama. Now, understand, I'm not complaining. Some people are worse off. Things are bad everywhere. It's been bad, bad. I get jobs. You know that, right? I pick 'em up in little ol' cheap restaurants and take-out joints. You know, they're places that sell hot dogs and 'sam-mages,' the kind o' stuff you and me like, right?"

"I like everything we eat when we go out, Daddy, except that tongue."

"Anyway, you remember that take-out place I took you to down on 14th Street, and we went back in the kitchen? Well, I was washing dishes and mop-ping the floor there. No, I don't mess with trying to get work in no expensive restaurant. They don't take no colored help. No way. So you think I'm gonna waste my time and theirs, or get into an argument over it? Nobody can't do nothing about it anyway. I just gotta settle for any little ol' thing that don't pay nothin' but what I can pick up easy. Then too, if I work in these cheap places, I can sleep later in the morning, 'cause they don't need me till just before noontime."

"That's right, that's better, Daddy. You're still home when Willie takes me to school in the morning. Oh, Daddy, you forgot. You didn't tell everybody here in the Grotto I started first grade."

"Hot damn, you're right. Listen, everybody, my little girl here is in first grade."

Applause swept through the bar. The bartender freshened my drink. The "regulars" shook my hand again. "Now them teachers'll have somebody to teach them somethin'." A man none of us had seen before in the Grotto, sitting conspicuously alone in the back, ordered drinks all around. His pearly cigarette holder glistened against his ebony fingers.

"Like I was saying, with these little jobs I pick up," Daddy was deter-mined to go on, "I get laid off as easy as I get 'em. Like that little shitty piece of a job I was on last week, the manager says, 'Dub, we got to let you go. We're not making enough to pay you.'" Daddy laughed out loud. "I said to myself," he went on, "'Man, as far as I'm concerned, you can stick this whole place up your ass.' Excuse my language, darling. To tell you the truth, sometimes I quit myself. You know, if they talk to me the wrong way, I'm not gonna take that crap. You see, you gotta understand, some people thought when we came North, things would be different. Well, not as different as day and night, but different. They thought we'd get work, and we'd be treated like we was human beings, not animals. And things are different in some ways. There's no signs up here saying 'Colored' and 'White.' Nobody's callin' you 'nigger' and 'boy,' at least not to your face, so you can be fooled, you see. You don't know what people are thinkin' while they're smilin' in your face."

"That's what this girl did to me in school, Daddy. She gives me a stick of gum, then she snatches my ribbon off my hair. I wanted my ribbon back, and I wanted to give the gum back to her, but I already had it in my mouth, chewing it, so it was too late."

"Yep, she took advantage of you. You didn't ask her for the damn chewing gum. Watch out for that. Don't take nothin' from nobody, you hear? If somebody comes up to you and offers you something, or just gives you something, you don't take it, if you don't know the person I mean."

"Well, what about that man sitting back there that gave all of you free beers just now, Daddy?"

"That's different. Men do that. You know, buy each other drinks to celebrate. But you don't take nothin' from him or no other man, you understand? Beside, he looks like he got plenty o' money to throw around in a bar. He's probably in the rackets."

"What's the rackets, Daddy?"

"It's makin' a lot o' money, darling. But it's makin' it the wrong way. You see, this is the way it goes." Daddy was halfway whispering. "People gotta have money to live. You can't get away from that. Jobs are too hard to find, 'specially if you're colored. So, what do you do? Well, there's the rackets. And I tell you, they're easy to get into. Easier than finding work, that's for sure. Makin' easy money is all around, on the street, in the stores, in any business you can think of up here in Harlem. Yes siree, easy to get into, but once you're in, they got you. You can't get out. The only way you get out is they drag you out after you're dead."

"How do you die, Daddy?"

"They kill you. And I'm not talking about the cops. It's the mob, the rackets that knock you off. You see, they're afraid if you pull out, you'll tell on them, so they have to bump you off. No, no, I don't want none of that stuff. What good is it to have a thick wallet if you're scared every minute you'll be a stiff the next minute? No, no, I want to stay alive, even without money. You got to be crazy to take chances on your life, gamble and get into shady dealings. Shit, I don't even play the numbers or shoot craps like you see the guys doing in the street. I'm gonna tell you the God's honest truth. I'm too scared to get mixed up with any dirty money."

"But you gamble, Daddy. You bet on the ball game."

"That's only 'cause I stand a pretty good chance of winning with you tellin' me how to bet. I stick with what I know I can do, like slicing meat, like roast beef, pastrami, and tongue. You can smell that good ol' fatty meat on my hands. Now, your Mama, she hates it." Daddy pushed his hands into my nose. "Tell me, what do you smell?"

"I smell greasy grease." I hated the smell too, but I didn't want to agree with my mother. I pretended it didn't bother me, but I felt nauseous. The bartender gave me spoonsful of a peppermint liquid to settle my stomach.

"Don't worry about me cuttin' up the tongue. You don't have to eat it," Daddy was saying. "Don't worry about nothin'. Whatever you want I'll try to get it for you. I'll always be here."

"And Willie too. Right, Daddy? She'll always be here too."

"That's right, darling. I'm so happy you got Willie. You're a lucky little booger. You know that? Yes siree. Sometime I stop and think about it. She's your Mama's sister, so even if your Mama's not with you, you got Willie. Hot dog, you are Willie's life. I tell you, you're the world to her. And she sticks with your Mama too. Did I ever tell you how me and your Mama used to try to get away from Willie?" Daddy wanted to whisper, but he had to talk loud because the noise in the bar was increasing. "I used to walk all the way from Batesburg to Leesville," he was saying, "you know, a couple of miles, to see your Mama. I tried to get to the church, where they had their school, before anybody else started walkin' home with her. I knew she'd go with whoever carried her books. We was twelve, maybe thirteen years old. Boy, oh boy, I was crazy about your Mama, and so was a lot of other boys around there."

"Who were the other boys, Daddy?"

"You wouldn't know 'em. They were just some boys who lived around Leesville."

"Were they as nice as you, Daddy?"

"No, no, not as good as me. I could play football. All they could do was plow. Anyway, I'd walk with your Mama down the road, you know, carrying her books. Well, Willie was always with her. She was two years older, but little, you know, like she is now. While we was walkin' along, with Willie followin' us, I was lookin' for sugar cane stalks, tall, thick, sweet ones, for me and your Mama to go behind where nobody could see us. But here come little Willie, hobblin' behind us, tellin' your Mama, 'Virture, you better go straight home, you know what Papa said.' That old man was mean and strict. First I didn't like it, then I started thinkin' when it's not me, then Willie'll be followin' and saying the same thing to some other boy who wants to go hide with your Mama. So I was glad Willie was with her. She kept your Mama in line. She still does. Yes sir, Willie's somethin', all right. She's not like everybody else."

"I know, Daddy. She's crippled. She's hunchback. That's why people look at her all the time." I felt a lump coming in my throat.

"How that make you feel, darling? Sorry for Willie?"

"I don't know, Daddy. Sometimes I get mad."

"I know, I know what you mean. You see, she didn't grow right. That's what happened. The bones in her body are all crushed together, too close, and they grew out o' shape, sticking out in the wrong directions, you know, so it's hard for her to breathe sometimes. There just ain't enough room inside her chest. That's what I think, anyway."

"But she's so smart, Daddy. Willie knows everything. She's smarter than anybody."

"That's right. You see, God said, 'She's got a bad body, so I'm gonna give her a really good mind.' You understand?"

"Can God talk, Daddy?"

"I don't know what the hell God can do. I'm just sayin' maybe that's the way it is, I don't know. But I do know you a lucky, blessed booger to have Willie. We all lucky boogers. But let's just suppose for some reason Willie's not around anymore. You know, if she had to go away. I'm still here for you. You know what I mean?"

"Willie'll always be around. You don't have to worry about that, Daddy. She takes me wherever she has to go. She takes me way down to Orchard Street when she has to buy fur and feathers for the evening dresses she sews for those ladies that dance in a long line. If Willie ever had to go away, she'd take me with her. I know that."

Daddy staggered and stumbled down Lenox Avenue on our way home from the Blue Grotto. The streetlights made the avenue look like the Apollo stage, a spectacle of people and activity, especially on warm nights. Familiar by day, the neighborhood changed scenery and lighting at night. The cast grew, they applied makeup, and dressed up. Faces of women that had been enclosed in window frames, like pictures on the wall looking down onto the street from second and third floors, became live, wiggly bodies at night. Stoops were crammed. Women as well as men congregated on the corners. I had a different role too, responsible for steering Daddy. Hand in hand, we zigzagged the sidewalk. He slumped from side to side like a rag doll. He stepped on my feet, so my socks were dirty by the time we reached 113th Street. I'll have to say I fell in the dirt in the park, I thought. We stopped, Daddy leaned against the hood of a parked car and gazed at the park.

"Didn't I tell you we were some lucky booger," he said. "Look at that. We got the park just a couple o' blocks away. From here the trees all thick and dark, make me think I'm lookin' into the woods behind Grandma Lyd's house in Batesburg. You know how I like them big, tall trees. And you like the park too, especially the lake, right? I could tell today when we took the rowboat out, and we took turns paddling around the lake."

"The best part is when you lay your oar down and I turn the boat around by myself. I can feel my end of the boat going in a circle. It's like dancing in the water."

"Yes siree, darling, you and me, we know how to be happy. We the best buddies. We stick together."

We bought Juicy Fruit chewing gum in the candy store. "This'll freshen our breath," Daddy said. "Nobody'll know we went to the Blue Grotto. It's our secret."

"I know, Daddy."

As we turned the corner on 112th Street, Daddy did a fancy pivot on the ball of one foot, lost his balance, and fell into the building. He scraped his head, and his forehead started bleeding. I started crying.

"Everything's all right. Don't worry about me. Your Daddy's fine," he was saying as he dabbed his head with his handkerchief and wiped the tears from my face. "I just got a little too happy, and I got dizzy. We'll just say I hit myself on the head with the paddle when I was gettin' out of the rowboat."

Spring 2000

Letter from Arcadia

HILARY SPURLING

EVERY TIME WE COME HERE, heading south down the coast from Athens, we pass a ghost settlement on a bare scrubby headland: tiered rows of blank house fronts with barred doors, shuttered windows, gaping balconies, and concrete colonnades exposed beneath a blazing sun and surrounded on three sides by sea. This is the Arcadian Village, built as a retirement colony for Greeks of the American diaspora. It has no shops or squares, no public buildings, no shady trees or gardens, not even any roads, just raw tracks gouged out of the rock. It is an eerie sight, untenanted and brilliantly lit like a de Chirico painting, waiting for inmates from another continent who dream of coming here to die.

Last night I heard the last dog bark and the first cock crow. I'm sitting now in early morning sun between the mountain and the sea on the terrace of a whitewashed stone house in Arcadia looking out over the broad blue gulf of Argos. Above me an amphitheater of olive-terraced hillside rises to sheer reddish ramparts that mark the foothills of Mount Parnon. This spiny finger of the Peloponnese was more or less cut off from the rest of Greece until they began blasting out a coastal road almost fifty years ago. Before that the only access was by foot or mule (which meant walking for four days through the mountains to the north) or by boat from the sea. Even now the road stops short halfway down the coast, where it meets the pass that twists inland to Sparta. Here in this ancient stony pocket people still speak Tsakonika, a language older than Dorian Greek, an oral fossil going back perhaps even before the Mycenaean script of Linear B. King Agamemnon must have sailed past this hillside on his way to rescue Helen from Troy.

Today Agamemnon's stronghold of Argos is the local shopping center (a huge joke for friends in the UK, where the Argos catalogue is Britain's nearest equivalent to Wal-Mart). It isn't easy to spot traces of the past in the drab modern towns of Argos and Sparta, but old people in our village still follow something very like the daily round described by Hesiod and Homer. For a thousand years, perhaps ten thousand, survival meant up to eighteen hours a day tending vines and olives, gathering branches for fuel and fodder, tilling the scanty soil beneath the olive trees to produce a barley crop—just enough to feed a household—that had to be threshed on circular paved floors cut out of the mountain and ground in stone mills planted outside each village on windy promontories above the sea. Goats gave milk, cheese, occasionally a kid to roast. Men fished, as they still do from the little wooden boats with painted hulls and fenders bobbing below me in the bay. This was the life of labor, monotony, and superstition that Hesiod complained about in letters home: "the unrelenting toil on the stony farm, the perilous commercial enterprises in small unseaworthy ships, the emigrant returning home in poverty."

That comes from the first lavishly illustrated bestseller to send its readers spilling out across this mountainy country, *The Glory That Was Greece*, published in 1911 (and still in print at the end of the twentieth century). Its author, J. C. Stobart, my husband's grandfather, said the air was then so clear and pure that he could look out of his hotel window in Athens and see hilltops in the heart of the Peloponnese. He was a young Cambridge classics don who tramped the hills long before the roads were built, watching the local people dance in rings and lines "just as they danced on the shield of Achilles," finding nature worshippers with mystic rites and snake-headed goddesses in still untouched Arcadia, admiring the newly excavated sanitary system of prehistoric Cnossos ("the world did not reach the Minoan standard of cleanliness again until . . . the late nineteenth century").

His was the first book we put on our shelves when we bought a goat farm in this village. Our first visitor was another Cambridge-educated academic, a distinguished retired professor from a great American university—I shall call him P—a character of Jove-like majesty and vigor, who made a dramatic entry on a cloudless blue-and-gold May day accompanied by drenching rain, lightning streaks, and claps of thunder. The freak storm came out of nowhere thirty minutes before he got here and subsided just as suddenly thirty minutes later. He admitted, when I asked him for an explanation, that his doctoral thesis was on Greek magic. Between them these two encapsulate the British love affair with Greece in the last century. Jack Stobart was one of a whole generation of classically trained young men who began opening up the Hellenistic world before WWI. My friend P belongs to a second wave of writers and adventurers who came after WWII, exchanging their own grey, ruined, and exhausted country for the exhilarating fierce bright clarity and simplicity of peasant life in the mountains and the islands.

Sitting here in the mornings on my terrace with its lemon tree, damask roses, cascade of bougainvillea, I watch the old women with their goats going up the mountain on donkey-back, sitting sideways on big wooden saddles, dressed in black with grey aprons and headscarves tied like jutting helmets. At night they come down again on foot behind what look like untidy moving haystacks of mulberry or bay. The donkeys, invisible now except for their neat small hooves, teeter in zigzags down the rutted path, carrying enough supplies to feed them for a week, like people lugging back provisions from the supermarket. The only traffic sounds in this village are goat bells, the soft slither of donkeys' hooves, and the occasional putter of a motorbike.

Donkeys are old people's transport. If you see one tethered beneath a tree, you know the elderly owner will be making hay nearby. A motorbike upended in the grass means a visiting son or grandson. There are no young men in this village, few women under sixty, and hardly any children. Once on the road to Sparta we were caught up in a flock of a hundred or more goats—rust, tan, chestnut, ginger, blackish brown—accompanied by two goatherds, aged about ten and five years old, with wooden crooks, tousled heads, and skin burned as dark as their goats' hides. Apart from these two little boys and a single teenage girl in jeans, I've never see anyone but old people tending the flocks or raking hay. The rest have moved out to the cities, or down the hill into new concrete homes strung along the shore where they build apartment blocks for summer tourists in their olive groves, drive cars or trucks, and grow plump little bellies, unlike their lean stringy grandparents, still stepping lightly up and down the almost vertical slopes between stone houses tucked into the mountain.

We bought our house from a couple of them. They spoke Tsakonika interspersed with modern Greek, and it was their son who signed the contract, either because they were too old to leave their mountain or because they couldn't read and write. The husband was in his late eighties, a white-haired patriarch beginning now to stoop and fade. His wife was ten years younger, tiny, erect, emphatic, moving gracefully on bare feet with a wispy white plait and a booming voice trained to carry from one hillside to the next. She told us—or we thought she did—that her name was America, a dream destination for Greeks in the 1930s when she was born. Their house, like all the others in the village, had an outside staircase and stone walls a meter thick. Most of the life of the household took place in the courtyard next to the vegetable plot and the domed brick oven. A dark opening led from it into the ground floor of the house, not much more than a storage cave, so low and dim you had to stoop and stumble over rocks protruding from the uneven earthen floor. Upstairs was a long high-ceilinged living space with a pitched roof, as big as a small barn or chapel, subdivided into many little rooms all tightly shuttered against the sun, crammed with gear—tools, cooking pots, rugs heaped on iron bedsteads—and richly painted, like a gypsy caravan, in chrome yellow with underlying streaks of spinach or deep glowing turquoise blue with cedar green shutters.

Outside was a small vine-shaded terrace overlooking the sea and above it an even smaller rickety platform on the roof. Rough steps led up from the courtyard below to two more yards hacked out of the mountain, one above the other, each containing a mighty wrinkled and corrugated olive. The larger of the two trees was said to be the oldest in the village, four or five hundred years old, a dense canopy of branches above a mass of twisted roots carved by time into knobs, crevices, and cubbyholes, used by the family as a capacious outdoor sideboard. They hung their coats or work trousers in its recesses, suspended ladders and spades from the branches, stowed bags and boots in the hollow trunk. Their back gate opened onto a narrow path leading to the village well between olive groves on one side and the olive-shaded goat-yard on the other. "You'll be able to keep a lot of goats up here," America said encouragingly the first time we met.

At that stage the idea of buying a house was still a barely formulated daydream. It was proposed almost as a joke by our friend A, when I said this unspoilt coast reminded me so much of the French Riviera a century ago that now might be the ideal time to buy something. "Why don't we?" said A. We made a list of pros and cons. Most of my pros ("Light. Sun. Sea. Heavenly beauty of the place") were smartly countered by J, who hates to travel ("It's a long way from Piccadilly") and can't be parted from his cat. "We couldn't bring the cat!" was a trump card that in his view put paid to the whole mad plan. "There are plenty of cats here already," I snapped back. We fell into a kind of counterpoint. "Seclusion and sea views," I wrote in the Pros column. "Almost inaccessible except by foot," he answered under Cons. "Mountain walks and healthy climbs" [me]. "Too steep for oldies" [him]. "We'd be able to keep coming here" [me]. "We'd *have* to keep coming here" [him]. "Cheap flights," A put in under Pros. "Airfares will go through the roof any day now" was J's response. "Let it and make lots of money," suggested A. "It'd cost more than we've got," J said grimly, "or ever will have."

Next day A came back from an evening stroll to say she'd met an architect with a pearl earring along the goat track opposite our holiday house. She flew home to London the day after, and that evening J and I met him too. Before we followed A back to London at the end of the week, the architect showed us a couple of houses up for sale. One was America's goat farm. J's resistance crumbled. The date was May 19, 2006. A month later A and I flew back to Greece for three days to finalize the deal. The deed of sale was translated for us over dinner in the village taverna by a friend, who warned us sternly at all costs not to touch the property given that we'd had no independent survey, seen no title deeds or proof of ownership, possessed no local knowledge, and hadn't even hired a lawyer to protect us. Neither of us slept that night. Before dawn I got up and waited on our tiny balcony for the sun to come up over the far side of the bay. A joined me. We made a pot of black coffee and gloomily compiled a second list of pros and cons. This time the cons far outnumbered the pros. But, as the list grew longer and more damning, the rising sun slowly turned the cliff opposite our balcony to gold. At half past eight we showered, dressed, and drove into town to buy the house. There was just time afterwards to raise a glass with America and her family, admire the view from each of the five terraces, and climb back down the hill for a last swim before the coach to Athens picked us up from the bus stop on the beach.

Et in Arcadia ego said the screensaver on the computer in the country lawyer's office where we signed the deeds. Until that fatal visit to Arcadia, the first and only time I'd ever been to Greece was when J and I came here as students in 1962. Like many of our postwar generation, we were in full flight from 1950s Britain with its bleak bombed cities, punitive restrictions on travel, food, and clothes, pervasive atmosphere of nostalgia, and a joyless puritanism. We had read Henry Miller, Lawrence Durrell, and Elizabeth David. We wanted to be writers too. Their sharp prose, luscious images, and dazzling evocation of simple pleasures—food, wine, sex, sunshine, sensuality—made a Mediterranean summer look like the essential start to any ad hoc creative writing program. We spent two months exploring the country by bus, foot, and ferries to the islands. We stared out to sea from the temple at Sounion, sat for hours watching the boats come and go below the harbor wall at Rhodes, tested the acoustics in the theater at Epidaurus, climbed into Mycenae after opening hours to see Agamemnon's tomb by moonlight.

We had no money, and in any case most of the hotels were still half-built, so we stayed in local peasants' houses, drinking retsina on the beach, living on olives, goat cheese, and tomatoes. Water was scarce, electricity supplies uncertain, indoor plumbing rare and ramshackle. Today even the most far-flung outposts have running water, street lighting, TV, and mobile phones. Our village in Arcadia is not so very different from the places we stayed in all those years ago, but cement mixers already trundle up these hills. Most days you can hear the distant whine and clunk of earthmovers, rock-blasters, and bulldozers. Builders' trucks edge along alleys barely wide enough to take a wheelbarrow, negotiating impossible corners, squeezing between stone houses at preposterous angles up perpendicular slopes.

It took the architect with the earring (he turned out to be half Greek, half German with a practice in Berlin) twelve months to transform our ex–goat farm into a writers' workshop. "Yours will be a pearl among houses," he said, and he was right. It still looks like any other village house with soft red roof tiles and whitewashed stone walls except for the paved terraces linked by flights of white stone steps, twisting and turning down the hillside through six or seven different levels to a pair of wrought iron gates made, like all the other massive village gates, by the local blacksmith. The space inside has been cleared and whitewashed to make a long airy light-filled room with roof and floor of chestnut wood, and spectacular views of sea and sky. A fine-drawn steel-framed staircase, welded to the wall in showers of sparks by the smith who made our gates, leads down to another light, cool space for bathrooms and bedrooms excavated from the mountain.

We start each day over coffee on the roof terrace, where you can still pick out the remnants of ancient village working patterns. A man with a donkey winds slowly upwards through trees on the far side of the hill. A deep raucous woman's voice calls across the mountain to some Gianni I can't see. On Mondays our aged barefoot neighbor lights a fire of twigs in her courtyard, heats water in a big blackened bucket, and squats over a tin basin on the ground to wash her husband's shirts and work pants. Often she hands us gifts over the fence: four new-laid eggs, a brown loaf still warm from her bread oven, a plastic bottle of retsina, a bag of oranges or a bowl of fat black olives from her tree. Another neighbor from two houses along fetches fluffy rabbits in a box from the farm lower down the lane. An hour later she has them butchered, skinned, and ready to roast in her bread oven. The day is punctuated by shouts, cries, and protestations. Even the body language of this neighborhood is a sort of street drama. Once we looked down from a walk high above the village to see a couple facing one another across their courtyard, motionless as statues, frozen in attitudes of passionate anger or appeal. The loud tirades of rancor and reproach I hear most days from next door sound more like Hecuba or Medea than my neighbor talking to her goats.

The collision taking place in this village between the old world and the new is brought home by the arrival of friends from Athens, bringing a man from Manhattan with them, a newly qualified young architect called D, on his way to spend a week touring the islands in a friend's father's private yacht. Our hospitality proves hopelessly inadequate. The supply of bottled water runs out, there is no air-conditioning, oranges and lemons on our neighbor's trees raise the dread possibility of wasps. D can't swim in the pellucid sea for fear of jellyfish or sit outside at twilight under the evening star in case there might be midges. He is suspicious of the local food. Whole grey mullet or stripy sea bass fresh from the sea, farm chickens with heads and feet attached, "roast kiddie" and wild mountain greens at the taverna, all fill him with foreboding. Like my own children, he belongs to a genera-tion with little or no sense of the past that is imprinted here on every stick, stone, and streambed. Apollo's rustic shrine in an oak grove on the next hill, Menelaus's tomb near Sparta, even the signposts to Epidaurus and Mycenae that we pass on the way here—none of it means anything to them. Suddenly I see this harsh dry landscape through D's eyes as hicksville, a sort of Texan backyard by the sea without even any oil wells.

That of course is how Arcadia always seemed to the unromantic Greeks from classical times onwards: a remote, crude, primitive place exemplified by its tutelary deity, Hermes, the rough and dodgy pre-Hellenic god of shep-herds, who strums an improvised, tortoise-shell guitar and is commemo-rated in these parts, according to J. C. Stobart, by piles of stones marking the edge of a road or the corner of a field ("his statues are three parts pillar to one part god"). Hermes's latest reincarnation in this village was made last summer by another of our neighbors, the Canadian sculptor David Moore. His installation takes the form of a long low curving trestle of rough planks surmounted at one end by a big battered wooden bust, roughly carved and painted here and there in patches of gaudy red and blue, like a ship's figure-head, with ram's horns, bulging pebble eyes, and a string of goat bells round its neck. A glossy lively mass of carob pods erupts like thick dark nerves or spilt intestines from the back of the brainpan. More pods, and whiskery tufts of tow-colored rope, protrude from cracks in the wooden body. There is something faintly sinister, even threatening, about this figure who clearly represents the village, or perhaps Arcadia itself.

At the far end of the trestle is a second bulky figure constructed from elaborately cut and folded sheets of tin, an angular, sharp-edged intruder in protective hat and goggles looming from behind a barricade of luggage crates and cases with a trail of shiny apparatus—measuring tapes and tubes, collecting boxes, books, and filing systems—strewn before him the length of the table. The two confront one another as if negotiating some sort of handover of power. When the piece was first shown in the art gallery at Nauplion—an austere, subtly lit interior that would not look out of place in London's Cork Street or Manhattan's Chelsea—the shabby baleful colored head seemed to shrink, growing tamer and less monolithic, more picturesque than menacing. Out of doors on the hillside in our village, where Moore originally planned to show his piece, it would have been the tinman's turn to look uneasy and defensive. That shifting balance could still tip either way. The week of Moore's opening saw the first of the fires that raked the western Peloponnese for weeks on end last summer. By the end of August the sky had turned red and black even over our untouched eastern coast. The wildness of this place is as exorbitant as its history, its landscape, its astonishing light and color.

Spring 2008

Letters from America

ALEXIS DE TOCQUEVILLE

ALEXIS DE TOCQUEVILLE was twenty-five years old in May 1831 when he and his friend Gustave de Beaumont landed at Newport, Rhode Island, after thirty-seven days at sea. Tocqueville was a deputy royal prosecutor, Beaumont his immediate superior. The two had been granted leaves of absence from their duties in the French judicial system to study American prisons, and a book-length report they co-authored upon their return, *Du système pénitentiaire aux États-Unis et de son application en France*, testifies to the earnestness with which they undertook their mission. But the letters they wrote from America show them avidly observing everything around them. Prison reform was their passport to the New World; it legitimated what proved to be a cultural enquiry of seminal importance.

The aristocratic family into which Tocqueville had been born shaped him more for caution than adventure. Having barely survived the Terror of 1793–94—unlike many of their close kin—his parents lived the life of cultivated Norman gentry. Count Hervé de Tocqueville was elected mayor of the town of Verneuil during Napoleon's reign but otherwise remained aloof from politics, concerning himself mainly with the welfare of a family that came to include three sons: Hippolyte (1797), Édouard (1800), and Alexis (1805). It also included a priest named Christian Lesueur, his own childhood tutor, who now tutored his children. At Verneuil, and wherever Hervé subsequently established himself, books mattered. The household Alexis de Tocqueville evoked years later was as hospitable to serious literature as it was fortified against current events. "Literature was one of the standing subjects of conversation. Every new book of any merit was read aloud, and canvassed and criticized with an attention and a detail which we should now think a deplorable waste of time." Hospitality extended beyond books to writers. Literature incarnate visited Verneuil now and again in the person of François de Chateaubriand, whose journey across America had inspired novels that would, when finally published in 1826, excite the imagination of young romantics.

With Napoleon's fall, history called old-line aristocrats out of the shadows. The restored Bourbon monarchy, mindful of sacrifices made to the throne during the ancien régime (above all, by Mme de Tocqueville's grandfather, Lamoignon de Malesherbes, who defended Louis XVI at his trial and followed him to the scaffold), appointed Hervé de Tocqueville to prefectships first in Burgundy, then in Lorraine. What this meant for Alexis was a life divided between his mother, who set up house in Paris, refusing to leave the Faubourg Saint-Germain, and his father, who took him under his wing when he turned fifteen. The division cut deep. In turn disciplined by a model of competent public authority in Hervé, and subjected to violent mood swings by the melancholic, irritable Louise—whose nerves may have been unstrung even before the trauma of her imprisonment during the Terror—Alexis did not live easily within himself. His intellectual brilliance, which led him in adolescence to challenge the pieties of his class, was nonetheless hostage to self-doubt, and never fought free of it. All this made for intense restlessness.

Left to his own devices, Alexis might have become a traveler the instant he was graduated from the collegiate school at Metz in Lorraine. But there was no question of travel until he finished law school, which he entered *à contre coeur*, lacking a better alternative. Back to Paris he shuttled in 1823, at age eighteen, for three years of drudgery at the École de Droit. In 1826, he defended theses in Latin and French, obtained his degree, and was rewarded by the family with a voyage to Italy and Sicily. His brother Édouard accompanied him. The young men spent four months abroad, taking notes, climbing volcanoes, and breathing free in what proved to be excellent preparation for Alexis's journey to America. When the voyage ended, professional life began. Hervé, now prefect of a region administered from Versailles, arranged to secure Alexis a niche at the court of general jurisdiction in his bailiwick. The council responsible for confirming such appointments included three members of the Tocqueville clan; council meetings were, to all intents and purposes, family reunions.

In 1830 history made the family reunion at Versailles a thing of the past. Dethroned during the July Revolution, Charles X was replaced by a constitutional monarch, Louis Philippe d'Orléans, whose father—dubbed Philippe Égalité—had joined the Jacobins advocating Louis XVI's execution in 1793.

Hervé, honored with a peerage under Charles, had had to resign his prefecture for a seat in the upper chamber of the legislature; now, under the Orléanist dispensation, he lost that as well. Nothing remained of a distinguished public career.

Alexis, in turn, sat on the horns of a dilemma, for the July Monarchy required Bourbon functionaries to take an oath of loyalty. It didn't matter that he held Charles X in low regard: pledging loyalty to Louis Philippe, a monarch whom his father couldn't abide, felt like an act of betrayal. But not to take the oath would cost him his job, and the specter of unemployment loomed even larger than the prospect of laboring without honor at chores that did not invigorate the better part of his intellect. How might he arrange to serve the new regime and not enforce its laws? The study of American prisons seemed a way out. But Alexis felt ambivalent about face-saving expedients. The turmoil of 1830 had not yet ended in 1831. Would this revolution follow the same course as that of 1789, he wondered? Would Tocquevilles who had escaped death almost four decades earlier survive this time around? Would he, who carried royal credentials to America, soon find himself in the vanguard of a new generation of émigrés? Was he a researcher or a fugitive? His letters from America, for all their exuberance, wit, and keen observation, would reflect those anxieties. *Translator's Note*

> On board the vessel *Le Havre*,
> bound for New York, April 26, 1831

To his mother,[1]

It is you, my dear Mama, to whom I wish to write first. I had intended to do so upon my arrival in New York, but I lack the courage to wait until then. Moreover, circumstances are favorable: since the wind speeding us forward is scarcely rocking the boat, my script may be no more illegible than usual. I should like to offer you a substantial letter, but I don't quite know where to begin. Not that anything of great moment has occurred since our separation, only that I feel I have millions of things to tell you. I shall therefore take the easy path and ramble.

---

1. Born Louise Le Peletier de Rosambo, Madame de Tocqueville was the granddaughter of Lamoignon-Malesherbes, famous as counsel for the defense of Louis XVI during the Revolution, who followed his client (and daughter and son-in-law) to the guillotine. Louise de Rosambo narrowly escaped the same fate. She married Hervé de Tocqueville, the scion of old Norman nobility, in 1793.

Papa will have told you how and at what time he bid us farewell at Le Havre. What he couldn't have reported was our sadness after his departure. Never have I felt such heartache. When he and my brothers left, the bond that tied me to all of you and to France went slack; and I doubt that any American city will ever seem as foreign and deserted to me as Le Havre appeared at that moment. After painfully killing three long hours, we boarded our vessel. Rumor had it that we would likely remain in Le Havre for six days. You can imagine how this news thrilled us. We threw ourselves onto our bunks and fell fast asleep, lacking a better alternative. At half past midnight, awoken by some noise overhead, I climbed through the companion hatch and realized that we were under full sail. A jetty lantern was still glowing on the horizon; otherwise no land was visible in the night, and I have seen no sign of it since. I hope, however, that it exists somewhere; for I am ill disposed to live this long on water. The threat of seasickness regularly sends me below deck. While Beaumont[2] has been his usual hale and hearty self, I spent two days in bed queasy and dejected. Only on the third did I take some interest in things of this world, and on the fourth I recovered. Most other passengers fared less well than I. We didn't really mingle until the sixth day, when everyone crept out of his hole. Let me assure you, we made a fine assemblage of pale, yellow, green faces—every color of the rainbow. I should like to acquaint you with the inhabitants of our little world, who, not counting a cow and a donkey, number exactly 181 by my reckoning, 30 housed in the cabin section, 13 in steerage, 120 in the bow, and 18 crew. I shall limit myself to a description of several cabin passengers—the vessel's aristocracy, as it were. In the cabin adjacent to our own is an important English landowner, M. Palmer, who has served in the House of Commons.[3] A very kind, knowledgeable old man, he has taken a liking to us and furnished us with useful information and excellent advice. He's the best of the lot. His roommate—a traveling salesman, to put it more bluntly than he himself might—is the buffoon. Not that he means to make one laugh. On

2. Gustave de Beaumont, Tocqueville's friend and fellow lawyer, who later married Clémentine de Lafayette, the marquis's granddaughter. He and Tocqueville were commissioned by the government of King Louis-Philippe to study the American penal system. The vessel on which they sailed was a 450-ton schooner, with an American captain and crew.

3. Charles Palmer was a retired major general, who had fought in the campaign against Napoleon. Representing Bath in the House of Commons, he owned considerable property there and vineyards in the Bordelais.

the contrary, he amuses us despite himself, being a very serious personage, whose entire conversation is wine and politics. And good Lord, what politics! Everything a fool would claim to know after reading *Le Constitutionnel*.[4] His pomposity has us in stitches. He always calls France "My fatherland," as in, "I'm visiting America to sell the wines of my fatherland." People give him a wide berth. He avenges himself by opening one of his bottles every day and hoarding it. Our other neighbor is M. Schérer, a man whose countenance is such that we couldn't face the prospect of conversing with him for three days; now we cleave together like three toes . . .[5] Except for his looks, which would be regarded as deplorable anywhere in the world, he is an excellent fellow. To be sure, he resembles in every way a thousand wastrels loitering about the streets of Paris, but we're glad of his company. He is fluent in French, neither dim nor bright, and happy-go-lucky. I must stop drawing these portraits or the letter will never end; suffice it to say that we are as diverse a conglomeration of animals as boarded Noah's Ark: a Spaniard, a whole French family, two Americans, a Swiss lady and her children. Relations are, by and large, easy and considerate, if not intensely amiable. We get along with everyone, and it is well that we do, for at sea one either befriends one's companions or fights. There is no middle ground. You'd be amazed, dear Mama, at the peculiar life one leads on this large oceangoing diligence! Being crammed together, constantly exposed, breeds an informality and freedom unimaginable on land. One lives in the midst of the crowd as if one were alone; some people read aloud, others play games or sing. While I write, my neighbor sups. If one feels impelled to do something—be it eating, drinking, or sobbing—one simply does it. Rooms are so narrow that one must step outside to dress, and, apart from putting on my breeches, I perform my daily toilette for all to see.[6] In short, we live, like the Ancients, on the public square. This is the true land of freedom. Its one drawback is that freedom can be exercised here only within the confines of a wooden box. Most of our companions therefore while away their time in the most trivial pursuits, distilling boredom drop by drop, as far as I can tell.

4. *Le Constitutionnel* was a left-leaning paper, patriotic and anticlerical, favored by the moderate, liberal bourgeoisie, which gained power and influence in the Revolution of 1830.

5. Édouard Schérer was a son of General Schérer, who had frontier commands during the Revolution and became minister of war in 1797.

6. Literally "face à Israel," or "in the presence of Israel"—from "coram Israel," a common expression in the Vulgate meaning "to appear in public."

We haven't been contaminated and busy ourselves much as we normally would ashore, weather permitting. We rise before dawn, work until break-fast at 9 o'clock; we resume work at noon and continue until dinnertime. After dinner, we speak English with whoever will tolerate our chatter, and retire at 9 p.m. This is not to say that we lack all external distractions. Every-thing in this world is relative. Think of the nuns [in the play *Ver-Vert*] all atwitter over the foul language of their pet parrot. That's precisely how mat-ters stand with us. We watch a cloud on the horizon or the trimming of the sails with absolutely rapt attention. The other day we spotted a barrel in the sea. It caused a general stir; pistols were produced; and we used it for target practice, making an infernal racket. Mine was the shot that pierced it. This has entered our annals as "The Day of the Barrel." Another sensation was Schérer's vizored cap being carried off by a wave. But unquestionably the most memorable event took place this morning when a gust of wind blew a charming little sky-blue bird, half dead, into our rigging. It's a species we don't have in Europe, and the Americans aboard immediately recognized it as one of their own. You have no idea how delighted we were with the little creature, which seemed to have been sent for the express purpose of announcing imminent landfall. We caught it and put it in a cage.

One week ago, on a delicious spring evening, our ship was plowing ahead, I'm not sure how, on a windless day in calm seas. Someone proposed that we dance. So Beaumont went off to fetch his flute, and a merry time was had by all, romping on the deck. If you want to know where this occurred, consult a map for the convergence of 42 degrees latitude and 34 degrees longitude! There, or thereabouts, was the dance hall. Man must be an animal heedless of all that may befall him to caper as we did over a bottomless abyss, under the vault of heaven, with death on all sides. But after all, is the same not true of the best furnished salon in the Faubourg Saint-Germain?[7] And then, one accustoms oneself to everything. I assure you that I no longer scan the horizon for land as I did our first day out; I am already quite used to seeing nothing around me but a more or less closed circle, with billowy clouds floating overhead. More than once, however, we have witnessed spectacles that deserve an artist's eye. One moonless night, for example, water began to sparkle like an electrifying machine. It was pitch black outside, and the ship's prow slicing through the sea spewed fiery foam twenty feet in either

---

7. The Faubourg Saint-Germain was a neighborhood of elegant mansions in Paris, inhabited mainly by the old-line aristocracy, including the Tocquevilles.

direction. To get a better view, I shimmied onto the bowsprit. From that vantage point, the prow looked as if it were leaping at me with a forward wall of glittering waves; it was sublime and admirable beyond my ability to evoke it. The solitude that reigns in the middle of the ocean is something formidable. During the first ten days of our journey, we regularly spied other sails; large birds tracked us and often perched on our spars; the sea abounded in fish. Beginning at around 30 degrees longitude, the vessels, birds, and fish disappeared. The ocean acquired a somber cast, but its monotony impresses one as vast rather than dull.

At the approach of the Banks of Newfoundland, we were buffeted by two gales, one lasting thirty-six hours. It was a repeat performance of what we experienced on the sea of Sicily [four years ago], with this notable difference that we were never in any danger of capsizing, as our sturdy vessel cleaved the tallest waves.[8] The real danger in those circumstances is of falling and breaking an arm or a leg. You can't imagine, dear Mama, what a toll is taken of one's energy by the continual effort to keep one's balance. I needed a sea voyage to acquaint myself with all the perils of distraction. If you daydream for a minute, you're liable to wake up on your backside, in which case you slide straight ahead until you meet a wall. At table, the diner opposite may receive a glass of wine in his face. Servants spill sauce down your collar.

Eventually, one grows used to all that. The thirty people at table end up regulating their movements, and we greet one another with the most agreeable decorum. Moreover, one endures these tribulations only in very heavy weather.

But to return to the Banks of Newfoundland, that is where birds and fish reappear, in particular one called the Portuguese man-of-war. It's a little fish with floating transparent membranes that catch the wind like sails. Then there are fish no bigger than a pinhead; they have the same properties as glowworms and in their millions produce an electric show of the kind I mentioned earlier. After fish and birds came kelp. It is said that this sea grass played its part in the discovery of America by announcing the approach of land to the mariners who first crossed the Ocean.

Today, May 4, the day on which I resume my letter, we are situated at 66 degrees longitude. New York is only 130 leagues away.[9] It will be a negli-

---

8. Tocqueville had traveled in Italy with his older brother Édouard in 1827.

9. The league was calculated differently at different times in different countries. Tocqueville's league was about 3 miles, or 5 kilometers.

gible distance if we strike a leading breeze, otherwise possibly a week's voyage. Meanwhile, we've already been 32 days at sea! Our fresh provisions are largely gone, and sugar is already rationed. Despite it all, you will believe me, I hope, when I say that my chief satisfaction upon docking at New York will not be stepping foot on American soil but receiving news from Europe. The packet that left Le Havre on May 15 will undoubtedly not have arrived, but other vessels that set sail eight or ten days after we did may have passed us. Only seeing you again, my dear Mama, could exceed the pleasure of reading letters from all of you.

From shipboard, May 9, 1831

To his mother,

Yesterday evening the first shouts of "Land Ahoy!" were heard, but one needed a spyglass to sight the shoreline. Today, at dawn, Long Island came into view. We are fast approaching the coast and can already make out greensward and leafy trees. It's a delicious spectacle. I must cut this letter short to join the celebration on deck. For once, the sea is not inconveniencing anyone.

From New York, May 14, 1831

To his mother,

When we first caught sight of Long Island, dear Mama, I hardly expected what would soon befall us. Once on deck, I realized that the wind, blowing from the east since morning, had shifted to the west. An hour later, it became violent and contrary. We were forced to tack, that is, to zigzag, but made no progress. As the morning wore on, our crew noted that the wind had settled "in a quarter," meaning that it would likely continue westerly for several days, to our dismay, for we had sick people among us, and had almost exhausted our fresh provisions; even wood and grain were in alarmingly short supply. Passengers therefore petitioned the captain to veer north and make for Newport. He agreed. So it came to pass that at nine in the evening of May 9 we dropped anchor in the outer harbor of that town, sixty leagues from New York. A fishing boat soon drew up and hailed us. Our delight at having reached land was such that all the younger folk and the captain himself crowded aboard the dory. Half-an-hour later, in damp breeches and on shaky legs, we were dancing jigs at Newport's dock, as happy as could be just to find ourselves back in the world. We then made our way to an inn, where the captain treated us to supper. What I personally relished most—you may not appreciate this—was the water we drank; the water onboard had become undrinkable (à propos of which I must tell you that the captain, excellent man and fine sailor though he is, had horribly mismanaged everything to do with the vessel's stores and comfort). As for my companions, they ate with two feet in the trough. Then, remembering "French gallantry," they and I bought a large quantity of fresh provisions, re-embarked, and reached our vessel at midnight. No one had yet gone to bed. In triumph we hauled our booty down to the ladies' saloon, and proceeded to sup all over again. When I say "supped," please understand that I refer, in my case, only to the conversational aspect of the meal.

The following day we visited Newport. To our indulgent eyes, the town seemed quite pretty. It is a cluster of houses no larger than chicken coops but very trim. Except that such neatness would be unimaginable in France, the inhabitants are not conspicuously different from French men. They dress like us, and their physiognomies are so various that one would be hard pressed to identify their national origin. I believe that this must be true throughout the United States.

After delighting for three hours in the sensation of walking on solid ground, we boarded the steamer that plies between Providence and New York. You would marvel at the interior of this immense machine. One detail will suffice: it contains three large saloons, two for men, one for women, where as many as eight hundred people eat and sleep comfortably. It completed the run of 60 leagues to New York in just 18 hours, despite choppy seas and contrary winds.[10]

This entire coastline of America is low lying and nondescript. Hardly a tree remains standing in a region densely wooded two centuries ago. We sailed between Long Island and Connecticut, and approached New York at sunrise, entering the port from behind. I don't know whether our view was colored by the experience of 35 days at sea and our recent passage down a drab coast, but I assure you that cries of admiration went up when we beheld the city's surroundings. Picture a sea dotted with sails, a lovely sweep of notched shoreline, blossoming trees on greensward sloping down to the water, a multitude of small, artfully embellished candy-box houses in the background—and you have the entrance to New York by way of the Sound.

10. River navigation by steamboat had made great strides since Robert Fulton accomplished the round-trip voyage between New York and Albany aboard the *Clermont* in 1807. The New York–Providence line was opened in 1822. More than 130 miles of its course took place at sea. Tocqueville's steamer, the *President*, had been put in service a year earlier. It was 413 feet long.

I was so struck by what I presume to be the commodiousness of these little houses and their excellent situation in the landscape that I shall try to obtain the design of several especially pretty ones; Émilie may perhaps find them useful for Nacqueville.[11] I have already been informed that they are not expensive; we have nothing comparable in France.

I must try to describe things more succinctly lest my letters swell into quarto volumes.

Here we are in New York. From a Frenchman's perspective, it looks disarmingly weird. There isn't a dome, a steeple or a large edifice in sight, which leaves one with the impression that one has landed in a suburb, not the city itself. At its very core, where everything is built of brick, monotony rules. The houses lack cornices, balustrades, carriage entrances. Streets are ill paved, but pedestrians have sidewalks.

Lodging was a problem at first because foreigners abound at this time of year and because we sought a pension, not an inn. At last we found one that suits us perfectly, on the most fashionable street in town, called Broadway. As luck would have it, M. Palmer, the Englishman I mentioned earlier, had already found accommodations in this boarding house.[12] Our shipboard friendship and especially the interest he is taking in our mission have led him to oblige us whenever and however possible. Best of all are the amenities offered by Americans. They beggar description. Men of every class seem to compete for the honor of being most cordial and useful. The newspapers, which report everything, announced our arrival and expressed the hope that people would come forward to assist us. They have outdone themselves. All doors are open, and welcoming hands extended at every turn. I, for whom diligences and inns have always been the tiresome appanage of travel, find these new conditions most agreeable.

One difficulty that has hampered us ever since we left France, and which we have begun to overcome, is language. In Paris, we fancied we knew English, not unlike collegiate school graduates who think that their baccalaureate is a certificate of learning. We were soon disabused of that notion. All we had was a basic vehicle for making rapid progress. We truly drove ourselves during the ocean crossing; I remember days on a windswept deck

---

11. Émilie de Tocqueville was a sister-in-law, the wife of his brother Hippolyte. She had inherited the chateau of Nacqueville, 8 kilometers from Cherbourg and near the Tocquevilles' chateau. There were three Tocqueville brothers: Hippolyte, born in 1797; Édouard, born in 1800; and Alexis, born in 1805.

12. The exact address was 66 Broadway.

translating English when it was difficult to hold a pen. Unfortunately, with so many French speakers aboard we could always fall back on our native language. Here the situation is different. As no one speaks French, we have had to give it up. Our conversation is entirely in English. It may sound pitiful, but at least we make ourselves understood and understand everything. Interlocutors even tell us that we show *great promise*. If we do end up mastering the language, it will be an excellent acquisition. The benefits we've already reaped illustrate for me the foolishness of a Monsieur de Belisle, who travels to lands where he cannot converse.[13] One might as well take strolls in one's room with the windows shuttered.

No doubt you would like to know, my dear Mama, how we spend our days. We rise between 5 and 6 and work until 8. At 8 o'clock the breakfast bell rings. Everyone convenes punctually. Afterward we visit several establishments to interview men with knowledge of matters that concern us. We return for dinner at 3 o'clock. Between 5 and 7 we put our notes in order. At 7 we go out and socialize over tea. This way of life is most agreeable, and I believe eminently sane. But it flouts all our assumptions. Thus, we were quite surprised at first to see women appearing at the breakfast table with faces carefully made up for the day. We are told that this is customary in all private houses. Paying visits to a lady at 9 in the morning is not thought improper.

At first we found the absence of wine from meals a serious deprivation, and we are still baffled by the sheer quantity of food that people somehow stuff down their gullets. Besides breakfast, dinner, and tea, with which Americans eat ham, they have very copious suppers and often a snack. So far, this is the only respect in which I do not challenge their superiority; they, on the other hand, reckon themselves superior in many ways. People here seem to reek of national pride. It seeps through their politeness.

Sunday, New York, May 15

I take up my letter again, dear Mama, after returning from high mass at a Catholic church five minutes from our residence. I carried the little book that Bébé[14] gave me and assure you that I was thinking about all of you during mass, of him and of you, dear Mama. I can't tell you how singularly

13. Bon Georges Charles Evrard de Belisle was Hippolyte de Tocqueville's father-in-law.

14. Bébé was a sobriquet for the abbé Lesueur, a priest who had tutored Alexis's father, Hervé de Tocqueville, and remained in the family as tutor to Hervé's three sons.

one is affected, when far from home, by all the religious ceremonies one has attended since childhood. At one point, with none but Americans around me, I fancied myself in France and was so persuaded of it that I spoke French to my uncomprehending neighbors. The church, a large one, was filled to overflowing, and the congregation more meditative than an assembly of French worshippers. We heard a good sermon on the subject of grace and were pleased to discover that we could follow it. Our intention had been to visit the bishop after mass, but he is in Europe right now.[15] We were told that his grand vicar, a good-natured, amiable priest named Power, would receive us splendidly, but Father Power was not at home when we called; we shall return tomorrow.

Catholics are firmly established in New York. They have five churches and more than 20,000 members. I have heard Americans say that converts are numerous. Their numbers are increasing in various parts of the Union, and I should not be surprised if a religion so beleaguered in Europe made great strides in this country. Every year another fifteen or twenty thousand Catholics arrive from Europe. They spread throughout the wildernesses of the West, where the need for religion is most keenly felt. They become fervent, if they aren't already, or their children do. So indispensable is a religious doctrine seen to be on this side of the Atlantic that Protestants themselves hold lapsed Catholics in low regard.

I thought these details would interest you.

I beg you, dear Mama, not only to transmit this letter to Édouard's household, but to ask Hippolyte how the arrangement sits with them. I prefer addressing only one person at a time and pouring out all my news. The thicker a letter, the less liable it is to go astray. Clearly, Beaumont and I have had nothing to complain about thus far. Launched on the most marvelous voyage imaginable, we enjoy privileges that travelers are seldom vouchsafed. Our brains are at work, we exercise our bodies, and time flies. But even the most beautiful things of this world have their dark side, and we cannot withdraw into ourselves without feeling pangs of anxiety. Almost two months and 1,500 leagues of sea separate us. What has become of you? What are you doing right now, as I calmly write this letter and gloat over my good fortune? What are my father's political circumstances? How is your health,

15. The bishop, Jean Dubois, had emigrated during the Revolution. At the time of Tocqueville's visit, he was in Rome raising money and recruiting priests for his diocese. John Power, the grand vicar, was an Irish priest who had been called to America in 1819 by the trustees of St. Peter's parish in New York. He was a theologian and renowned preacher.

dear Mama? How is good Bébé carrying his eighty years? Is Alexandrine feeling better or worse? What are my brothers doing, and Émilie? What, finally, is the state of France? I ask myself these questions during the day; they return at night and prey upon my mind. We are dying to hear from you, but when we do, our happiness will be cheated by the realization that your news is five weeks old or more. How many changes, how many revolutions can take place during that interval! Last year, between July 26 and August 8, less than a fortnight, was there anyone in France whose life had not been turned upside down?[16] I'm sure you want to know what we plan to do next, but we haven't made any definite decisions. We think we'll remain here for another three weeks or so. We would like to visit Boston, then, after coming back, to set out for a little town 100 leagues northwest of New York called Auburn, which is the site of a very famous penitentiary.[17] In this land, there is incredible contempt for distances. The immense rivers, some of which we've seen meeting the sea, and the canals built to connect them make it possible to travel day and night at 4 leagues an hour, on boats as commodious as houses, with no bumps or relays. Thus, people do not say that one is 100 leagues away from one's destination, but 25 hours.

My first letter went to father on the Liverpool packet, which I was sure would be the quickest, most reliable carrier. I hate to think of you anguished by our long silence and hope that M. Hottinguer has reassured you.[18] May this be a lesson to you: whatever is said about the ease with which one now crosses the ocean, it is still an enterprise fraught with imponderables. One cannot fix its duration. And besides, if a letter should miss the packet, there will be a further delay of two or three weeks, or sometimes a month.

Here I am at the end of this immense letter. I could relate many other things, for we are all eyes and ears. Eventually I shall relate them, little by little. Tell Papa, Bébé, my brothers and sisters that although the letter is not

16. On July 26, the Bourbon monarchy issued its last edicts. A revolutionary uprising followed on July 27–29, known as "Les Trois Glorieuses." On August 8, Louis-Philippe acceded to the throne as a constitutional monarch. Tocqueville's father, who had been an important prefect during the Restoration, lost his post and his seat in the Chamber of Peers. Unemployment was rife. Riots continued to break out in major cities, often resulting in the destruction of church property.

17. The penal system at Auburn required inmates to work in common during the day and live isolated from one another at night.

18. Jean-Conrad Hottinguer was a prominent French banker of Swiss origin, the cofounder of France's first savings bank, the Caisse d'Épargne et de Prévoyance.

addressed to them, I had them in mind when writing it, that I think of them incessantly, that nothing in life will make me happier than clasping all of you to my bosom.

Good-bye, my good mother. I have not yet forgotten your parting recommendation, and never shall, I hope. Beaumont almost cried when he read what Bébé wrote in the book he gave me and has asked me to tell him that he will never forget the sentence at the end, which refers to both of us.

Please keep this letter. It contains details I haven't had time to note and with which I shall take pleasure revisiting at a later date.

I've folded it peculiarly in order to include one to Louis de Kergorlay; I don't know his whereabouts and am afraid my letter might go astray. Be so kind as to have it handed to him in Paris or posted out of town, if you know his address.

New York, May 28, 1831

To his brother Édouard,

I thank you, my dear friend, for the letter that crossed on the April 15 packet. You know how precious your communications are to me, and especially one that comes from so far away. You are, as I said to Alexandrine, more present in our mind than what we see every day. Do not fail, therefore, to write us long, very detailed letters whenever the opportunity presents itself. It's the surest way of making us happy. Moreover, you can well believe that in our present state, we want to know more about French politics than we extract from newspapers. The latest reports bode well for the preservation of peace. I hope to God that they are right. Our last French paper dates to April 15, when government securities were rising, the Austrians were evacuating the Papal territories, and the ministry seemed to be growing stronger, although the language of the press was quite violent, and there is still mayhem in the streets. Yesterday we received the April 24 issue of English papers; we learned, to our utter astonishment, that the Chamber of Deputies was *suspended* and not *dissolved*. This measure took us completely by surprise and, insofar as one can judge such matters from abroad, I do not consider it wise. It seems clear to me that the present Chamber does not sway public opinion in the least, and that newspapers, by exploiting the legitimate case to be made against it, will lose no time casting discredit on the very *moderation* that this Chamber represents.

The radical press will step backward the better to spring forward. I believe that there has never been a more propitious time for elections than now: everything points to the disadvantages of anarchy, and the lower classes are more fearful of disorder than of the privileges enjoyed by the upper crust.

But I recur to what I said above, that it is impossible to judge from afar. I am anxious to know the language of French papers; they must be gushing over the top. Apparently, England hasn't fared brilliantly either. The whole nation is embroiled in a terrific struggle, and there's no telling where the movement will stop.[19]

Here we are truly in another world. Political passions are only superficial. The one passion that runs deep, the only one that stirs the human heart day in and day out, is the acquisition of wealth, and there are a thousand ways of acquiring it without importuning the State. To draw comparisons between this country and Europe and to entertain the idea of adapting to one what works for the other is blindness, in my opinion. I thought so before leaving France; I am confirmed in that belief the more I examine the society in the midst of which I now find myself. This is a world of merchants who give some thought to public affairs only when their work affords them the leisure to do so. By the time we return to Europe, we will, I hope, have acquired all we need to address this subject knowledgeably: no one is better set up for the study of the American people than we are. Our mission and our letters open all doors; we rub shoulders with all classes; all possible documents are furnished on demand; we have come for only one reason, to accomplish a serious goal. Our minds are constantly straining for the acquisition of useful knowledge; it is an immense labor, but not at all painful because ideas are entering us through every pore and as many of them in a salon or on a walk as in the privacy of our study.

But will we have enough time to bring this enterprise to fruition? One need not be clairvoyant to foresee events that may call us home. We ponder that every day, and the thought often leaves us momentarily disgruntled with our labors.

My dear friend, I must ask a favor of you and beg you to do it as soon as possible, though it will put you to some inconvenience. Among other things that are exorbitantly expensive in this country are gloves and articles of silk. Ballroom gloves that cost 45 sous in Paris cost six francs here and are shoddy. Since we are forever attending social functions and will be even

19. The movement to which Tocqueville alludes led to the Reform Act of 1832 and fundamental changes in the electoral system of the United Kingdom.

more sociable this winter, you can imagine that we would be ruining ourselves if we had to purchase new gloves every two or three days. We shall be saving money by having them sent from Paris, despite the postage and custom duties. What I need are two dozen yellow kid gloves, the best possible, and half-a-dozen brown wool gloves. Please include a pair of silk openwork stockings for evening wear and one or two black silk neck cloths. Here, black neck cloths are worn at soirées.

Beaumont will enlarge upon what he would like, and Monsieur Hagdé will give you money for his purchases. You would pack everything in a tight little case and send it to me in New York—I'm not entirely sure how, but it should be easy. As for my hand measurement, you will certainly find some old gloves in my room, and in any event, our hands are almost identical. As for Beaumont, he claims that if you go to his haberdasher in the Palais Royal, Chez Irlande, the *demoiselle* on duty knows his hand perfectly well. Of course, you would send this package only if the state of affairs in Europe should lead you to believe that our sojourn in America will not be cut short.

Adieu, my good friend; I embrace you lovingly and swear that not a day passes without my thinking about you, your wife, or your daughter. I am handing my pen over to B.

Sing Sing, June 3, 1831

To his father,

You will never guess, my dear father, where on earth I have ensconced myself to write this letter. I sit at the top of a rather steep hill. In the foreground, one hundred paces below me, is a country house, where we lodge. Beyond it, the hill slopes down to the Hudson. More than a league wide[20] and covered with sails, the great river runs north into a range of high blue mountains and disappears. Its banks are a scene of bustle and prosperity delightful to observe. And overhead is an admirable sun whose rays, filtering through the humid atmosphere of the region, bathe everything they touch in soft, transparent light. You may infer from this lengthy description that its author has a panoramic perspective. Indeed he does, for an enormous sycamore shades the summit of my hill, which rises higher than others round about, and I am perched in its branches to avoid the heat. That is where I am writing to you. You see how well I mesh with the landscape.

20. Tocqueville states "five quarter leagues," or more than three and one-quarter miles.

Now I must tell you where we are, and why we have come. Sing Sing, thus named after an Indian chief who lived here sixty years ago but whose tribe has since retreated further inland, lies on the Hudson 11 leagues north of New York. The town has 1,000 or 1,200 inhabitants. Its famous prison, the largest in the land, houses 900 inmates and abides by the American penal system, which it is our mission to study in depth. We have been here a week already and feel an extraordinary sense of well-being. The hectic life we were obliged to live in New York, the number of visits we made and received every day began to tire us. Here our days are at once blissfully serene and well employed. We live with a respectable American family, who show us every possible courtesy. We have made the acquaintance of several villagers whom we shall see again when we are free to do so. The rest of our time is spent in visiting the prison, in taking notes and collecting all the practical ideas that the penal system can provide. The alacrity with which government agents supply every kind of document we may require makes our task much easier. Unfortunately not everything has been documented. Broadly speaking, I would say that, where administration is concerned, this country and France have gone off the edge, but in opposite directions. While among us, government meddles in everything, here there is not, or appears not to be, any government at all. Alike the virtues and defects of centralization are seemingly unknown; there is no mainspring regulating the machine's moving parts, with the result that in many specific ways overall performance cannot be judged. One issue of paramount importance is recidivism. There are no records that would help us determine satisfactorily the number of convicts reformed by prison life. You will appreciate that for us such information is vital.

Our impression of the prisons we have visited makes a very long story. I'd rather not launch into it with you, lest you conclude that our eyes are fastened to the penal system and to nothing else in America. That is not the case, I assure you; on the contrary, our time here is employed in many different occupations, which may be why it seems to be slipping away so terribly fast. I believe that even if we don't produce something acceptable about the United States, we shall not have wasted our time by devoting ourselves to the study we have undertaken. Our one aim since we've come here has been to comprehend the land we are exploring. We cannot accomplish that goal unless we disassemble society *a priori* and identify the elements that constitute it in France so as to pose questions useful for an understanding of America. The enterprise is difficult but alluring: it has enabled us to discern a great many details that go unseen when one doesn't analyze the mass and suggests any number of practical ideas that would not otherwise have crossed our minds. Knowing as we do exactly what we want to ask, the most humble conversation is instructive, and I daresay no man, whatever his social rank, is incapable of teaching us something.

This life, which is a boil of physical and intellectual activity, would make us quite happy were it not for the chasm that separates us from France. The thought of your remoteness spoils everything. I have said it already, dear father, but I feel compelled to repeat myself—living so far from those one loves is being only half alive. Given our cerebral existence, in which the heart counts for little, I despair of conceiving anything but arid impressions.

Since we are now little more than "probing machines," you will perhaps ask me, dear father, what we find most noteworthy in this land. I would need a volume to tell you everything. Or to tell you what I think today. Tomorrow I may no longer agree with myself, for we are definitely not systematizers. Among ideas that preoccupy me, two bulk large, the first being that this population is one of the happiest in the world, the second that it owes its immense prosperity less to its characteristic virtues, and even less to a form of government intrinsically superior to all others, than to its peculiar conditions, which result in perfect accord between its political constitution and its needs and social state. This may sound a bit metaphysical, but you will understand better what I mean when I observe, for example, that nature provides so well for human industry that there is no class of theoretical speculators. Everyone works, and the vein is still so rich that all who work it succeed rapidly in gaining the wherewithal to achieve contentment. Here, the most active minds, like the most tranquil characters, have no void in their lives to fill by troubling the State. Restlessness, which harrows our European societies, seems to abet the prosperity of this one. Wealth is the common lure, and a thousand roads lead to it. Politics therefore occupies only a small corner of the canvas. I have no doubt that it does more stirring up in the most ostensibly peaceful European state than in the entire American confederation. No newspaper, among those we read every day, devotes as much space to matters of general import affecting government as to the price of cotton. What space remains is monopolized by discussions of local interest, which feed public curiosity without in any way causing social turmoil.

To resume, the more I see of this land, the more convinced I am of this truth, that there are virtually no political institutions radically good or bad in themselves, and that everything depends on the physical conditions and social state of the people to whom they are applied. I see certain institutions work here that would predictably work havoc in France; while others that suit us would have evil effects in America. And yet, unless I'm sadly mistaken, man is not different or better on one side of the Atlantic than on the other. He is just differently placed. At some later date I shall tell you what strikes me in the American character.

Right now, I bear a strong resemblance to "Master Crow, perched in a tree," don't you think?[21] On that note I shall finish my oration. I am so *snug* on my branch that I run the risk of falling asleep—in which case I might, like my friend Robinson Crusoe, shout "My dear parents!" and wake up on the ground. I have therefore decided to climb down. I shall finish the letter tomorrow.

Auburn, New York, July 17, 1831

To his mother,

Here I am almost 80 leagues farther from you than a fortnight ago, my dear Mama; I detest the thought that letters take three days more to reach us. Letters being an integral part of our existence now, we are highly sensitive to the least delay. Would you believe that we have not yet received mail sent on June 1? It's been more than three weeks since we've seen anything in your hand; I assure you that we are very far from inuring ourselves to this silence.

We left New York on June 28. Our voyage began on a distinctly sour note. The steamboat we boarded that evening was to sail up the North River and stop at West Point. West Point, which figured importantly in the American war, is not only an historical landmark of note but one of the country's most picturesque sites. We counted on arriving at night and spending a day there. Well, in mid-voyage we learned that our boat would go straight to Albany. We were thus in the position of a man who, having taken the wrong diligence, travels to Rouen rather than Compiègne, except of course that one can get off a diligence en route. We could only resign ourselves to our fate. And West Point was not the only omission. As the boat sailed at night and reached the city of Albany at 5 in the morning, all the spectacular scenery of the river passed us by.

There our misfortunes ended, and the trip became most agreeable. We remained three or four days in Albany, to cull the statistical documents we needed from the central government of the state of New York. I think we'll need a crate for all the notes, books, and pamphlets swamping us.

21. The first line of La Fontaine's fable, based on Aesop's "The Fox and the Crow."

We attended the July 4 ceremony in Albany. July 4 is the anniversary of the Declaration of Independence, and Americans hold a parade and religious ceremony to commemorate the event. Shall I describe this parade, which we followed for two hours under a splendid sun? I'd rather describe our visit with the Quaking Shakers.

The Shakers are a kind of religious community of men and women who farm in common, take a vow of celibacy, and have no private property. One of their establishments lies in the middle of the woods three leagues from Albany. We arrived there on Sunday, at around 10, and immediately went to the temple, which is just a large room, very neat, with no altar or anything to suggest the idea of religious observance. After half-an-hour, two groups of Shakers, male and female, entered the room by different doors. Men formed up at one end, women at the other. The men wore what looked rather like the stock costume of our playhouse peasants: white shirts with flowing sleeves; grey, wide-brimmed felt hats; loose-fitting vests with pockets. Their attire was all purple, but for the shirts, and almost new. The women wore white. They ranged from very old to very young, from ugly to comely. The very old sat up front, the young behind them; and men arrayed themselves likewise. These groups faced each other wordlessly, waiting for inspiration; when, after five minutes of total silence, one man felt the spirit rise in him, he stood and gave a long, rambling talk about the religious and moral obligations of Shakers. The groups then launched into an earsplitting rendition of the shrillest song I've ever heard. Especially fervent members nodded the beat, which gave them somewhat the appearance of those porcelain Chinese figures with tilted heads on our grandmothers' mantelpieces. Until then the ceremony was no more exotic than a Jewish Sabbath. But once the singing was over, the two groups merged into one line. Five men and as many women backed up against the wall and began to sing something in a lively, impetuous rhythm. At this, men and women, young and old began to caper breathlessly. The sight of old folks with white hair keeping up with the others despite the heat and their exhaustion might have been droll if it weren't pitiful. From time to time, the dancers clapped their hands. Picture Frenchmen romping in the Dunkirk Carillon, and you will get a good idea of this event.[22] When the dance stopped momentarily, one member

22. Dating to the fifteenth century, when the belfry of Saint-Éloi in Dunkirk acquired its bells, the "Dunkirk Carillon" was the most boisterous of French country dances.

of the congregation improvised as best he could a short religious speech; the dancing then resumed, only to stop time and again for more sermonizing. Among Shakers, there is no priesthood: anyone can say what he or she thinks appropriate. After almost two hours of this frightful exercise, they placed themselves two by two in a circle, men and women together. They then pressed their elbows to their sides, extended their forearms and let their hands dangle, like the front paws of trained dogs forced to walk on their hind legs. In this posture they intoned an air more lugubrious than all the others, began to walk all around the room, and continued thus for a good quarter-hour. One of them made a little speech explaining that the Shaker sect was the only path to salvation and admonishing us to convert, whereupon the community withdrew in perfect order and silence. I suppose the poor devils had to rest. But just imagine, dear Mama, what queer byways the human mind can take when left to its own compass! There was a young American Protestant with us, who said afterward: "Two more spectacles like that one and I'll become a Catholic."

We quit Albany on one of this country's diligences, which are called *Stages*. They are carriages suspended on nothing but leather straps and driven at a fast trot on roads as deplorable as those in Lower Brittany. One feels quite rattled after a few miles. But the new scenery took our minds off our physical discomfort. It was our first venture into America's hinterland; until then we had seen only the seacoast and the banks of the Hudson. Everything here was quite different. I believe that in one of my letters I complained of finding almost no more woodland in America; I must now make honorable amends. Not only does one find wood and woods in America, but the whole country is still a vast forest with man-made clearings here and there. From atop a church steeple, one sees trees as far as the eye can reach swaying in the wind like waves of the sea: everything bespeaks newness. Settlers establish farms by cutting down trees to within three feet of the ground. Soil is tilled between the stumps, and eventually crops grow up around them. They pock the fields of grain. What is more, wild plants continue to germinate in soil cultivated this way, with the result that every plot is a confusion of wheat stalks, saplings, tall grass, and creepers. Men forever struggle against the forest in a contest from which they don't always emerge the victor.

But if the country is new, one observes at every turn that those who have come to inhabit it are of old stock. When, after traveling on a rough road and crossing a kind of wilderness, one reaches a farmhouse, one is amazed at encountering more evidence of civilization than one would find in any

French village. The farmer is neatly dressed; his dwelling is perfectly clean; there is usually a newspaper near to hand; and his first subject of conversation is politics. I can't remember where it was—in which obscure, unknown corner of the universe—that one such farmer asked us in what condition we had left France; how we viewed the relative strength of parties; and so forth. A thousand questions, to which I replied as best I could while laughing to myself over the incongruity of the questioner and the place of our interview. The territory we have just crossed was formerly inhabited by the Confederation of Iroquois, about which so much has been heard in the world. We met the last of them during our passage; they go begging and are as inoffensive as their forefathers were fearsome.

We occupy rooms in a magnificent hotel at Auburn, a town of 2,000 souls, all of whose houses are well-stocked shops. Auburn, where, twenty years ago, people were frequently off hunting bear and deer, is now the hub of intense commercial traffic. I'm almost accustomed to this phenomenon of society growing like rank vegetation. I surprise myself speaking as Americans do and calling some establishment very old when it's been in existence for thirty years.

Adieu, dear mother, and all my love. Embrace my father for me and the good abbé. Pass this letter on to Édouard's household, and tell them that I shall write soon. Give my news to Hippolyte. We are leading a life so fraught, so ridden with tasks, that I can't really produce more than one letter at a time.

On Lake Ontario, August 21, 1831

To his mother,

When I was on Lake Ontario, dear mother, I wrote a letter to my father, who must have told you about the voyage we improvised during the first fortnight of this month. At Buffalo, your letters of last May 27 awaited us and, despite their date, gave us indescribable pleasure. I had gone so long without seeing anything of my family's script. I can tell you how touched I am, dear mother, at receiving mail from you in each delivery. I am aware that writing tires you, which makes your letters all the more precious to me. Also, thank the entire household on my behalf.

After an hour in Buffalo, we headed for Niagara. We could already hear the falls two leagues before reaching them. They sounded like distant thunder, and in fact Niagara is an Indian word that means "thunder of the waters." I find the expression wonderfully apt. (Indian languages are full of images far more poetic than our own.) We advanced toward the noise, unable to imagine how close we were to its source.

Indeed, nothing prepares one for the spectacle. A large river (which is only Lake Erie brimming over) slowly flows across flatland. The terrain remains featureless right up to the cataract itself. We arrived toward dusk and postponed our first visit until morning. August 18 dawned a splendid day, and we set out early. I will unavoidably wax pathetic in describing what we witnessed. I believe that the falls surpass everything said and written about them at home; they surpass anything one's imagination conjures up beforehand. The river divides as it nears the abyss and forms two falls separated by a small island. The broader is shaped like a horseshoe a quarter of a league in width, which is to say more than two times wider than the Seine. When the river arrives, it spills over the edge to a depth of 149 feet. Vapor rises from the bottom like a cloud, with an enormous rainbow framed against it. One can clamber quite easily to the tip of a rocky spur that juts toward the falls. Nothing equals the sublimity of the view one has out there, especially at night, when the bottom of the abyss disappears and the rainbow is moonlit. I had never seen a nocturnal rainbow. It is much the same as the diurnal, but perfectly white. It arched from one bank to the other. About the cataract: walking behind that curtain of water strikes one at first as a dangerous maneuver, but it turns out not to be. We took perhaps one hundred steps before the cliff wall bellied in front of us. Now and again a sun- or moonbeam penetrates the deep, dreadful darkness of the place, everything suddenly becomes visible, and one feels that the whole river is crashing down on one's head. It's hard to convey the exact impression produced by this shaft of light; after allowing you to glimpse the vast chaos all around, it delivers you again to the shadows and din of the waterfall. We remained at Niagara for a full day. Yesterday we set sail on Lake Ontario.

This account of the wonder that filled us at Niagara may lead you to a false conclusion about our state of mind. Far from being tranquil and happy, I have fallen prey to deeper melancholy. At Buffalo, I found news of Europe and France in various newspapers. From the many small circumstances they report, I form the picture of a country in crisis and of civil war itself looming near, with all the danger that that presents for those I hold dearest. . . . These images interpose themselves between me and everything I set eyes upon, and I cannot, without a profound sense of something very like shame stand in awe of these American falls, knowing that the fate of so many people hangs in the balance.

Aboard *The Fourth of July*, November 26, 1831

To his brother Édouard,

I begin this letter, dear brother, aboard the steamer taking us from Pittsburgh to Cincinnati. I shan't finish and date it until I arrive at the latter city in a few days. Right now we are on the Ohio River, which is already as wide as the Seine at Paris, though still quite some distance from its juncture with the Mississippi.

What I see are the world's most beautiful mountains. Unfortunately, they are covered in snow, for winter has finally reached us. We encountered it in the middle of the Alleghenies, and it has stayed with us ever since. But we are fleeing it, and a week from now it will no longer present a threat. Pittsburgh is the former Fort Duquesne. There was real genius in the way Frenchmen situated their military outposts here, before the war of 1754. When the interior of the North American continent was still terra incognita to Europeans, the French established bases in the middle of the wilderness, from Canada to Louisiana—a string of small forts which, now that the country has been mapped to a fare-thee-well, are recognized as ideal sites for cities whose fortunes depend upon their ability to attract commerce and command the navigation of rivers. Here, as in many other circumstances, we worked for the English, who profited from a vast scheme of our devising. If we had succeeded, the English colonies would have been hemmed in by an immense arc, with Quebec and New Orleans its two extremities. The French and their Indian allies would have been at their back, and Americans of the United States would not have rebelled against the mother country. They all recognize this. There would not have been an American revolution, and perhaps not a French one, or not the revolution that played out as it did.

The French of America possessed within themselves all the resources to be a great people. They are still the finest offspring of the European family in the New World. But, overwhelmed by numbers, they were bound to succumb. Their abandonment is one of the most dishonorable episodes of Louis XV's inglorious reign.

I have just seen in Canada a million brave, intelligent French, made to constitute one day a great French nation in America, who live rather like strangers in their own land. The conquerors control commerce, employment, wealth, power. They populate the upper classes and dominate all of society. The vanquished, wherever they don't enjoy decisive numerical superiority, are day by day losing their customs, their language, their national character. There you have the effects of conquest, or rather, of desertion.

Today the die is cast: all of North America will speak English. But aren't you struck by men's inability to foresee the ripples of a present-day event, to sense the eternal danger of regretting or rejoicing without discernment? When the Battle of the Plains of Abraham, the death of Montcalm and the shameful treaty of 1763 placed England in possession of Canada and of a country bigger than all of Europe, which formerly belonged to France, the English exulted almost fulsomely. Neither the nation nor its greatest men suspected then that, by reason of this conquest, the colonies, no longer dependent upon the mother country's support, would aspire to independence, that independence would be a fait accompli twenty years later, with England in economic tatters after a disastrous war and facing an immense new nation on the American continent, English-speaking but her natural enemy, almost certainly destined to usurp her lordship of the seas.

On the Ohio River, November 28, 1831

To his sister-in-law Émilie,

I would like to write to your husband, dear sister, but I don't know where my letter would find him. The last news from France suggests to me that he has undertaken a long voyage of necessarily indeterminate length. You know that I have never approved of such capers; they seem to me useless at best; but at a distance of 2,000 leagues from one's friends, one is not well placed to offer advice—it would arrive after the event. I can therefore only confine myself, limply, to hoping that all turns out for the best.[23]

You know, dear sister, that we have revised our travel plans and will probably be back in France sometime during the month of April. I trust that you will understand all the considerations that have led us to shorten our sojourn in America and that you will not greet us with a sour face. The truth is, it would be unfair, in the first place because we have acted for the best, and secondly because we shall be so happy to see you again that a less than joyful response from you would be sheer ingratitude. The day I set foot on French soil again will be a beautiful day indeed. You who *live in the country* have no idea what it's worth; on the contrary, speaking poorly of it is one of your favorite occupations—I can attest to that, having heard you deliver long tirades against it. Well, I believe that a voyage abroad would change

---

23. Tocqueville is referring to plans for a royalist uprising in Brittany, associated with the clandestine return of King Charles X's exiled daughter-in-law, the Duchesse de Berri.

your opinion. I've already *knocked around* this world quite a lot. I've encountered people in different positions, but nothing of what I've seen proves to me that any other nation is fundamentally better off than we. Here, for example, I observe a marginal display of all the nasty political passions that come so glaringly to light during our revolutions. But I shall stop there, for fear of *falling* into lofty political, philosophical, metaphysical, economic, and moral considerations from which I could not extract myself before putting you to sleep. I was saying that America is not worthier than France. The example I shall adduce is *the fair sex*, to use the language of madrigals. I confess that from a certain point of view, this land is the El Dorado of husbands; one can almost certainly find perfect happiness in it, provided one totally lacks romantic imagination and asks of one's wife only that she prepare tea and raise one's children—the sovereign duties of conjugal life, as we know. In these matters, American women excel. They are reasonable people, eminently *reliable*, as they say, who confine themselves to their teapots and stay indoors once they've pronounced the famous "yes." I grant that this is an undeniable advantage. Despite it, however, I often find myself wondering whether, at bottom—note well the "at bottom"—there isn't a prodigiously close resemblance to European women. Don't regard me as a peevish philosopher disappointed in love, I beg of you, but listen to my reasons. I shall enumerate them. My first and principal reason is that they are all, before they become wives, consummate flirts. Properly speaking, love plays no part in this, which makes for a tranquil society. I have not heard about a single drowning or hanging in the entire Union since the Declaration of Independence: people don't fight or throw fits. Young women are perfectly free to choose, and their choice is always the swain whom the family notary would have recommended, if consulted. You see that I am impartial; if they are outrageously flirtatious, I note that they are *reasonably* so, as they never fail to set their cap at men who, quite apart from their social rank (an advantage often much exaggerated in Europe), are in easy circumstances. This reflects honorably upon their rectitude. But it remains to be understood how such perfect domesticity is accomplished, how these women cease to be coquettes from one day to the next. How does one explain a change so sudden and punctual? If it occurred once, by chance, I would believe in a miracle, but when it repeats itself every day, I am confounded. Might one suspect, might it not be possible to imagine, might we not have some reason to think— you see how circumspect and suitably dubitative I am—that the cure is only apparent and that the coquetry still exists, though unable to display itself? The fact is, and this has been remarked by all travelers, that married women in America are almost all weak and languishing. For myself, I am tempted to believe that they are ill of repressed coquetry. Why not? Isn't it commonplace to see men green around the gills with repressed ambition? Let it be said that this is pure conjecture, and I don't attach great value to it. But even so, it's already enough to prove that, all things considered, one is better off living in France than in America.

I don't know how I can have the courage to talk such silliness with you, dear sister. One should refrain from writing frivolous letters when one is 2,000 leagues from home; by the time my chuckles reach Europe, you may be in tears over something. This thought haunts me. I never laugh wholeheartedly here, always fearing that at that very moment a terrible misfortune has struck me on the other side of the world. It is also true that the world has never seen a family like ours: a collection of old crocks worse than any found in a hospital. I have yet to receive, in the past eight months, a single letter that contains this one little phrase: "Everyone is faring well." Yet I don't think they were laying it on too thick in portraying their decrepitude.

When I arrived here, dear sister, I found one of those letters from you only you can write, testifying so lavishly to your affection for me. Although our friendship already goes back quite some time, that testimony gives me as much pleasure now as when I first received it. One of the things I most regret about not being in France is being unable, at difficult moments, to offer your husband my advice, and to offer all of you the services that warm friendship can render. But patience! I shall soon be home, and we must hope that we are not yet done with revolutions, so that, in another one, we may regain what we've lost. I am going to address this letter to Nacqueville once again and hope that it succeeds better than the last in reaching you. How wise of you to love Nacqueville! At the present time, one cannot do better, I believe, than to stay put there quietly and await *one's day*.

Adieu, dear sister, I embrace you with both arms and all my heart.

Memphis, December 20, 1831

To his father,

The place from which I write, my dear father, may not be on your map. Memphis is a very small town on the banks of the Mississippi, at the far southwestern edge of the state of Tennessee. We've been here for several days. By what chance, you ask, are we in Memphis rather than in New Orleans? Therein lies a long, pitiful tale, which I shall attempt to relate as succinctly as possible. I wrote my last letter to you when I was sailing down the Ohio and about to arrive at Louisville. There I expected to find a steam-boat ready to make the six- or seven-day voyage to New Orleans. But during the night of December 4–5, the temperature, which was already low, fell so precipitously that the Ohio, despite its strong currents and its width, froze, trapping us in ice. You should know that Louisville is in the same latitude as Sicily. It doesn't often freeze there, to say the least, and no one could remember ever experiencing such cold before the end of January. That's what I call *good luck!* In any event, we managed to get ashore, where we learned that Louisville was 9 leagues distant. A local frontiersman, a big bruiser, offered to transport our trunks to the port in his cart. Our travel-ing companions, who numbered ten, did the same as we, and off we went, on foot, across mountains and woods that had never, since the beginning of time, been visited by a loaded wagon. It rolled, thanks to the audacity of our driver and to some strong shoulders occasionally put to the task. But we were marching in snow knee high. The journey became so strenu-ous that our companions began to drift off, one after another. We, on the other hand, persevered and finally arrived at Louisville toward nine in the evening. The following day we learned that the Ohio was frozen solid, that we would have to establish winter quarters in Louisville or turn back. But there was another alternative. At a small town called Memphis on the banks of the Mississippi in the state of Tennessee, all steamboats plying the river replenish their store of wood. We were told that if we found our way there, we could surely resume our journey waterborne, since the Mississippi never freezes. Because this information was conveyed by eminently credible peo-ple, we acted on it straightaway and left Louisville for Memphis. These two cities lie about 150 leagues apart; we had to travel that distance on the most abominable roads, in the most infernal carriages and, above all, the most dreadful cold imaginable—the natural order seemed to have been upset for our particular discomfort. Tennessee is in about the same latitude as the Sahara Desert. Cotton is raised there, as well as other exotic plants, and when we crossed the state, it was 15 degrees below freezing; no one had ever seen anything like it.[24] Finally arriving at Memphis, we learned that several miles upriver, the Mississippi itself was unnavigable; one could see icebound steamboats sitting as motionless as rocks. We must now plan ahead. If, after several days, this freakish cold doesn't let up, we shall forego our voyage to the South and make for Washington by the shortest route possible. I will say

24. Celsius –15 degrees is +5 degrees on the Fahrenheit scale.

this: apart from the frustration of having our projects more or less thwarted (through no fault of our own), we do not regret our trip through the forests of Kentucky and Tennessee. We acquainted ourselves there with a breed of humanity and a way of life completely unknown to us. The only inhabitants of that region are men called Virginians. They have preserved a moral and physical identity all their own; they are a people apart, with national prejudices and a distinctive character. There, for the first time, we had the opportunity to observe the social consequences of slavery. The right [north] bank of the Ohio is a scene of animation and industry; work is honored, no one owns slaves. But cross the river, and you suddenly find yourself in another universe. Gone is the spirit of enterprise. Work is considered not only onerous but shameful: whoever engages in it degrades himself. The White Man is meant to ride horseback, to hunt, to smoke all day long; using one's hands is what a slave does. South of the Ohio, Whites form a veritable aristocracy which, like every other, marries low prejudices to lofty instincts. It is said—and I am much inclined to believe it—that these men are incomparably more sensitive to issues of honor than their counterparts up North. They are straightforward, hospitable, and value many things higher than money. They will end up being dominated by the North, however. The latter grows richer and more populous by the day, while the South, if it grows at all, grows poorer. Inhabitants of Kentucky and Tennessee live scattered in vast forests and deep valleys. It was there, one evening after a long day, that we happened upon a log cabin with chinks on every side through which a big fire could be seen crackling. We knocked. Two mongrels, as tall as donkeys, rushed to the door. Their master followed, roughly shook hands with us, and invited us to enter. Picture a fireplace half the width of the room, in which a whole tree was burning; a bed; a few chairs; a six-foot-long carbine; a hunter's accoutrements hanging on the log wall and dancing in the draught. The mistress of the house sat near the hearth, with that quiet, modest air so characteristic of American women, while four or five robust children were frolicking on the floor, in light summer clothes. Sitting on their haunches under the mantelpiece of the chimney were two or three Negroes who looked as if they had been shivering ever since Africa. Our gentleman played the host nonetheless easily and courteously for his house being a hovel. He hardly stirred, mind you, but the poor Blacks served us at his behest: one presented us glasses of whisky, and another corncakes and a plate of venison. The third was sent off to fetch more wood. The first time I heard this order given, I assumed that he was going to the cellar or a woodpile; no, the blows of an ax echoing in the woods soon informed me that a tree was being felled for our benefit. That is how things are normally done here. While the slaves were thus occupied, the master, quietly seated in front of a fire that could have roasted an ox down to its bones, majestically wrapped himself in a cloud of smoke and between each puff entertained his guests with an account of his most memorable feats as a hunter.

I must recount one more little anecdote, which will tell you at what price a man's life is held here when he is unlucky enough to have black skin. About a week ago we faced the Tennessee River. The only means of crossing was a paddle steamer operated by two slaves with a horse. We ourselves made it over, but since the river was full of drift-ice the master hesitated to transport the carriage. "Rest assured," one of our traveling companions said, "that should the boat sink, we will compensate you for your horse and slaves." This argument seemed irresistible: the carriage was loaded, and sailed across.

On the Mississippi, December 25, 1831

To his mother,

At last, at last, my dear Mama, the signal is given, and here we are cruising down the Mississippi, as rapidly as possible under the combined influence of steam and a strong current. We were beginning to despair of ever escaping the wilderness. If you take the trouble to examine your map, you will see that we had reached a pretty pass. In front of us, the Mississippi half frozen and no boats launching; overhead, a Russian sky, pure and frozen. We could have retraced our steps, you say. But that option was fast disappearing. During our sojourn in Memphis, the Tennessee had frozen, and carriages could no longer cross. So there we were, in the middle of a triangle formed by the Mississippi, the Tennessee, and impenetrable backwoods to the south. We might as well have been marooned on a rock in mid-ocean, inhabiting a world made expressly for us, without papers, without news of the rest of mankind, and facing the prospect of a long winter. That is how we spent a week. I must say, however, that except for our anxiety, those days were not disagreeable. We were staying with good people, who did their utmost to ingratiate themselves. Only twenty paces from our house was the edge of the world's most beautiful forest, a sublime place, picturesque even under snow. We had rifles and plenty of powder and lead. A few miles from the village lived an Indian nation, the Chikasaws; once on their land, we always found a few natives happy to join us in the hunt. Hunting and warring are the sole occupations of the Indian, his pleasures as well. For large game we would have had to go too far afield. Instead, we killed a great many

pretty birds of a species unknown in France. We found this highly diverting, though it didn't do us much credit in the eyes of our allies. I killed
red, blue, yellow birds, including parrots with plumage more brilliant than
any I had ever seen. That's how time passed, lightly at any given moment,
but with the future weighing upon us. At last, one fine day, we noticed a
wisp of smoke on the horizon, over the Mississippi; the wisp soon became
a cloud, out of which loomed not the giant or the dwarf of fairy tales, but
a large steamboat chugging up from New Orleans. It dilly-dallied in front
of us for a quarter hour, as if wanting to keep its intentions secret. Would
it stop, or continue on its way? Suddenly, it blew like a whale, made straight
for us, smashed the ice with its heavy hull, and docked. The whole population gathered at the riverbank, which, as you know, once formed the edge
of our empire. All of Memphis was astir; the bells weren't rung because
there aren't any, but the assembly shouted hurrahs! and the new arrivals
knelt down on the shore after the fashion of Christopher Columbus. We
weren't yet saved, however, for the captain had Louisville, north of us, as
his ultimate destination, while we had our sights set on New Orleans to the
south. Fortunately, there were about fifteen other derelicts not wanting to
make Memphis their winter quarters. We exerted collective pressure on
the captain. What did he think he could accomplish up the Mississippi? He
would unavoidably be halted by ice. The Tennessee, the Missouri, the Ohio
were frozen. We all swore we had witnessed the situation for ourselves. The
ice would not only stop his vessel but almost certainly damage it, or worse.
We had only his interest in mind—his rather than ours, of course . . . The
spirit of altruism lent so much color to our argument that the man began
to waver. Even so, I am convinced that he would still have gone forward,
but for a felicitous event, thanks to which we have not become citizens of
Memphis. As we were parleying on the riverbank, we heard an infernal
racket in the nearby forest: drumbeats, the neighing of horses, the barking
of dogs. At length, a large group of Indians emerged—old people, women,
children, with baggage—all led by a European, and came toward us. These
Indians were Chactas (or Tchactaws), to pronounce it as Indians do.[25] À
propos, I shall tell you that Monsieur de Chateaubriand behaved a little like
La Fontaine's ape; he didn't mistake the name of a port for that of a man,
but he gave a man the name of a powerful nation of the American South.
You would like to know, no doubt, what these Indians were doing there and

25. The appellation generally used today is Choctaw.

how they could serve us. Patience, I beg of you; since I have time and paper today, I don't want to hurry.

You will learn that the Americans of the United States, a rational people without prejudices, known for their great philanthropy, conceived the idea, like the Spanish before them, that God had bestowed upon them, as an unrestricted gift, the New World and its inhabitants.

And listen to this: it having been demonstrated that one square mile could nourish ten times more civilized men than savages, it followed logically that wherever civilized men settled, savages had to make way for them. What a splendid thing is logic. When the Indians found themselves a little too near their white brethren, the president of the United States sent them a message explaining that, in their own interest naturally, they would do well to retreat slightly westward.[26] The region they've inhabited for centuries belongs to them, no doubt: no one denies them this incontestable right. But it is, after all, uncultivated wilderness—woods, swamps, very poor land really. Beyond the Mississippi there is, on the contrary, splendid terrain which the European will never reach, where game have never been alarmed by the sound of a woodman's ax. Pioneers are separated from it by a hundred leagues. Throw in various gifts of inestimable value, calculated to buy the Indian's compliance: casks of whisky, glass-bead necklaces, earrings, and mirrors. What clinches the argument is the insinuation that if Americans meet with a refusal, force may be applied.

What to do? The poor Indians carry their old parents in their arms; mothers hoist their children onto their shoulders; the whole nation begins to march, taking their most cherished possessions with them. It abandons forever the soil on which its forefathers lived for a millennium perhaps and settles in a wilderness where the Whites will be harassing it ten years from now. Can you see what becomes of a high civilization? The Spanish are real brutes, unleashing their dogs on Indians as they would on ferocious beasts; they kill, burn, massacre, pillage the New World like an army storming a city, pitilessly and indiscriminately. But one cannot destroy everything; fury spends itself. Indian populations that survive end up mingling with their conquerors, adopting their customs, their religion; there are several provinces today in which they hold sway over those who subdued them in the

---

26. Tocqueville is referring to the Indian Removal Act, signed into law by Andrew Jackson in May 1830, which led to tens of thousands of Indians emigrating westward in what was described as "a trail of tears and death." It is estimated that 40 percent of the tribes died en route. The Choctaws were removed in 1831, the Chickasaws in 1837.

past. Americans of the United States, being more humane, more moderate, more respectful of law and legality, never bloodthirsty, are more profoundly destructive of the Indian people than Spaniards. And one cannot doubt that within a century there will no longer remain on the North American continent a single Indian nation, nor even a single man belonging to the most remarkable of Indian races. . . .

But I've left my story behind. I was writing about the Chactas, I believe. The Chactas form a powerful nation occupying the border country of Alabama and Georgia. This year, after protracted negotiations, they were persuaded to leave their homeland and emigrate to the west bank of the Mississippi. Six or seven thousand Indians have already crossed the great river; those appearing in Memphis came there with the intention of following their compatriots. The government agent who accompanied them, with authority to pay their passage, hurried to the riverbank upon hearing that a steamboat had arrived. The fee he offered for their transportation sixty leagues downriver fixed the wavering mind of the captain. He gave the signal to depart. The bow was turned south, and we cheerfully climbed aboard, passing passengers on their way down the gangway who, instead of going to Louisville, found themselves, poor souls, obliged to await the spring thaw in Memphis. So goes the world.

But we hadn't yet left; we had to board our exiled tribe, its horses and dogs. Here a truly lamentable scene unfolded. The Indians advanced mournfully toward the riverbank; first came the horses, several of which, unaccustomed as they were to the forms of civilized life, took fright and leaped into the Mississippi, from which they were rescued with difficulty. Then came the men, who, in the customary fashion, bore nothing but their weapons. The women followed, carrying children tied to their backs or swaddled in blankets; they were also loaded with bundles containing all their wealth. Last of all, the old people limped along, with help. Among the latter was a woman 110 years old. I have never seen such a horrifying figure. She was naked, except for a threadbare blanket revealing, here and there, the scrawniest body imaginable. She was escorted by two or three generations of grandchildren. Having to leave one's land at that age and seek one's fortune in a foreign country—what an abomination! Amidst the old people was a young woman who had broken her arm a week earlier; for lack of care, the arm had frozen beneath the fracture. She was obliged nonetheless to join the march. When everyone had passed, the dogs approached the bank but refused to go farther and protested with hair-raising yelps. Their masters dragged them aboard.

This whole spectacle had an air of ruin and destruction; it spoke of final farewells and of no turning back. One felt heartsick watching it. The Indians were calm, but somber and taciturn. One of them knew English, and I asked him why the Chactas were leaving their land. "To be free," he replied. I couldn't get anything else out of him. We shall deposit them tomorrow in the backcountry of Arkansas. One must admit, it was a singular chance that placed us in Memphis as witnesses to the expulsion, one might say the dissolution, of the remnants of one of the most celebrated and oldest American nations.

But enough about the savages. It is high time I returned to civilized folk. Just one more word about the Mississippi, which, in truth, hardly deserves more than that. It is a large, yellow river, gently rolling through the emptiest of unpeopled countrysides amidst the forests it floods in the spring and fertilizes with its muck. There is not a hill to be seen, only woods, more woods, yet more woods: reeds, vines; profound silence, no vestige of man, not even the smoke of an Indian camp.

Washington, January 24, 1832

To his father,

This letter, dear father, will perhaps be the last I write to you from America. Praise the Lord! We plan to sail on the 10th or 20th of February from New York; and thirty days being the average length of crossings, we shall arrive in France toward the 10th or 20th of March.

At this moment I am revolving many ideas about America. A fair number still reside in my head; I've scattered the seed of many more onto notepaper; others crop up in summaries of conversations I've had. All these raw scraps will be served up to you. You will not find them interesting in themselves but will judge whether something of value can be drawn from them. During the past six weeks of our journey, when my body was more tired and my mind more serene than it has been for a very long time, I have given much thought to what might be written about America. Drawing a complete picture of the Union would be an utterly impractical venture for someone who has spent only one year in this immense country. I believe, moreover, that the boredom of such a book would match its instructiveness. One might, on the contrary, by being selective, present only that which is pertinent to our own political and social state. The work would thus be both of permanent interest and of moment. There you have the general idea, but will I have the time and capacity needed to furnish it? That is the question. Something else preoccupies me: I shall write what I think or write nothing at all, while bearing in mind that wisdom does not want every truth aired. I hope that we shall be able to speak about all that at our leisure two months hence.

We have been here for a week and shall stay on until February 6. Our sojourn is useful and agreeable. Gathered in Washington at this moment are all the eminences of the entire Union. It remains for us only to elicit from them ideas about what we don't know, but in conversation we go over more or less familiar ground and concentrate on doubtful points. It's a very useful kind of counterproof. We are always treated with great respect and courtesy. Yesterday, the French minister introduced us to the President, whom we called "Mister" with perfect ease. He, in turn, greeted us in much the same way that he does his familiars, shaking our hands. He makes no distinctions among people. . . . A visit to Washington gives one some idea of how wonderfully well-equipped men are to calculate future events. Forty years ago, when choosing a capital for the Union became a matter of public concern, the first step, reasonably enough, was to decide upon the most favorable location. The place chosen was a vast plain along the banks of the Potomac. This wide, deep river bordering one end would bring European goods to the new city; fertile fields on the other side would keep markets well provisioned and nourish a large population. People assumed that in twenty years Washington would be the hub of the Union's internal and external commerce. It was bound, in due course, to have a million inhabitants. Anticipating this influx, the government began to raise public edifices and lay out enormously wide streets. Trees that might have impeded the construction of houses were felled by the acre. All this was nothing but the story of the milk-jug writ large:

> *Il était quand je l'eus de grosseur raisonnable.*
> *J'aurai. . . .* [27]

The farmer's wife and Congress reasoned in much the same way. The population didn't come; vessels did not sail up the Potomac. Today, Washington presents the image of an arid plain scorched by the sun, on which, scattered here and there, are two or three sumptuous edifices and five or six villages that constitute the city. Unless one is Alexander or Peter the Great, one should not get involved in creating the capital of an empire.

---

27. The verses are from La Fontaine's fable *La Laitiére et le Pot au Lait*, in which a farmer's wife balancing a jug of milk on her head as she walks to market daydreams about all that the sale will buy her: more chickens, a pig, a cow and her calf. She jumps for joy at the prospect and spills the milk. "[The pig], when I bought it was reasonably fat. / When the time comes to sell it . . ."

I've backed myself into such a corner that I don't have time to discuss the memoir you sent me. But I hope to be with you a week or ten days after this letter arrives, and I shall dilate upon the subject more satisfactorily than on paper. What I can do right now, my dear father, is thank you; your work sheds light on subtleties that help me understand the administration of this land. One's mind, as you know, is enlightened only by comparing one thing to another. Your memoir has already served as the basis for many very useful questions. You say in one of your letters to me, dear father, that you are counting on me to do something beneficial in this world; I desire it no less than you, dear father—even more for your sake, I swear, than for my own. Embrace Mama for me, and my brothers and sisters. May God preserve you all! The thought that henceforth I shall not take a step that doesn't bring us closer to one another makes me happy.

From America, [date undetermined]

To Mary ("Marie") Mottley,[28]

. . . And what would I reproach you for? For having introduced me to the only real happiness I've known in this world, for having enabled me to develop a great interest in existence, for having endured uncomplainingly the rough edge of my violent and autocratic character, for having subdued me with sweetness and tenderness. To my knowledge, those are the only reproaches I can summon. You have done still more for me, my beloved friend, another service I've kept for last. You have steered me away from a path that might have been my undoing. You have opened my eyes to what there is of nobility, generosity, and I daresay, of virtue in true love. It is my belief, I swear it, that my love for you has made me a better man. I love what is good more for love of you than for any other reason. The thought of you elevates my soul; I would like to make you proud of me and give you fresh proof every day that you were not mistaken in choosing me. Finally, I have never been more disposed to think of God, more convinced of the reality of another existence than when I think of you. You have been able to observe with what singular pleasure I converse with you about the gravest questions of life. You alone in the world, *without exception*, know how matters stand in the deepest recesses

28. Tocqueville met Mary Mottley in Versailles, where she and the unmarried aunt who had brought her up lived as members of an expatriate English colony. Born in 1801, she came from a naval family, her father having been bursar of the seaman's hospital at Gosport. Tocqueville married her in October 1835.

of my soul; you alone are acquainted with my instincts, my hopes, my doubts. If ever I become Christian, I believe that it will be through you. What I write here, Marie, is not an improvisation; these are thoughts long harbored . . .

Haven't you noticed, my tender friend, that we experienced our happiest moments when we spoke least. I have often thought that during those instants something happens that is said to happen after death: our two souls chime without having recourse to the senses. Each of us enjoyed his own happiness and the other's; our souls communicated sensations, sentiments, ideas a thousand times more swiftly than in words, and yet the most profound silence reigned between us. How can one understand such pleasures when one has never loved? How can one ever forget them once one has felt them? For myself, if I were unfortunate enough to die before seeing you again, dearest one, what I would miss most would not be the pleasures that attach most men to life, no, assuredly not, I would experience only one desperate regret: that of not being able to feel again this delicious tristesse of love, of no longer hearing that inner voice of the soul. I would miss not the joys of the world but the very sorrows of a loving heart and the soft sighs it cannot stifle.

I love you as I have never loved in my life. My reason and my heart are at one in adoring you. I wasn't suddenly taken captive: you won me gradually by revealing a little more of yourself each day. You conquered my soul, you made it yours; you now reign over it as absolute mistress. I love you as one cannot love at sixteen, and yet I feel, when I think of you, all the generous passions, all the noble instincts, the absolute detachment from self that are normally the attributes of love only at that age.

I don't know why, Marie, men are fashioned after such different models. Some foresee only pleasures in life, others only pain. There are those who see the world as a ballroom. I, on the other hand, am always disposed to view it as a battlefield on which each of us in turn presents himself for combat—to receive wounds and die. This somber imagination of mine is home to violent passions that often knock me about. It has sowed unhappiness, in myself no less than in others. But I truly believe that it gives me more energy for love than other men possess.

[Translated from the French by Frederick Brown]

Autumn 2009

historic syncretism that is endemic to Syria: known as the Gate of the Sun during the Roman Empire, Bab Sharqi is composed of a second-century triple Roman arch topped by a precariously placed medieval mosque, put there by the great Arab leader Nur ed-Din. A weird sight indeed, but entirely typical of the complex layers of historical accretion that have gone into the making of this ancient Levantine city.

Damascus and Aleppo each lay claim to being the oldest continually inhabited city on earth, with lifespans of somewhere around eight millennia. No one has ever been able to determine which is actually older, since both sites are so densely inhabited that excavation possibilities are limited. But clearly both cities are extremely ancient, and they offer the extraordinary spectacle of life being lived, totally unselfconsciously, just as it has been for hundreds and even thousands of years. In Damascus and Aleppo the souqs (markets), houses of prayer, and khans (caravanserais) are still being used for their original purposes. The ancient souqs are not tourist traps (except for certain sections) but are places where people do their everyday marketing. The khans of the old cities are still in use, though mopeds, minivans, and the occasional donkey are housed in them rather than the camels for which they were intended.

Archaeologists have long been at work in Syria, but the digs only began to be professionalized under the French mandate, with the creation of the *Service des antiquités* in the late 1920s. It was this body that founded the great museums of Damascus and Aleppo and some provincial ones as well. Most digs involving foreign universities or museums went on the spoils system, according to which the foreign institution would get half the takings and the other half would go to one of the Syrian museums. Though as a result many of the country's treasures reside at the Louvre or the Yale Museum of Art, the remaining artifacts are of a richness that can scarcely be conceived. In the Damascus Museum there is enough to keep even an only mildly interested tourist busy for days. Among the exhibits there is a cuneiform tablet showing the first known example of an alphabet in human history—and not only that, but another showing the first musical note. There are entire tombs dug out of the desert at Palmyra, complete with funerary sculpture quite unlike anything we have ever seen—a touch of Roman, a touch of Etruscan, a touch of Persian, all combined in an idiosyncratic local style. There is the extraordinary third-century synagogue of Dura-Europas, of which more below. There is the Hall of Mari, containing that city's charming Mesopotamian sculptures, four thousand years old. There are rooms and rooms of Hellenistic and Roman-era sculptures and mosaics, objects that also spill out into the enormous garden. The Roman and Byzantine sculptures from the Hauran district south of Damascus, all in the region's harsh black basalt, are probably unique in the world.

And the Aleppo Museum is just as remarkable. A ninth-century BC stele with a symbol of the moon goddess—almost exactly like the Muslim crescent. Some very early pottery, seventh or sixth millennium BC, that I would have sworn was pre-Columbian. Quantities of cuneiform tablets, some conveniently translated for the viewer, from excavations conducted in the region by Agatha Christie's archaeologist husband Max Mallowan. Hundreds of cylinder seals of marvelous beauty and delicacy. Lion statues from the weird neo-Hittite site (which we later visited) of Ain Dara. Documents from the royal archives at Ebia, one of the oldest collection of written texts anywhere in the world. A fine Hellenistic mosaic of Cassiopeia, who looks rather like a stripper popping out of a cake.

Even the provincial museums are superb. At Suweida south of Damascus there are wonderful sculptures and architectural details from the Nabatean and Roman periods; at Shahba, formerly Philippopolis (hometown of Philip the Arab, who became the Roman emperor in AD 244), we see a lovely collection of classical mosaics. The mid-size city of Deir ez-Zor along the Euphrates has one of the most delightful museums I have ever been in, crammed with pieces garnered from the many Mesopotamian archaeological digs. Here we see the tiny object supposed to be the first known image of a human face that is lifelike and expressive. Here, too, are murals from the royal palace at Mari, showing King Zimri-Lim paying homage to the goddess Ishtar, and a re-creation of Zimri-Lim's archive with its 15,000 clay tablets. At the out-of-the-way town of Ma'arat al-Numan (principally famous as the place where in 1098 some cannibalistic Crusaders dined on Saracen flesh), we are taken to a sixteenth-century madrasa that also serves as a museum of mosaics. All the mosaics here are Byzantine, all in good condition; some are extremely large, taking up entire walls. They are local works, having all been discovered by farmers ploughing their fields. In its entirety this is a collection that would be the envy of the Met, the Louvre, or the British Museum.

At Aleppo we fall in love with a group of statues that were taken from the neo-Hittite site of Tell Halaf along the Euphrates. This mound was excavated before and after the First World War by a German archaeologist, the Baron Max von Oppenheim—the last, apparently, of the great amateurs. The statues are comical, cartoonish, as stylized as anything by Botero or

Remains of the Roman Temple of Jupiter, Damascus. © Peter Aaron/OTTO.

Henry Moore. We are charmed by them and also by the archaeologist himself, who appears in several photographs with his arms flung affectionately round one or other of these weird beings. There is a cautionary tale attached to the Tell Halaf sculptures. Von Oppenheim, according to the booty system, took a number of them back with him to Berlin, where he created a special, state-of-the-art museum for his treasures. A good idea, one would have thought; but not so many years later they were blown to smithereens by a bomb during World War II.

In Damascus, our hotel is in the eastern part of the Old City, traditionally the Christian quarter. It was here that St. Paul was brought after his great revelation on the road to Damascus; it was here that he lodged with a local Christian, Ananias. Ananias's house, or at least his basement, still stands; we enjoy our visit there, thinking it not unlike some of the Christian catacombs we have seen in central Italy. Mark Twain visited the place too: in *The Innocents Abroad* he commented that "There is small question that a part of the original house is there still; it is an old room twelve or fifteen feet underground, and its masonry is evidently ancient. If Ananias did not live there in St. Paul's time, somebody else did, which is just as well." It was near this house, somewhere along the ancient city wall near Bab Sharqi, that St. Paul was lowered in a basket to escape the Jewish population who were angry at his proselytizing.

The author William Dalrymple, who traveled throughout the Middle East visiting Christian communities and wrote a fascinating book about his trip, remarked that no one who has visited Damascus can fail to be impressed by the confidence of the Christians there. It's true. The Christians, a motley mixture of Maronite Catholic, Greek Catholic, Greek Orthodox, Armenian Catholic, Armenian Orthodox, Syrian Catholic, and other sects, have their businesses all up and down Straight Street—"the street called Straight" of the New Testament, which in Hellenistic times was the principal thoroughfare of the city's Hippodamian grid and later, under the Romans, became Via Recta, the city's *decumanus maximus*. It's still more or less straight but now looks more medieval than classical, accretion and clutter over the course of centuries having severely narrowed it; the Ottomans, during the four hundred years of their dominion over Syria, built overhanging terraces that make it almost claustrophobic. Straight Street was certainly never designed for automobile traffic, and now the stream of cars forces pedestrians to press up against the walls to avoid being mashed. The theater built there by Herod the Great no longer stands, but there is a lovely Roman arch square in the middle of the street, impeding traffic, and the remains of the classical columns that used to line the Via Reeta are piled up hugger-mugger. This is the first example of something we will notice throughout our Syrian travels: the conquerors there, whether Greeks, Nabateans, Romans, Arabs, or Turks, have seemed content to leave the traces of earlier dispensations undisturbed. They build around them, or next to them, or on top of them, but they appear to have had no iconoclastic impulses, no need to destroy traces of earlier faiths and creeds.

The Umayyad Mosque, the spiritual center of Damascus, is itself the ultimate illustration of this principle: it has been invented and reinvented for centuries, and each time traces of its earlier incarnations remain as part of the building's fabric. A thousand years before Christ, the Semitic god Hadad was worshipped here; centuries later, the city's Roman conquerors converted the site to an enormous temple to Jupiter. The Byzantine emperor Theodosius turned Jupiter's temple into a Christian church dedicated to St. John the Baptist, whose head supposedly reposes within it. (John, or Yahya as he is called in Arabic, is worshipped by both Muslims and Christians.) It remained in operation as the Church of St. John throughout the first decades of the Muslim regime in the seventh century, then in the early eighth century was chosen as the site for the great mosque the Caliph al-Walid planned to build as a testimony to the might of his dynasty, the Umayyads, who took Damascus as their capital. Though the Umayyad Mosque has now stood for thirteen hundred years, the propylaeum to the Roman temple still stands, rearing high over the open square and the high-arched entrance to the splendid nineteenth-century covered market, the souq al-Hamadiye. The pre-Muslim Greek inscription can still be read in the mosque's wall: "Thy Kingdom, O Christ, is an enduring Kingdom, and Thy dominion endureth throughout all generations."

Now this comes as a bit of a surprise. After all, here in America we have been shown films of the Taliban blowing up ancient Buddhist statues in Afghanistan. We assume that countries with a rich pre-Islamic heritage are at risk. And Syria *does* have a rich pre-Islamic heritage. Its ancient cities along the Euphrates were rightly called the Cradle of Civilization. Hittites and Egyptians duked it out here. So did Assyrians and Chaldeans. The Phoenicians settled along the coast, trading with cities up and down the Mediterranean. The ruined Phoenician city of Ugarit, which was possibly the first great international port in history, enjoys special renown as the place where the alphabet was first invented—the original, one and only alphabet, which the Greeks borrowed and disseminated throughout the Mediterranean world. The Latin and Arabic alphabets, among all the others, are its descendants. The cuneiform tablet found at Ugarit, now in the Damascus Museum, shows a system of thirty symbols or "letters," each associated with a particular phoneme. This is the first extant example of the alphabetic principle.

Great Colonnade, Palmyra. © Peter Aaron/OTTO.

Syria was part of the Greco-Roman world for a thousand years, from Alexander's victory over the Persian Empire at the battle of Issus in 333 BC until the Arab conquest in the seventh century AD. It was incorporated into the Seleucid empire founded after Alexander's death by his general Seleucus I Nicator, becoming an integral part of the Hellenistic world. The mercantile Nabateans were active here as they were farther south in Petra and founded the city of Basra, south of Damascus. Conquered by Pompey the Great in 64 BC, later taken by Mark Antony and presented to Cleopatra as a wedding present, Syria was retaken by the emperor Augustus and made one of the principal provinces of the Roman Empire. A century later, Trajan annexed the southern part of the country and created the province of Arabia. The eastern part of Syria was the easternmost boundary of the Empire, coming right up against the hostile Parthians and, later, the Sassanian Persians.

The Romans took over Hellenistic cities like Damascus, Apamea, Lattakia, and Aleppo, rebuilding them along Roman lines with straight, wide thoroughfares and large-scale religious structures. In the ruins of Apamea one can still see the layout exactly as it was planned: this, surprisingly enough, is what Damascus' classical Via Recta must have looked like before it became medieval Straight Street. Palmyra, halfway between the coast and the Euphrates in the middle of the desert, on the way to Iraq, is in my opinion one of the wonders of the world: an entire classical city abandoned and left to the desert sun and sands for the better part of two thousand years.

The transfer of the Empire's capital from Rome to Constantinople in 395 brought Syria closer to the center of power. Syria was thoroughly Christianized by the middle of the fourth century, the country covered with countless monasteries, churches, pilgrimage centers. The Syrian monks were notorious all over Christendom for their extreme asceticism (the rationalist Gibbon was particularly scathing on the subject of these "horrid and disgusting" anchorites). The most famous of all these "athletes of God" was the Syrian St. Simeon Stylites, who flaunted his piety by standing on a pillar for the better part of forty years. The pilgrimage church of Qalaat Simaan that was built up around the famous pillar after the saint's death consists of a gigantic cruciform structure made up not of one but of *four* large basilican churches; it was the largest church in Christendom until the construction of Hagia Sophia. In Western Europe, there would not be a comparable piece of architecture until the late Middle Ages. These surprisingly well-preserved ruins are one of the major tourist attractions of the country; its architecture poised halfway between the classical world and the Gothic, with distinct traces of both, the church sits high on a promontory overlooking the fertile Afrin Valley. Olive groves lie all around.

Qalaat Simaan and the pilgrimage city that grew up around it are just one, albeit the most spectacular, of the 700 so-called "Dead Cities" that dot northwestern Syria: they are essentially ruined Byzantine towns, deserted since the depopulation of the area during the century or so before the Arab conquest. There is more intact Byzantine architecture here, it turns out, than in any comparable space in the world, though it is of a more rough and provincial variety than the magnificent urban specimens one can still see in Istanbul. The builders in these out-of-the-way spots made free use of the ample limestone composing this northern *massif*, developing a style that looks almost like some ancient version of Lego, with large limestone blocks piled squarely atop others. Houses, public baths, taverns, churches, inns (the Greek word *pandocheion*, we discover, is the original for the Arabic word *funduq*—hotel): all are composed in this rather basic geometric style, a little like ancient Sears houses.

I guess what surprises me is not only that so many of the pre-Muslim sites still exist, but that they have been so carefully and lovingly preserved: that while the country is most definitely a part of the Arab world, the Syrians are also very proud of the region's rich, cosmopolitan history. Look at Dura-Europas on the Euphrates, for example, an eastern border outpost that for many years was fought over by Romans and Parthians. After AD 164 an important garrison town, Dura fell to the Sassanian Persians a century later and was thenceforth abandoned. It can still be visited, a lonely and windswept place overlooking the oozing, mud-colored river.

What's so interesting about Dura is what the excavations tell us about the region and the nature of multiculturalism in this easternmost end of the Roman world. Between 1923 and 1937, French and American archaeologists dug at Dura, making some remarkable discoveries that can be read about in an entrancing account by a member of the Yale team who was there throughout the proceedings: *The Discovery of Dura-Europas* by Clark Hopkins. What stunned the archaeological community at the time was the astonishing coexistence of religions in this relatively small community. There was a rich variety of pagan sites at Dura, with temples to Zeus Theos, Adonis, Artemis, Zeus Kyrios, Hada, Atargatis (the so-called "Syrian Goddess"), Zeus Megistos, and to the Palmyrene gods that were worshipped by the Palmyrene merchants living there. There was a Mithraic temple. There was a freestanding Christian church, the first example of such a church (as distinct from a room inside someone's house) to be found in Syria. Most astounding, there was a sizable synagogue whose walls were covered in frescoes unique in Jewish history, for they depict human forms in scenes from the Old Testament—the only such "graven images" that have ever turned up. According to the original agreement, Yale was supposed to get these frescoes, but the Syrians insisted on hanging onto them. Reconstructed, the synagogue is the centerpiece of the Damascus Museum. A smaller replica of it has been built at the Jewish Museum in New York.

Another fascinating place along these lines is Bosra, which boasts four "cities": the Nabatean, the Roman, the Byzantine, and the Arab, all built in the black basalt of the Hauran district in southern Syria. The city has pre-Nabatean origins—it was founded in the Seleucid period and taken, at one point, by Judas Maccabeus—but the earliest structures now visible are Nabatean, from the century before and the century after Christ. The Romans made the city the capital of their province of Arabia and installed a legion, greatly expanding the town; the large Roman theater is still in use as the home of a summer music and dance festival. In Byzantine times, Bosra became the seat of a bishopric and later an archbishopric. Its church became one of the greatest cathedrals of the east, as large in its day as Hagia Sophia. Finally, under the Arabs, the city continued to flourish as a stop on the pilgrimage route to Mecca.

The layers of the town are interwoven and superimposed on one another: Roman temple, Nabatean house, Byzantine church, Muslim madrasa, all make up part of a weird syncretic whole. Amazing, really, that the Christian rulers did not destroy the pagan temples, or the Muslim overlords tear down the Christian sites. On the contrary, here as elsewhere they have been well preserved, and one of the churches is especially important to Muslims because of its association with the Nestorian monk Bahira, famous for having recognized the teenage Muhammad as a future prophet when the boy was visiting the town with his merchant father.

Muslims revere Jesus, John the Baptist, and the Old Testament prophets and see Islam as the culmination of the Judeo-Christian tradition rather than a deviation from it. Christians and Jews, of course, see it as a heresy. But it is certainly a surprise to see Muslims praying at certain Christian sites, such as the various shrines to St. George, who is holy to Christians and Muslims alike. If anything, a spirit of ecumenism seems to be cultivated here— just as well since the religions are so interwoven. On the slopes of Mount Qassioun there is even a cave said to be the spot where Cain killed Abel—or Qabil killed Habil, according to the Muslim Hadiths. Here Syrians of every faith come to pay their respects, and for good measure Abraham and St.

Roman amphitheater, Palmyra. © Peter Aaron/OTTO.

George have also been associated with the site. We were welcomed there by a gentle Imam, who sat on a deck chair next to his dozing cat.

Both Christians and Jews were originally tolerated by Muslims, by order of the Prophet: they were *dhimmi*, "people of the book." "Dispute not with the people of the book," Muhammad said, "save in the fairer manner, except for those of them that do wrong; and say, 'We believe in what has been sent down to us, and what has been sent down to you; our God and your God is one, and to Him we have surrendered.'" Christians seem to thrive in Syria today. But what of the Jews, whose local roots go back even further than the Christians and who for so many years seemed to get on better with the Muslim overlords? Jews lived in Syria from ancient times. Abraham is supposed to have come to Aleppo to milk his cow (the Arabic name for the city, Haleb, derives from the word for milk). The principal synagogue of Aleppo is said to have been founded by King David's general Joab about a thousand years before Christ. This tale is somewhat dubious, but the original structure certainly dates back as far as Byzantine times. Jews traditionally did better in the Muslim Middle East, where their rights were respected, than they did in Christian lands. After the Crusading armies conquered Jerusalem in 1099, for instance, they slaughtered Jews indiscriminately, and it was to Damascus that the survivors repaired for asylum. Pogroms and blood libels against

Jews were unknown in early modern Syria. The first such event, a blood libel in 1840 called "the Damascus Affair," was instigated by Christians rather than Muslims, and when there were bitter anti-Christian riots in Damascus in the wake of modernizing reforms undertaken by the Ottoman sultan, the Jews were not assaulted.

The medieval rabbi Benjamin of Tudela, visiting his coreligionists in Syria in the twelfth century, surmised that "it's in the national character of the three peoples that there's greater affinity between Jews and Muslims than between Jews and Christians" and ascribed this fact to the nature of the religious practices, the Jews' and Muslims' trading customs, and their shared interest in science, medicine, and technology.

So what went wrong, and why are Syria's synagogues now boarded up and deserted, its Jewish population dispersed? It seems to have been due to the simultaneous rise of Zionism and Arab nationalism after the First World War. Palestine was viewed as an integral part of Syria, of *bilad al-Sham*, the Arabic name for Greater Syria, and the anti-Jewish sentiments that arose in twentieth-century Syria were anti-Zionist rather than anti-Semitic in the racial or even the religious sense. Everything came to a head in December 1947 when the UN General Assembly passed its resolution enabling the creation of the Jewish state in Palestine. Rioting broke out in Aleppo, with synagogues being burned down and priceless Torahs and other sacred items destroyed. Syrian Jews began fleeing the country, but the borders were closed to them, for the authorities did not want them emigrating to the Israel that they, the Syrian government, refused to recognize. Jews were not physically harmed—they were allowed to keep their businesses and continue life as before—but they were denied exit. Over the next few decades all but a handful of Jews got out of the country.

My husband, who is Jewish, loses no time apprising the various people we meet in Syria of this fact, but no one seems particularly interested or makes any comment. He also frequently hazards the remark that it was too bad our two countries aren't better friends. Almost invariably, whoever he is addressing will say, "Oh everyone knows that's just politics, *not people*." But people at home, we reflected, *don't* know that, or believe it. In Syria the man in the street differentiates between government propaganda and reality: after decades, centuries, of authoritarian government, well aware that their press is not free, the Syrians approach its dicta with skepticism. In America we believe that we have a free press and tend to accept the spin put on the news by politicians and media.

Syria is generally described as a police state, which is true insofar as the government seems to have unrestricted rights. The first Assad and now the second both chose to leave in place a 1963 "state of emergency" declaration for which there is now clearly no legitimate reason; and in 1968, still before the first Assad assumed power, a special court was set up to try people accused of dissent or offenses against state security: the Supreme State Security Court. The SSSC still exists, under the control of the executive branch of government, and Syria's prisons contain quite a few people found guilty of convenient but vague charges like "spreading false news," "weakening national morale," and "inciting sectarian sentiments."

But this is not quite like the old Soviet empire, where the feeling of being watched was pervasive, where visitors had to worry about their rooms being bugged and locals were afraid to talk with them. It is not even like modern Egypt, where the police and military presence is everywhere evident. With the exception of traffic cops there is no visible police presence here at all, and the fact that everyone we meet wishes to talk to us makes it seem very unlikely that many people are systematically watched. Strangers invite us to sit down with them at table, to dine in their homes, to visit with them at restaurants. And they don't just want to exchange platitudes: they want to make meaningful connections, to talk about poetry, philosophy, history. We are nervous about bringing up the subject of Syrian politics, but occasionally it arises anyway. When we speak of American or world politics, our new Syrian friends discuss these subjects eagerly and knowledgeably. They seem to have a broader understanding of world events, despite their "unfree" press, than we do with our "free" one. Speaking of which, we notice that Al Jazeera is an excellent news station with no extreme political bias that we can detect—not unlike the BBC in fact, and certainly superior to CNN. So far as we can gather, the rule in Syria seems to be that unless you get involved in politics, the police will leave you alone.

In the bar at the Baron Hotel in Aleppo we meet two young girls, both studying Arabic at the University of Damascus. Hannah, 24, is American; she hopes to stay in Syria to teach English. Freya, 18, is English, a delicate-looking blonde. She is doing a gap year before beginning her studies next fall at the University of Bristol. She says that her father has taken her and her brothers on several holidays in the Middle East, determined that they will not grow up to share their culture's popular anti-Arab prejudice. Hannah and Freya live in international student housing, have made plenty of friends, and are having a wonderful time. The good thing about studying in Damascus, they say, is that the local kids actually want to meet them and socialize with them. This was not their experience in Paris. They also find the place remarkably safe. Several years ago, while in college, Hannah went on an American-sponsored student tour to Israel. She tells us that a number of the other kids were forbidden by their parents to venture into Arab neighborhoods like Jerusalem's Old City because they were supposed to be dangerous. Hannah finds this incomprehensible.

They are dressed, by the way, like college students at home. And since I'm on the subject, what *about* that question about whether we have to wear headscarves, since that is the one question that absolutely everybody asked us, the one and only subject that seems to be of universal interest to Americans? Well no, we don't. If you go into a mosque you are required to, but they generally have robes specially reserved for tourists. (At the Umayyad Mosque they have marked a "Putting On Special Clothes Room" for the purpose.) Otherwise the headscarf is optional in Syria, a matter of personal choice. Of course nothing is ever that simple, and people usually end up conforming with the rules of their community. Most Muslim women here (though not Christians) do wear the scarf; not many, though, are fully veiled. My daughters flat out refuse to modify their everyday dress, which happens to be jeans with ordinary shirts, open-necked collars, and rolled-up sleeves. The only reaction this garb occasions is open admiration from the men, though (unlike other Mediterranean countries I have been in) this is only expressed in polite ways; no one ever, ever pinches or gropes.

Back in New York, lots of people tell us we were "brave" to venture to such a scary place. We hear this even from people who should know better: an eminent historian, for instance, who has done lots of work on Middle Eastern history. Before I left for Syria, I mistrusted the mainstream American news media. Now I hold them in contempt. I won't let them dissuade me from exploring any other countries. Next stop, I hope, is Iran. Or maybe Uzbekistan.

Spring 2010

Tremblement de Terre!

The Gods Turned Their Faces Away: Letter from Haiti

HERBERT GOLD

A BON VOYAGE wish from a neighbor on Russian Hill in San Francisco: "I hear you're going to Haiti? Have a nice vacation." Another bon voyage message from Port-au-Prince from the director of the documentary I'll be appearing in: "We can't avoid the smell of human shit anyplace."

I used to express my long fascination with Haiti by describing it as the tragedy you can dance to and entitled a book *Best Nightmare on Earth*. But irony at Haiti's place on earth no longer seems possible. Suffering has shaken this brave people, with all their wit, talent, and charm, into a darkness almost impossible to measure.

The flight to Port-au-Prince was filled six months after the earthquake of January 2010, during terrible times, with Haitians heading home to check on families, to help, and perhaps some to profit. Uneasy sleepers, mouths agape, lay slumped and dreaming of their future here or their past.

Also there was a scattering of white travelers, representatives of various aid groups, the religious ones evident in the wearing of symbols, clutching of Bibles, short haircuts, grim do-gooding frowns or blissed-out do-gooding smiles fixed on their faces; also briefcase- and laptop-bearing NGO functionaries or volunteers. And a few odd seekers, plus at least one diehard nostalgist.

From the air, the city of Port-au-Prince was silent, of course, like any city. On its hills near the bay, leading up to the mountains beyond mountains, it looked almost one-dimensional, with some structures still standing like sentinel columns. Then, as we headed down for landing, skeletons of buildings appeared, emerging from piles of rubble, amid a few scattered, apparently intact survivors.

A renowned furniture designer, who liked to sit in his love seat with very young girls, found one he liked, bought a house in Petionville, married her. Unfortunately, in the way of human flesh, she grew old—about fifteen; but fortunately, he had deep feelings for her family, divorced her, married her younger sister, and waited while still younger sisters ripened on the vine.

A woman from Minneapolis, recently divorced, came for an extended visit because she wanted to live in an "oral language culture." I assured her that every culture, not just Minneapolis, has an oral language; even nearby St. Paul, for example. She was displeased but soon found a stalwart Haitian practitioner of oral language. A more hardworking anthropologist, fluent in Creole, a young scholar with graduate degrees from CUNY, was now doing postgraduate research in a village near Port-de-Paix. He was dreading the visit of his conventional Jewish parents because they would be meeting his pregnant bride, by whom he already had several children. He was serious about fieldwork, and also about teaching his wife to read and write in Creole, her native oral language.

Over the years, I've met a select group of art collectors, admirers of painting, sculpture, and the densely worked beaded voodoo flags; also harvesters of street art and crafts, which could be bought for a few dollars and sold in Key West, Miami Beach, and Provincetown resort shops. These art miners included a couple of former ballet dancers, who gracefully and enterprisingly danced to Haiti for vacations which they supported by selling their crops back home. And, increasingly, drug traffickers, taking advantage of porous Haitian law enforcement. I also knew a defrocked English banker, employed by the Duvaliers, father and son, who arrived every few months with his girlfriend and his whisk broom to sweep up any money rattling around the national treasury. Hearing that I was driving to Forêt des Pins, high in the mountain above Port-au-Prince, above Petionville, even above Kenscoff, the money-laundering banker asked me to buy him a couple bottles of *sellé bridé*, a milky substance with a dark curl of some kind of root at the bottom of the bottle. "Best in the whole world for—" and up, up, up into the air he raised an erect finger.

In the fifties, as a young student, I was proud to be invited to join the Cenacle des Philosophes in Kenscoff, a cool village on the mountain above Port-au-Prince; honored to be among a group of retired judges, government officials, and coffee dealers. We discussed world issues. These distinguished friends, plus the American, drank our good dark-roasted Haitian coffee in the unappreciated center of the world. It was decided by us that Haiti could be the *trait d'union*, the hyphen, making peace during the Cold War between the USSR and the USA.

My son Ethan, who has visited Haiti with me several times, listened to me point out where old friends lived or played or solved world problems, and he finally said, "Dad, you're seeing ghosts." Haiti and nostalgia for Haiti still washes over some foreign fanatics, while the elements of flood, poverty, corrupt politics, and now this ultimate disaster wash over nine million people, brave and talented amid the folly of themselves and the gods.

During one of my frequent journalistic visits to Haiti after the expulsion in 1986 of Jean-Claude ("Furniture-Face") Duvalier, known to others as Baby Doc, I couldn't help noticing a beautiful young woman, taking breakfast every morning at a table near mine on the terrace of the Oloffson. We shared admiration of the splendid Haitian coffee, the papaya, mango, and pineapple fruit plate, sometimes the special Oloffson French Toast. I was reporting on the political turmoil, but distracted by the portfolio of papers she studied, both of us occasionally looking up to appreciate the early morning freshness.

In the natural evolution of things, we shared news of our reasons for being in Haiti. She was Argentinean, heading out every day to dig for brutalized bodies which had been buried during the Duvalier regime, trying to identify them, trying to identify the killers. Never in the United States, or at least not in the coffeehouses and taverns of Cleveland, New York, and San Francisco, had I ever met a graceful, warm-hearted, dark-haired, tender-spirited, civic-minded, and lovely young Argentinean woman who gave as her profession "forensic archaeologist." The inscriber of this confession is also not immune to the allure of Strange.

In addition to sex, of course, there was music, art, buried pirate treasure to be sought even if not found, and surreal politics to entertain active spirits. Brutality and hardship did not impinge on visitors unless they cared; most didn't.

When I first lived in Haiti, friends with a pirate treasure map invited me along on a trip across the island to Port-de-Paix to help them dig, but all I gained was a nearly fatal case of blackwater fever, malignant malaria. Exotic travel had its risks, even before the AIDS epidemic. I didn't know that the pirates had apparently buried the treasure with thirteen upright slaves to provide a curse on treasure embezzlers a couple of centuries later. In the rich anthology of human desire, there are always unexpected surprises.

During this visit in 2010, a couple from Normandy with a boy and a girl—pigtails, pink ribbons, impeccable new clothes every morning—were waiting at the Oloffson for their adoption papers to be stamped properly, notarized, signed, confirmed. The little girl often screamed, for no apparent reason, and then abruptly stopped, as if a switch were clicked. The solemn little boy came and stood by those taking meals on the Oloffson terrace; stood, stared, crawled into laps. Both children seemed to be about three years old. The French couple had visited Haiti several times and thought they had completed the adoption process, but now the orphanage decided they needed more papers, stamps, notarizations, approvals, before they could leave.

They waited. This middle-aged couple was stuck at the Oloffson, hugging and kissing the two children, who were often on the move in the swift way of very young kids everywhere. I admired the patience of sudden new parents. The boy needed a kidney operation as soon as possible. He was age five, not three, as I had thought.

"Did you choose these two?" I asked.

"No. The *orphelinat* did."

The children had already learned to clink glasses in morning, orange juice toasts, like playful little French children. Question: How did this Frenchwoman from Normandy learn to braid and tie pink-ribboned pigtails for a tiny Haitian orphan?

Cameron Brahman, a Canadian who used to manage the Katharine Dunham estate in Port-au-Prince, billed as "the largest urban forest in the world," a collection of destroyed buildings and odd crumbled trophy statuary, now exports toy tin-painted tap-tap buses, witty examples of Haitian craftsmanship. Steadily on his computer or his cell phone, busy despite the ambient tropical languor, Cameron seemed immune to the siesta habit. "Business," he explained. Or: "My wife." She was waiting for him in Toronto.

In the evening, at the Oloffson bar, he was still lively and jolly, keeping his laptop and cell phone close by and handy, although there was plenty of turmoil in this traditional pot-au-feu gathering of politics, negotiation, flirtation, and energetic fun or, at least, distraction-seeking. One evening Cameron was accompanied by Reginald Jean François, a burly resident of Cité Soleil, the most dangerous slum in Port-au-Prince. He is the artist who constructs these toy tap-taps, using tin pulled from dumps and debris, painting them with traditional inspirational or prayerful messages, such as JESUS IS GOOD in English, or BON DIEU BON, a Creole incantation. Discovered by Cameron, Monsieur François told me he lived for a time in the

States, practiced a criminal trade, not fully defined ("J'étais un bad guy"); was deported. Then happened to find a Bible in a garbage barrel and happened to read it. It was God's will that he find Jesus. For everything, and especially the earthquake, Jesus has a reason, an excellent reason we know not of, because it is not within human power to know what His reasons are. "He is good, so I know this. It was all good." Monsieur François didn't pause but stared into my eyes. "It is beyond understanding."

I agreed that it was beyond my understanding.

I hoped it could be revealed to those who were former souls on earth, loving others, probably damaging or nurturing some, enjoying rice and beans, papaya, *clairin* (the raw white Haitian rum) on holidays, working day after day—growing up and growing older—that is, *living.*

According to Monsieur François, the perished ones were not nowhere people but elsewhere people. "Bon Dieu Bon!" he said.

I had seen a sign on a former, now collapsed, church: Jesus Église à Louer.

On tap-taps with people hanging from every available space: "THANK YOU ST. ANDRÉ."

"BON DIEU BON"

"PROMESSE DE DIEU"

"LA VIE EST DRÔLE"

Yes, it is.

A blind guitarist, waving his cane before him, was led up and down the stairs to the high terrace on the "maternity ward," where so many have stood to look out over the city, the port, the sea. In the afternoons, he sat there, picking at his guitar. A bottle of Prestige, the local beer, stood within reach when he paused in his improvisations, waiting while the flap-flapping of a United Nations helicopter passed above. He had the undernourished, skeletal, harassed look of a man for whom satisfaction of the simplest need was a continual strain. The first time I asked if we could record and speak with him for the film, he said, Maybe later. Just then he was busy.

He played and stared with sightless eyes over the destroyed city. He couldn't see it, but the sounds from his guitar clearly stated that he knew what there was down below.

"I don't like to intrude," I said.

With great affability and a broad smile, meeting my eyes with his blind ones, meeting them approximately, he said, "You already did that."

"So would you like—?"

He was softly fingering his guitar, gently rocking in his chair, smiling with amiability, kindness, and gentle refusal. "Occupé," he said. He was occupied in his own tranquil universe of melody.

Travelers over the years have been bewildered by the pell-mell bustle, noise, and confusion of street life in Port-au-Prince and then at other times the tropical somnolence. Both existed, and still do. When I first lived in Haiti, there were so few automobiles that often I recognized the driver of an approaching car. Sometimes the driver could be seen talking to no one visible; this meant his lover spotted the automobile of her husband and had ducked down to be invisible. (Once a confused wife made a regrettable error, recognizing the car of her lover. When she ducked down, her husband instantly pulled out his pistol and shot her.)

In those years the streets were crowded with burros and, especially during the night, silent processions of peasant women, "*Mesdames* Saras," carrying vegetables in baskets on their heads to the Marché au Fer, the Iron Market, for sale in the morning.

There were also jollity, desperation, the struggle for survival, the ceaselessness of that struggle. There still is.

Paul Morand, a French travel writer—racist, semi-fascist, tainted during World War II with collaboration—described in his book *Hiver Caraibe* a world of elegant, Francophile, generally lighter-skinned landowners, coffee exporters, generals, politicians, a traditional inherited elite which aimed to be au courant with Paris. (They were more au courant and *bon ton bon chic* with nineteenth-century Paris.) In 1953 what he described still existed. One of my neighbors was a doctor-lawyer too rich and elegant to practice either profession but showed respect by adhering to the high standards of his profiteer ancestors by always wearing a tie like the one he had worn at the Sorbonne, tight despite the heat. It's not generally hot in nineteenth-century Paris.

After my treasure hunt in 1954, when a sudden high fever appeared during a five-day holiday and all the available practicing doctors seemed to be on vacation, he consented to feel me all over, diagnose malaria (noblesse oblige), and ask me if my heart hurt. I said everything else seemed to be burning, but my heart didn't hurt. "Alors! Tant mieux!" ("Well! So much the better!") And then he bid me a charming farewell.

Eventually I found an actually practicing doctor. The Haitian medical school of that period had expertise with tropical diseases. Paul Morand's nostalgia for a class system reminiscent of slavery also existed among the elite, although some of their ancestors were slaves. One effect of the upheavals since the Duvalier reign, starting in 1956, has been an evolution toward American influence, in addition to exploitation and violence as an underclass imperfectly moved toward power. Different exploitations, of course. The archaic hangover was replaced by other hangovers, further disasters.

"AN EMPTY SACK CAN'T STAND"—a Haitian woman whose husband and children were crushed by the *seisme*.

Six months after, the streets of Port-au-Prince might be cleared, except that tents, tarps, and makeshift lean-tos have sprung up because the million and a half homeless people have no other available space. Also wreckage continues to spill from destroyed buildings, erupting onto the roads as if by volcanic movements. Men with buckets and shovels and bare hands only dent the piles of debris. Rubble removal is blocked by lack of equipment, lack of coordination among the aid groups and chaotic remnants of government, lack of sites to put the rubble. Bodies still reveal themselves. The living need to be resettled.

Anarchy shouldn't be said to rule because the word "rule" suggests a comprehensible pattern.

A perception of the uncoordinated efforts of the hundreds of groups which have sprung up with money, the best of intentions, and incoherent vision can be gained from a large English-language help-wanted advertisement in *Le Nouvelliste* for Compassion International, listing the ten requirements for an "EARTHQUAKE RESPONSE AUDITOR," beginning with:

"1. Mature Christian person, based on Evangelical Christian values; has a personal relationship with Jesus Christ."

Over the years, I've seen Buddhists, Scientologists, Yoga therapists (!), and New Age mystics troop in, sometimes on weekend expeditions to cure hunger, illness, and destitution by rescuing Haitians from their prevalent faith in the traditional voodoo gods. The Catholic Church has conducted a centuries-long campaign to exterminate a syncretic religion which traveled from Africa and thrives in the Caribbean. More recently, Evangelical Christians and Mormons have established a presence, although Haitians tend only to add, generously as is their wont, in exchange for food, medical care, and hymns, whatever new faith is offered to the entrenched pantheon of Damballa, Erzulie, and their troupe of attendant *loa*. "Jesus bon," admits a Creole proverb, "mais Damballa puissant." (Jesus is good, but Damballa is powerful.) On Sunday mornings I would watch voodoo adherents thronging to the church in Kenscoff, its masses conducted by Breton priests, after Saturday nights celebrating the power of Grande Erzulie, the goddess of love, whose symbol represents orgasm but whose image was an icon of the Virgin Mary. These long Saturday nights–Sunday mornings served as a kind of insurance or (mixed metaphor warning) a form of covering all bases.

Years ago, Jasmin Joseph, one of the great painters of the postwar Haitian Renaissance, sold me a painting of white rabbits in plastic clothes and heavy horn-rimmed glasses, two of them kneeling, all of them clutching what look like Bibles, amid a group of sleepy, heavy-lidded, bored brown bears, lounging at their ease. There are no bears in Haiti, and I don't recall ever seeing rabbits, certainly none with horn-rimmed glasses. I said to him: "These are white missionaries and these are Haitian bears." He looked bemused by the idiocy of my question. "No, bears and rabbits, m'ami, bears and rabbits."

Jasmin Joseph wore heavy horn-rimmed glasses, but I could never imagine him as a white rabbit.

Not just normal life, but the extraordinary life of Haiti is crowded with normal idiocy and surprises, a gift of the gods even now to bring comedy into the world, no matter what. Taking a rum punch on the terrace of the always-falling-down Hotel Oloffson sat an elderly German tourist, tall, stooped, with sparse, hanging, stringy hair, who had just arrived and was enjoying his drink of welcome. He was happy to be here. "I come for twenty-five years! Such these are beautiful girls!"

The hotel never quite falls down, and the seekers of Strange never quite abandon it. But on this visit, amid the ruins and suffering, the words "I am a tourist" are among the strangest I've ever heard. The next morning, out on the road in front of the collapsed school named after the poet Roussan Camille, the retired Herr Professor was asking to take a photo of a girl on the street. She was a pretty child, perhaps fifteen or sixteen. "Oui," she said. Then he tried to kiss her. She scrambled away, giggling, "Non! Non! Non!"

This would-be swain, at least fifty years older, couldn't catch her. My friend Aubelin Jolicoeur—Duvalierist, journalist, occasional official greeter, art dealer, father of at least eleven children, and indefatigable dancer and squire for lonely American women—named "Mister Haiti" by the above-signed—might have arranged things better for Herr Professor. Aubelin, alas, who had seemed immortal, was not.

In Haiti I've learned to welcome untragic news among the dire events. Sarodj Bertin, Haiti's beauty queen, almost won the Miss Universe title at the Mandala Bay Resort in Las Vegas. "She carried the ribbon of Haiti on her chest," reported *Le Nouvelliste*, Haiti's premier newspaper's own chest bursting with pride: "She was there to conquer!" And she might even have won Miss Universe! For the glory of Haiti! (Except that she didn't.) But my old friend Theo Duval, once Ambassador to the United Kingdom, reminded me, in case I'd forgotten, that the Haitian flag had been planted on the moon. (Except that it was an old-model flag.) Theo has been asking me for years to tell an astronaut to install the non-obsolete correct flag.

Sarodj Bertin is the daughter of an assassinated lawyer. The Miss Universe contest was sponsored (owned) by Donald Trump. The winner was Miss Mexico.

The divide between life and death in Haiti makes the gods seem frivolous. Miss Haiti competes in Las Vegas while severed limbs, crowned with maggots and flies, can still be found within the rubble of Port-au-Prince, Gonaives, Leogane, and Jacmel. Life and death live next door. Death dies for a moment if we find distraction, so I was relieved to see children playing amid the collapsed scramble, older boys kicking soccer balls, and a sweet child giggling and running from an avid sex tourist.

Infected with the well-known Haitian Presidential Disease, the Haitian-American hip-hop performer, Wyclef Jean, discovered the usual symptoms of infection—that he alone had all the attributes necessary, charisma, divine appointment, and acute hearing to detect the call of the People, plus in his case surely including a unique skill at rapping. There were elections scheduled for November 2010; he might even have won, although several other messiahs, plus some competent and qualified candidates, were on offer.

The case of the attractive performer has much precedent here, including the well-spoken and folk-singing previous messiah "Titid," Jean-Bertrand Aristide, who is now singing his siren songs from South Africa; a rapid parade of handsome, self-appointed generals: the voodooesque medical doctor and torturer François Duvalier, "Papa Doc"; then detours into the holding patterns of Papa Doc's moronic son, and brief interregnums of academics, such as the army-selected sociologist Leslie Manigat, who explained to a group of journalists: "Democracy is a bay-be. If the bay-be is not perfect, do you strangle the baby? Do you tear the baby to bits? No! You feed the baby, you rock the baby. . . ."

I was distracted by his crooning and gentle rocking motions for the precious small burden of democracy and failed to take down his entire declaration.

A competent technocrat with a reputation for honesty, Mare Bazin, failed several times to be elected, probably because not only was he trained

Letter from Indonesia

CHRISTIAN N. DESROSIERS

DARKNESS WAS ALREADY GATHERING in the sky when I boarded a bus in Medan bound for Aceh. And by the time we had pulled away from the terminal, past the smoggy factories and fluorescent malls, the lunch counters, fruit vendors, car washers, beggars, out of the crowd of motorcycles and onto a slender road flanked by sunken rice fields, it was deeply night. I had some anxiety about my destination. It had only been a handful of years since the Indian Ocean had surged in, swallowing up Acehnese coastal towns and cities—countless lives—and as long since that catastrophe had necessitated an uneasy ceasefire between the Indonesian army and separatist paramilitaries. The rebels, operating under the banner of the Free Aceh Movement, or GAM, had fought to secede from Indonesia on the grounds that the Jakarta government disregarded their best economic interests. That fighting had spread across three decades and from time to time overflowed from the mountainous interior into terrified population centers along the coast. More recently, the area has seen the arrival of Jemaah Islamiyah, an al-Qaeda affiliate that seeks by violent means to establish a unified Islamic state out of Muslim-majority areas scattered throughout the region's various nations. A paramilitary training camp run by these Islamists had been discovered and shut down last year, and it was likely that more existed. This confluence of secular separatists, Islamist radicals, and outsized natural disaster made the region especially interesting to me. I was living several hundred miles and an island away in a small industrial city on Java, teaching at a private Islamic school, and had interrupted my work for this attempt to understand to what extent the rumors which circulated freely about life there either did or did not obscure its true dimensions.

When, at dawn, we arrived at the outskirts of Banda Aceh, the capital of the province, I saw impressive post-tsunami reconstruction—sturdy new buildings and wide, smooth roads—but overshadowing such hopefulness was my understanding of the forces, natural and man-made, that threatened from the mountains and the sea. I had been the only Westerner on a bus brimful of Sumatrans and Acehnese. Across the aisle a neatly dressed middle-aged man had, for the entire eight-hour journey, balanced on his thigh a drooping, languid infant. He had the twin bruises on his forehead that are the ornaments of pious Muslims, earned by many thousands of prostrations on hard mosque floors. Beside him sat his headscarfed daughter, who periodically broke the long silences of the bus ride to vomit into a bag. My own neighbor had been a young Acehnese laborer who worked in Medan and was now returning home for a short visit with relatives in Banda Aceh. He was poor; his clothing was of bad quality, and he traveled with no bags. We chatted intermittently, and I shared with him the crackers I'd brought. He spoke to me in a guilty tone about many family members who had perished in the tsunami. He was 23, my age precisely, and as is always the case in these situations, a thought lingered in my head about how differently life had treated us. Standing outside at a rest stop just after midnight, he offered me a cigarette, and though I do not smoke, I accepted it. I was overcome by a nebulous and ridiculous guilt and somehow felt that accepting a gift from an impoverished friend eradicated our inequality, or else absolved me of the crime of being fortunate by comparison. And the nonsensical thought led me to ponder how heavily the dead weighed on the hearts of those like him, who had survived the war and the tsunami. Infinitely more substantial, how could a person barter away that guilt?

Near a vegetable market, I found a room in a small guesthouse with NO UNMARRIED COUPLES neatly printed in Indonesian on a card at the front desk. And after some haggling with a mechanic who ran a shop nearby, I was able to rent his motorcycle. I took it out into a low mountain range that defined the city's western boundary. Reliably, every few minutes, I came upon another army garrison. Small outposts are ubiquitous in Indonesian cities, but here in the Acehnese frontier they were more numerous and more menacing; the drill yards were full of commandos bearing their assault rifles and performing manly drills—a conspicuous bulwark against secular and Islamist threats. Such sights made it difficult to take seriously billboards paid for by Aceh's tourism ministry which encouraged travelers to "Feel the Harmony."

When I broke out to the other side of the mountains, I stopped at a roadside shack for a meal of coffee and fried noodles. I was the only customer, and the cook expressed surprise that I, an American, had come alone to Aceh. "Do you feel safe here?" he asked. I asked him if there was any reason why I shouldn't feel safe. At this he laughed and said that he supposed there wasn't.

Back at my guesthouse, I passed several mosquito-ridden nights mingling with the other guests. There was a man, moon-faced and sad, in town to see a family member who was ill, and from Mecca a traveling salesman promoting amulets and natural medicines which, he said, had magical healing properties. Often, we were joined by a youthful provincial senator who was in town for a conference. The senator quickly became fond of me and invited me to accompany him back to his home district on the aircraft he had privately chartered. I turned down the offer and would later wonder what I had missed. I talked with each of these people as well as with others, smoked cigarettes, drank tea, and became increasingly impatient: they all were either unable to tell me anything specific about GAM or were feigning ignorance.

Then one night the owner of the hotel introduced me to another guest: a government deputy willing to talk about his past as a GAM paramilitary. The ex-guerilla swiftly qualified his willingness, saying that if he wanted to answer my questions, he would, but if he did not want to, he wouldn't. He had been a foot soldier in the insurgency. He had a sturdy body, and it was easy to imagine him slogging through jungled mountains. He told me stories of the time before the Helsinki "Memorandum of Understanding," when the Jakarta government was making great profits from the region's natural gas and leaving none of it for the Acehnese. Running water and electricity had been scarce and the Acehnese very poor. When I pressed him with questions about separatist remnants, he was as masterful in the art of dissimulation as any guerilla, retreating behind a polite smile that conveyed the air of sufficiency without answering the questions. I asked him if he and most other former rebels were happy with the terms of the Helsinki MOU, which had given the Acehnese a certain percentage of revenues from natural gas. He pursed his lips for a moment, pondering, and then said that most Acehnese civilians were happy to see the end of the fighting. It was an evasive reply. But are the soldiers happy? "No," he admitted. "Most of us are not happy." He seemed uncomfortable to be admitting this and, talking late into the night, I let the conversation move to other subjects. By the next morning he was gone.

Centuries ago, at the height of its power, the Sultanate of Aceh dominated this portion of the world by virtue of its control of the Strait of Malacca which, then as now, was the crucial channel for trade between the Far East and Europe. The advantages of such a strategic asset were realized most successfully in the sixteenth and seventeenth centuries by the eminently shrewd Sultan Iskandar Muda—literally, "Young Alexander"—who expanded both the boundaries and the wealth of the empire, and under whom the Acehnese Sultanate flourished as a center of Islamic art and theology. But, soon after, Aceh's star dimmed. After Iskandar Muda's death, factional conflicts weakened the Sultanate, and, despite fierce resistance, Aceh found itself first under the heel of the Dutch and then, later, Java-based Indonesian nationalists. The region's special dispensation to apply sharia law, a concession granted to twentieth-century separatists, was the sole living legacy of its proud Islamic past.

The center had become an extremity: Jakarta and Kuala Lumpur and Singapore now dominated the region, their influences towering over any quaint reminiscences of the Sultanate. When I visited, despite the post-tsunami surge in development, Banda Aceh was as expansive and empty as any frontier city. Punishing heat drove most people out of the streets in the daytime, and at night the city maintained its docility. But small distortions, details just on the other side of normal, transformed it into an uncanny place. Hundreds of vessels had been swept inland by the tsunami, and two remained. I visited them one day, one after the other. The first was a fishing boat that had come to rest atop a house. The boat had decayed in the intervening years, and permanent scaffolding had been erected to preserve it in its improbable location. There was a plaque commemorating the disaster. Deeper inland, imposing itself on the village clustered tightly against it, was an enormous freighter. A man loitering nearby informed me that four houses had been crushed beneath it, forever entombing whoever had been at home that day. I climbed atop it and, gazing at the coastline miles away, tried to imagine an ocean swell powerful enough to deliver it so far inland.

The freighter was both a memorial to the past and an ominous suggestion for the future. There had been no warning then; would there be one next time? This kind of memory mingled with fear was part of the psychology of the place. The elegant tsunami museum, that along with the main mosque anchored the city, was built with excessive sturdiness. And on the outside a spine of concrete stairwells led up to an evacuation roof. Out near the jetties the tsunami research center was similarly constructed, and in front of it lay the flood-ravaged husk of a rescue helicopter.

I took shelter from a sudden downpour in a small government office and there met M., a clerk in his late thirties. "You have come to the proper place at the proper time," he said when I asked if it would be all right to query him about GAM. M. liked to talk and was inclined to do so dramatically; he had learned his English from old American westerns and spoke with a cowboy's lazy vowels. Because it was toward the end of the workday, most of the other employees had gone home, and it was safe to talk here. He told me to go ahead, to ask him any question I had, and in the same breath warned me to be careful about whom I asked these questions, noting that police and military were fond of inventing "visa problems" for foreigners who were too curious. As he said this, a clerk brandishing a handful of documents hurried into the room. He looked at the clerk, then he looked at me knowingly. We exchanged his mother tongue for mine. He said: "But don't worry: no one else here speaks English."

M.'s eyes were double-ringed. The black dots of the pupils were circumscribed first with a thick, deep brown band which was itself circumscribed by a slender ring of pale blue. The pupil and the inner band were almost indistinguishable in color; the effect was that his eyes seemed at all times to be extremely dilated, lending him an owl-like watchfulness, a bottomless gaze. He smoked cigarettes constantly, lighting each with the dying embers of the one preceding it. He was tall and thin and small featured. I knew that centuries ago there had been European merchants in this area, and when I remarked that he resembled a Westerner, he confirmed my suspicion, telling me there was Portuguese blood in his family. There were others like him though the tsunami had erased the town in which most of them had resided. But it was his view that the event was not entirely a disaster. "God blessed us with the tsunami," he said; "if it did not happen, we would still be fighting."

For non-militarized citizens the era of conflict had been a terrible one, and confusing. M. had once been shot at. He had been driving home from fishing at the jetty when soldiers in Indonesian army uniforms stopped him at a checkpoint. They ordered him out of his car and waist-deep into the sea with a handful of others who had been detained. The soldiers were searching for a rebel commander by the name of Muharram who was said to be in the area and demanded that these people reveal his whereabouts. No one knew or was willing to speak, so the soldiers began firing automatic weapons over the heads of the half-submerged civilians, hoping to intimidate one enough to start talking. This went on for hours, then, abruptly, without having gotten their information, the soldiers released them. M. told me that Muharram went uncaptured for the duration of the conflict, then, with a laugh, he added that Muharram went on to become a major elected official in the new special autonomy zone.

But M. said that he was not sure that the soldiers had truly been with the Indonesian army. Both sides worked to deceive civilians. Government commandos disguised as rebels would harass people in order to turn the population against the separatists. Rebels disguised as government commandos would do the same for the inverse effect. And then of course there were times when the Indonesian army and the rebels dressed only as themselves. Civilians had no way of knowing which side to blame for which crimes.

I repeatedly met with M., and, with some frequency, he brought me to his favorite coffee shop, where we would pass hours making small talk over coffee and a variety of fried, sugar-glazed breads. Around us, people filtered in and out, and M. seemed to know all of them. We sat with a friend of his who boasted to me that, "Hindu, Buddha, Christian, Islam," he'd read the entire quartet of Karen Armstrong's books on the world's major religions. He liked the books very much and said that all of the religions follow the same god. M. had his own ideas; he said to me: "Your country practices some ways of Islam, like helping the poor, but they are not Muslim. They are kafir." He spoke proudly of Aceh's Islamic character, and of the goodness of the people here, but then spoke darkly about a group of what he called "illegal Muslims" who honored foremost not the Prophet Muhammad but the Prophet Abraham. Not wishing to have a theological discussion, I left the comment alone.

Later, we passed another rainy day at the coffee shop and saw someone M. did not know. Two tables away an ancient-looking white man in dripping clothes sat alone. A peculiar sight in Indonesia as most expatriates are wealthy and conspicuous about it. If I had wanted to think logically, his soggy clothes, single rolled-up pant leg, and hair matted thick with rainwater would have led me to the conclusion that he had been riding his bicycle through the foul weather; but at the time, with no bicycle in sight, and as wet, disheveled, and unexpected as he was, he appeared to me as a man having just washed in from the sea. M. had seen him here before and wanted to speak with him. "Perhaps we can do business together," he said (M. was always looking for ways to supplement his wages). It became clear that he wanted me to make the introduction. When the man shuffled by our table, I reached out to him: "Where are you from?"

He was from Australia but had been living in Indonesia for thirty years, and his name was Ibrahim. He was affable and spoke in a warm, grandfatherly way. He moved frequently throughout the country, working odd jobs, most often as a translator. M. saw his chance, pried for business leads, and found one. Ibrahim was bringing in a large group of Western tourists and needed someone to handle logistics. To iron out the details they switched into Acehnese, which Ibrahim spoke fluently. For a few minutes I was left to sip my coffee and idly observe the rain that fell outside.

An Arab name being so unusual for a Westerner, I asked Ibrahim if he was a Muslim convert. He replied that he followed "the religion of Abraham," and that his birth name had been Clive. M. was silent. Jews, Christians, and Muslims, Ibrahim went on, all came from the same tradition. He asked me: "What was Jesus?," and I knew that he wanted me to say that Jesus was a Jew, but, regardless of its historical accuracy or inaccuracy, I knew that most Indonesian Muslims vigorously maintained that all the prophets, extending to Adam himself, were Muslim. I said that I didn't know. He smirked boyishly, then exclaimed, "Jesus was a Jew!" "Jesus was Muslim," M. objected. There was silence: neither wished to offend the other. After a moment, I spoke up, steering the conversation to a neutral topic.

Later, taking a ride together in his pickup truck, M. said to me darkly, "I don't think I can offer Ibrahim my cooperation. He follows a false religion."

The day before I was to leave, M. and I took a drive in his pickup truck down Aceh's west coast to visit his aunt and a family friend M. said I would be interested to meet. Green mountains, blue waters, gray rocks—it was beautiful country painted in broad strokes. We traveled along roads cut into the mountain slopes that periodically opened up into small coves with flat, grassy coastline. Glancing up the mountainside from these vantage points, I was able to gain another purchase on the scale of the tsunami. Thirty meters up, M. pointed out to me, there was a boundary in the vegetation; below the line was young growth and above it was the taller, older growth that had escaped the water. Everyone living in this area would have been pulled out into the Indian Ocean. At one time these empty fields comprised homes, farms, and some hotels. "If Aceh were Bali, this would all be redeveloped by hotels," M. said. "But we don't sell freedom here." He paused in order that I appreciate that he was talking about American culture—my culture—full of the sex and alcohol he had seen in Hollywood movies. He added: "Freestyle life."

Before long we had made it down into the southern tracts where mountains gave way to plains on which there were new, sturdy, and tightly clustered towns. Among these were neat enclaves of identical houses, white with green roofs and white with maroon roofs. These had been part of the disaster relief effort by the government of Saudi Arabia, which had proudly stamped its national crest on the front of each home. There were other settlements paid for by the Turkish government and bridges and roads built with American money.

M.'s aunt lived in a wooden, single-story home in an outlying village. She was light skinned and blue eyed, and she told me over tea that as recently as her father's generation, groups of Acehnese had been able to speak Portuguese. But these communities had clustered along an area of the west coast that had been erased by the tsunami. M.'s friend dropped by. This friend, M. told me, had been a GAM spy. The man was so mild and ordinary-looking that he would be difficult to describe—and in fact ordinariness is the extraordinary asset of that profession. I asked the man about GAM. He replied curtly that it had ceased to exist, which was neither avoiding my question nor quite answering it. "I don't believe him," M. said to me in English so that neither his aunt nor his friend would understand.

We spent several hours with M.'s friend walking about the town and its coastline. On a hilltop there was the ancient tomb of a Muslim holy man, and on the beach pottery fragments from a Portuguese settlement that had been here centuries ago could be turned up as easily as seashells. Neither of these interested me; I wanted to know more recent, more secret histories, but my new companion either knew nothing of interest or was very good at his job. He admitted only that during the years of open conflict he had lived in Banda Aceh and contributed to the resistance by passing to the rebels information on government troop movements. When I asked him whether he retained his earlier occupation, he smirked and shook his head. I understood that it was not a question of if but of *to what extent*. But even that question might have been irrelevant: there is an immense difference between mustering the cunning to stage guerilla attacks on the Indonesian military and the ability to govern a breakaway state within reach of Jakarta, whose military, already considerable, has designs on growing to rival that of China. Nor are Indonesia's allies in the global "War on Terror" keen on losing a portion of a client state to Muslim radicals—and these days, military technology and economic interdependence being what they are, global concerns, with rare exceptions, trump those of local disputes. I hoped, for M.'s friend's sake, that the rebels had the wherewithal to recognize this, and the lack of breaking news coming out of the region led me to believe that they did.

Our return trip would take several hours, so we said our goodbyes to his aunt and his friend in the early afternoon. With my departure from Aceh imminent, in the car I became more aggressive with my questions. Why had M. disbelieved his friend? M. explained that when the MOU had been signed, a major commander went into hiding and remained hidden somewhere in the mountains. And from time to time in the newspaper there were stories of weapons caches being uncovered by the Indonesian army. (A few months after I departed, the city was reminded that munitions are plentiful: in connection with political unrest, there would be two grenade blasts. No suspects were arrested.) I read from M.'s face that he was pleased by the thought of a continuing resistance. Why had he never joined the separatists? He said that, as a government employee, he would have lost his job. "But even though I never joined, GAM still likes me," he said, "because they know I am not a corrupt person." Evening was falling, the monkeys had come out to the road as if to supervise our departure, and M., hoping to be home before night, increased his speed. At one point, as we skidded around a mountain switchback, M. looked at me and said, "Beautiful, but dangerous." He was speaking about the roads, but his words could have been for Aceh itself, and I pretended that they were.

Winter 2012

The Lighthouse at the End of the Hudson

ANTONIO MUÑOZ MOLINA

Suppose one can keep the quality of a sketch in a finished and composed book?

—Virginia Woolf

1

For some time, I went down to the edge of the Hudson, to run along a path that then reached north to 125th Street and now extends up to the George Washington Bridge. Heading south, the path borders the river through Battery Park, at the tip of Manhattan. My home is near the river, on West 106th Street, named Duke Ellington Boulevard. Duke Ellington lived in the mansion around the corner on Riverside Drive. An old newsreel shows his funeral procession heading up Broadway to the Cathedral of Saint John the Divine. Almost every day the weather allowed, I would pass Duke Ellington's mansion's corner in my running clothes and shoes, and I would cross the park, Riverside Park, to go down to the river's edge. At the park, the esplanade covers the tunnels for the railroad line that begins at Penn Station and heads north to Albany, the state capital, to Niagara Falls, to the border with Canada.

2

The vault of the bridge, almost a tunnel, frames the first sight of the Hudson, confined by the ugly apartment towers and the cliffs of New Jersey. A Willem de Kooning painting titled *Door to the River*: to push a door and suddenly find oneself before the glow of the river. At the end of this arch of shadow lies a brightness that changes each day. Gray brightness of cloudy

253

days, blinding on sunny mornings, red and golden in the afternoons, arctic on snowy winter days when the landscape disappears underneath the whiteness and naked trees become the black scribbles of Henry Callahan's photographs. On sunny days, the river lights up beyond the arch of the tunnel like a sheet of steel waving in the wind. Spring, summer, autumn are the luxurious seasons of colors. Winter is the austere age of drawing. But David Hockney says that there is color in winter too: *Even in dull days there is a lot of color if you look. The trees only go black when it rains.*

3

If you look. I would run and think I was seeing everything. It took me just a few years to realize I was barely noticing anything. A few years and the pain in my knee and the sole of my foot that forced me to stop running. How I've longed for the elastic pounding of heels against hard but not rigid soil that gives in gently under each step, unlike asphalt; the passage from fatigue that seems undefeatable to a sudden burst of unexpected lightness; the flood of endorphins that widens the lungs and makes one sensitive to the smell and texture of air in dilated nostrils. Once I was running up the river's edge, and a storm surprised me. It was summer, and I was grateful for the first tepid drops that hit my face, the smell that came up from the earth and the river. The agile fingers of the rain drummed across my shoulders, on my chest. The wet cotton of my shirt stuck to my skin.

4

A moment later my hair was dripping and my shirt was soaked. I shielded myself under an immense elm that covers the path with its crown. Toward the river, its branches reach over until they touch the water. Sheltered by the tree, I felt gratitude for its powerful and benevolent presence. The rain clinked against the leaves. Parallel to the path by the river flows the other incessant river of traffic on the West Side Highway. Beyond that, higher, over the crowns of Riverside Park's oaks and maples, the towers of Riverside Drive are outlined as cliffs and lighthouses, with rows of windows where the last red glow of the afternoon fades away. When the rain stopped, I continued to run, and I quickly recognized the pain in my knee and the sole of my foot. From that day on, I would look at the elm for a moment each time I ran past it and almost greeted it like the friendly stranger one becomes used to recognizing on the street. When I ran, I did pay attention to the trees, and I liked knowing almost all of their names, in Spanish and English. The eye truly discerns a tree only when we are aware of its name: the elms, the oaks, the acacias, the maples, the cherry trees that give their name to that stretch of the esplanade, *the Cherry Walk*. I would think about the tradition of trees as a source of wisdom in so many primitive cultures.

5

I thought I saw the river. I absentmindedly imagined its monotonous course to the sea. When I ran heading north, I could see the silhouette of the George Washington Bridge in the distance. Le Corbusier used to say that it was the most beautiful bridge in the world. I never went too far on these runs. I didn't even know that the path extended to its very columns. Or that there is a lighthouse under the bridge that has been there since long before. Now that I know that the lighthouse is there, and I've visited it many times, my gaze has focused, and I can make out its shape from far away. We see things if we know they exist. I would see the silhouette of the bridge soften in the mist or sharpen in days of luminous clearness. While I ran, I would look at the flattened soil or the stretches of pavement ahead of me and at the buildings on Riverside Drive. The Riverside Church tower and the round structure of Grant's Tomb served as markers of distance covered. I didn't know that peregrine falcons nested on the top of the church tower. I didn't know that falcons in New York fed on sparrows and pigeons and on small rodents. I had never looked at a falcon, perched on a branch in front of me, still, his round eyes fixed on mine, solemn and condescending as a god, like the black obsidian falcons from the Egyptian wing at the Met.

6

As I ran I would notice the things people dispose of as they leave the river's edge. Food containers, plastic bottles, soda cans, beer bottles, newspapers, plastic bags, religious pamphlets. A plastic bag or bottle takes about five hundred years to decompose fully. I loved the path so much I was offended by the lack of respect toward a place of such beauty. Sometimes I would pick up a bottle or a can and take it to the nearest trashcan. As a gesture of restitution to the path and the river, of respect to the elm that had sheltered me from the storm. Once I carried a half-finished beer bottle, and the runners and cyclists that passed me shot disapproving glances in my direction: a wanton runner quenching his thirst with beer.

7

But I didn't see much more. During that time my own obsessions enclosed me, and I ran as if inside a bubble or a bottle. The obsession with keeping track of time as I ran, with how long it would take me to become exhausted, with making it as far as Grant's Tomb, with feeling the beginnings of pain in my knee or the sole of my foot. My own obsession with being foreign: passports, visas, legal procedures, the wait for the green card. Faster runners, cyclists would leave me behind with the murmur of wheels after a warning bell. There is no stealthier machine than the bicycle. Or I would pass slow runners with faces red from exertion who seemed to drain their last reserves of energy attempting to escape death as it trailed closely behind. The afternoon's final ray of sun would shine across the highest windows of buildings, and just before it dissipated, it seemed as if the river stream was set ablaze.

8

Thoughts flow not to the rhythm of a race but to that of a walk, says a book I am reading. Our hunter ancestors often prevailed over animals not by shooting arrows but through their endurance, running after them until they collapsed. *My only comfort is in motion*, writes Dickens in a letter. When not restlessly imagining his characters in motion, pen hastily scratching paper, stopping only for a dip in the inkwell, Dickens continued moving, walking through the streets of London, and the rhythm of his step punctuated the creations he would pour into his novels as soon as he returned to his desk. Dickens' novels are full of people who walk the streets of London. Before him, Thomas De Quincey had walked through that city best, intoxicated with opium, terrorized by the multiplying faces of strangers, by the multitudes of faces in which he could never find the only one he wanted to see, that of his beloved Ann, the young prostitute who had taken care of him. The pain forced me to stop running, and I rarely frequented the path by the river. Meanwhile, I got used to taking long walks. There is a different flow to thinking and seeing when one walks instead of runs. It's more difficult to remain in that trance one disappears into while running, in which there is actually little thinking and not much seeing beyond what is needed to avoid falling or getting lost. Walking fast and noticing what I see without reducing speed, I've managed to write a whole article or section of an essay or a novel in my head. My only comfort is in motion. In the morning, as soon as I've finished breakfast, I'm agitated by the desire to go outside. I stir around the house like a nomad burdened by sedentariness. Sorrow most easily condenses into a cloud in domestic air, especially during winter, in a city of exaggerated heating. Walking fast, one can escape. Depression loses one's trail for a while.

9

I again found myself outside, filling up my lungs with the first medicinal gulp of cold air on a January morning, and I took off, stepping on crunchy snow, headed toward Duke Ellington's mansion's corner and the stone steps that go down to the park and the path by the river. A day or two before, I had returned to New York after an absence of many months. I didn't pass a single person. I was bundled up like an Arctic explorer. Hands in gloves and gloves in jacket's pockets. Hat on my head, covering my ears, under the hood. Collar up and buttoned over my mouth, breath dampening the coarse fringe of my scarf. The crunch of steps on snow as marked in the silence as the naked shapes of trees in the whiteness or in the low and smooth gray of the sky. Bird calls reverberating as if in a vault. Each distinct and all pronounced by invisible birds. Only a few times have I walked through a park or the woods in the snow, and I've barely ever stopped to identify the songs or species of birds. I see one, atop a scrawl of a naked branch. I see it because its plumage is blue and its crest is black. Seeing a bird or a tree and not knowing its name is not really seeing it. I now know that these blue birds are *blue jays*.

10

To the south, a handrail encloses the path by the river. When someone is leaning on it, it seems as if he were looking out on the deck of a transatlantic ship. In the distance, the parallel lines of the handrail and the path get lost in fog. There are no footsteps on the snow. The fog has also erased the other edge of the river and the bridge. The river emerges, immense, from the very fog, limitless like the ocean it flows into farther down. A ship's siren howls in the fog. A moment later the ship emerges from the fog, a blunt and black barge carrying mountains of minerals or junk. A beautiful word materializes in the imagination like the ship or the sound of its siren: *foghorn*. We would have to search for a Spanish translation that definitive and exact, a drumroll of two syllables that would not be possible in our verbose language. *Cuerno de niebla. Claxon de niebla. Sirena de niebla. Nieblasirena. Sirenaniebla.* Kindred sirens can be heard far away, especially at night, when American trains sound their horns.

11

I remembered, in previous winters, seeing large ice floes going downstream. I remembered or, rather, I thought I had seen them. But what I see today I have never seen before. It is not a river flowing downstream, dragging flat ice blocks. It is not a river flowing downstream. It is a lake of sorts or a still ocean because there is no edge on the horizon. It's not still: it undulates like a spine. It's an extension of blocks, of pieces of icebergs, stuck to each other, juxtaposed, colliding, something like a valley of marble shredded to pieces after a cataclysm, a prairie of ruins getting lost in the fog. Like noticing the arrival of a glacier with a casual glance. It is the ruins of a city's palaces and temples, of an entire civilization. Sometimes piled one upon another, as columns or roofs, as facades broken into pieces, or separated by cracks that still maintain an outline where they were fractured. Moving, if I look carefully. Moving very slowly toward the ocean like the glacier that millions of years ago lodged this same channel in the Hudson. Moving with the slow undulation of the robust, primitive backbone the width of the river might possess. The words come back to me: *ice floes.*

12

I only stop noticing the movement when I'm not walking. Once the noise of my boots crushing the snow and the whooshing of my pants and jacket stop, I'm able to hear something. When the river sounds. What you hear is the ice. Fragile collisions between ice blocks, brushing, crunching, something being torn apart, rushes of water or compressed threads within ice cracks. That secret murmur comes from the whole river. There is nobody else along the path, and that makes it more forceful. I can hear it better as the path gets farther away from the highway and traffic. Even better when there are no airplanes crossing the river in the direction of LaGuardia Airport. In the halt of my footsteps, in the silent parenthesis, emerge crushing and crackle and grazing and fracturing and the crash of the colossal traveling city of ice ruins.

Yesterday I could not recall the word, *témpano.* Wanting to conjure it, I could only get close, *bloque de hielo, plancha de hielo,* even its equivalent in English, *ice floe.* And I needed it so I could really see what I hadn't seen before: the whole breadth of the Hudson, as far as the opposite edge, turned into a great plain of ice, yet not smooth but as if made up of ice debris of every size, some like sunken walls of houses made of ice collapsed into themselves, like ruined cities of ice unraveling as far as the eye can see, to New Jersey, in the direction of the ocean, or upstream, toward the silhouette of the George Washington Bridge subtly drawn in the fog.

Témpanos: finally, the exact word. *Témpanos* of all sizes, dissolving into splinters or into a gray pulp of ice, broken into uneven blocks, covered with snow. I was walking on the path along the river, and it was only when I stopped that I perceived it: the plain of ice was moving, with mineral slug-gishness, the current dragging it, and as I paid more attention, the move-ment became more singular: the blocks near the edge remained motionless, or almost; they advanced more rapidly as they drifted away to the river's center, or more accurately, less slowly. And each ice floe had its own move-ment, distinct from the rest, colliding with others, brushing against them. If just slightly slower, the movement would have been imperceptible to the eye. And as I stopped I noticed something else: you could hear the ice. In the interludes between bursts of traffic on the nearby highway or between the sound of airplanes climbing over the river, there was a permanent sound, a rupturing of sorts, scrapes, cracks opening deliberately, quiet blows. I remembered that background noise that according to astronomers is the Big Bang's fossil reverberation. It seemed as if I were listening to a geological murmur, like that of tree roots trembling under the earth. There was no one else listening to that sound in the whole length of the snowy path.

13

From memory emerges the accuracy of a scholastic definition, explained and learned word by word, copied with meticulous calligraphy on a black-board, on a wide-ruled notebook. There are crucifixes above the board and on the teacher's desk, and on one side a portrait of Franco and on the other one of José Antonio Primo de Rivera. There is a globe in the corner. Old oilcloth maps hang on the walls. Their cracks blend in like geographical accidents: the shaded outline of mountains, the palest river valleys.

—What is a river?

—A river is a continuous stream of water that flows into the sea.

—Or into another river.

14

> Nuestras vidas son los ríos
> Que van a dar a la mar
> Que es el morir.
> Allá van los señoríos
> Derechos a se acabar
> E consumir.
> Allá van los ríos caudales,
> Van los ríos medianos
> E los chicos.
> Y en llegando son iguales

Los que viven por sus manos
Y los ricos.[1]

15

Childhood memory deposits, fixed with awe, with the strangeness of half understood words. Iceberg. *Témpano*, with its coldness and its ice shape. *Carámbano*: in bleaker winters past, icicles hung like stalactites in the gutters. The large earthenware pot, broken in half, that served as cistern in our corral at home was covered with ice in the morning. The green water became hazier under its strigose surface. A river. A continuous stream of water that flows into the sea. Or into another river. We would learn the names of all the main rivers in Spain and recite them from memory. The Miño, the Duero, the Tajo, the Ebro, the Guadiana, the Guadalquivir. Continuous streams of water in the brown and ochre of a dry country's map, the oilcloth quartered as if with slopes of ravines without water, just the northern front shaded in green, where the ocean's blue was also more intense. Spain borders north with the Cantabrian Sea, west and south with the Atlantic Ocean, east with the Mediterranean Sea. The blue of the Cantabrian and the Atlantic looked like the fake blue of the sea in adventure films. In a few films, white men were outfitted in red coats and three-cornered hats and the natives in leather pants and jackets and moccasins, carrying axes with feathers, Mohawks on their shaved heads. They would run, gliding through thick forests, or row canoes across very wide rivers that at some time could have been the Hudson. Typical Westerns took place in sun-flooded, desert landscapes, but the

---

1. Our lives are rivers, gliding free
    To that unfathomed, boundless sea,
    The silent grave!
    Thither all earthly pomp and boast
    Roll, to be swallowed up and lost
    In one dark wave.
    Thither the mighty torrents stray,
    Thither the brook pursues its way,
    And tinkling rill,
    There all are equal; side by side
    The poor man and the son of pride
    Lie calm and still.
        —Jorge Manrique, trans. by
          Henry Wadsworth Longfellow

most mysterious ones featured the deep dimness of the woods that for us could only exist in the movies.

16

In the summer, on Saturday afternoons, when the hot and humid air acquires a tropical density, there are musical performances by the river's edge, at the foot of a slope next to the tennis courts. The slope itself functions as an acoustic box. Musicians play with their backs to the river. Jazz music sometimes scatters in the wind. The human voice that sounds like a sax and the sax with the quality of a human voice dissolve in the river's breeze and blend into passing ship sirens and the squawks of seagulls. The sun sets as the music continues. The crowd is scattered across the slope, sitting in groups, with the static calmness of a Seurat painting, colors dissolving into light fog, women's print dresses. When it becomes night and the musicians start putting away their instruments, luminous scribbles of fireflies fill the air. Virginia Woolf: *the idea of some continuous stream, not solely of human thought, but of the ship, the night, etc., all flowing together: intersected by the arrival of the bright moths.*

17

Past rivers of my life. The Guadalquivir was not that river from maps but a brightness as of sheets of broken mirrors in the bottom of the valley that separates my native city from the Cazorla and Mágina mountain ranges. North of the Jaén province, among hills with red soil stitched together with olive groves, the Guadalimar was a slow and ochre river one would see on the train coming back from a trip. My father gave it a name that was not on the maps or in the school encyclopedia: *el río colorao.* In Granada, the Darro is an agile aquatic snake at the foot of the hill from where the Alhambra rises, and soon after, a river buried below asphalt, under slabs of pavement at Plaza Nueva and the provincial narrowness of Reyes Católicos Street, under the path known in Granada as the Embovedado. Poor Ángel Ganivet, a local from Granada, saw his native irritation flare up in his Baltic exile with the felony of covering up the river. *Los dos ríos de Granada*, says Lorca. *Uno llanto y otro sangre.*[2] When my oldest son was only a few months old, and I was a municipal employee who wrote in the afternoons, I lived in a building by the edge of the Genil River. Its precarious stream was visible from my window.

2. The two rivers of Granada / one tears, one blood.

One winter it rained and snowed a lot over the Sierra, and with the melting ice the Genil flowed so tumultuously you could hear it in the background all night long. In fiction, experience transmutes according to laws similar to those that originate in dreams: once I wrote a story about a man who lived alone on a high floor near a river and the roar he heard in the darkness when he couldn't fall asleep was the same that had kept me company on nights of insomnia that winter when my oldest son wasn't even a year old.

18

The great European rivers: those from my first trip outside Spain, to Italy, at twenty-two, backpacking, with my friend Nicolás Latorre, closest of friends at an age when friendship is truer and wiser than love, as it is learned first. I had never seen broadness as majestic, force as solemn, the Arno in Florence, first, and then the Tiber in Rome, its water ochre and greenish, as monumental as its bridges, creating foam as it crashed into the pillars' angles, the Arno and the Tiber accentuating the pure happiness of being in Italy, awe and the desire to see more leading me, as if the rivers were carrying me. In the mornings, my friend Nicolás and I would sit on the parapet of the Ponte Vecchio to warm up under the blond sun of Florence, so it could take away the humid cold of the tent where we slept, so poor in Italy we couldn't even pay to stay in the campgrounds. We fed ourselves on canned sardines and cured meat we had brought from Spain, the cheapest mortadella, on grapes we bought by the pound from any street vendor. Sitting in the sun on the parapet, we would look at the Arno as we passed between us the milk carton we would get for breakfast.

19

Alluring names of rivers. On the dry land of our town, the world maps at school nourished our imagination and, without realizing it, we tasted the poetry of river names as we recited them from memory. There isn't any great river that doesn't have a memorable name: the Arno, the Tiber, the Seine, the Thames, the Nile, the Rhone, the Vistula, the Elbe, the Danube, the Yangtze Kiang, the Ganges, the Mississippi, a name so long and full of i's and s's it's as if it begins flowing in saliva inside the mouth, the Río de la Plata, the Paraná, the Orinoco, the Amazonas. I conjure up names, and I'm carried by the currents of remembrance: the Somme, the Loire, the Volga, the Amur. We would learn its source and its mouth and the sea or ocean in which it ended and the kilometers of its expanse or its width. Which one was the longest river in the world, the Mississippi or the Nile? The Nile began in the Mountains of the Moon. They were verbal rivers, sinuous lines on maps, names. Back then there were a lot less images. The rivers of literature: the Thames, when I went to London for the first time, it was Dickens' river, and it belonged to Conan Doyle and Chesterton's enigmas of dazzled reason; the one the sailor Marlow traveled upstream on a boat in *Heart of Darkness*, in Buenos Aires, at the Costanera, the first time I visited the city, in the apocalyptic spring of hyperinflation and election propaganda and streets covered with wood planks and shaken by the constant roar of generators, I leaned to look over the river's edge and recognized the precision of a verse from Borges:

> *Y fue por este río de sueñera y de barro*
> *Que las naves vinieron a fundarme la patria.*[3]

20

I've learned the name given to the Hudson by the Lenape people, who inhabited the island of Manhattan when the first Dutch settlers arrived: *Muhheakantuck*. River that flows in two directions. River that comes and goes. But the intensity of meaning weakens when it has to be distributed among more words. Muhheakantuck. *Rioquevayvuelve*. I had the reason for that name in front of me, and it took me long to see. I didn't see the river before me but the abstract image of a river, the definition of a word. The Hudson sometimes goes to the sea and other times comes back. Muhheakantuck. The word itself says it. It took walking there and transiently exiting the hermetic bottle of my obsessions to see that sometimes the river's stream goes backwards, pushed by sea currents. That close to its end, it ceases being a river to become an estuary, and much of what I see is salt water. That, and not just because of the direction of the wind, is why it sometimes smells so powerfully like the ocean on days when the tide and fog come from the south. The air tastes like salt and algae. The objects the river carries downstream come back the same way. The coming and going of its name is that of a breath. Also that of the tides and of seasons. Systole and diastole. Night and day. Any objects thrown in the river will remain there a long time. Going up and down. Returning just before reaching the ocean. A storm throwing them against granite blocks piled up at the shore. Sent sailing by a high tide.

---

3. And was it along this torpid muddy river
   that the prows came to found my native city?
   —trans. by Alastair Reid

The blow of a wave or a low tide leaving them once again stranded ashore. Staying there for weeks or months. The sun dries them and gives them the texture of bones.

21

Each day, the river is the same, and it is a different river. It's many rivers simultaneously. I hadn't noticed that the river can go up and down not in a successive way but at the same time: the tide pushes up, the current goes down; the water ripples in the wind from the northwest to the southwest, the current flows at the same time. A garland of trash and dirty foam circles parallel to the shore between a current going down and one going up. Currents are thin rivers circulating within the river. You will not walk by the same river twice. Every hour of the day changes the wind and changes the light, and the river possesses a different color and moves in a different way. Today a powerful wind blows from the other shore, northeastern wind, and great waves crash against the slope of rocks on this side. Metallic sparks jump from them under the slanted afternoon sun. Instead of flowing along the riverbank, the water breaks against it like the sea against a boardwalk. And since the tide is high, the waves splash my face and almost reach the path. The foam sometimes leaps to windshields on cars on the West Side Highway, the other incessant river that goes in two directions, tires giving off a sound like that of fabric tearing as it adheres to the wet pavement. The river of burnt gasoline and carbon monoxide runs day and night along the Hudson. But looking more closely, I notice two simultaneous movements in the choppy water: while coming to the shore propelled by the wind, the current continues to travel down. River that moves in two directions. And when it hits the shore it carries with it old tree trunks and broken-off branches that crash against the rocks with the fatalism of shipwrecks. The wind violently bends naked shrubs and tree branches that curve toward the water. The inclination of branches modeled by the wind's persistence is a photograph or an x-ray of its invisible and constant thrust.

22

A very large man or a very large woman approaches, arms swinging. From a distance, the very small head and the enormous oscillating and shaking body don't let me identify sex. Neither do the loose breasts spilling over the stomach under a workout shirt. Arms swinging, puffing, sweating, and closer up I can see that it's a woman and not a man. White iPod headphones hang from her ears.

23

Seagulls flap their wings and squawk high up in the wind, as if under the arteries of a vault. They motionlessly glide in vertical air currents. They plummet to a floating island of branches, dry leaves, garbage. With still majesty, they swing over whirlpools at the river's edge, their shapes like spindles sharpened by wind and water, pieces polished and rounded by millions of years of evolution, much more slowly than the old tree trunks that have been in the water for long, eroded by it, soaked, thrown against rocks in high tide, run aground for days or weeks or months, drying in the sun, later rescued by the current, going down to the sea but not getting lost in it, returning, in the direction of the same forests where they originated, where they were chopped down and turned into beams or torn off from the trees by a hurricane or by the blow of lightning.

24

Pascal: *Les rivières sont des chemins qui marchent et qui portent où l'on veut aller.*[4] Henry Hudson traveled up the river in September 1609 believing it was the road that would allow him to circle around the north of the American continent and reach China. Just a few years later, as Henry Hudson led another voyage searching once again for the passage to Asia, he fell victim to a mutiny by his crew, who finally abandoned him at the bay that now bears his name. Nothing else was ever known about him. When he was abandoned, his son was on the boat with him.

25

Odd people by the river's shore. The ones who seem transplanted from another world. An elderly man advancing to the edge with slow and brief steps, opening his legs in a particular gesture. Before the water, his legs apart, his eyes half-closed, he moves his hands horizontally in delayed tai chi movements. An old man in a black suit, wearing a black hat, a black tie, black shoes, his hair white and his face very red, his legs bent, wiping a handkerchief over his forehead, looking as if he had come from a wedding or a funeral in a small town on the Mediterranean coast. For a moment, that grandfather, with his reddish peasant's face and his faint white hair, with his bent legs, has become the ghost of my paternal grandfather, who died twenty-five years ago.

---

4. Rivers are roads which move, and which carry us whither we desire to go. Trans. by W. F. Trotter.

26

Cry Me a River. Write Me a River. Write me a river, don't describe it to me. Narrate it, make it sound in my ears, let the smell of mud and algae inundate my nasal passages, let its current take me away. *The voice of many waters,* says the book of Genesis. The magnanimity of accepting everything and carrying it. The river as that old well-built bearded man from Roman mythological sculptures. The Old Man River of the blues. And the movable darkness that must be at the bottom, the silt between gray and greenish, sunken objects, the heaviest, skeletons of dead bodies never found, the drowned ones and the murdered ones, old electrical appliances thrown into the river under the cover of the night, the gun a murderer threw over the railings of the G. Washington from a moving car or from the edge of a dock, the millions of leaves from all the winters that were so soaked and sinking and have rotted in the silt in the bottom of the river and are part of it, blind fish feeding on debris, the submarine plains and slopes of oysters, if any are left, that for centuries filtered the river water to maintain an extreme purity and were then harvested or extinguished because of pollution, gigantic tires that sometimes surface when the tide is very low, entire tree trunks that have been simplified and petrified, shoes missing their mates, shells from zebra mussels that invaded the Hudson in the eighties, and having colonized everything and exterminated almost every other form of life, then extinguished themselves by eating each other because there was no other food left. Write me a river. Write rivers of ink. Writing as a river that hasn't stopped flowing since I've had use of reason, a river of chalk on blackboard, of pencil on ruled school notebook pages, of typewriter ribbon, of fountain pen, of cheap pen, of extra fine Pilot marker: how lengthy and sinuous must be the river of all the words one has been writing throughout one's life, the river of each and every one of our steps.

27

On September 9, 1609, Henry Hudson captained the *Half Moon* as it headed for the first time through a river that as far as the crew was concerned didn't have a name and gave no indication of where it led. The river, already as wide as an estuary, measures almost two kilometers from one edge to the other. The *Half Moon* measured less than thirty meters from prow to stern. We can no longer imagine what it would be like to venture into a landscape that has no familiar characteristics or names, that does not exist on maps. An officer named Robert Juet kept a journal onboard: *This day the people of the country came aboard of us, seeming very glad of our coming, and brought green tobacco, and gave us of it for knives and beads. They go in deer skins loose, well dressed. They have yellow copper. They desire clothes, and are very civil. They have great store of maize or Indian wheat, whereof they made good bread.*

28

The smell of nature on the American continent at that time was so profound that navigators perceived it even before they had spotted solid ground. The smell of the woods. *A sweet smell of flowers came from the earth*, writes Columbus in his diary. Glimpsing the tree-covered coast in the distance, Giovanni da Verrazzano says he sensed "the sweetest odors." Verrazzano is now the name of another extremely beautiful bridge that unites Brooklyn and Staten Island, a bridge of lines so simple it could be a Platonic bridge, a bridge that could be a Brancusi sculpture. After a long voyage and the surely foul odors emanating from the ship's interior, the crew of the *Half Moon* smelled the grass and flowers as they went upstream. Dutch settler Adriaen van der Donck writes in his diary: *The air in the New-Netherland is so dry, sweet, and healthy that we need not wish that it were otherwise. In purity, agreeableness, and fineness, it would be folly to seek for an example of it in any other country.*

29

The country is full of great and tall oaks. Robert Juet's journal aboard the *Half Moon*, September 4, 1609.

30

Going down to the river has become a habit, a mania, an idée fixe. If I don't have a lot of time, I cross Riverside Park and the tunnel and stop for a few minutes by the shore and return home as rapidly as I've come. I don't take more than half an hour. I check to see whether the tide is high or low: when it is very low, blocks of algae-green rocks and heavy objects that are usually submerged appear, truck tires, for instance, iron beams, an entire engine, a refrigerator stripped of its door. When the tide is very high, the water almost reaches the path, and the river is swollen like the belly of a woman about to give birth. I stand at the edge for a while: I examine the current, smell the air, look to see if there is a lot of trash. Sometimes the Hudson looks so clean, it would seem to be a river that precedes human presence, and other times it's a junkyard, depending on the day, or on the tides, the wind, who could know. A lace of foam extends across two or three meters from the edge for many days. The foam is the color of snow on the sidewalk that won't melt after a few days: a filthy white that is almost gray, a gray of filth and of a rat's back. Owing to some principle of fluid mechanics, the foam adopts shapes akin to leopard or zebra spots.

31

As I walk, very closely to the handrail, I don't take my eyes off the garland of dirty foam, the thin river of trash that circulates parallel to the edge, swinging in the current, sometimes broken by it, disarranged in discontinuous threads. When I find myself engrossed in the catalog of things that make up the garland of trash, I walk without seeing anybody I pass, cyclists and runners I could crash into. If I had a notebook and a pencil with me and I could write without diverting my eyes from the water and without stopping, I would make a complete list of everything I'm seeing. Sometimes what I do is take quick photographs with my BlackBerry, so many that I never get to review them and even less to transfer them to the computer or to attempt a selective classification.

32

A condom. A faded tennis ball, torn like orange peel. An inverted water bottle. A large yellow plastic lid like the ones from big jars of olives. A red construction hat that oscillates like a half-shipwrecked canoe. Another condom. A ripped bag of potato chips. A large bag from Duane Reade drugstore, the red and blue of the logo already somewhat dull. A plastic cup from McDonald's that still has a straw stuck through the lid, like a small mast. A baby's stroller's seat pad. A Tetra Brik that has lost any traces of branding. An almost new tennis ball, greenish yellow and shiny. A golf ball atop a wave's crest. A woodblock with burnt borders pierced with a large rusty and crooked nail. A double page with *New York Post* headlines so soaked it is starting to disintegrate. A gasoline can. A plastic watch with a pink band. Half a compact disc. A thick biker's glove that surfaces in the water like the open hand of a drowned man. A shrunken athletic shoe and its sole coming apart. A condom that must have been in the water so long it has dilated to impossible dimensions.

33

The day after Valentine's: a long-stemmed rose with great red petals half plucked and the remainder of a cellophane sleeve floating in the river with the ghastliness of a suicidal woman.

34

Among the blocks of granite and concrete that compose the shore are holes filled with rat nests and cracks that have trapped some of the smallest objects that the river tosses or that were left behind when the tide got lower. Bits of chip bags, toy car wheels, chopped-off Barbie doll heads, pen caps, pens advertising restaurants or banks. Plastic bottles, mostly. Encrusted in almost every crack on the rocks at the Hudson's shore are one or many plastic bottles in various degrees of decay. Small water bottles, some still with a quite visible label, others opaque and fractured by the passage of time, by the constant cycle of water immersion and sun exposure that makes the material more rigid and takes away its transparency, after erasing any labels. Water bottles that evoke bottles with messages from a shipwreck. Bottles, lids, plastic lighters, hotel minibar liquor bottles, cut-up shoes, old sneakers, shrunken, sneakers that have lost their shoelaces or that have lost everything except the sole. Pieces and lumps of plastic that have lost any recognizable shape after many years between the shore and the water. And much closer, if you crouch down and dig in the cracks, always with the fear of encountering a rat's snout, increasingly smaller flakes of plastic, rusty and deteriorated coins, particles that get mixed with grains of sand and splinters of granite, that will return to the water and end up in the stomachs of fish or of seagulls or of the geese that go up to the path to sunbathe, chemical components that never dissolve, that will reach us through a chain that begins with plankton and fish.

35

But what the river takes and brings most, more than plastics, the river that comes and goes, what it leaves ashore when a wave breaks and what it recovers later when the tide rises, is wood, wood in every stage of transformation, from the closest to its origins to the most degraded, from a swollen sage branch full of leaves that are still green, cut off by the wind, to a tree trunk that already has the texture of fossil matter, to a beam from a building built a century or two ago that remained standing for a hundred years and was demolished or destroyed by a fire in such a way that it still shows black burn marks. Pieces of wood drift up and down the river: sometimes aligned in a current that crosses precisely through the center of the river, beams and trunks and sheets in a severe formation that looks like an invading army, in water that is between green and gray and under an opalescent sky of bellicose metals.

36

Time, great sculptor, says Marguerite Yourcenar. The river is the great sculptor of wood. A whole tree chopped by a storm or toppled by lightning falls into the river; after some time and going up and going down and almost reaching the ocean and being pushed back upstream by the tide, it slowly becomes an abstract form, the naked sculpture of a tree. It loses all specificity: its leaves, of course, its slight branches, its bark. It will take years or decades. It gradually dismantles until it bears the extreme starkness of a tree silhouette. Drenched with water, dried in the sun ashore, later dehydrated by the sun, polished as it brushed against water, returned to the current by the clash with the edges of stones at the shore, it finally acquires the whiteness of raw bone, the light gray of ashes or minerals. The trunk, the forked crown like two arms amputated at half length, nothing more. The tree is no longer elm or beech or maple or any of the tall and great oaks that covered the island when Henry Hudson arrived. It is nothing more than a tree, the vestige of a tree, the fossil testimony of a tree. How to know which hillside upstream it sprouted from when a seed that fell on the ground, was nourished by the organic rotting of leaves that accumulated through the years, autumn after autumn, winters of snow and rain and animal footprints. How could I possibly trace the biography of that tree trunk that I've seen for the first time this morning, catapulted near the edge of the path in the tempest, still drying in the sun, well-built and cast away, like Ulysses on the shore of the Phaeacians.

37

A woman stands atop the concrete blocks that jut from the river's edge. People usually sit there to read, or to look at the water, or to type on an iPhone. There is also the occasional sunbather in the summer. One season, at that same spot, as I ran I would see an older man meditating in perfect lotus posture, his back straight, his legs crossed, the nape of his neck lightly angled, the palms of his hands on his lap, thumbs touching. Today I see the woman who is so close to the edge I'm afraid she might jump. She has her back to me: she holds something in her hands. Since I'm carrying my BlackBerry, it occurs to me to take a picture. I get closer, and I see that she has thrown into the water whatever it was that she had in her hands: something white, with thick pages, a notebook that sways on the foam of waves breaking by the shore. The woman turns and sees me. She has curly hair, a round and tranquil face. I say, "Can I ask you something?" She nods. "I saw you throw something into the water. Could you tell me what it was?" "That's between the river and me," says the woman, polite but conclusive. *That's between the river and me.*

I continue my walk, and I hear somebody call me. It's the woman with the notebook. "I'm sorry if I was rude. Why were you asking me that?" "I come to the river almost every day. I observe what people do." "It was a manuscript for a book. I'd take notes and write drafts on that notebook. I have the complete book on my computer. Now that I've finished it, instead of keeping the notebook, I brought it for the river."

38

Yesterday fog covered the Hudson, after several sunny days. The bridge and the opposite shore were practically invisible in a gray that in the distance blended into the calm gray of the water, almost as still as a lake in the windless afternoon, in the freezing point of the tide. Unmoving river that doesn't come or go, swollen river, broadened, almost overflowing at the shore, almost reaching my feet on the path, bulging and heavy as the belly of a woman about to give birth.

39

Driftwood. Wood drifting, branches by the shore dried to the gray whiteness of bone, whole lengthy tree trunks going down the current's center like vessels and run aground between two rocks and oscillating perpendicular to them, with the agitation of docked gondolas, beams of fallen or burnt-down or demolished buildings, squared shoes with bent nails that went through their soles, logs insects drilled for years that then fell in the water, sticks like the knobbly staffs of prophets in the desert, their cylindrical pieces like drums or like buoys, sheets of bark that have acquired a mineral texture, sharp splinters with missing points that became holes that suddenly turn them into the head of an animal with sharp pupils and a large snout, the organic shapes that the drift itself has modeled from wood: bare sticks with a serpent's wave, with a serpent's eye, with a fissure at the end that is the serpent's mouth. One afternoon, among the rocks on the shore, a piece of a beam, broken in a peculiar way and grazed by the oblique sun, appears exactly like a whale's head, its round eye almost under its hump, its lower jaw narrow and hanging. I get close, I take a photograph, another photograph, from another angle, so absorbed it takes me a while to notice that a smiling black woman is curiously watching what I'm doing, an expression of anticipated tolerance on her face.

—What do you see there?

—That piece of wood. It looks just like a whale's head.

—You can see some strange things when you look through somebody else's eyes.

And when I put away my BlackBerry and continue along the path, the woman stays back there, still looking at the block of wood in which she now sees a whale.

40

My memory serves me well when trying to recall the moments when I learned certain words. I first found *driftwood* in a book that I bought in a secondhand store in London, twenty years ago, during a very rough time in my life; I lacked any fixed center, I, who so poorly tolerates irregularity and uncertainty. It was John Franklin's diary of his first Arctic expedition. My English was much poorer then. Driftwood was one of those words that appear and reappear until the lazy reader has no choice but to look in the dictionary. Finding pieces of wood drifting in that Arctic solitude could be a matter of life or death: the difference between having fire or not. I was going between transitory housing and hotel rooms, and Franklin's book was a pillar of sorts. It was small, hardcover, with very clean typography, with a particular smell of aged paper, as it must have been over a century old. I would bring it with me in my coat pocket and at nighttime would leave it on bedside tables that rarely ever belonged to the same rooms. Driftwood.

41

Driftwood is wood that has been washed onto a shore or beach of a sea or river by the action of winds, tides, waves or man.

Driftwood: n madera f de deriva.

But translating one word using multiple words, two dry syllables into seven, would be to relent. One day, during a walk by the river's shore, I coined an exact equivalent, a word that doesn't yet exist in Spanish: *maderiva*.

42

To drift. To let go: led by the river's current, by the impulse of steps, of the elastic pounding of heels against flattened soil, soil thick with humidity and leaves that the same steps have been pulverizing, transmuting into fertile ground: to let go in the fortuitousness of thoughts, in word associations; in the liquid river sprouting from the tip of a pen, sharp as a burin, in the murmur it produces when it slides across the smooth and solid pages of a notebook. To let go so that writing might happen by itself, so that it may unfold without a design like the dirty foam garlands and soaked leaves and wood drifting along the river's shore. Writing that walks and flows, stream of consciousness, river novel, novel river, *flujo de conciencia*, flow of ink forming words like a meander, a humble substitute for the Chinese or Japanese calligraphy pen brush, writing and drawing both, instantaneous writing, shorthand of the here and now.

43

Writing of somnambulism and rapture: *Howl, Paterson, Leaves of Grass, El don de la ebriedad, Livro do Desassossego, Dirección única, Le spleen de Paris, Poeta en Nueva York, The Bridge, The Day Lady Died*. William Carlos Williams, so reticent, his exterior manner that of the respectable New Jersey pediatrician, immediately celebrated the hallucinatory excess of *Howl*. The generosity of this veteran and consecrated poet toward a practically unknown young man, from the formal doctor with his gray suit and his tie to the practically unknown young man, the bearded homosexual beatnik from the Village, recognition imparted by Williams from profound fellowship, indifferent to appearances, or rather respectful of them, the two men accepting the differences between them, recognizing themselves in the other not in spite of but precisely because of these, because they widen each personal condition. It is Haydn's generosity toward Mozart: the humility of the teacher who recognizes the eruption of a much younger talent.

44

Preparations for a walk. I wake up early, and as I look out the window, the block across the street is drenched with sun. The clothes people wear along the wide and tranquil sidewalk of 106th Street, along Duke Ellington Boulevard, are my weather indicator: somebody wears just a shirt to walk the dog; a cyclist passes in a light athletic jacket; a young woman with bare legs. The poplar in the patio behind the kitchen hasn't yet sprouted new leaves. In spite of the continuously mild weather of late, the trees of New York preserve their naked branches, scribbles against the very blue sky. On some branches, plastic bags trapped after the wind has picked them up undulate like Tibetan flags for months or years. More or less faded or torn, unthreaded from being out in the open, some like algae hair, like submerged white heads of hair. Plastic that infects the air just as it does the river's water and the shore's soil and roots.

53

Baudelaire: *Mon cher ami, je vous envoi un petit ouvrage dont on ne pourrait pas dire, sans injustice, qu'il n'a ni queue ni tête, puisque tout, au contraire, y est à la fois tête et queue, alternativemente et reciproquement.*[6]

54

To see everything, to hear everything, to pay attention to everything. To the sounds of the river water crashing against the shore and of car tires sliding across the wet asphalt on the highway, of runners' soft footsteps and of stealthy bicycle wheels, and of airplanes flying upstream over my head, one after another, coming from the ocean, climbing in a straight line until turning east when they're up by the George Washington Bridge, on their way to LaGuardia Airport. To see the small Mexican immigrant sitting alone on a flat rock in front of the water, keeping close to him the old bicycle which he might use to do deliveries for a restaurant, immersed in what longing, in what solitude as unapproachable as the scale of the landscape and the width of the river. To see the young blonde woman leaning over her book as she reads, instantly acquiring a possibility of beauty that actuality might refute if she were to turn in my direction. To hear the wind among still bare branches that lean toward the water, or the others, the ones that could be x-rays of the direction of the wind, the ones that have straightened as they've grown. To listen to the murmur of splashing water and of soaked beams hitting the edge of rocks at the shore, over and over again, with each wave that pushes them, just as it models them and wears them down.

55

Fernando Pessoa: *By art I mean everything that delights us without being ours—the trail left by what has passed, the smile given to another, the sunset, a poem, the objective universe. To possess is to lose. To feel without possessing is to preserve and keep, for it is to extract from things their essence.* I have walked along another estuary, wider even than the Hudson's: Mar da Palha, with its gold straw radiance, across the stairs of Lisbon, the mouth of the Tagus.

---

6. Dear friend, I send you a work no one can claim not to make head or tail of, since, on the contrary, there is at once both tail and head, alternating and reciprocal. Trans. by Keith Waldrop.

Coat, l
wine, s
It was
spots o
the Go
artist r
tied w
less: li
day, li
tide in
of air
bottle:
ing fr
swellin
more
pling
arose
iron b
sound
side th
instea
a view

60

Then,
foot o
lighth
into li
simul
seem
ture l
never
the e
at the
so str
edges
the li
the ir
rocks

56

Today I walk north. Yesterday, I went down to the island's southernmost end. Yesterday it was warm, and the wind brought sea mist with the smell of algae. Today it's cold again, and the wind comes from the plains and the interior lakes, from the Canadian frontier and the Arctic Circle. I put on my coat, and if I take my hands out of the pockets, they freeze. I have on my black sneakers and the seventies style coat that I bought at a secondhand store ten years ago and haven't stopped wearing since. I like the tenacity of things that last. Using them wears them down, cracks them, models them, like the weather and the sun do to my face and the river to the tree trunks it carries from one place to the other and deposits at the shore and retrieves from it. The coat is missing a button, and there is a hole in the right pocket. The shoes have carried me with invariable equanimity during times of darkness and of elation that wouldn't attenuate. They have stepped across the Atlantic dunes of Doñana, the dried leaves of the forest in Inwood, the sidewalks of Barcelona and Bilbao, the well-trod ground of Parque del Retiro and the Botánico in Madrid, the fragrant meadows of the New York Botanical Garden. When I take them off at night, I leave them at the foot of the bed. A Zen teacher said that shoes must be taken off at night with reverence, in gratitude for all the leagues they have covered for us.

57

Looking down at the ground. Stepping on soil freshly moist from rain in Riverside Park. The path has become a great puddle. The soil can't absorb any more water and overflows with it. The rain has soaked and tenderized whatever leaves are still left in winter. By now, the dried leaves from the fall have accumulated in successive layers and have a consistency close to dust, to the fertile ground they're becoming. Fallen, pushed by the wind, drenched in the rain, buried under ice, softened when ice has melted and mixed with mud, stepped on by people and animals, hardened and brittle once more, covered in snow, soaked again more slowly and gradually as it melts. The patchwork of leaves possesses a materiality that can only be discerned when walking with our eyes on the ground, absorbed in it, lost in its baroqueness of diverse species of leaves, lumps of soil, rocks, broken branches, innumerable fragments of the most tender branches broken under the weight of the snow or with the blowing of the wind, branches that fell this winter and past winters, a good amount eaten away by parasites, drilled into by insects, flakes and splinters of wood, bits of tree trunks, warped more as they increase in

size,
keep
time:
snou
a sna
shar

58

In m
grou
Smal
penc
a po
capit
elem
perh
ing t
fossi
Ther
I tak
strar
by a
or a
from
if I c
It's i
coin:
foun
shin
as I
five
swea
com

59

A fri
ton
stray
West

skins, with festoons of fox, wolf, and lynx hides hanging from the rafters, dim light gleaming on the polychrome mounds of fur.

Living there in the 1940s and '50s, one could see how Europeans and Eastern colonials must have felt as they traveled west in the eighteenth and nineteenth centuries. It didn't seem possible that one could diminish the seemingly endless supply of land and animals through hunting, trapping or fishing, through building towns and highways, through mining and logging. In most settlements in Alaska when I was a child, the wilderness was virtually at the end of every street. In winter when things got rough, moose would wander into town to be chased through backyards by neighborhood dogs. Everyone had a bear story or two, usually as a result of fishing expeditions, for bears love fish even more than we do. One high school buddy was literally run over by a bear that didn't realize they were both stalking the same caribou. After the collision, each sat up to see the other and find their quarry dashing over a hill in the distance. Another classmate, of my college days, was chased down by a good-sized black bear while surveying near Fairbanks. Grabbing him by a leg, it shook him the way a dog does a stick until he fainted. Whether puzzled or disappointed, the bear lost interest in the limp rag-doll result and wandered off, leaving my friend with a bad knee thereafter.

An engineer with whom I worked had been treed by moose and bears numerous times. Once, somehow, while still wearing a pair of skis, he even managed to scamper up one of the scrawny black spruces that occupy millions of acres of the Territory to get out of harm's way. On another occasion a family friend retreated prudently from a fish-filled stream only to have a bear he'd encountered follow him to his truck. Willy jumped into the cab locking the door. The bear followed and, climbing into the bed of the truck behind him, began to gnaw on the cab in an attempt to open it like the wrapping of a tasty morsel. Upset about what was happening to the finish of his shiny new vehicle, he shot the bear through the rear window and drove back to town to get it replaced, dead bear still in the back.

As children we all knew about bears. Blackies were a nuisance and could be found around garbage dumps without fail. Grizzlies, the big silvertips, were most feared. It was commonly held that if a grizzly entered one's cabin through a door in search of food, it would more than likely exit through one of the walls, leaving a heap where your home had been. All in all, it was great not to see some of the wildlife—bears, wolves, wolverines, or one of the most dangerous of all, a cow moose with a calf—just as it was fun to see others, such as foxes, caribou, mountain sheep, or a bull moose feeding belly-deep in a pond with sheets of water cascading from the broad antlers as his head came up with a mouthful of water lilies, their dripping stalks dangling from his muzzle like giant pasta.

It's worth noting the diet of the giant brown bears of southwest Alaska. In the Kodiak Island Wildlife Preserve alone there are over 3,000 bears. This is more large carnivores than in all of East Africa. Then there are all the bears in the rest of Alaska. When Kodiak bears first come out of hibernation, they eat grass for about a month while waiting for fish to arrive. Once the various types of salmon—reds, silvers, kings, coho, humpies, dog, and chum—begin their runs, the bears feast on fish for several months. After that it's time for berries, which they eat for another month. At any time they are happy to add ants, field mice, young deer and caribou, or birds' eggs. I once came across a place along the Wood River near Naknek where a bear had successfully managed to dig out an entire colony of bank swallows, feasting on all their eggs. The result of this near continuous and omnivorous activity is that Kodiak bears have a healthy and well-balanced diet: first salad, then meat (fish mostly), and finally fruit, albeit each for at least a whole month at a time, and in that order.

Humans are fond of salmon also. When I was young it was so plentiful and common that I came to despise it. The Natives around Bristol Bay and all along the coast of the Bering Sea caught modest quantities in set nets along the shore and mouths of the rivers. Those in the Interior used fish wheels (traps) farther up the Koyukuk, Kobuk, Yukon, and Tanana rivers. In southeastern Alaska, the canneries of American corporations had built enormous fish traps across the mouths of nearly every major river that captured the vast majority of salmon attempting to return to spawn, resulting in a devastating decline in the population. While this was bitterly fought by Native Alaskans, residents, and particularly the seasonal fishermen who came north to fish every summer, corporate lobbying in Washington, DC, kept the traps in place. The first official act of the state legislature and governor in 1959 after statehood was to ban commercial fish traps, which saved the Pacific salmon runs in the Gulf of Alaska and at the time reportedly created 6,000 jobs for fishermen. Around Bristol Bay, which has the largest runs in the world, large quantities of salmon were hung up to dry and mostly used for dog food. On the Kenai Peninsula in those days salmon coming up streams from the Anchor River to spawn were so plentiful in places they would fill the water to the point where their backs could be seen rising above the water with some even pushed sideways out onto the bank. By the time the fish made it hundreds of miles up the rivers to the Interior, they were too beaten and torn up to be considered for much of anything other than the dogs. I remember friends after a weekend of fishing on the Kenai driving around with a pickup truck full of salmon and giving it away half a dozen at a time. In those days salmon fishing wasn't really considered sport. In the cannery communities of the coast, it was and still is business and employment.

Rainbow trout and Arctic grayling, however, were considered tastier and more challenging. As a small boy, I admired the grace and colors of grayling more than any of the other the fishes I knew: small and brownish with purplish sides spangled with blue-black spots and a tall sail-like dorsal fin covered with midnight blue spots encircled by rings of crimson-lake, they fought fiercely before one could tire and land them. Wading into cold glacial rivers and streams to fly fish in the Alaska Range and the Interior or the lakes north of Katmai and west of Iliamna and east of Bristol Bay, whether in frequently squally weather or blissful sunny days, was always fun, and hard work, and produced fabulous food. Here one also found lake trout, the largest and tastiest of all American freshwater trout. There were other fish, of course, particularly great northern pike, Arctic char, and Dolly Varden, each in its region and environment. The idea of *catch and release* was decades off in an unimaginable future. As an eight-year-old, I began my fishing days walking to a small nameless creek a mile or so from our house at Mile 26 (from Fairbanks on the Alcan Highway). Here I learned that a foolproof way—even if unsporting as I came to see later—to catch any fish is to put salmon eggs on a hook of any kind or size. Fish find them irresistible much as many of us do caviar.

In late summer at the end of the twentieth century in a broad area north and west of the dormant snow-covered cone of Mt. Iliamna, only a short hop from Dillingham, Naknek, and Bristol Bay, one could find dozens of fishing parties composed of well-heeled businessmen, executives and guides, numerous cabins, lodges, boats and floatplanes. The Tikchiks, a series of interconnected lakes, had become known as some of Alaska's most productive and desirable fishing territory that is now on the map of those who compare notes in men's clubs and boardrooms of Manhattan and Chicago, in sports bars and airplane lounges in Seattle and Washington, DC. Part of its renown is due to the fact that here one finds rainbows, Dolly Varden, grayling, great northern pike, Arctic char, and various salmon in season. On the Labor Day weekend of 1959, after a summer of working as a project engineer in Dillingham, I and an acquaintance hired Harvey Stovall to fly us into the Tikchiks. At the time there were no structures and virtually no people at all, only fish, birds, bears, a lot of water, brush and muskeg stretching to the Alaska Range far off in the distance to the south and a vast level horizon stretching to infinity in all other directions. There was only one tent and an old-timer who was about to come out for the winter. "Blackie" had been there all summer with Lady, his black lab, fishing, poking around, and hiring out as a guide to the few parties who come from Bristol Bay and Anchorage. We camped with him for three days, fishing all day. We caught one large fish after another of every variety. It was a truly unforgettable experience even for someone raised in Alaska who'd been fishing for years. No wonder it has since become one of the more treasured and expensive retreats for those who care about such things.

☙❧

Mile 26, where we lived for several years, was a military construction site in the woods of the Tanana Valley. My father and a couple of other men were in charge of building what became Eielson Air Force Base, a mainstay of the Strategic Air Command in the Cold War with the Soviet Union. Partly because of haste, and partly to insure that the construction equipment wouldn't stall and stop running as the men changed shifts, it was kept running virtually 24 hours a day. In spring there still was an amount of snow and ice around; and when the second shift operators of the Caterpillar tractors, scrapers, and trucks arrived to take over, they would find animals, mostly caribou and moose, standing around the engines warming themselves.

The pressure of a dynamic environment populated by a plethora of creatures pushing against one's daily routine was something we took for granted. The world was alive, and you had to pay attention or it could, and most probably would, bite you. Forest fires started by lightning strikes were common, earthquakes frequent—plus there were several dramatic volcanic eruptions west of Anchorage in the Aleutians and on the Alaska Peninsula that coated the city and woods with ash. While not so dramatic as the giant eruption of Katmai that buried several villages and towns on Kodiak Island and along the Shelikof Strait as decisively as Pompeii at the turn of the last century, they were sufficient that one summer, while I was on a survey party for several weeks running line along the base of the Chugach Mountains near Anchorage; every time we cut trees or brush we stirred up clouds of fine choking volcanic dust. There were floods as well in some locations annually. Nature may be beautiful or even sublime, as nineteenth-century aesthetes and philosophers believed, but it is not cute or pretty, and it certainly is oblivious of us. Nature is neither friendly nor cruel, words that have been used to describe it—it just *is*. As a colleague recently remarked about the Katrina hurricane, "That wasn't a *natural* disaster, it was a *human* disaster. Katrina was an example of nature being very energetic."

Every spring in the north when snow and ice begin to melt, and the waters that have been locked up for many months flow together on the way to the sea, there are all manner of flood events, large and small. Thousands of miles of ice sheets on all the rivers and streams are overtaken by water flowing beneath and above them as they begin to rot, fracture, and break up into blocks, pans, floes, and fragments that at times are enormous. Soon this almost inconceivably colossal realm of slush, ice, and water all begins to shift and move downstream everywhere, headed for the sea. In the towns of Alaska, spring breakup makes for great lotteries with much fun known as ice pools, consisting of great speculation and substantial financial prizes for people to bet on. Spring breakup also makes for the creation of countless ice jams and pileups that cause frequent floods in historic settlements that, with the exception of some seacoast villages and towns, are nearly all on rivers. During one of the floods, when I was a child, as the whole world seemed to be melting, I recall seeing the *Emma R*, a stern-wheel riverboat, tied to a streetlight on what normally would have been Front Street in Fairbanks. A day later the road south of Fairbanks was washed out at a place called Moose Creek near our home. Several of us who'd made it to school that morning with our driver as he forded the rising water had to be flown home in an old C-47, where we remained until the Tanana River returned to its banks a week later.

All the rivers in Alaska are still quite wild and dangerous. Bitterly cold with snow and glacier melt, fast moving, laden with tons of silt, and filled with surprises such as submerged and floating logs, sweepers (fallen trees), and debris, with constantly shifting channels and gravel bars, they are tricky to navigate. No one enters them on purpose, for most who fall in die. Expert river guides and Natives proceeded with caution on the rivers; still there was a fair amount of river travel in summer. Yet in those days many of us knew of someone who was surprised and upended, losing all his gear, and in some cases worse. The father of one of my closest friends was drowned in a fishing accident the summer after second grade, and I remember numerous disasters, near tragedies, and accidents involving the rivers around us in the Interior. The accident most feared by trappers was to fall through rotten ice into a creek or river in late winter with a sled and dogs. While the wild animals may be fierce on occasion, the landscape, so beautiful, can also be deadly.

Hunting in the fall was as thrilling as it was humbling. Millions of birds that had spent the summer feeding and raising their young across the Arctic were on the move. I'll never forget dawn one September morning on the tide flats near the mouth of the Susitna River when the entire sky turned black and deafening with geese from horizon to horizon as they lifted off and began to wheel about above me. I had been spotted by one of their canny sentries while attempting to sneak up a slough from Cook Inlet hoping to bag one or two. Later that day I nearly shot a swan when a group of them suddenly exploded a few feet in front of me from a bunch of tall grass on the margin of another meander. The enormous mass of white feathers immediately overhead, however, instantly told me this was no goose. As on all such trips, whether hunting ptarmigan in a gray half-light and new snow at Twelvemile Summit north of Fairbanks—a week earlier it would have been easy to see them in their fresh white winter plumage against the russet heath and crimson berry leaves, but now it was nearly impossible to see them—or hunting willow grouse (we called them spruce hens) in the birch and spruce forests of the Tanana Valley where the mottled birds were perfectly disguised to help them blend into the visual welter of autumnal leaves, branches, twigs, moss, and brush—we usually went home thoroughly exhausted but with ample food for several delicious feasts.

While grouse and ptarmigan were all around, they were quiet and furtive. In contrast, throughout the Territory on myriad lakes across the Interior in late afternoon and for several hours, one could be jolted out of quietude by the haunting strangled call of a loon. It is hard not to love the peculiar deep round sound of its unforgettable wind instrument and the pullulating rhythm of its call as it echoes from the hills around a lake in the early evening as the silver line of its wake slices across the golden reflection of a still forest and sky in the mirror surface, the low-slung black bird with its white necklace effortlessly gliding along.

In the wilderness, when humans have yet to begin to concentrate upon work and it is difficult to see and focus one's eyes in the hazy light of early morning, so many creatures are up and about: caribou, moose, foxes, rabbits, weasels, beavers, bears. There are others, however, particularly songbirds, that go about their business in the heat of the day. One particularly strong memory of life in the bush is that of walking back and forth all of one summer across an open meadow on the edge of the woods in the warm sun listening to horned larks (we called them meadow larks, but Sibley and others today don't). Their glorious long and melodic song ends with a trill. Unlike European counterparts made memorable by Ralph Vaughan Williams' composition *The Lark Ascending*, whose song is delivered high in the air as they do indeed rise, larks in the North—and in the rest of the

West—do so while sitting on the ground in the grass and low shrubs where they feed and nest. Their long chirrs and melodies spring up out of the earth in various spots across a field as they assert themselves and contest with each other. It is a heavenly and joyful sound like no other and spreads a harmony and delight through the air across the bush. I was eight years old, blissfully alive and bathed in bird song, as free as my vocal companions in the light summer breeze.

Wherever one is in Alaska, whether in the valleys and ranges of the Interior or on the Arctic coast, out in the Aleutians or in the rain forest of Southeastern, throughout the summer one is surrounded by birds, an infinite variety and quantity, much in the manner of those who moved West in previous centuries accompanied by vast herds, colonies, and flocks of animals. Fewer and fewer Americans today have the pleasure of hearing a high haunting sound approach as if from nowhere and of gaping heavenward in the autumn as formations of geese, cranes, and swans stretch across the sky heading south. In the lower 48 today, instead, nuisance flocks of resident Canadian geese hang about the suburbs polluting parks and corporate campuses and are all that people there know. Strangely enough, I don't remember when or how all these birds arrived in spring. They must have snuck past at night headed to the Arctic prairies in small groups and silent bands or something. Suddenly one day in late spring they were all back. Only a few months later, when the weather abruptly turned crisp and masses of gold and russet appeared on the hills among the waves of black spruce, they appeared en masse, for several weeks, drifting south. And then they were all gone until next year. A few days later snow flurries would begin and winter would descend.

Weather

People who learn that I am from Alaska nearly always ask, "Wasn't it cold? What was it like?" The answer is, yes, in the winter it was cold, but in summer in the Interior it was warm, at times downright hot (at least to us), and the wind would blow dust for days on end. Puzzled, they ask where dust could come from in the subarctic. The answer is not only did it rise up in waves from gravel streets, roads, and construction sites throughout the Territory, but also in great clouds from thousands of acres of sand and gravel bars in the network of rivers, sloughs, and deltas that sprawl across the Territory from Canada and the Interior to the Arctic Ocean and Bering Sea.

It is true. The winters were very cold, dark, and long. Fairbanks was colder (as was much of the Northern Hemisphere) when I was young than it has become in recent years. It was cold in the winter, bitterly so. At times the mercury in thermometers simply disappeared and temperatures stayed between 20 and 40 below for a week or two at a time. There are hundreds of tales of hardships and heartaches, of difficulty and death that have to do with winter in the wild: everything from cabin fires to drunks freezing to death in the snow on the way home from a friend's place or a bar. Dozens of times the van taking us the 26 miles to a two-room school in 40 below zero weather broke down, and the driver had to walk for help while we sat huddled in the dark in the paralyzed unheated vehicle until he returned with help or a different vehicle. On a couple of occasions, one or more of the kids had to be carried off the van with frostbite when we finally reached home late at night.

Climate is what you expect. Weather is what you get. One is a record and statistics, a description and numeration of past experience smoothed over into averages and probabilities. Each day, however, turns out to be a sequence of unique conditions and events, a combination of sun angle and direction, temperature, season, and the residue of yesterday's events. In the North everyone listened to weather forecasts attentively to hear just how bad or not it might be each day and night, and then went out to see what would really happen. Later we listened again to learn what it was that we'd just experienced. Increasing cold, oncoming storms, high winds, snow or rain, more of the same, or clearing, or a warming trend for a day, a few days, a week, or a month. Or rain again. More, heavy at times, thunderstorms, a gale, also fog for the week, or overcast for week after week. It affected life and work. In the woods one summer, running line with a survey crew in the Chugach Mountains, it rained every day in the month of August, much as I remember it also did up in the Interior in July a few years earlier. Rain every day for 30 days in a row. Everything was soggy and rotting. The streams and lakes were brimming full. All the vegetation was wet. After the first week we gave up wearing rain gear as we were completely soaked anyway with sweat from the work of clearing a line through the dense undergrowth and tangle of fallen logs, branches and trees, devil's club, shrubs and ferns. We were going to be wet whatever we did, all day every day, so we abandoned our slickers and rain pants and worked less encumbered in sodden jackets and trousers. Water in its many manifestations was present everywhere in the Territory. The seasons I spent out on Bristol Bay it was cloudy and windy, and rained part of every day. Fog and clouds came up out of the ocean to the west and blew onto shore continuously. A constant sequence of squalls, showers, wind, and dazzling patches of sunlight explained why old-timers occasionally referred to that portion of water north of the Aleutian Islands as "the smoky sea."

There were ramifications to the cold as well; among them were: the freezing over of all of the lakes and rivers; snow for months on end; human activity moving almost exclusively indoors; a set of devices and rituals having to do with starting and keeping automobiles running; and numerous strategies for resisting the cold, ranging from layers of clothing (scarves, inner mittens and outer shells, long underwear, sweaters, jackets, hats, parkas, fleece-lined boots to go over shoes or mukluks) to excessive intakes of coffee and alcohol. Social life revolved around stoves and coffeepots.

My first winter in Fairbanks was bitterly cold, even by northern standards. A week after we arrived in December 1946, my parents walked home from an evening out on the town only to discover that it was 69° below zero, which explained why they thought it seemed really cold. They'd walked back to the camp we were living in across the Chena River from the commercial downtown of Fairbanks. In summer the river divided the town into two halves connected by only one bridge. This continued until the late 1950s when a second one was built. Things were completely different in winter when a number of streets that led down to the river connected across the ice to others on the opposite bank. Then for many months pedestrians and cars moved back and forth in all directions on the rock-hard ice, and the town was integrated spatially despite the cold and its being plunged in near perpetual darkness. The river became a road and our central civic space. A large area was cleared for ice-skating near the bridge at the heart of town. The starting and finish lines for the North American Championship Sled Dog Races, which took place in March every year during Winter Carnival and predated the more recent "Iditarod" race that begins in Anchorage, were located here. During this event, Fairbanks's answer to Mardi Gras, there were Eskimo games, parties, and various entertainments, including pari-mutuel betting on the races taking place on the river in the middle of town. Like the potlatches and fur rendezvous of the nineteenth century in regions farther south, these were festive events heralding the end of the coldest weather and trapping season as animals began to lose their dense winter coats. Movement nearly everywhere would become extremely difficult as the thaw began and much of the land became an endless terrain of bogs, streams, and difficult rivers. It was a festive time, and people came once a year from far and near to powwow, gossip, party, trade, shop, get drunk, win some money, spend some money, get news, and see relatives and old friends. The Natives—Eskimos, Aleuts, and Athabascan Indians—the subtleties and nuance of their many language groups and historic names and identities largely unrecognized to whites at the time—came from all over the Interior as well as from the Arctic slope and coast. Among other things, the races brought the best mushers from around the Territory with families and friends in their furs and calico-covered traditional parkas from missions and settlements on the Kuskokwim River and Brooks Range, from Eagle and Old Crow, from Anaktuvuk Pass and Shismaref, from Nome and Kotzebue, Fort Yukon, Tanana, and Nenana, Bethel and Point Hope. Many of them were fierce competitors and represented their Native communities in ways similar to basketball teams in the States: Andy Paul, Silas John, Simon Paul, Paul Silas, Raymond Luke—a biblical roll call of names acquired in mission school, with an occasional Anglo like Gareth Wright from Nenana—were household personalities thanks to the detailed radio and newspaper coverage. For three days they would set off several minutes apart every morning from a starting line on the ice on the river near the bridge in Fairbanks and disappear, racing against the clock. Reports during the day from various mileposts kept everyone in town abreast of their times and progress. Late in the day they would all come back, some with a dog or two in the sled. They had to return with all the dogs. If their feet became too cut up by ice or they became exhausted, the drivers couldn't just cut them loose for the time being. The weather varied from year to year from balmy and sunny to blizzards or 35 below. Unlike the Iditarod race of today, named after a remote region southwest of Fairbanks once only reached in winter by sled teams, a contest that also tests the skills and mettle of both humans and dogs, these earlier races before and after World War II were as much about community and annual cycles of human contact as the Palio in Siena or the footraces and games of ancient Greece once were.

Old-time freight drivers in ankle-length fur parkas and fur hats with long leather bullwhips organized the drivers and teams to depart in order. But what seemed truly special were the teams of dogs. Dozens of teams of these handsome animals would be scattered all along the river curled up in lines and clusters in the snow, noses tucked under the curl of their tails, exhausted from running 35- to 40-mile legs of the multi-day race. There were always dogs around wherever one was in Alaska. Having joined humans at some point in late Neolithic times, they were very useful to have around given the prevalence of wild animals and the need for their help at times. They also provided company for people on their own, often in trying circumstances. There were all sorts of dogs, most notably huskies, Siberians, and malamutes, as well as dogs commonly associated with hunting such as pointers, retrievers, setters, and spaniels. In the 1940s sled dogs were still in use for hauling freight in the Interior and in western and northern Alaska. Racing for fun and money was just beginning. Kennel clubs with registered breeds weren't yet on the scene, so the dogs used for hauling tended to be big, heavy, and to my eyes fearsome-looking mixed breed creatures. The common husky at the time was a relatively short, stocky dog with brown or yellow eyes. They tended to be tan or brown with beige chests. Malamutes, our high school mascot, were tall and rangy, with black on their backs and gray or white undersides. Their facial markings were inevitably a black mask of sorts, and their eyes were brown. Of all the somewhat domesticated dogs, they most closely resembled wolves in their height and length. Siberian huskies were smaller, thin, pale gray and buff, with distinctive pale blue eyes. Many people in Fairbanks between 1946 and 1950 still kept teams of dogs. One that I remember clearly was that of Jackie Landrieu. Leonhard Seppala had left his dogs to her when he left town and retired to Tacoma, Washington, a few years earlier. Seppala, a Norwegian immigrant, was the crucial driver who mushed 340 miles round trip through a raging blizzard across the ice of Norton Sound and through the Interior from Nome to Nenana and back to carry the diphtheria serum that stopped an epidemic there in 1925. Jackie, like many in town, was still outraged that credit for this feat in the press Stateside had been given to the man who only carried the serum from Fairbanks to Nenana (only 55 miles' distance) and that a statue had been erected in New York's Central Park to honor Balto, the wrong dog, instead of to Togo, Seppala's lead dog whom he was forced to retire after the exploit due to the strain of the effort.

As even children know, a lead dog is chosen for intelligence, experience, and its ability to obey and comprehend both the driver and the terrain as it unfolds. For this reason all manner of dogs have ended up in the role. Gareth Wright, who won the North American Sled Dog Championship Races several years in a row, had an Irish red setter for his lead dog. His team, like other winners of the era, consisted of a group of mixed breeds that weren't as large or heavy as the freighting and pack dogs. I recall with affection one dog named Buck, part wolf, part malamute, who had been shot in the hip and walked with a limp. He seemed to me to be an exceptionally handsome and gentle creature. By the mid-1950s many of the racing teams, however, were composed of the swifter, lighter Siberians. One other feature of these animals should be mentioned. Sled dogs can't bark. Lying in bed at night, one can hear them howl, however. They can create an ungodly ruckus when a bunch set to doing so. Even so, it's not as chilling as when one hears wolves with their long-drawn-out howl, gradually sinking into a low grainy moan. Still, the sound of dogs could pose difficulties in trying to relax and fall asleep.

Summer was different. In Fairbanks sled dogs slept and ate, tried to find shade, often digging deep holes in the ground into which they crawled to cool off in the small shade it afforded and by being closer to permafrost. Some broke loose and wandered about and were a nuisance. On the Bering Sea and along the Arctic coast the Natives fed those that they kept tied up on dried salmon. Some turned their dogs loose in the spring forcing them to forage for themselves, resulting in their reverting to a less domestic and fairly wild state. In the autumn they were rounded up, caught, and beaten back into submission to form working teams. For this and various reasons, wild dogs were always an issue one had to be aware of as a child. Like many young Americans from the 1920s through the 1950s, I was encouraged to sell newspapers to produce my own spending money. Few of us had allowances, and those who did found the sums less than they wished to have. Goods of all sorts, even comic books, were expensive on the frontier. Delivering the evening paper throughout a neighborhood was one thing in the States but an entirely different thing in Alaska, especially in the winter. Not only were the temperatures, snow, and ice fog an issue, so too was the darkness. Trudging along at 30 or 40 below with a bundle of newspapers in the gloom, I was perpetually on the lookout for wild dogs that tended to gather and prowl about in packs like wolves. An avid reader of comic books, I'd seen a series of advertisements on their back pages for flashlight batteries that depicted adventurers holding wild animals (mostly mountain lions in the illustrations) at bay with the unfailing beam of their flashlights. This was my security. Armed with a flashlight and fresh batteries, I would set out from home into the darkest depths of my snowbound paper route. Oddly enough, I have no memories of delivering papers in the summer even though I know that I did, as it simply wasn't stressful. On several occasions I did run into stray dogs, more than once in a pack. Flashlight in action, I stood my ground, I believed like some character out of Kipling. The dogs did, indeed, go away. Later I found it was as much from standing my ground and staring them down as anything. Unfortunately, every few years, a child was seriously attacked, mauled, or in a rare instance killed, but as I now know, they were smaller than I was, showed their fear, and ran, turning themselves demonstrably into prey for the feral animals.

Another lesser-known aspect of social life in Fairbanks at the time was how teenagers took cars out on the frozen river at night (maybe half the time it was only afternoon, but it was always dark after school in winter). We raced about, and with an appropriate spin of the steering wheel the driver would send tons of steel spinning harmlessly around in circles amid much shouting, squeals, and shrieks. The worst that could happen was their parents' automobile would end in a snow drift, upon which those aboard would get out, push the vehicle back into the clear, and drive off with laughter, only to hit the brakes purposefully, spin the wheel, and drift off out of control again. This activity also occasionally took place south of town in late April during the senior class picnic at a lake named for President Harding (who died on his way home from Alaska). It was more iffy than the river in mid-winter as the ice was starting to melt and patches of water had appeared. I remember watching from shore wondering if the gorgeous new car belonging to someone's parents was about to be dropped into ten feet of water, but the ice, groaning and cracking, held on the afternoon my class partied there. We all knew of other adventurers who weren't so lucky.

Everyone in the north has dozens of stories about winter pleasures, misadventures, and common experiences such as the ice fog. Every winter from time to time, when it was particularly cold, a thick blanket of ice fog would form and hang over Fairbanks and the Chena River Valley, sometimes lasting for several days or a week. The cause was simply a stationary front with a complete absence of any wind and the freezing of moisture rising in the air and its accumulation as crystals around particles of smoke and exhaust from all of the fires and motors, combined with frozen steam from local power plants. On occasion a major contributor also was the foul-smelling cloud rising from a crew that went about with a boiler on a sled thawing out sewers by forcing live steam into them with pipes and hoses. These plus the accumulation of all of our breathing, heating, and the vehicles in town created a frozen version of smog. It is hard to describe how thick it was, but some of the descriptions of London in Dickens' time sound familiar. As it coincided with the darkest time of the year, it was particularly smothering. I recall innumerable times walking home from school or after-school part-time work when I could only see streetlights if I was immediately underneath them. Even then they only made a dim glow above, which barely reached me. I thought it was spooky, but no one discussed it much, except to say, "The ice fog's thick today," a version of the sort of stoic behavior and laconic remark traditionally associated with folks Down East or in Scotland.

Snow wasn't as much of an issue in the interior of Alaska as it could be in other parts, especially those near any portion of the thousands of miles of coastline. I learned while still in grade school that snow would always arrive to cover the ground by my birthday in the second week of October, that it would stay for the winter and last until spring in late April. In Fairbanks it rarely snowed when colder than 20° below zero Fahrenheit, so a weather report predicting snow was always welcome as it meant it was going to warm up. The phrase "clear and cold," however, could be the introduction to a forecast of a week of minus 30° or colder. In Fairbanks the snow almost never amounted to more than a couple of feet at a time, and often was no more than a foot deep in many places. Repeated plowing, however, created awkward humps and mounds along streets and roads, with an irritating effect upon pedestrian life in town. One was always clambering over rotting drifts and filthy piles of mashed-down snow and ice at intersections. Likewise snow in the Interior wasn't usually very wet, due to the generally dry continental aspect of the region. This meant that it was fairly worthless for snowballs, fort building, and the like. In the first year after we moved there, I was disappointed to find that it was nearly impossible to make an igloo with it.

Along the coast it was different. One winter while visiting my family who'd moved south to Anchorage (in the independent spirit of those on the frontier I'd refused to move with them so continued my last two years of high school in Fairbanks 350 miles away largely on my own staying with friends), it started snowing on Christmas Eve. How lovely we all thought. It snowed on, becoming heavier through Christmas Day, and kept snowing for several more days. By the time it stopped, the city was buried under about six feet of snow, which then began to drift and blow, in some cases up to fifteen and twenty feet. I recall walking on top of the crust (one could have built an igloo with this) beside a canyon carved out by snowplows. I reached up and touched a streetlight. Anchorage received 156 inches of snow that winter, which was a bit much even for seasoned sourdoughs. On the other hand, I can't remember Anchorage ever getting colder than 25° below, the reason that those north of the Alaska Range referred to the region from Anchorage south as the "Banana Belt." This area, also known as the "Panhandle," extends south nearly a thousand miles from Anchorage and shares a coastal climate that supports what amounts to a giant and continuous rainforest extending from Kodiak Island in the Gulf of Alaska to northern California. The annual rainfall in Ketchikan from 1949 to 2005 averaged 152 inches per year. Snowfall on the other hand was only 36 inches a year. From ice-free year-round ports in the south to inaccessible towns trapped behind hundreds of miles of pack ice along the Arctic coast across the north, from rainforests to tundra, a seemingly endless expanse of valleys and hills, mountains, rivers, and lakes in the Interior, from tide flats to fjords, it is hard to convey how truly diverse and enormous Alaska is. With this ecological and topographical variety and the sparse settlement of the Territory before the advent of satellites and widespread use of computers, it was difficult to predict accurately what to expect in the weather more than a few hours or a day or two in advance. Alaskans were always prepared for just about anything to happen, and suddenly. People grumpily remarked that Siberia, along with the Arctic Ocean, Bering Sea, and Gulf of Alaska, were endless sources of storms and foul weather, which to a degree is true; at least that's where they came from.

One side effect of snow at the times when there is a lot is the difficulty of navigating in canyons made by snowplows for the roads and rails. The deep snow channels they form become a problem when moose, often on the brink of starvation and struggling to travel about in the deep snow, choose to use cleared roads or rail tracks to get about. Inevitably there are accidents and collisions. One winter trip by rail from Anchorage to Fairbanks we counted more than fifty moose before we gave up counting halfway. The train stopped several times having hit one and another of them. Each time it took a while to resume moving as the crew had to get out and dig a hole big enough in the snowbank beside the track to shove the large dead animal off the track. Later a work crew would come along, pick up the frozen carcasses, take them to town, and donate them to orphanages, hospitals, and retirement homes for meat. In the winter of 2005–6, over 180 moose were killed in accidents on the 600-mile-long system of the Alaska Railroad.

Once snowbanks become higher than 4 feet tall they make driving in winter difficult. When one approaches an intersection, there is absolutely no way of knowing if someone is moving along in the other street or road. The only solution is to approach slowly, stop, and then inch out until one can see into the other canyon. If someone is barreling along in it, there is an inevitable collision, especially if the driver hits the brakes and goes into a skid. I don't know of anyone in those days who hadn't run into a snowbank, gotten stuck, or spun the car around a time or two while driving in Fairbanks.

Another side effect of snow included the use of skis for airplanes, although we never skied much ourselves in the Interior because it was too cold. From the first decades of the twentieth century, there had been considerable use of small airplanes, especially those that use floats to land and take off on water in the summer and skis in the winter. Interestingly enough, Alaska benefited from aviation early in its infancy, with many pioneers of the industry living and flying there. Billy Mitchell, the father of modern aerial warfare and the US Air Force, was born and raised, and began flying in Nome, west of Fairbanks. Some of the earliest regularly scheduled freight, mail, and passenger services occurred there, along with numerous developments in instrumental and cold weather flying. Air travel proved to be a nearly miraculous way to move about the vast Territory and to connect the small population separated by vast distances and terrain nearly impossible to traverse conveniently any other way. By the end of World War II, flying had become a way of life in the north, and the amount of traffic since has been remarkable. When I was in college in the late 1950s, one-third of all the licensed float planes (no one ever calls them "sea-planes") in the United States were located on Lake Spenard outside Anchorage. While the exploits and skill of Alaska's bush pilots may be well known, less advertised are the many accidents and tragedies that have occurred, in no small part due to the difficulties of flying in the Arctic weather and terrain. Will Rogers and Wiley Post were killed in one of these mishaps, and there are wrecked airplanes of all sizes and periods, military and private, scattered about. All of us knew of someone who didn't come home.

The most recent mechanical aid to travel in the north at another scale and for shorter distances has been the snowmobile. These loud and dangerous mechanically propelled sleds, now ubiquitous in the north around the globe, were decades away in the future when I was there. In addition to having a negative effect upon wildlife, shattering the quiet of the winter landscape, and adding to pollution with their inefficient petroleum burning engines, they have virtually ended the use of dogs for any substantial work, only for racing. Just as autos ended centuries of human interaction with horses, leaving them largely only for recreation and sport, so too snowmobiles have ended a partnership with dogs in Alaska that began sometime near the end of the late Stone Age.

Then there were ice worms. Even as a child I knew that people were pulling my leg when they told me about ice worms and glacier bears. Alaskans like to tell tall stories to cheechakos (newcomers), a tradition of the American West much appreciated and utilized by writers from Mark Twain and Bret Harte to Thomas Pynchon and the current generation of cowboy poets and songwriters. A favorite tale at the time told of an Air Force mechanic who'd pumped several hundred gallons of aviation gas into a plane before he realized it was a mosquito. When I was first told there were worms living in the ice of glaciers, I dismissed it as more nonsense. So too, I rolled my eyes about a group of bears living on glaciers that were supposedly blue.

nice pair of Native mukluks to wear when we were to be out for an extended period, whether playing or for work. My favorite pair that I had through grade school was fairly conventional with tough soles of fur-seal hide. The upper parts of the boots, which came partway up my calves, were made of caribou with the fur on the outside and lined with wool flannel. One added felt insoles as a cushion and for extra insulation underfoot. As was often the case, there was a decorative geometric band of embroidery on flannel trim at the top where they were tied around with handwoven cords that ended in pom-poms of red wool. My mother had a lovely golden pair made from spotted seal with embroidered Native wild flowers on a wool flannel panel over the top of the foot. Knowing that they had been made by hand, that the soles had been cured in urine and then softened by Native women chewing on them, who then carefully sewed and embroidered them through the long winters in the villages on the Bering Sea, added to their special quality.

Wolf or wolverine fur, because the long outer guard hairs are hollow unlike most hair, offers a layer of insulation and was used by Natives for the trim on parka hoods that one pulls close about the face in the colder weather. None of this, including a scarf wrapped around my nose, however, helped when I first began to wear eyeglasses in the winter of 1950. The frames and rims were metal and gold-plated as was common. Plastic frames, which were somewhat better, were a few years off (along with television) in high school, even though they still had a wire core. It is hard to describe how painful the two tiny nosepieces felt while standing beside the road in 30 or 40 below weather waiting for a bus to go into town. When one finally hove into view, its two headlights made the most striking star patterns of the Hallmark Christmas card sort. I could never figure out if it was my frozen glasses or the frozen air that caused the effect. Squinting only increased the starburst effect.

Another aspect of the cold was that sound traveled great distances, especially at night. One could lie in bed and hear the decking rattle on the bridge in town several miles away as cars passed over it. We also believed we could hear the northern lights as they moved and wavered overhead. Did we really hear them? It hardly seems possible as they are caused by a bombardment of energy as it enters the ionosphere. In any case they were beautiful and came in several varieties of mysterious spectral effects. One was the corona, a big wobbling blob of light overhead, which filled a vast portion of the sky. This came in either a pale red or a pale yellow-greenish white color. Another form was that of streaks—lines like great thin brushstrokes or attenuated fingers or whiskers, also in a pinkish red or pale yellowy green that stretched across the sky. The third and nearly everyone's favorite form was what we called curtains, which is an apt description. Like infinitely huge curtains hung from far above the planet, these contained red, green, yellow, and white colors in bands similar to a rainbow. All of these manifestations could be dynamic and show movement. The latter at times would actually wave or ripple slowly like cloth in a light breeze. It's mesmerizing to witness. While standing out in the cold looking up at the black star-filled sky, we never ceased to wonder at this pale but vast panorama of light. At times someone would say, "Listen, you can hear them." And we would all believe we could hear them crackling far above. On the other hand one didn't know what to do with the experience. It was cold, and inevitably one turned back to the task or journey at hand, or retreated indoors. By the mid-1950s a group of geophysicists at the University of Alaska near Fairbanks were studying them. Sleeping near their gear, which was mounted outside on the roof of a university building, they were reputed to leap out of bed like firemen when detecting devices told them a display had begun, and rush to the roof to turn on their recording and measuring equipment. Today, after decades of satellite observatories and progress in many aspects of astrophysics, these lights are undoubtedly only a footnote in science, a mere luminescent side effect of greater processes to do with the cosmos, but they can still be an exciting show to mere mortals as anyone can testify who has flown recently in the winter months and has watched their fellow passengers peer raptly out the windows after the pilot has announced that the northern lights can be seen off to one side of the airplane toward Minnesota (or Canada, Maine, Germany, Japan, or wherever one is at the time).

⚬⚬

Alcohol and drinking are a noticeable aspect of life in the north, whether in Alaska, Russia, Finland, Sweden, Denmark, Norway, or Scotland. It is tempting to say that it has something to do with the climate. The use and abuse of alcohol is a familiar topic to anyone who has ever spent more than a few hours in Alaska. It has been as devastating to the Native people there as everywhere else in America. Despite the common notion that drink warms you up, the truth is that it only makes you unaware of how cold it is by befuddling the nervous system. Every year people are found dead, frozen to death, who were walking home from a heavy bout of drinking. Crimes of passion, fights, and feuds fueled by alcohol were common enough. There were mundane and spectacular shootings to be dealt with by the US Marshal (we were a Territory, truly the "last frontier"), the father of one of my classmates. From the first week there in December 1946, I can remember many

5th and Wickersham. Fairbanks. 24 July 06. one of the quiet streets that still maintains the dignified calm of the neighborhoods of Fairbanks

sessions sitting high on a barstool between my parents at Johnny's Tavern with workers from my dad's office. They were drinking what became a favorite drink, hot buttered rum. It was dark outside as usual and rather dark inside. There was a certain consistency of darkness with only a few neon lights glowing outside and matching ones from a jukebox and the back bar inside. There was a proliferation of bars: the Mecca, the Vet's (Veteran's), the Wagon Wheel, the Pioneer, the Pastime, and Johnny's were the most popular in town. Some, like the bar in the old Pioneer Hotel, had elaborate late Victorian furnishings, heavy wood carvings and mirrors that had come from the East or Europe around the Horn of South America by boat during the gold rush and shipped up the rivers by stern-wheelers. These bars were gathering places where men went in search of news, passed the time of day, amused themselves playing cards and pinball machines, told stories, and listened to music. Out in the bush a drink with a visitor to your cabin was even more precious.

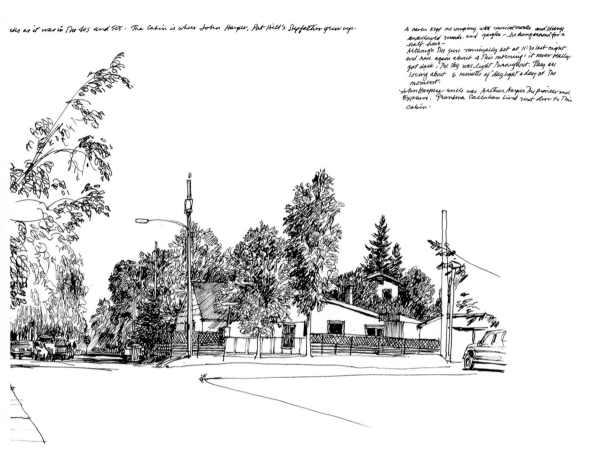

this as it was in the 40s and 50s. The cabin is where John Harper, Pat Hill's Stepfather grew up.

A raven kept me company with musical croaks and strange swallowed sounds and gurgles – we hung around for a half hour –
Although the sun nominally set at 11:30 last night and rose again about 4 this morning, it never really got dark, the sky was light throughout. They are losing about 6 minutes of daylight a day at the moment.
John Harper's uncle was Arthur Harper the pioneer and Explorer. Grandma Callahan lived next door to this cabin.

Bars were also great places to sell newspapers in the late afternoon, something I learned in fifth grade. One could buy a bundle of papers at the pressroom of the *Daily News-Miner* for a nickel apiece. It was a remarkable scene with the presses churning away, Linotype machines with hot lead, ink-covered men, noise and trucks with the newsboys in a group together noisily gambling and pitching coins toward one wall with the one landing closest winning each round. With a bundle of between 20 to 50 papers— whatever I could afford or carry—I'd head out to the streets to hawk them, accosting everyone on the sidewalks and going into shops, cafes, and eventually bars. At first it seemed rather daring to me to go alone at that age into a darkened bar in the afternoon to confront hardcore drinkers, many of whom had been at it since morning or lunchtime. Inevitably several would buy the paper, often with a sizable tip, most commonly simply giving me a silver dollar rather than the dime it cost. There was little small change around anyway and no paper single dollar bills anywhere. Here in the bars one met a motley crew of prostitutes, hopelessly addicted Eskimos and Indians, and various versions of down-and-out white male alcoholics. The bartenders were dour, scowling at us kids. An additional frisson added to being out of bounds, and the payoff was the music. Here one heard the latest popular records, especially what my father scornfully called "hillbilly music": the fathers of modern country and western—Hank Williams, Hank Snow, Ernie Tubb, Red Foley, Bob Wills, the Sons of the Pioneers, and Les Paul and Mary Ford. It was sad and lonesome, whiney and lowdown. On occasion I found people playing this music live, usually a scrawny Indian standing on the back bar with an electric guitar singing to himself in the mirror and no one paying much attention.

Vegetation

If asked what do Robert Frost, Boris Pasternak, and Ingmar Bergman have in common, one answer would be: birch trees. Many aspects of life are circumpolar: geology and soils, climate and weather, plants, animals, birds, fishes, and insects. The grouse in Scotland, Finland, Siberia, Alaska, and Canada, the heathers and heath, the berries, flies, and mosquitoes, even the people, the Laps, Ainu, and Inuit, have either spread from place to place or evolved in parallel. One common denominator of the North is the ubiquitous presence of birch forests. Few trees are as graceful or as graphic as birches with their pure white trunks, black branches, and delicate leaves that shiver in light breezes and turn a clear golden yellow in autumn. Whether casting blue shadows on snow in winter or silhouetted against black spruce, their scrawny constant companions across the taiga, they form a key element of the mental map of those who live in the North. Whether the shocking uprooting of a young birch tree in Bergman's film *The Virgin Spring* by a distraught father or Frost's young boy climbing to the top of one only to bend it playfully with his weight, or the crystal light in their ice-glazed branches in *Doctor Zhivago* as the title character retreats to the country from the upheaval of the Russian Revolution, birch trees carry an emotional weight for northern dwellers. Birches were planted as street trees in residential neighborhoods of Fairbanks in the 1920s, '30s and '40s, partly for practical reasons—they were one of the only shade trees that could be grown to any size in that region, and shade, especially there so near the Arctic Circle with the omnipresent summer sunlight, was desirable in the summer. Also they evoked a memory of traditional American towns in New England and the Midwest with their graceful ranks of elms and oaks, maples and ashes that had successfully softened and sheltered domestic and civic life for two centuries. The street trees of Fairbanks were clearly the gesture of a community asserting its cultural legacy and survival, even a presumptive hegemony in the face of the vast wilderness on all sides.

For many, birches represented firewood as well. A number of Scandinavian immigrants had drifted into the region, and there were several men known as Ole or Swede, along with some Finns who introduced saunas, now an established feature of many cabin sites throughout the Territory. One was an ancient woodcutter who came into town occasionally for supplies and the comforts of civilization. What was his life like, I wondered, out there alone in the bush cutting trees and splitting endless cords of wood? Did he have to keep moving as he cut down all the birches in a particular area? Did he have a cabin? How did he get the wood out and bring it to town? Whom did he sell it to? What sort of money did he make? I tried to imagine him alone with a saw of the sort we called a Swede saw and a double or single bit axe. Did he have a stock of extra handles? Wedges? Sleds? Dogs? I never knew. I just saw him occasionally in town, tall, thin, wearing a wool plaid jacket over tin pants (moisture-resistant gabardine twill lined in flannel), with grizzled white stubble of several days' length, and a flat cloth cap. It was a look adopted by teens and rock musicians two decades later in Seattle and a few years after that by Ivy League students and now seems somewhat ubiquitous. He was a creature from the past like medieval swineherds who lived a drifting life in the forests outside town, or the trappers who showed up in late winter with their furs.

Not that there weren't other trees and plants. Alders were the preferred wood used for smoking salmon or any other meat. But for children birches were companions and a vital furnishing of our playground. The subarctic is bursting with life. In spring avalanche lilies come up through rotting snow in the mountain meadows as everything thaws and life returns. An extraordinary variety of berries, leaves, and seeds provides ample food for the myriad creatures that move about the landscape—several varieties of blueberries, low bush and high bush cranberries, red and black raspberries, salmon berries, Saskatoon berries, elderberries, snowberries, bearberries, and rose hips, for example. A wealth of flowers too plentiful to list populates hills and meadows. A favorite example was the violet expanse of iris extending as far as the eye could see across the flood plain of the Susitna River in early summer. This surplus of life, this generosity of foliage, finds expression through one species and community of plants after another. Examples range from the Sitka spruce forest that covers the islands of the Gulf of Alaska and extends south into British Columbia, Washington, and

Oregon where it merges with other species—Douglas fir, cedars, hemlock, and, eventually, redwood in northern California. One of the last stands of old-growth trees left in North America, this forest has been under attack for over a hundred years, with whole areas the size of Southern states destroyed. Entering it is to plunge into a world festooned and swaddled in moss and lichen, dripping above and spongy below. Shafts of green and yellow light shift about and slant down through the heavy canopy. An ecological community as extensive and oppressive as that of the tundra on the Arctic coast and equally harsh, it supports a limited handful of animal and bird species that include, in addition to bears and beavers, the petite Sitka deer, a few siskins, creepers, and the pileated woodpecker of the Northwest. With the demise of the ivory-billed species in the South, this is America's largest and most spectacular woodpecker—its enlarged head and pointed red crest, the inspiration for the manic bird of animated Saturday cartoons of a generation ago. The sudden and loud report, a deep rapid, round knocking sound, as these furtive birds signal their peers of their whereabouts, or the quieter chipping and chunking as they go after ants and beetles, sending bark and chips flying in their attack upon one of the ancient trees, is enough to startle and delight anyone within hearing. Only occasionally does one actually see them as they glide silently between the trees. Immediately following their explosive knocking, a deep quiet returns relieved only by the soughing of treetops high above in the wind and the repeated creaking of branches rubbing somewhere nearby.

In contrast to the filtered light and water-soaked blankets of moss on the forest floor that one finds on the islands and mountains of southern Alaska, farther north one can move for hundreds of miles through valleys and hills scraped by glaciers, exposed, frozen, and baked by the sun and wind. Here, between rivers, streams, lakes, and bogs on the granite slopes and the outwash of gravel and clay, one finds a scrubby land of heaths, heathers, grasses, sedges, rushes, flowers, shrubs, and patches of struggling forest of spruce, birch, and alder. This is the taiga, stretching for thousands of miles across the north where millions of the pencil-thin, slow-growing spruces are spaced apart atop deep peat beds that fill ancient glacial pothole lakes.

In late summer, lying on my back in a mattress of ground-hugging bushes, I would reach out in all directions and rake in handfuls of blueberries for a half hour at a time before moving to a fresh patch. Listening to the steady chipping of birds, I'd study the sky. Some weeks it was totally devoid of clouds day after day. The sun at that time of year circled the sky, dipping low toward the horizon in the north late in the evening, only to hesitate briefly before climbing back to blaze intensely through the next day as well. This may be the thing I miss most about not living there anymore: the summer light, the midnight sun. There is absolutely nothing like it. It invigorates and bathes one in a clear limpid light by day and a magical golden haze by night. Parents give up trying to get children to sleep and simply let them run around until they keel over, putting them to bed in rooms they struggle to make dark with window shades and lined draperies. Like bears and other creatures nearby, everyone eats continuously—fattening up for the long winter of darkness, sleep, and leaner fare. A favorite late summer dish on Bristol Bay and along the Bering Sea was Akootuk, a concoction of huckleberries, seal oil, and sugar. Occasionally referred to as Eskimo ice cream, it was originally made by emptying a five-pound sack of sugar to form a small mound in the center of a washtub, then filling the tub with huckleberries or blueberries and pouring in quantities of seal oil. This was stirred with a wooden paddle carefully so as not to break or mash the berries until it was thoroughly mixed and set outside to chill and stiffen into a soft sticky mass. It was then ladled out like porridge and eaten as a favorite dessert. By the late 1950s, the recipe had been updated with Crisco substituted for the seal oil, which had become less available due to the change in lifestyle and decline of ocean hunting by Aleut and Inuit. It was mixed gently by hand in a large bowl until all the berries had a light coating of lard and sugar and put in a refrigerator to set. Served in bowls with milk, half-and-half, or even whipped cream poured on top, it is an incomparable treat. As recently as the mid-1970s, there was at least one café near the ferry terminal in Seattle where Alaskans could find this dish on its menu.

Color

The Alaskan flag was designed in an intuitive stroke of genius by a thirteen-year-old Aleut boy in an orphanage in Seward in a contest in 1927. It is blue and gold, two colors I associate most with the Territory. The flag shows the Big Dipper, Ursa Major—the large bear—and Polaris, the North Star. How apt. No color is more present in the north: the huge blue sky of day and night combined with the color of the mineral that drew tens thousands to the wilderness streams, goldfields, frontier camps, and towns. So too beneath the omnipresent heavens throughout the extent of Alaska are countless lakes, rivers, bays, and the ocean with their ever-changing shades, deep fjords and kettle holes of blue. There are as well the blue of miles and miles of iris in annual drifts in the estuaries, and the state flower, the forget-me-not, with its tiny pale blue blossoms, in contrast with the scale and crushing weight of icy blue glaciers. This pale spooky blue at the heart of the ancient ice is oddly similar to that of the small and intent eyes of Siberian huskies. The most common color one sees at a social gathering in the summer is that of blue—blue jeans, denim jackets, bib overalls, blue work shirts, blue wind-breakers, and parka shells. In the Interior and Arctic winter at times, the sky when not dark is either a bluish haze above a pinkish, cream horizon or a golden shimmer of light in fine crystals. Cobalt, ultramarine, cerulean, aqua, slate, chalky—blues with tinges of red and purple, with hints of green and brown, unimaginable and familiar blues in all seasons and weather, overhead, underfoot, in the distance, pale and intense. Blue.

Early images and depictions of the North were almost always in black and white as a result of the paper and ink as well as of printing and engraving for the press. Early photographs in books and journals by Arctic explorers and adventurers were also in black and white, at times profoundly beautiful with their velvety blacks and sharp whites (I'm thinking particularly of the work of Bradford Washburn). Even so, there are greens, tans, ochers, browns, occasional reds, even startling whites among the animals and landscape, while spring floods and regions of grasses, shrubs, and trees turn after only a brief time to a palette that ranges from dusty pale straw through yellow to brilliant gold. Whether the long golden haze of the midnight sun that bathes the entire north in the evening for several months or the brilliant reflection from peaks as it sets at other times, or the color of the hills in the Interior in autumn, as the birches and heaths turn, or the color of the clouds of dust and insects that blow across the vast river deltas and bars north of the Alaska Range, or the speckled chests of meadow larks and spruce hens with a ring of amber around their pupils—gold is the complement to the omnipresence of blue.

White to an artist is often a starting situation, the color of paper or a primed canvas. Once it is covered, no matter how lightly, it is gone and can't be recovered. White is frequently thought of as the absence of color. To science and physics, of course, it is the presence of all colors, a fact that seems counter to our experience and practical lives. In winter, however, snow can remind us of this truth, albeit often in subtle ways that we rarely stop to observe, since they are most obvious during the daily ritual of sunrise and sunset, which near the Arctic Circle occurs commonly in the midst of the workday throughout the winter, leading many to miss it by not looking up from their tasks in time. Like the iridescent feathers of some species of birds, snow has no color in itself. The dazzling colors we see in the spray and ice, snow and clouds are simply colors refracted by scores of miniature prisms from the pure clear invisible light spectrum.

Life is possible on our planet because of the sun and water. In Alaska a person annually experiences these two important phenomena in alternating extreme aspects of their possibilities. In November, December, January, and February one rises in the dark and goes to work or school in the dark. At some point in mid- to late morning—a little before noon—the sun comes up and skids along just above the horizon in the south, and then before it even seems like afternoon it sets and one works and departs in the gloom. In the shoulder months, however, when there is still plenty of snow and it is clear and cold and the sun is beginning to climb halfway back up the sky, it can be dazzling. Then in late February and early March on spectacular days there isn't just one sun, but there can be two, or three or even four. These are the "sundogs." Due to the refraction of light in what seems like a snow globe of infinitely fine-grain suspended ice crystals high in the atmosphere, the sun appears to have companions, other suns to its left and right, and on some more rare occasions, above and even below it when high enough. As a child I thought they were magical and probably a lucky sign, especially when more than one appeared.

ᗴᘜ

Recently and at fairly regular intervals, I hear declarations that there is no such thing as wilderness anymore, that nature is over, and that the entire world is now a cultural landscape, that humans have affected or changed everything on the planet. I've also noticed that there are a great number of people who think that we are somehow separate from nature. While there are aspects of truth in the first thought, the second remark is ridiculous. Admittedly, we have had a debilitating effect upon the planet, destroying species, wrecking ecosystems, and poisoning vast tracts of land and the waters, and are seriously and alarmingly heating the atmosphere. Our impact takes many directions. A few years ago, the Alaska Native Service issued a warning to women along the Arctic coast that they should probably refrain from breastfeeding their newborn infants because a high strontium 90 count had been detected in their breast milk. It was radioactive. This was a result of eating caribou that had eaten sphagnum moss that had absorbed radioactive fallout from Russian aboveground nuclear tests. We are part of nature. We are in nature all the time, all of us, even in the heart of our cities—subject to the laws of physics, chemistry, and biology—whether we realize it or not. Many people in the cities of the world today are so busy, so distracted and hard-pressed, or so self-involved that they are unaware of nature, to the point where they even think they don't need it. Such foolishness.

Flying from the US to China on a polar route, one sees below the vastness of Canada, Alaska, the ice pack, Siberia, and Mongolia. Hour after hour peering out the window there is wilderness and nature extending to the horizon. Flying to South or Central America likewise one sees an amplitude of remote forests, rivers, and mountains. While primitive society may hardly exist anymore (with the exception of a handful of small relict tribes here and there in the forests of Asia, Africa, and South America), and our trash may be everywhere, even in the middle of the largest oceans, there is still an enormous extent of wild and resilient nature. In the long run we may render the planet uninhabitable for scores of creatures and ourselves, but nature will then once more reassert itself in various forms and manners without us.

I don't hunt anymore. It made sense when I lived on the frontier, but not much where I live now. I sometimes do, however, wish there could be a mass slaughter of the white-tailed deer that are destroying the eastern woodlands, parks, and landscapes. Such population explosions that occur in the absence of predators are something not experienced in the wilderness. While nature is dynamic, not stable, it also has mechanisms for recovery and refreshing itself. I don't miss guns, even though they were omnipresent in my childhood. They were useful and at times absolutely necessary in the wild. In cities today their only function is shooting people, which is clearly not a good thing. Leave it at that. After I left Alaska and had been outside in the States for about ten years, I came to be able to eat salmon once again and now consider it tasty. I don't get into the wild often these days but feel at home and enjoy hiking in the woods or merely sitting on the side of a mountain, or the rare treat of fly-fishing in a cold clear stream when I can get there, or more simply just sitting listening to a stream. I can see how for some, contemporary catch-and-release fishing is entertaining, but I don't like it much. The original and sole purpose of hunting and fishing was all about food. For most of us that's no longer necessary, but the idea of not being able to eat a tasty fish one catches ruins it for me.

Eventually after coming out to the States, I became a landscape architect and have spent the last thirty-five years primarily working on the design of urban public spaces. There is no question in my mind that Frederick Law Olmsted was right about the need to bring aspects of nature and its processes into our cities. Society mustn't be forced to choose between nature and urbanity. We can and must have both. Great cities like New York,

London, and Paris do have both. This does not mean that we should imitate nature, but rather that we should engender aspects of it that are sensually and aesthetically stimulating, such as the play of light and the sound of water, vegetation with all its textures, movement, and seasonal change, the spatial amplitude and variety of natural materials, their diversity of form and scale. While I know that art learns from art, in the beginning it learned from nature. A visit to the caves of the Dordogne or the halls of the great ethnographic and anthropological museums around the world confirms the powerful influence and authority garnered from nature by our ancestors in all regions of the world. It is good to remember that all forms employed in art exist in nature, and it is for us to discern, to learn from them, and to use them for our purposes.

In addition to this primary and fundamental aesthetic necessity that natural phenomena fulfill for humans, the pleasure and beauty they generate, it is critical also that we enfold aspects of natural processes into our cities that can help to render them healthier and safer, that will aid in purification and circulation of air and water, and that assist with cooling in summer and insulation in winter, as well as providing environments for exercise and play, for social activity in healthy settings. We need nature. It doesn't need us. The sooner we realize this, the sooner we will have a chance to survive with health and a high quality of life as individuals and as a species.

☙❧

The history of Alaska in recent centuries has sadly followed the general pattern of European exploration and colonial exploitation, one of devastating Native populations and rapaciously extracting and exploiting any and all natural resources for the use and profit of a population far away. First came the Russians, who decimated the sea otter population and enslaved the Alutiiq people until they successfully revolted. Then came the miners of the 1898 gold rush, first to the Klondike and then to Nome and Fairbanks. Next were the fisheries and timber outfits. World War II and the subsequent Korean and Cold Wars brought the military and more boomers, workers, drifters, and settlers. The North Slope oil was not a surprise to Alaskans. We knew it was there. During and after World War II, the Navy had a group of technicians and scientists at Point Barrow under the operational name PET4. PET stood for petroleum. That they were involved in oil exploration was understood. That anything could be successfully produced and somehow gotten to market seemed largely infeasible at the time. While we went about our lives, however, yet more portions of the Territory were crisscrossed and mapped every summer by crews from the US Geological Survey (USGS). In the summer of 1954, while staying for a time in Manley Hot Springs, I asked a member of one of their crews what they were doing. The engineer pointed to a hill across the river and said, "See that?" "Yes," I replied. "Well that's all tin." Several years later, I was working in Dillingham on Bristol Bay. A group of geologists from what was the Standard Oil Company at the time (now ARCO) were staying in the same rudimentary hotel that I was. They were renting planes for weeks on end at $100 an hour, an extravagant sum at the time, and spent many evenings in their rooms after dinner typing. "What's up?" I asked one day. Looking me over, the young bearded engineer replied, "You ever heard of the Gulf of Mexico?" "Of course," I said. "Well kid, it's full of oil, and the ocean near here is a similar formation to the Gulf of Mexico, and it's a hell of a lot bigger." "Oh," I said.

The summer of 1959 was the last one I spent working for the Alaska Highway Department. I'd begun after being graduated from high school four years earlier when it was still the old Alaska Road Commission, a step-child of the Interior Department, set up to minister to a distant territorial situation. Each year our survey crews pushed farther out from the major towns and cities, laying out and building roads in the woods. Part of our group was dispatched to Mt. McKinley Park to improve the road through the park with new bridges and to push key sections east and south into the Kantishna area and toward Paxson Lodge on the Richardson Highway, the only road connection between Anchorage and Fairbanks. Our group was running line out of Wasilla north to connect the park from the south. Out on Bristol Bay we were also working on roads between Naknek and King Salmon as well as from Dillingham to Aleknagik and the Tikchik Lakes. Classmates from Fairbanks were working on a road from Livengood north of Fairbanks to Manley Hot Springs. A network of roads and highways was being created to link up and connect central and important parts of Alaska. None of us really envisioned that we were witnessing and were part of the ending of the old Alaska. A few years later the North Slope Oil development took place, and a road was finally pushed through from Circle north of Fairbanks to the coast of the Arctic Ocean east of Point Barrow.

And now the North is melting. For anyone still skeptical about climate change, I suggest a trip to the circumpolar North. The phrase "You can't go home again," which usually refers to the social changes in a childhood setting and to an evolution of personality, also implies the physical alteration or destruction of a formerly beloved locale. In the case of Alaska, while much remains enormously wild and as grand as ever, it is also obvious that dramatic change is taking place. The climate has been changing rapidly, more so in the Arctic and subarctic than anywhere else in the world. It is warmer every year, and the earth is melting, literally. This was clear to me fifteen years ago in March of 1998 when I returned to Fairbanks for a few days' work. Curious to see old haunts of my youth, I set out to re-explore the town. The temperature was so balmy that I walked about in a light jacket with it open, as one might on a fine spring or fall day in New England or the Pacific Northwest, not Alaska. "How odd," I thought. In the 1940s and '50s it would have been well below freezing—somewhere between 10° and 30° below zero. We would have been wearing fur parkas and mukluks. Here I was in street shoes and an open windbreaker with my shirt exposed to the weather! Strange, I thought. Several years later in 2006, I returned in June to see some old friends. Driving out of town down the Alaskan Highway to visit a lake where we'd built a camp as Boy Scouts, I noticed that the telephone and power poles were leaning about in all directions, some about to fall over. "What on earth?" I exclaimed. My childhood pal said, "Oh, it's the permafrost melting." What I was witnessing was the great unlocking of thousands of years of frozen land that is taking place across the entire north around the globe, but most notably in Alaska and Canada.

As a young person drawing the world about me, I recorded the swaybacked profiles of numerous cabins. These seemingly solid structures made of stiff log construction were commonly known to be settling and sinking as the frozen earth and ice beneath them thawed in response to many long winters of fires and heating within. Now the entire land is doing so. Recent scientific studies reveal that the permanent polar sea ice is at the smallest extent it has been for the past 2,000 years and is continuing to shrink at a rate of at least 12% per decade, but may even be accelerating. Glaciers are melting and retreating on every continent. A most spectacular and most studied retreat is occurring in Greenland, but also in Alaska. Places I knew 50 years ago such as Portage Glacier near Anchorage are almost unrecognizable now. Villages and towns on the Bering Sea are starting to abandon their ancient sites in a move to higher ground as the sea has already risen there and continues to do so. A recent survey of 41 permafrost scientists in the journal *Nature* predicted that at the current rate between 48% and 63% of the terrestrial permafrost will be thawed to a depth of 3 meters (11.6 ft.) by 2100. This means that about 10% of the stored organic matter on earth will be released into the atmosphere, a portion of which will be methane, which in turn will contribute further to the intensification of global warming.

During the last ice age, the Pleistocene Epoch, when herds of camels and horses roamed central Alaska and humans moved along the coast and into the valleys, the Arctic Ocean and North Pole were free of ice. A lot of the moisture we know as glaciers and lakes on the continent to the south were formed as all that water came down in the form of rain and snow in what we refer to as temperate latitudes. While history doesn't repeat itself, it "rhymes" as Mark Twain once quipped. I doubt we'll see glaciers forming in the US as a result of the melting and unfreezing this time; the recent dramatic and sudden increase in climatic perturbation suggests that all that water will be in circulation in the oceans, altering their temperature and currents, and in more generous quantities of storms in the northern hemispheres.

What all this means for migratory animals, birds, insects, and plants has been widely discussed and debated, but one thing certain is change. Nature is dynamic, and humans have given it a big additional push. I feel fortunate to be a child of the North and to have seen it as it was and probably will not be again for many centuries, if ever.

Spring 2013

Letter from Tasmania

DAVID MASON

YOU FIND YOURSELF thinking *England*. Then you think *No, Wales. No, Scotland*. But despite a very British culture, Tasmania is none of these. Nor is it the Pacific Northwest, though its vast tracts of rain forest and giant ferns remind me of home. Tasmania, the Australian island state situated 150 miles south of the mainland, is wonderfully other.

You know you're not in the Northern Hemisphere when looking at the night sky, locating the Southern Cross and the Magellanic Clouds. And you know when you see the gum trees turning red with new growth in spring instead of red with death in the fall. The world's turned upside down.

A eucalypt forest is far more multifarious than I realized. Diverse types of gum trees appear to mimic deciduous foliage from all over the earth. Then in another glance they are visibly *not* European, *not* North American, *not* of the Indian subcontinent, but a forest you can see into, the trees tattered and shedding—perfect fuel for regular bushfires. And it smells better than any perfume I have ever known. If I could bottle the smell of a eucalypt forest in spring, I'd be richer than Ralph Lauren.

Nearly 45 percent of Tasmania is set aside as parkland, much of it UNESCO World Heritage. Some of the world's tallest eucalyptus trees grow there. Saving the Tasmanian wilderness from exploitation and development was a milestone in the environmental movement, foundational for Australia's Green Party. The current conservative government, however, seems dead set on rolling back those gains.

Reading about these developments, Americans must adjust their vocabulary. Here the conservatives are the Liberal Party, while the liberals are Labour. Here Liberals might say with our Republicans, "Drill, baby, drill." Tasmania's economy is the weakest in the country, but to lose its old growth forests would create a crisis of another kind—an identity crisis. Just what is Tasmania? The license plates say, "Your Natural State." Lose the nature and what have you got?

You've got a lot, it turns out. A city on the rise in Hobart, some fine smaller cities and great cultural institutions—yet it all seems Tasmanian because you are never far from the wild, the constant variation of peak and valley, the bush-like wave on pale-green wave of life.

We arrived on this heart-shaped island by ferry, *The Spirit of Tasmania*, in December—summer Down Under. Already we had camped in our van for two weeks, traveling through southeastern Australia, and had experienced rising heat. In Victoria's Grampians National Park the heat excited cicadas till their vibrations were literally deafening, and we wore earplugs to hear ourselves think. Yet during our first night in Tassie, as the state is affectionately known, we were snow-drenched in Cradle Mountain National Park—a place that definitely made me think *Scotland*, except for the wombats like miniature bears grazing in the alpine meadows and echidnas sniffing ants from rotten logs in the bush.

The island has been cared for. People clearly take pride in the land, yet its history has been violent. Tasmania's Aborigines were wiped out by disease and massacre. The last full-blood Tasmanian Aborigine, a woman named Truganini, died in 1876. (Some argue that the last person of full-blood was Fanny Cochrane Smith, who lived into the twentieth century.) Now mixed-blood Aborigines claim the heritage—including land rights and social benefits.

Tasmania is both familiar and estranging, cozy and mildly dangerous—all snakes in Tassie can kill you. The land feels deliciously passed over by modern abrasiveness, quite suitable for Hobbits and recluses. My wife was born here, in Hobart, the daughter of an English colonial mother and a father descended from a transported convict. Isolation from the rest of the world once made Tasmania an ideal prison, but the same isolation now seems idyllic.

As we drove the small, winding roads, one startlingly beautiful view of mountains and paddocks full of sheep or cattle following another, I began to call it "The land that time forgot."

Early European exploration of Australia was a comedy of errors. Everyone assumed a *Terra Australis Incognita* lay down there somewhere, but globe-circumnavigating vessels kept missing it. Landings on the continent took place as early as the sixteenth century, but none of them resulted in colonies.

Tasmania was officially "discovered" first. Abel Tasman found it in 1642 and called it Van Diemen's Land in honor of his employer, a governor of the Dutch East Indies. The English landed in the 1770s and were more assiduous than other Europeans in their colonization of the continent. Robert Hughes's superb history, *The Fatal Shore: The Epic of Australia's Founding* (1987), tells how Australia was first used as a series of work camps for transported criminals. Between 1803 and 1853 some 75,000 convicts were transported to Tasmania alone. One early prison at Macquarie Harbour on the west coast was guarded by headlands and rip tides difficult to pass and surrounded by a wilderness in which escaping convicts starved or were reduced to cannibalism before being captured, flogged, and resentenced.

When you consider that some transported criminals were petty thieves, others political dissidents from Ireland, you can see even more the injustice of the penal system. Ships carrying prisoners to this unknown land were often recommissioned slavers, so overcrowded and unsanitary that typhus killed many on board.

Perhaps Dickens' Magwitch came to Tasmania. Remember the Hulks near the mouth of the Thames where Pip first encountered his convict:

> By the light of the torches, we saw the black Hulk lying a little way from the mud of the shore, like a wicked Noah's ark. Cribbed and barred and moored by massive rusty chains, the prison-ship seemed in my young eyes to be ironed like the prisoners.

In *Great Expectations* the policy of transportation is not merely a plot device but creates a form of social equality the young snobbish Pip needs to learn.

Another novel, Marcus Clarke's Tasmanian classic, *For the Term of His Natural Life*, is often melodramatic, Gothic in sensibility, but notable for vivid descriptive passages and impressive reportage, like this about the "classless society" of a convict ship:

> Old men, young men, and boys, stalwart burglars and highway robbers, slept side by side with wizened pickpockets or cunning-featured area-sneaks. The forger occupied the same berth with the body-snatcher. The man of education learned strange secrets of housebreakers' craft, and the vulgar ruffian of St. Giles took lessons of self-control from the keener intellect of the professional swindler.

Australia's convict past contributed to the social leveling you still feel among its people today, a lack of reverence for money or station or power, anarchic humor and the culture of mateship. Australians don't make a lot of idealistic noise and would never call themselves, as Americans are wont to do, "the greatest nation on earth."

Marcus Clarke was remarkable. Born and educated in London, he emigrated to Australia and tried to learn farming in Victoria, but was soon writing stories instead of tilling the soil. A brief visit to Tasmania in 1870 inspired him to write his most famous book, which was serialized in the *Australasian Journal* over the following two years. Clarke wrote a lot, but money troubles followed him and are said to have helped cause his death at only thirty-five.

Halfway through our month in Tasmania, we visited one of his novel's settings, Port Arthur, the most famous prison on the island and now a World Heritage site on a serene harbor tucked into the western flank of Carnarvon Bay, roughly one hundred kilometers southeast of Hobart. The Commandant's spacious house and gardens look out on Mason's Cove where longboats would have moored, and nearby are several large prison complexes, a hospital, an asylum, a huge Victorian garden, and a well-appointed church. Port Arthur looks like a ruined English village rather than the setting of hard labor and floggings. The brick buildings reflect evolving theories of incarceration. Should men live under constant watch as in Jeremy Bentham's Panoptic Prison, or should they be left in solitary confinement—Benjamin Rush's theory—to take stock of their sins and repair themselves? What is a person? Novelists and jailers ask the same question.

Escape from Port Arthur was impossible. As Clarke puts it,

> The Peninsula of Port Arthur was admirably guarded, signal stations drew a chain round the prison, an armed boat's crew watched each bay, and across the narrow isthmus which connected it with the mainland was a cordon of watch-dogs, in addition to the soldier guard.

That "Dog-Line" at Eaglehawk Neck was a gruesome barrier with a dozen poorly fed Cerberuses snapping at anyone trying to get past.

Across from Mason's Cove lies Puer Point, a boys' prison, and just off that a tiny Isle of the Dead. The latter proved well worth a boat trip into the harbor for the tour. Convicts carved the headstones for people of all classes buried there; the misspellings and chiseled corrections are hilarious. A deceased school inspector was "Sincerily regretted by all who knew him." Another fellow was remembered as a "Businessman, Forger, Convict and Author." On a tour of the isle, the novelist Anthony Trollope asked the Irish gravedigger in residence why he did not keep a vegetable garden. The wizened convict pointed to the ground, reminding Trollope what was already planted on every square inch of land.

Port Arthur is also the site of Australia's worst mass murder. On April 28, 1996, a young man named Martin Bryant drove to the park with a bag of guns and started shooting. He killed methodically all of that day and into the night and the next morning before being captured. Among those he shot point blank were two little girls, Madeline and Alannah Mikac, after first shooting their mother. At the end of the massacre thirty-five people lay dead, twenty-three wounded. He chose Port Arthur for the same reason it had made a secure prison—his victims would have no way of escaping.

We had talked about this at a dinner in Hobart, where a new friend of ours recalled hearing "There's a surfie down in Port Arthur with a gun." Common associations of surfer culture with something illicit come to mind, yet all the surfers I have known are people of quiet integrity. Like fishermen, they have sea knowledge and look out for each other and help the young learn their skills. Martin Bryant was no "surfie."

The cafe where he did much of his killing has been turned into a memorial and a meditative space in the park. On three of the four sides of a fountain you can read these words:

MAY WE WHO COME TO THIS GARDEN CHERISH LIFE
   FOR THE SAKE OF THOSE WHO DIED

CHERISH COMPASSION FOR THE SAKE OF THOSE WHO
   GAVE AID

CHERISH PEACE FOR THE SAKE OF THOSE IN PAIN

In America massacres nearly as bad as Port Arthur are now regular occurrences, and our gun laws hardly change. But Australia is a different sort of society. As my wife puts it, "There's no freedom at the cost of other people." America says, "Don't tread on me, and don't mess with my rights." Australia says, "Yes, but look out for your mate at the same time." It's an ethic partly born of the country's convict past.

The Port Arthur Massacre caused immediate national soul-searching, after which Australia enacted some of the toughest gun control laws in the industrialized world. A nation that began as a prison has produced one of the most stable, law-abiding societies on earth.

Martin Bryant came from New Town, a neighborhood of Hobart where some of our family live and where my wife's childhood school was located. She and her half-sister would take the city bus in from Berriedale, their suburb farther north, to face the strict discipline and love of the nuns. We arrived in Hobart during the Christmas holiday, just before the summer exodus of January in which many Australian families hit the road and pack the nation's campgrounds. My wife had not been back to her birthplace for three decades, and she wanted me to see how beautiful it was.

Walking through New Town, we saw the hospital where she was born as well as her school with its Eucharistic motto: *Sursum corda* (Lift up your hearts). The school was closed, but on the office door we read another motto of a sort common in Australia yet nonexistent in the United States: "As you take your next step, remember the first people who walked this land."

Hobart is my idea of the Goldilocks city—"Just right." With a population of more than two hundred thousand, it is large enough for good food and other cultural amenities, complex enough for the usual social problems and dramas, but small enough to be crossed on a bike. Hobart lines the Derwent River—really a large estuary snaking out to Storm Bay and the open sea. On the west side of the Derwent you have Mount Wellington, first noted by William Bligh on one of his voyages. To the east lies Mount Direction like a beacon of the future.

From her bedroom in Berriedale, my wife as a little girl used to look out on a peninsula jutting into the Derwent. It was a magical and forbidden place for her with an Italian villa and vineyard. Children used to catch pollywogs just below its bluff, but they never trespassed. Now the grapevines remain, but the villa is gone, and in its place the world's strangest art museum has been built.

MONA—the Museum of Old and New Art—is the brainchild of Hobart's most controversial citizen, David Walsh. As it happens, he is exactly my wife's age and also grew up Catholic in a troubled Hobart family. In his youth Walsh rejected the Church and cultivated two different tastes of his own, for art and mathematics. His taste in art is anti-academic, to say the least. He despises the hushed reverence with which most museums treat their treasures and wants art to be a more open playground.

His skill with mathematics made MONA possible. According to "Tasmanian Devil," a profile of Walsh by Tassie novelist Richard Flanagan (*The New Yorker*, January 21, 2013), Walsh is a leading member of a gambling syndicate called the Bank Roll. Walsh's algorithms have allowed the syndicate to win huge fortunes at casinos and betting operations around the world.

Walsh built MONA mostly with his own money, and the museum is his Wonderland as much as the people's. He lives in a rooftop apartment with various windows to the underworld he has built, rather like the Wizard of Oz behind his curtain. You can see the extremity of my allusions: Lewis

Carroll, Hades, and L. Frank Baum rolled into one. On the day we were there, Walsh could be seen out on the grounds, engaged in conversation with museumgoers. Tasmanians enter for free. The rest of us pay admission, but MONA still needs millions to stay afloat. Nobody knows what its future will be.

For the present moment, however, MONA is marvelous. The exhibit we saw was titled "The Red Queen" after Lewis Carroll, and indeed, entering the building is like going down the rabbit hole. Instead of a monument to imperial taste rising from manicured grounds, MONA asks you to descend deep into the peninsula, either by spiral staircase or elevator, following giant walls of rock into Hadean depths. There you find art by painters like Australia's Sidney Nolan in proximity with stranger things—a mummified possum whose open abdomen emits a flurry of insects, an "affectionate couch" named Zizi who makes sweet gurgling sounds when you lie on her, two giant Buddhas—one of metal, the other made of incense ashes—facing each other in a dimly lit space. There's a wall of water spelling words from news headlines that fall and disappear (as news headlines are apt to do), another wall of projected language and numbers defying comprehension. Both walls invite children and grown-ups to stand in front of them and pose or perform, becoming part of the art, part of the challenge of finding meaning in a data-saturated world.

As a museum devoted to sex and death, MONA has its share of controversial exhibits. One of the basement toilets, for example, is a satirical masterpiece. An unsuspecting patron enters the toilet and takes the accustomed seat, noticing a small pair of binoculars on the counter. Nothing to read, so he naturally looks through the binoculars and soon notices something, an illuminated object across the room. Very quickly he realizes the object he is staring at is nothing other than a human bum. Soon after, he realizes just whose bum it is, conveyed back to him by a system of mirrors and lights.

"Poets should go and sit in the third toilet on the right," a friend later said in another context. "Most of them are only looking up their own arseholes." I couldn't agree more.

MONA's partially lit spaces expose the observer-participant to both life and art. The open rooms and pools of illumination allow you to see multiple exhibits at once, sometimes reflecting each other or the people viewing them. There's no respectful distance between art and its viewer. Nothing is labeled. You hold a small iPad as you walk, accessing information only when you want to know more about the works you are seeing. Some of the exhibits are intensely moving. In a room full of old TVs, each one showing a film in which a person from a Turkish village relates his or her life story, you find yourself equally moved by the faces of museumgoers in old armchairs watching these films, or nodding off in front of them.

I was both taken and taken in by the life of the imagination, feeling an unexpectedly sacred energy in the vital irreverence of art. MONA is the only museum I have ever visited that did not at some point fatigue me. The land that time forgot has none of the smugness of cultural capitals, but plenty to teach the world.

What was my favorite day in Hobart? The day we rode bikes to MONA and had a coffee on the grounds while chooks wandered among customers gazing across the Derwent from beanbag chairs? Or the day we rode down to Salamanca Place at the harbor and wandered the Taste of Tassie Festival and the old city? On that day the winning boat in the Sydney to Hobart race sailed in.

My wife had known Bob Thomas, one of the world's legendary skippers. In the 1998 race when six sailors died and five yachts sank in a harrowing storm, Thomas lost his instruments but got his boat safely to Hobart using dead reckoning—a feat few others could perform. This year the winning boat was *Wild Oats*, owned by businessman Bob Oatley. We saw it finish just before sunset—its big grey sails and red 7 visible for miles against the hills of Hobart. The mainsail was reefed because they had hit a gale in Storm Bay. I told you—in Tassie you are never far from the wild.

For ten days over Christmas we camped on South Bruny Island, visible from Hobart but a world apart. We stayed in Adventure Bay, a place so little populated we could still imagine the masts and rigging of Cook's and Bligh's ships anchoring there in the eighteenth century. We took a boat trip into the Tasman Sea, then farther to the Southern Ocean, where we saw dolphins, seals, and albatrosses. We hiked to the Fluted Cape with its wild orchids and she-oaks and kookaburras. On our way back to camp we found ourselves diverted into an abandoned campground at the foot of the hill. Its buildings—office and toilet blocks—were all intact, though spookily overgrown, and its orchard and paddock were full of wallabies, including two with white fur and pink intelligent eyes. These are the rare painted wallabies of South Bruny. They were like spirit animals, tolerating our presence for a long time before disappearing into the last red light and tall grass where we could not follow them.

Our final campsite on Tassie was far to the northeast, the Bay of Fires, so named because early sailors could see the lights of Aboriginal campfires along the coast. The coast is sacred ground, and I can see why. The beach is bleached white like soft salt crystals. You walk barefoot on the granite headlands at each point and feel the primordial sleeping animal of the earth under your soles. Sometimes Australia seems the beginning of the world.

Tassie is difficult to describe, though excellent writers have lived here, including the late Christopher Koch, best known for *The Year of Living Dangerously* (1978), and the poet James McAuley, one of the geniuses behind the Ern Malley hoax of 1943. The fine philosophical poet Gwen Harwood, who lived much of her life in Hobart, once wrote,

> Language is not a perfect game,
> and if it were, how could we play?
> The world's more than the sum of things
> like moon, sky, centre, body, bed,
> as all the singing masters know.

She's channeling Wittgenstein. Me? I'm trying to channel Tasmania.

Summer 2014

Homesick for Sadness

A Childhood in Incompletion

JENNY ERPENBECK

WHAT WAS I DOING the night the Wall fell?

I spent the evening with friends just a few blocks from the spot where World History was being made, and then: I went to bed. Yes, I slept right through this bit of world history, and while I slept, the pot didn't just get stirred, it was knocked over and smashed to bits. The next morning I was told we wouldn't need pots any longer.

In the society I was born into, the government's most exacting critics had surpassed their own government in their capacity for hope. I'd learned to hope, and also to understand what it meant for something to be provisional, and to have other ideas, and to wait. And now? Now the ones whose ideas had been criticized all those years were being not just replaced but canceled out. And the critics were left sitting in an empty theater. There was a lot of talk of *freedom*, but I didn't know what to do with this free-floating concept suddenly drifting about in all sorts of different sentences. The freedom to travel? (But what if you couldn't afford to?) Or the freedom of expression? (What if no one was interested in my opinion?) A freedom to shop? (But what comes after the shopping trip?) Freedom wasn't a gift, it was something you paid for, and the price of freedom turned out to be my entire life up till then. The price of freedom was having what had just been the present a moment before suddenly relegated to the past. Our everyday life was no longer everyday life; it was an adventure that had been survived, our customs now a sideshow attraction. Everything that had been self-evident forfeited its self-evidence within the span of a few weeks. A door that opened only once every hundred years was now standing ajar, but the hundred years were gone forever. From this point on, my childhood became a museum exhibit.

When I picked up the newspaper not long ago, I read an obituary for my elementary school. It's true, a few former students had gotten together and published a death notice for the building where I'd gone to school for eight years. *In loving memory we mourn the demolition of our school.* These former students—now adults, of course—spoke in this unusually long death notice not only of their grief, but also of their everyday lives in and with this school, which had been constructed in 1973/74 in the valley between the East Berlin high-rises of Leipziger Strasse and the tall edifice of the Springer Publishing house in West Berlin. After the fall of the Wall, this building—a standard-issue postwar monstrosity—housed a high school for a decade or so, then was abandoned, then stood empty for another ten years, in the course of which it was overgrown with trees, bushes, and weeds. A silent place, its grounds covering nearly a square kilometer if you count the sports area, just around the corner from the hustle and bustle of Checkpoint Charlie, the world attraction for visitors trying to get a sense of what the Wall felt like. And just a quarter of an hour by foot from Potsdamer Platz with its palaces of glass.

Where else in all the capitals of the Western world might one possibly find a wasteland like this—earth lying fallow, dead, a defunct bit of everyday reality left over from another age? Ground Zero in New York became a construction site as soon as the rubble was cleared away, and a museum was built at its edge in memory of those who lost their lives in the attack on the World Trade Center. But no one died in our school. There had been, thank God, no war fought there, no attack. Once the building had been abandoned by school officials, all that could be seen in it was this new society's appetite for developable property in a prime location.

When I go to inspect the ruins, all I find still standing is a fragment of the rear staircase. These were the stairs that during my childhood still led up to the chemistry and biology labs. During recess, the boys from my class would stand in a tight circle in the alcove between the outer wall of the stairwell and the building proper, turning their backs on all the rest of us so they could smoke in secret. When one of them became *my boyfriend,* I was the first girl allowed to stand there during recess with the others, turning my back on everyone else.

When a wall collapses, when a ceiling crashes to the floor, what happens to the curve of space-time?

The disappearance of a place always occurs in two phases. I realize this only when I see, piled up beside the huge pile of rubble, the limp heap of red rubber mats that used to cover the sports area of the schoolyard. The first phase: the emptying out, becoming overgrown, collapsing but still remaining there—and then the second: the being swept away and replaced by something new. Only after the sweeping, the clearing up, the being disposed of can something else replace the thing that used to be there.

This desolate fermata in the district Mitte had nonetheless remained a sort of placeholder for my memories of the school, which—as is the wont with schools—was not always a happy place. As a wilderness in the middle of this quickly gentrifying neighborhood, this square kilometer was also something like a bygone era that gets stuck in the contemporary moment's throat until finally it can be spat out.

Only after the surface has been smoothed and scoured can the place that has disappeared and the time that disappeared along with it set off on their final journey, the journey to a purely intellectual realm, if you will, and from then on they exist nowhere else but, for example, within the convolutions of my brain, and in those of others, where they find in the memories of this or that person their final refuge.

The open area in front of the main entryway was just big enough to allow all the students in the school to assemble there in rectangular formation for the flag ceremony. But we also gathered there when the principal had sounded the fire alarm as an exercise. And starting in April or May, we would assemble there for another purpose as well: jumping according to strict, self-imposed rules over elastic bands that had been knotted together and stretched between two pairs of girls' legs. This was done with elastic designed for the waistbands of underwear, and at the time the game was known as *Gummihopse* (elastic hop)—these days it's called *Gummitwist*. Level One: with the elastic at ankle height; Level Two: at the knees; Level Three: the hips. It was easier to carry out the various maneuvers required in this game with each foot separately than when you had to keep your feet pressed together as you jumped over the elastic. The stairs that led from this site of games, assemblies, and fire alarms up to the main entryway is where the yearly class photos were taken as well, with the taller kids standing on the steps behind the smaller ones, like in choir.

A schoolyard large enough for all the kids to assemble in rectangular formation for the flag ceremony (*Where's my blue pleated skirt? Where's my cap? How come it won't stay on? C'mere, I'll stick it in place with a barrette. Stop, it hurts!*),

Class picture 1976/77. The author is in the top row, fifth from the left. Reprinted by permission of Jenny Erpenbeck.

a schoolyard like this is covered with paving stones, and because it's paved, it's perfect for jumping over a piece of elastic stretched between two pairs of girls' legs. Saluting the flag can be a part of everyday life, just like a game that girls play when the weather is finally warm enough for knee-highs.

In the place where this schoolyard used to be, there are no longer any children, and the words "flag ceremony" have now been phased out, rubble words. In the place that used to be kept empty so that orderly assemblies could take place there, chunks of concrete from the building are now piled up. This heap of concrete has something to do with me: one of the pieces, I see, has small blue tiles from the girls' bathroom stuck to it. Did I like this bathroom? Is it even possible to like a bathroom in a school? Aren't I looking forward to the future, to the light-flooded apartments or offices, for example, that will soon rise in the place of this erstwhile Socialist school bathroom? Edifices of granite, steel, and oak replacing the classroom walls with their bulletin boards featuring articles with headlines like *Mere Sparks Gave Rise to Flames!*, and soundlessly closing elevator doors in what used to be open air where children responded to the exhortation: *For peace and Socialism be ever prepared!* with a snappy or sleepy: *Always prepared!* Was that it? Strangely, it's not so important whether the thing being replaced was delightful or deplorable, good or evil, honest or dishonest. It is simply a matter of the time that once passed in this familiar way—this way familiar to me—and still lingered in these spaces. What is at stake is time that used to be the present: a universal present that happened to contain my own private one. Time that included a particular notion of the future, a notion familiar to me, even though this future still lay far in the distance. *Even the future isn't what it used to be*—a brilliant observation by Karl Valentin. Meanwhile I know what became of that lofty future we were being prepared for in this school. The long haul, often referred to by Brecht's phrase the *labors of the plains*. These plains were too extensive. But now? Now we have a future again. Or have present and future been conjoined for all eternity? And when the ruins are cleared away once and for all, will the past have been cleared away too? Are we now arriving in a time that will retain its validity for all time?

Now that the basement that sometimes was transformed into a vaccination center, and the cafeteria that sometimes still served dishes like blood pudding with sauerkraut, and the auditorium where our pictures from art class adorned the walls have all become a pile of rubble, I can see that in accordance with the two phases of disappearing I mentioned before, my mourning too has two phases. With the gradual disintegration of this place, I was first just concretely mourning the loss of the vaccination center, cafeteria, and auditorium—not the rooms themselves, of course, but these rooms as the gradually rotting backdrop for the quotidian reality of my childhood—as though a reality like this, long gone, might retroactively grow old and weak.

But now that the rubble is being swept aside, a more fundamental sort of mourning is beginning within me, one that extends beyond my own biography: mourning for the disappearance of so visible a wounding of a place, for the disappearance of sick or disturbed objects and spaces that bear witness to the fact that a present can't just come to terms with everything, finish it off, settle things once and for all. In this second phase, the phase of *cleansing*, I mourn the disappearance of the incomplete, the broken, of what has visibly refused to let itself be incorporated—the disappearance of dirt, if you will. In places where the grass just grows, where garbage piles up, a relativizing of human order sets in. And given the fact that we ourselves are mortal, every one of us, this is never a bad thing to ponder.

When the Socialist architects tried to lock out evil spirits, there was fortunately not enough concrete, or else it sprang a crack. It was also more than anyone could achieve at one go. Replacement parts were problematic. And besides: To whom does the *property of the people* really belong? Whose business is it? During my childhood, everything I saw in this city bore witness to how little time separated the present day of the Socialist experiment and the present day of wartime. The incomplete and the vision of a lofty future, ruins and the construction sites of the new world still existed side by side, always open to view. *Arisen out of ruins and toward the future turned* was the first line of the GDR's national anthem—one could not be imagined without the other, no future without ruins. And a child starts by learning only through the things that are *there*, children learn by seeing what is *there*, the things that exist side by side. Stories get added to this only later, and one's own experiences. For children, ruins from another age that they find waiting for them when they are born—just like hospitals in which they have not yet seen anyone close to them suffering, or cemeteries in whose earth they have not yet had to bury a friend, a grandmother, a grandfather, father or mother—are not yet sites of mourning. Not even sites of fear, because a child does not yet have enough experience to be afraid. What I'm going to call my love of dirt, the incomplete, and ruins was still pure and untainted when I was a child, and my learning took place only through the presence of damaged places and sites of this sort, through their very existence and the fact that I was sharing my life with them.

During my childhood, ruins were an everyday sight—these very ruins that had cost me nothing since I had been born into their reality. Didn't my first rendezvous with the aforementioned boyfriend from my class at school take place in the ruins of the German Cathedral, amid the weeds and jagged blocks of stone? Hadn't I climbed a birch tree whose strong branches reached to the second floor of the ruins of the New Museum, making my way to the half of the museum corridor that still remained, in order to look at statues no one else knew about? These statues were supposed to be torsos, but a war that had nothing to do with them had truncated them further. Hadn't my father, every time we drove past Alexanderplatz in our Trabi, pointed out the construction fence across from the Red Rathaus, reminding us of the mummies dating from the Biedermeier period that he had found as a student in the catacombs of St. Nicholas's Church, undamaged by bombs, which were no doubt still buried beneath the rubble of the bombed-out block? I knew the bullet holes around the foundations of Humboldt University and the State Library and all the other grand edifices of Berlin's Mitte neighborhood, I always knew what it looks like when a tree starts growing out of a roof gutter, knew what it's like to look out your window at an air-raid bunker, and knew the faint differences of hue that made it possible to look at an old tile-covered wall and see where there used to be a bathroom, a kitchen, a pantry. Girders. Charred beams. Walls with nothing behind them. Rooms in which dead pigeons get rained on because there's no roof. Firewalls that create attractive silhouettes at sundown. Roped-off properties. Vacant lots and dead ends in the middle of Mitte.

As a child, I loved the ruins. They were secret places, abandoned spots where the weeds grew as high as your knees, and where no grown-ups would follow you. Sometimes they were dangerous places, too, places with gorgeous views, places where we could make discoveries that belonged to us alone. Peaceful places where nothing happened except that clouds passed by overhead. Places from where you could look up through several floors and burnt-out window frames and see the sky. Places where shepherd's purse grew—you could eat the hearts. They were places that were landscapes in the middle of the city. It was many years before I realized that these places so familiar to my childish gaze were in truth a bygone era that had been wiped out, an era that sticks in the contemporary moment's throat until finally it can be spat out. To be sure, there was one difference: At the time, it didn't cost anything to have the ruins there. Time wasn't moving forward, it was at a standstill. No one talked about money. The private ownership of property had been abolished. Real estate was nothing more than real.

Probably it was during this period that I learned to live with the incomplete and also with the awareness that buildings that have been constructed for all eternity do not last for all eternity. Not until I was grown did I learn that Hitler had planned the monumental buildings for his "Thousand-Year Reich" in such a way that they would make excellent ruins when the thousand years were up. Looking at the ruins of Berlin at the time, it was easy to study what remains when a cupola is destroyed, or a department store; one could learn without much effort that it was perfectly possible to live in the bottom two floors of an apartment building even if the top two floors had been destroyed by bombs. And this knowledge is of a sort that cannot be forgotten again. Even today I find myself automatically converting shopping arcades into the ruins of shopping arcades, I make clouds of dust rise up in elegant boutiques, imagine the glass walls of office buildings splintering and raining down, leaving behind naked offices with no one sitting in them. I know perfectly well what it would be like if all the rubber plants in living rooms and all the geraniums on balconies dried up because there was no one left to water them, or because the ones who were left behind had more urgent matters to attend to than watering the plants. I see fountain basins filled with debris, see streets that are impassable, and consider which pieces of my furniture might be left standing on a bit of floor if the apartment itself no longer existed. I've always also known how the people sitting across from me on the subway—children, teenagers, or adults in the prime of life—would look at the age of 80; I couldn't help converting these people into their own ruins: the infirm, wise, ravaged, or overripe ruins of faces and bodies, I knew all about the decline awaiting them and kept seeing it in different forms. This compulsion has remained with me to this day, as if the decline of all that is were just the other half of the world without which the rest too would be unthinkable.

And at the same time, I myself was living in the middle of a construction site that could only be there because before it there had been nothing or almost nothing left—without my being conscious at the time of what I was experiencing. That's no doubt how it always is: It takes you an entire lifetime to make sense of your own life. Layer after layer, knowledge piles up atop the past, making it look again and again like a brand-new past you have lived through without actually knowing it.

I begin my life as a schoolgirl, then I grow, and the buildings surrounding ours grow as well. My own conscious life was accompanied by the Socialist life of Leipziger Strasse, which today leads to Potsdamer Platz but at the time came to an end at the Wall. Today I know that one hundred years ago, Leipziger Strasse was a narrow, popular, and highly populated commercial street filled with tobacco shops, horse-drawn streetcars, sandstone curlicues on the buildings, and women with fancy hats. There were still Jewish-owned textile mills in the neighborhood at the beginning of the 1930s. But by the time of my childhood, none of this was left, and I didn't know there was something missing, or someone. Today I also know that the tall buildings, like the one I lived in, were constructed with propagandistic intentions as a response to the Springer Publishing headquarters on the West side of the Wall, but as a child, I simply enjoyed all the lights we could see on the other side from the terrace above the 23rd floor. As schoolchildren, we read the time for our Socialist recess from an illuminated clock display in the city's Western half that was visible from our side of the Wall. That the building to which this display was affixed also bore the illuminated letters "B.Z.," advertising a newspaper we'd never heard of, was of no interest to us. For our Sunday walks, my parents would bring me to the end of Leipziger Strasse, to the area right in front of the Wall, where it was as quiet as in a village, there was smooth prewar asphalt there, perfect for roller-skating, and here was also the final stop on the bus line, no through traffic beyond. This was where the world came to an end. For a child, what could be better than growing up at the end of the world?

When I was a child, the one-half of the city was a whole city for me, and even today it's only my mind and not my feelings that understand that the city is only now functioning again the way it was built and intended. For example, I can drive down Chausseestrasse a hundred times—a street that leads from the East Berlin district Mitte to the district Wedding in West Berlin, now a perfectly normal street again—and one hundred times I will be driving through a border crossing. This growing-together-again of the city is for me not a growing-together-again, it's a perfectly arbitrary addition, just because as a child I didn't experience the two halves of the city as belonging to a single city. I see how in the half I know so well the functions of a capitalist metropolis move back into the buildings that belonged to them fifty years before and suddenly comprehend that these buildings knew more all along than they were able to tell me. One building bears the inscription "House of Switzerland," and I'd always wondered why this oddly constructed building, planted amid all the Socialist linden trees with a grocery store on the first floor, bore such a name. Now the building is back in the hands of the banks and insurance companies that first built it. And still: something I failed to learn with the feelings of a child still eludes me now, with my grown-up feelings. Someone like my old neighbor, who always bought his breakfast rolls across the street before the war—in a place that suddenly became the West and inaccessible—no doubt had the inverse experience. With his childhood feelings he got to know all of Berlin, and for him, the Wall can only have been a subtraction for those twenty-eight years.

When I was a child, I didn't distinguish between the ruins left behind by the Second World War and the vacant lots and absurdities of city planning that came about when the Wall was built. For me, with my 1970s childhood, the buildings still bearing inscriptions in the *Fraktur* script so beloved of the Nazis ("Molkerei" or "Kohlehandlung") long after the dairy and the coal merchant had closed up shop, were just as familiar a sight as the blocked-off entrances to the subway stations that had been closed when the Wall went up. The wind blew old paper and dry leaves down to the foot of these stairs that no one descended for thirty years. The sounds made by the West Berlin subway lines that ran beneath East Berlin without stopping could sometimes be heard through the ventilation shafts all the way up to where we children of the East were standing, and we also knew the warm air that would waft up to us from these inaccessible tunnels. But we learned that just as municipal dairies and coal merchants could disappear forever, there were also paths beneath our feet that were not meant for us, even that there were airplanes flying above our heads in which we would never travel. We heard the workmen on the construction scaffolding in West Berlin hammering and drilling and knew that an entire world that seemed so close could still be inaccessible.

At the same time, though, we learned that if you look at it from the other way around, besides the world we knew, there was a second world that existed quite close to us. We learned without learning—only by existing in this city and living this life—that the things you could grasp were not all there was. That other worlds were hidden in the earth we walked over and in the sky whose clouds drifted untouched above East and West alike. For me as a child, an empty space did not bear witness to a lack; instead it was a place that had either been abandoned or declared off-limits by the grown-ups and therefore, in my imagination, belonged entirely to me.

Often, visiting my grandmother, I would stand in the living room behind the curtains, looking at the large building that could be seen behind the Wall, *over there*. It might have been a school, or a barracks. In the mornings, the sun would shine brightly on its walls. I liked this building and wondered what sort of people lived or worked there. The wall separating me from the part of the city where this building stood, and the barbed wire barrier in front of the Wall, and even the strip of sand under the barbed wire, which probably had land mines hidden in it, and the border guard who was patrolling right beneath where I stood, were of far less interest to me. While my grandmother was cursing because a dustrag she had hung over the railing of the balcony to dry had been blown down into the border strip—now it was lost to her forever—I stared at this building. In the evenings, its windows remained illuminated for a long time, every window with the same neon light, so probably they weren't apartments after all. An empty space is a place for questions, not answers. What we don't know is infinite.

My aunt, the one who always sent me the greatest "West packages" from the other half of Berlin, lived on Sickingenstrasse. The address was on the package. Sickingenstrasse. My entire childhood I thought it was the "trumpeter of Sickingen" in the legend, but really it's the "trumpeter of Säckingen." And the trumpeter of Säckingen—as was clear to me even then—could not possibly be the same trumpeter I was thinking of when I sang the "Song of the Little Trumpeter": "Among all our co-omrades, not one was so fine, as our little trumpeter, the Red Guard's pride and joy, the Red Guard's pride and joy." But for a child it's not particularly surprising for the Baroque bourgeois trumpeter from Säckingen to be singing Erich Weinert's Communist trumpet song in the inaccessible Sickingenstrasse in West Berlin, a song that used to move me to tears every time, and so for me, as a child, Sickingenstrasse was a lovely street, a lovely street in the inaccessible West, where everything was fragrant with Ariel laundry detergent and Jacobs Krönung coffee, while the little trumpeter dies a heroic death, melodiously, as well he must.

After the fall of the Wall, I then visited my aunt at some point, and of course Sickingenstrasse turned out to be not lovely and fragrant but instead loud and dirty, and my aunt's apartment was in a modest 1950s housing block, a dark one-bedroom flat with low ceilings, a wall unit, collectible teacups, and an L-shaped sofa. I peeked behind the window curtains and saw the building across the way with its sign reading "Unemployment Office" and the many sad-looking men standing in front of it, apparently waiting for the office finally to open. Even with the window closed, I could hear the din of the nearby freeway in my aunt's quiet living room. The newly accessible West didn't look, smell, or sound anything like the West still blossoming inside my head.

On the other side, though, the Unknown filling up with stories like a vacuum was probably just as great. East Berlin was gray, said people who had ventured from the West into the city's Eastern half. Only now am I able to imagine what an adventure it must have been to pay your entry fee and then find yourself in the forbidden zone. When as a teenager I lived near the Friedrichstrasse border crossing, Westerners who hadn't managed to spend all the money they'd been forced to exchange sometimes handed me twenty-mark bills. These Westerners looked as though they were a little ashamed to be treating me like a beggar, and they also looked as if they didn't have a clue as to how things actually worked here in the East. They looked as if they were glad to be able to go back to where they knew their way around.

At the same time, East Berlin, it seems to me today—now that I know the West perfectly well—probably wasn't much grayer than the city's Western half; it's just that there were no billboards and neon signs hanging on the bullet-pocked walls in front of the vacant lots full of rubble. Admittedly, the plaster was crumbling from the walls of buildings in Prenzlauer Berg, and some of the balconies were no longer safe to stand on, true. The front doors of the buildings were never locked because private property was not an issue, and for that reason drunkards would sometimes take a leak in the entryway, I'll be the first to admit it.

But I remember above all—leaving aside the question of the grayness—a sort of almost small-town peacefulness that made a deep impression on me as a child, a sense of being at home in a closed-off and for that reason entirely safe world. Seen from the outside, there may well have been something exotic about our Socialist reality, but we ourselves saw our lives as neither a wonder nor a horror—life was just ordinary life, and in this ordinariness we felt at home. The only thing that connected us children with the so-called wider world out there was, on the one hand, the West packages (which not everyone received) and, on the other, *international solidarity*, the worldwide struggle for the release of Luis Corvalán or Angela Davis, for example, which we as schoolchildren translated into readily comprehensible "sandwich bazaars" or "scrap material collections." My parents filled their home with Biedermeier furniture and used money that weighed no more than play money. The lack of agency didn't hurt as long as there was no agency. As a child, you love what you know. Not what grown-ups think is beautiful, or strangers; no, you simply love what you know. You're glad to know something. And this gladness sinks into your bones and is transformed into a feeling of being at home. As for me, well, I loved this ugly, purportedly gray East Berlin that had been forgotten by all the world, this Berlin that was familiar to me and that now—at least the part where I grew up—no longer exists.

When my son and I are in the country in the summer, sometimes we roam around, crawling under fences that have been blown over and knocked full of holes to access abandoned plots of land once used for company holidays, we open the doors of empty bungalows, they aren't even locked, and silently gaze at the carefully folded wool blankets at the foot of the bunk beds, the curtains that were neatly drawn shut before some departure long, long ago, and the Mitropa coffee cups that someone washed and put away in the kitchen cabinet twenty-five years ago. Without saying anything, he and I gaze at all these things that have been preserved unchanged as if by a magic spell, ever since the last Socialist vacationers spent their holidays there just before their companies were "phased out" at the beginning of the 1990s, transforming an absence that was to last only two days into an absence forever.

Now forever it is time for "milk break" in the museum of my memory. I am drinking vanilla-flavored milk from a small triangular container, the opening gets soggy as you drink. I am thinking of the mechanical pencils we would take apart to use the barrel as a blowgun for launching little balls of paper, of the notes we would write and pass around, the fits of hysterical laughter that would overwhelm my best friend and me in the back row. I can still remember how we rocked in our chairs or propped open our pencil cases to play with pins, buttons, and erasers behind them, and I can also clearly remember the morning when I had to show up for school with glasses on my nose, and everyone said I looked like Lilo Herrmann, the antifascist resistance fighter whose picture was in our textbooks and whom we had declared hideous on account of the horn-rimmed spectacles she wore. My most vivid memory, though, is of the day when I stood up in the middle of class, walked across the room, and slapped the face of the boy who was always teasing me, to get my point across—and then got slapped back by him: an extremely unchivalrous and therefore unexpected revenge. When recess came, the red mark on my cheek was still visible. A few days later, it seemed perfectly understandable that this boy should be my boyfriend.

The place where all of this took place is now as flat as a book that's been closed again. I am standing beside it thinking: That's where I learned to read. A desert isn't the opposite of a mountain, it's a mountain that's been scattered, mountain climber Reinhold Messner once said. My perfectly normal schooldays, which in the end were not very different from a thousand other schooldays, became extraordinary thanks to the destruction of the site where they took place and the disappearance of the society that left its mark here. All these things that can no longer be seen here are now inside my head, more vivid than ever. Of course, this will only be the case for a certain length of time, for memories are inscribed in mortal flesh, and so the older I become, the more blurry and indistinct they will become, until eventually they will be swept away along with me, so that in the place where I used to walk around with my memories of all sorts of things, someone else will be able to walk around, remembering something else.

[Translated from the German by Susan Bernofsky]

Winter 2015

Letter from Athens

Logbook I, Days of 2016 (and Moments Before and After)

A. E. STALLINGS

13 June 2018 This is my third Ramadan in Athens. I'll be glad when it is over tomorrow night. I'm not fasting, not being Muslim, but the days are long and hot, so hot, and I start to recognize a certain worn, patient suffering on some of the faces I pass through the day, and also the relief of those carrying bags of skimpy shopping toward nightfall to whatever Iftar dinner they can cobble together. A few years ago I would not have noticed—a skinny Pakistani immigrant who has perhaps made some change today by washing car windows at a shade-less street corner, hastening through the street with his bag of festive groceries—fizzy lemonade, potato chips, perhaps some dates, some Arabic pita bread—at sundown. I think travelers (and thus refugees) are, in theory, given a dispensation from the daylong fasting and abstaining from water, but it is also a way of clinging to normalcy, dignity, home, and God, of course, among some who might seem forsaken. Some of the older children at the squat where we volunteer are observing, and we see it is with pride that they explain that not even a drop of water may pass their lips.

When I think about it, of course, Ramadan has been celebrated in Greece for centuries. Byron and Hobhouse first arrived in Ioannina during Ramadan in 1809, surprised to find it a time not only of quiet days but raucous evenings as Turks fired guns at the moon and neighbors feasted and visited one another. Naturally, the scene winds up in *Childe Harold*:

> LX.
> Just at this season Ramazani's fast
> Through the long day its penance did maintain:

Tents aligned outside a port building at Piraeus. Photo credit: Adrianne Kalfopoulou.

> But when the lingering twilight hour was past,
> Revel and feast assumed the rule again:
> Now all was bustle, and the menial train
> Prepared and spread the plenteous board within;
> The vacant Gallery now seemed made in vain,
> But from the chambers came the mingling din,
> As page and slave anon were passing out and in.

I post "Eid Mubarak, Y'all" on Facebook, to a dozen likes from fellow volunteers, and a trickle of thank-yous and hearts by names in Arabic and Persian script, some people I know from the squat, or Melissa Network where I teach a workshop, or refugees who have made it as far as Germany or Sweden. Sometimes I communicate with kids who have made it into "Europe" on FB Messenger. This is the only time I use emojis—we send each other hearts, or funny cats, or winking faces. How are you? How are you? Fine. Fine.

25 November 2015 It is my first visit to see what is happening at the port of Piraeus as the ferries come in, full of refugees from the islands (from Syria, but also Afghanistan, Iraq, Iran), who have reached Europe and plan to walk to Germany. I am going because it is happening in my town, I want to see it firsthand, not just from footage on a television broadcast. This perhaps is the upshot of being married to a journalist. As a writer I think, perhaps I will write about it. (This is, unfortunately, our nature.) But I am there with a group called Carry the Future that passes out baby carriers. I follow them on Facebook, I've given some money to the cause, I've "liked" things. One day, Maureen fires back on the post—"I don't need 'likes,' ladies, I need extra hands." So one bright November morning we meet her down at the passenger terminal E-1 in Piraeus waiting for ships to come in, while sorting through bags of baby carriers. It turns out I am already friends with two people on this "team"; we take a photo of the five of us, feeling strangely giddy to be out under blue skies on a November morning waiting at a port for people we've never met. It will turn out that each of these women will spend the next several years engaged with refugees in Athens or at camps outside of Athens.

I'm worried about passing out the baby carrier. Do you just walk up to someone with a baby, and say, here's a carrier? We are actually supposed to demonstrate the carriers and strap the babies in. The BabyBjörns I understand, having used them with my own babies, but some seem bizarrely complicated or perplexingly simple systems of slings or straps. In the end, it is such chaos, and of course the arriving parents are often more adept than I at figuring out a baby carrier. But at least I give a few away.

Wealthier refugees have taxis or cars waiting for them; they will drive away to decent hotels before continuing their journey. (A reminder that "refugee" is not a socioeconomic status.) Others scramble for the port bus that will take them to the train station. There is no government agency nor any NGO waiting for them; they simply walk off the boat (or are carried or are pushed in strollers or, sometimes, wheelchairs) and make their way past people in red hats trying to sign them up for cellphone plans and travel packages and bus tickets to Eidomeni.

11 December 2015 We have a successful day passing out baby carriers at the port. It is overwhelming to see people pour off the ferries in scenes shockingly reminiscent of the Asia Minor refugee influx of 1922/23. The exchange of populations meant 1.2 million ethnic Greeks, who had never set foot on Greek soil, arrived in Greece with nothing to their name, wearing headscarves and fezzes, many flooding the port of Piraeus, which became a tent city. But people are happy if tired, they have reached Europe. Welcome, we say. A photo posted to FB of me handing a baby carrier to an attractive smiling couple and their child, the wife looking chic in her purple headscarf, while my own hair is wild with the wind, is enormously popular—so many heartfelt likes and messages of gratitude and encouragement. This is at the beginning. The longer we work with the refugees, the longer we have been at it, the less approval we garner, from social media or elsewhere. Going down once or twice to the port to lend a hand is one thing, bravo. Allowing this chronic situation to take over a portion of your life is something else. *What is wrong with you?*

4 January 2016 Arrivals in Piraeus: *Mykonos*, from Chios and Samos, with 688 refugees; *Ariadne*, from Lesbos and Chios, 1,880 refugees.

14 January 2016 In late 2015 and early 2016, I am on a list to receive daily posts from Piraeus Solidarity and other volunteer groups on the number of arrivals daily from the islands, a Homeric Catalogue of Ships (the *Blue Star 1*, the *Blue Star 2*, the *Nissos Mykonos*, the *Nissos Rodos*, the *Ariadne*, the *Diagoras*), from Lesbos, Chios, Samos, Leros, gates of arrival (E-2, E-1, E-7), the times and the number of refugees onboard. Volunteer groups are meant to organize themselves to meet the ferries, offer what assistance they can (sometimes there might be a donation of oranges or apples to distribute, or toothbrushes and hygiene kits, or breakfast-in-a-bag).

The *Diagoras*, coming from Kos/Leros (one of several ships that will arrive today in Piraeus), is packed with refugee families, children, and babies, including a two-week-old infant. A Syrian man politely offers Maureen and me some of his food-aid juice, in thanks for Maureen's managing to get the devilishly packaged thing open. In a separate incident, I have never seen a man so thrilled at the sight of an apple: "An apple! An apple! I am so happy because I am hungry!" A middle-aged lady in a leopard-print hijab steps off the boat and meets my eye as if she knows me. I realize I am wearing a leopard print baseball cap. Salam, she says. Do I say, *Here, have an apple?* Welcome.

22 January 2016 It is a Friday morning; I've just got my children off to school. The news all over my local FB feed is that two separate Aegean shipwrecks near Greek islands have left 42 refugees dead, including 17 children, enough to fill a classroom. These are the drownings we know about, of course. Other boats sink without witnesses or survivors. Small bodies wash onto desolate shores nibbled by fish; fishermen draw up the faceless drowned in their nets.

The rector of the University of the Aegean (based in Mytilene on Lesbos), Stephanos Gritzalis, distressed at the spate of drownings, quotes a line from Aeschylus's *Agamemnon* (659–60), "the Aegean blossoming with bodies." It is an intertextual quotation, though, since George Seferis uses the ancient Greek verbatim in his famous "In the Manner of G. S." (Keeley-Sherrard trans.):

> and if we see "the Aegean flower with corpses"
> it will be with those who tried to catch the big ship by swimming
>   after it
> those who got tired of waiting for the ships that cannot move
> the ELSI, the SAMOTHRAKI, the AMVRAKIKOS.
> The ships hoot now that dusk falls on Piraeus,
> hoot and hoot, but no capstan moves,
> no chain gleams wet in the vanishing light,
> the captain stands like a stone in white and gold.
>
> Wherever I travel Greece wounds me,
> curtains of mountains, archipelagos, naked granite.
> They call the one ship that sails Ag Onia [Agony] 937.

7 February 2016 Urgent! 20 or more families are stuck at the port, as there are various bus strikes. They are being housed in the passenger terminal at E-1 in Piraeus, but the building isn't heated. Emergency calls go out for food and for sleeping bags. It's a Sunday, usually a date night for me and my husband, but I persuade him to go down to the port instead to check on how Maureen and other volunteers are doing, what the situation is. (Since my husband is a journalist, we sometimes go to the port together, for our disparate reasons.) I bring markers and paper for the kids; as Maureen points out, one of the problems is just boredom, there is nothing to do. I imagine my kids, weary and whining and are-we-there-yet-ing on a brief car trip; I can't imagine what this journey is like. (Another friend, Eileen, has been organizing the making of and passing out of activity kits—with markers and paper—to children in transit since 2015.) The children (and some teenagers) seem delighted to have something to do; girls in bright new hats draw me pictures of flowers, a boy, 11 or 12, draws pictures of tanks and a helicopter and machine guns, all with eyewitness accuracy. He is shy and proud and gives me his pictures. Two Greek grandmothers who have come along to help and entertain the kids get involved, telling the children to tidy up, to put the caps back on the markers. It is a moment of insight: I can see that something in the kids relaxes when they are being told off by the familiar grandmothers—themselves probably descended from Asia Minor refugees—in frumpy black. There's a reassuring normalcy to it. We are no longer in a war zone, this is a place where the caps go back on the markers, so they can be used again. (This becomes a sort of philosophy then for our activities with children: the caps-back-on-the-markers theory.)

16 February 2016 Many times people do not even come into the passenger terminal, which is set up with some supplies, and bathrooms, and electrical sockets for recharging, and a little warehouse of clothing and shoes. Since the boat is delayed, I am helping to sort donations in the warehouse: these range from beautiful new hand-knit baby sweaters to the bizarrely inappropriate—stilettos, bikinis, evening dresses, used thongs. We are trying to pack up boxes of gloves and hats and socks and boots to send to Eidomeni, where people are freezing in the rain and mud at the border, hoping to cross over into the Republic of (Northern) Macedonia. An older man and a teenaged boy come up to the counter—the boy needs a jacket or outer layer, he's only in a T-shirt. (People's clothes are soaked on the journey over in dinghies, and then they often have to make do out of boxes of donations.) It's easy to fetch out an old tweed jacket or an ugly sweater; the father is tired and grateful, but the kid is clearly mortified to have to wear these items. And then I realize he's about my son's age; my son wouldn't be caught dead wearing this. It crosses my mind—what's it like to be a teenager *and* a refugee? One mortification after another. While an efficient volunteer shouts from back among the boxes, "We aren't a shop, you know!," I manage to scramble back into the bags I've been sorting and locate the one arguably "cool" item of warm clothing I've come across, a thick black hoodie. It's too big, but that's OK. The kid's face is still something of a blank, but he takes the garment with a glimmer of satisfaction.

18 February 2016 Closure of the Balkan route; refugees can no longer walk out of the country, and populations start to build up at ports and borders.

6:55 *Blue Star 1* E-2
9:40 *Diagoras* E-1
23:35 *Nissos Mykonos* E-7
Many refugee arrivals are expected.

20 February 2016 The *Ariadne* arrives tonight at 10:00 at E-1 with 1,900 refugees onboard.

22 February 2016 *Blue Star Patmos* arrives in E-1 at 19:00 today with 1,277 refugees onboard.

25 February 2016 URGENT UPDATE:
    The *Blue Star 1* arrives from Lesvos & Chios at 06:30 with 1,355 refugees onboard.
    The *Diagoras* arrives from Dodecanese at 11:55 with 691 refugees onboard.

26 February 2016 Marie and I decide to join Maureen at E-1, which is now crowded with families and children. We will, in theory, distract children while she works on sorting the warehouse. We realize there will not be enough markers or paper (though we've brought activity kits), so try sidewalk chalk, and balloons, and singing songs. The songs are hugely popular—most of the kids seem to know the ABC song or even "Frère Jacques," and quickly learn others. One of our participants is a cute smiling kid with crooked teeth and wild hair. He hangs around us for an hour or so. As we are about to leave, a woman comes up, distraught. I can't figure out what is the matter. Finally she shows us a photo of the kid on her phone. She's lost him. She, Marie, and I run wildly through the terminal looking for him among families camped on little squares of floor, demarcated by lines of duct tape on the floor, which also delineates imaginary passageways. We realize in the chaos how easy it is for a child to wander off, or to be taken by someone, the panic compounded by being in a strange land in a language you don't understand, to have escaped war only to lose a child in a crowd. In the end, she finds him, he was with other family members on the other side of the terminal. The look of sheer terror drops from her face, but everyone's hearts are still pounding.

28 February 2016
23:50 *Nissos Mykonos* E-7 Lesvos, Chios, Samos

1 March 2016 Needs list posted for port:

Bottles	Tea/sugar
Pacifiers	Baby formula
Bottle brushes	Nuts (almonds, walnuts, etc.) for
Soap	pregnant/lactating women
Diaper cream	Latex gloves
Pampers for one-month-olds	Paper cups/plates
Talc	Plastic knives and forks
Toothpaste/toothbrushes	Salt and oil
Strollers	Chickpeas
Water	Lentils

3 March 2016 Four of us—three writers and an artist—the novelist Cindy Camatsos; the poet Adrianne Kalfopoulou; and artist and graphic designer Marie Howarth and I head to Piraeus to do some art activities with the kids staying near the E-2 passenger terminal (or the Stone Building), as E-1 gets more attention from volunteer groups. (The port is filling up, with strikes affecting bus services, and temporary border closures.) Today, the group is mostly Kurds from Iraq. We have drawing paper and markers, homemade bubble solution. Some of the drawings are of weeping figures, with names printed above them. Two older boys with excellent English help us to translate and organize the little kids. Upon being asked where he hopes to get to, Wasam says, brightly, "England." (Usually, the answer is Germany.) We wish him well. On the way back into town on the train, Adrianne and I are sitting near an extended Iranian family. At the Omonia metro station, where they need to change trains, half of the family accidentally gets off on one side of the track, and half on the other; the impassable gulf and tracks yawn between. There are looks of bewilderment and panic at the separation in this strange new city, with its incomprehensible signs. Adrianne and I try to tell one group to stay in place while we go get the other group to reunite them. We end up as turned-around and frazzled as they, in the confusing layout of the station, though in the end everyone is together. When I get home, I go to bed for three hours.

4 March 2016 I'm meeting up with some volunteers from Melissa Network at Victoria Square briefly to do some drawing out on the square with families camping there. It's on my way to another appointment, at the swanky café, Zonar's, just two stops away. I've brought along sidewalk chalk, which is an efficient and portable means of entertainment. Hopscotch, it turns out, is a universal children's game, and children try to teach me numbers in Farsi. I am surprised to run into Wasam, whom we had met at the port the day before. How are you? All the optimism has drained from his face. He bursts into tears. Arriving in mainland Greece is not the end of a difficult journey and struggle, but the start of another. An hour later I am in one of the most elegant and storied of Greek cafés (it was founded 75 years ago, though has moved location), sitting on a chair upholstered in green velvet, meeting with a writer from Crete. When I stand up, I realize there is gum on the plush chair—I must have sat in something on the pavement at Victoria. There is no way to remove it. The squalor sticks; I carry it with me.

20 March 2016 Today everything changes, something cracks. The borders with Europe slam shut, perhaps forever. Murmurations of rumor swirl among refugees and volunteers. From this day, the tent city at Piraeus will grow from scores to five thousand within weeks. Seeds of despair are sown in the muddy fields to the north at the border town of Eidomeni.

The day after, the Greek President, Prokopis Pavlopoulos, sends out a press release for the joint observation of International Poetry Day and Fight Against Racism Day (and also first day of the new Turkey-EU "agreement"), quoting Thucydides, and ending with ten lines of Seferis's "Last Stop" (here in the Keeley/Sherrard translation):

We come from Arabia, Egypt, Palestine, Syria;
the little state
of Kommagene, which flickered out like a small lamp,
often comes to mind,
and great cities that lived for thousands of years
and then became pasture land for cattle,
fields for sugar-cane and corn.
We came from the sand of the desert, from the seas of Proteus,
souls shriveled by public sins,
each holding office like a bird in its cage.

(The President bolds the last two of those lines for emphasis.) I would add
the whole poem of course bears rereading, eerily topical, with such lines as:

"The same thing over and over again," you'll tell me, friend.
But the thinking of a refugee, the thinking of a prisoner, the
     thinking
of a person when he too has become a commodity—
try to change it; you can't.

"Last Stop," Cava dei Tirreni, 5 October 1944

In the EU-Turkey deal, refugees are certainly commodities and not persons.

23 March 2016 The port has become increasingly chaotic, as more and more
people are stuck there, living in tents if they can get one. 5,000 people from
different war-torn regions side by side, nervous about their future, suspicious
of each other. Our last visit to the port, organized by our artist friend Eileen,
included a near child-riot over balloons, and I somehow ended up holding
a baby for an hour, not knowing to whom he belonged, and getting a little
worried when it came time to leave. (Finally, an older sister fetched him out
of my arms.) But today a squat is opening up much closer to me and many of
the other volunteers, in central Athens in an old school. It's almost walkable,
although I usually take a taxi as I am carrying games and activities. We imagine it will be good to see families and children more than once, develop relationships perhaps, offer a little stability. The rooms are bare (people are still
in tents, making room partitions out of the ubiquitous grey UNHCR blankets), but clean. It is indoors. There is plumbing. A desperate message over
one of the FB groups has brought us there—they need a hand with the kids,
who are using medical gloves as balloons and are generally bored and underfoot as they (anarchists, solidarity groups, students, volunteers, refugees) try

to set up the building. That's what we do! We come with markers and balloons and watercolor paints and reams of Ikea paper. After a couple of hours, the families want to be left alone to celebrate and settle in—they decorate the rooms with our balloons. On the balloons one father writes, in English and Arabic, Thank you, Yunan! and also draws what is clearly meant to be a Greek flag in blue and white. (The proportions are wrong; he emphasizes the cross.) Yunan or variations on Yunan (Yunanistan) are what countries to the east of Greece call Greece. It's evidently a corruption of "Ionian." A Syrian man, a painter who goes by Kastro, and who seems to be in charge, comes up to us and is unhappy we haven't taken better care of the children's drawings, some of which are now ripped or wrinkled.

One of the fathers, tall and melancholy, turns out to be a sculptor from Syria. He explains he works on a very small scale. All his work had been lost in the war. It is as if he has walked out of a Cavafy poem. Or rather, as if we are all wandering inside a Cavafy poem. Sometimes people I meet inadvertently quote him. One young man tells me, "I will go to another land."

4 April 2016 Visit the squat with volunteers busy with art activities, math and writing sheets. Pleased it goes so well, how it is even educational. On the other hand, plumbing situation at the squat dire. The drains keep blocking (word on the street is that it was outdated plumbing that condemned the old school in the first place), and no one can use the showers; it is also a hot April. Toward the end, I am smiling and communicating with two of the mothers (who are sisters). One of them has enough English to ask if she can come to my place and take a shower. I know they are miserable, being unable to shower. Why not? OK, I say. But then she wants to bring a child with her. OK, I say, but only two people, I can only take two. A translator comes over, and we go over this again. She goes off to get ready and comes back with laundry as well. I start to become uneasy. When I hail the cab, it is the woman and four children who try to get into the cab. I can't take four, I try to explain. A taxi will not take five people in Athens. The cab driver indeed refuses, and in the meantime, we are blocking traffic. Horns are honking. I panic and tell them they must get out. In a moment that haunts me, I stay in the cab, and it drives off. It is horrible. I have humiliated her. I have mortified myself. She is angry and hurt. I have behaved terribly. Over the next few days, I practice "Ana asfa," to an Arabic voice-recognition app on a website till I think I can be understood: I am sorry. I think of never returning to the squat. When I do return, I offer her a small gift and utter my sentence. She quietly refuses the gift and walks away.

5 April 2016 Invited by Nadina Christopoulou, I have started doing poetry workshops at the Melissa Network for Migrant Women near Victoria Square. At first, the participants are economic migrants—an Albanian cleaning lady who is, in Albania, a famous poet; Filipino women who have left their own children and homes in the Philippines to clean houses and care for children in Greece. (The Filipino community organization is among the most effective and long-standing in Greece.) One woman writes a letter afterwards to Melissa with her impressions—"What is a cleaning lady doing in a poetry workshop? But when we were doing the 'make a list' activity, I was like 'ok that was easy' and when everyone started sharing thoughts and everyone just kind of listen to what one wants to say I felt this confidence of opening, and just say what is in my mind. For the years of working inside a house, I got used to obeying orders, never being asked of my opinion on matters, so I developed this feeling of insecurity." Soon, the sessions expand to include refugee women.

14 April 2016 The photos from this day at the squat are sunny and color-saturated. The memories are dark as well as bright. Yazan, a 10- or 11-year-old Syrian boy, about my son's age (it dawns on me that I tend to bond with boys my son's age and girls my daughter's age) with good English, has been a favorite with volunteers. He is polite and helpful, turned out in good clean clothes. It is unclear whom he is with at the squat—a father, an uncle? Once I bring a small basketball of my daughter's along. Could I get him one just like that? He would pay for it, he insists proudly, he has money to pay for it.

This day he works for a long time (with the artist Marie) on a picture of a house. It is a vivid green, there is an apple tree in the grassy yard, curtains swag across the windows, and high blue clouds. His name is written carefully in Arabic and in English on either corner of the sky. I don't know much about children's art, but we have noticed certain patterns. At first, the children draw national flags. *This is where we are from.* (Sometimes these are aspirational flags, such as the flag for Kurdistan.) Later come the houses. Sometimes there are mountains and rivers in the background. Sometimes there is a car in the driveway. Sometimes there are birds. But there are never any people. These are, I think, dream houses. Houses of the past, houses of the future. But no one lives in them now, or yet. Mohammed, a boy in dirty clothes who barely speaks (it is unclear whether this is a speech impediment, a developmental issue, or perhaps some trauma, or all of the above), and who often loses his temper, is the same age. This day he is in dirty mustard-colored sweatpants. He has been doing better lately—he absolutely quieted down and fell into rapt concentration with some knitting lessons (interestingly, quite popular with this set of boys). Everything seems to be going well, but then Mohammed accidentally steps on Yazan's carefully colored picture. Yazan screams and leaps up and clutches Mohammed by the throat, with a tirade of Arabic. Volunteers wrench the children apart, and Marie manages to reassure Yazan about the fate of his picture, dusting off the faint footprint on his dream house. But Mohammed is on the steps, sobbing with more desolation than I have ever seen from him, inconsolable. His mother and his little brother surround him and walk with him into the squat. I will never see Mohammed or his family again. My last image is of him downcast, head in his hands, inarticulate with grief.

3 May 2016 Today's arrivals:
06:55 *Blue Star 1* E-2 Lesvos/Chios 560 refugees
09:40 *Diagoras* E-1 Rodos/Kos/etc. unknown number

23 June 2016 I have made the mistake of bringing some donations to give out at the squat; I ought just to drop them at the office, but the Afghans keep complaining that the Syrians get everything (in future I will take all inter-squat gossip with a grain of salt—how am I to know or judge?)—girls quarrel over who gets the black pants. The sisters Aqdash and Moskan keep asking for the sunscreen I have brought, or anything else I might have to pass out. Aq. is usually aloof (indeed, I have never really seen her smile). Both sisters are striking, with jet-black hair and expressive eyes. M. is the same age as my daughter and greatly resembles her, only darker. The sisters are gesticulating wildly and uttering a torrent of urgent Persian (or rather probably Dari, which if I understand aright is a dialect preserving the vocabulary and pronunciation of medieval Persian). I am flustered and lose my sangfroid, eventually walking off with everything and plunking it down outside the office, from which it may be distributed or may disappear. I leave feeling badly about losing my cool. I will be better with them next time, I promise myself.

But I will never see them again. What they were trying to explain is they were leaving, if I had anything to give them, it was now or never. They have made their way into the squalid, overcrowded camp at Elliniko (the site of the old abandoned airport, now a terminal for exile and the stranded), and from there to somewhere in northern Europe. I still think of Aq. with her stern intelligence and unsmiling beauty, her fashion sense so that, even among the secondhand clothing donations they had to dress out of, she only wore edgy combinations of black and purple, her purple-and-black hijab always matching her long-sleeved checked shirt and her slim black pants.

7 July 2016 We're celebrating three birthdays at the squat—Narges and Maedeh each turn eleven within days of each other (and mine just passed). N. and M. have the typically prickly relationship of other middle-school-aged girls, a mixture of affection and envy, fondness and competition. N. is the beauty (sometimes decked out like an Afghan princess), M. the brain, having picked up English and being evidently a math whiz. (I set her double-decker multiplication problems in three digits, she does them at lightning speed, and then I find I cannot check her answers without a calculator.) Both are from Afghanistan, though they appear to be from different ethnic groups, M. is Hazara, a persecuted group from Bamiyan. (The preferred fake passports for Hazaras trying to smuggle themselves farther into Europe are evidently Chinese and Korean.) I make cupcakes so there are enough for everyone, Judi brings a cake, Mar has some presents and decorations. This first time I bring cupcakes to the squat, it seems a bit surreal—though I am tickled to be baking cupcakes for refugees, instead of some silly PTO bake sale. My husband is bemused. At the squat we discover it is also Hamza's birthday, a Syrian boy, and we try to find something in our bags of activities for a present, but he seems pleased when we make him a construction-paper crown. Some of the children speak Persian (or Dari), and some speak Arabic, some Kurdish. Among themselves they develop a sort of lingua franca out of Greek and English phrases. "What does 'malaka' mean?" the kids ask me early on. It's the most common Greek curse word.

13 July 2016 Piraeus Solidarity: Current needs at the port of Piraeus:

Shorts (all sizes) for men & children	Razor blades
	Tea bags
Sandals & flip-flops (all sizes)	Sugar
Plastic basins for washing clothes	Baby formula nos. 1, 2 & 3
Washing powder	Spray, etc., for mosquitos
Rope for drying clothes	Sunscreen for children & adults
Brooms & dustpans	Toilet paper

14 July 2016 I supervise some reading with a 13-year-old boy, Wasim, at the squat. His English is excellent. We talk for a while about his life. He misses his cat, which they left in Damascus, and his guitar. He has spent three months in the squalor of the tents in Eidomeni. He still seems hopeful, somehow. I am going to the States, and he wants me to bring him back a guitar, preferably an electric guitar. He wants me to walk with him past the music shops that are around the corner from the squat, to look at the guitars. To this day I regret I did not get him a guitar or at least sign him up for some lessons. It will be his birthday while I am out of the country. But when I return, he has moved on from the squat to some camp. I do see him again—many months later, after he and his family have been at the camp, still waiting to get to Germany. He seems a different kid, less outgoing. How is he? How has he been? He turns away, dashing tears from his eyes with the back of his hand. I never see him again.

8 October 2016 Melissa poetry workshop—one of the first with the group of refugee women. Most are from Syria or Afghanistan, the class contains Arabic and Persian/Dari speakers. When I introduce the idea of poetry (Sha'ar, in both languages), I talk first about lullabies and children's songs, such as the ABC song for remembering the alphabet. One Afghan woman points out that, under the Taliban, song was forbidden, and I realize that even my most basic introduction to poetry is fraught. As with earlier sessions at Melissa, I start with list poems, as anybody can make a list; lists don't require syntax or grammar yet tend to tell a narrative. As people stay longer at the port, the lists of needs coming over the social media transom keeps changing: sleeping bags, coats, then sunscreen and flip-flops; soap, lice shampoo, scabies medicine; pregnancy tests, diapers, baby formula.

We start with group activities. What are the items that make a home? At first the women suggest basics: shower, bathroom, rest. But they quickly get the gist of the activity and expand on this. Kisses, school. Books, television, music, perfume, flowers, a goldfish. Birdseed (for the bird, a girl explains).

Make-up was also forbidden under the Taliban, and I realize that for many of these women, lipstick or nail polish is not a luxury or an oppressive necessity, it is subversive, a kind of liberation. When Valentine's Day swings around in 2017, I am able to give out a batch of new lipsticks donated by the New York City lipstick entrepreneur Poppy King. Women apply it, delighted (the room I teach in has a large mirror), and one leaves kiss marks on her notebook.

One Afghan girl, Sakina (about 16), loves rock-and-roll and Jackie Chan movies (movies were also forbidden under the Taliban), and her poems

Lipstick distribution at the poetry workshop on Valentine's Day. Author A. E. Stallings in top photo with arm raised. Photo credit: Dr. Nadina Christopoulou. Courtesy of the Melissa Network.

often reflect this, with a mischievous sense of humor. Composing an acrostic poem based on her name, she ends:

> Kung-foo
> In the
> Night.
> Am I a good girl?

21 October 2016 Art and activities with volunteers at the squat. The family of Narges, Afghans, all get involved in painting with watercolors. Narges's grandmother especially likes the art activities. She looks like she could be 100 years old, but I think she might be closer to 60, as later we find that N.'s mother herself was only 14 when she married; N. is 11. Mostly the mothers paint abstract flowers. But N.'s mother paints another scene—of her, her three children, and her mother in the dinghy that brought them to Greece. The mother stands at the front, holding something and pointing ahead. There is a sail or flag that looks like the Greek flag. The other figures look down or stare ahead, expressionless and hunched into their orange life jackets.

The ancient grandmother paints a strange figure that could be a folk pattern on a traditional carpet.

Mar, the Spanish volunteer and art therapist who is at the squat daily, asks the children to paint scenes from their journey or their homeland, something I have to say I would be nervous about doing; she says it helps them process it. These are often terrifying. A kindergartner who can barely draw a stick figure draws a scene of a boat at night being fired upon with water cannons by the Turkish coast guard. There is a brown stick figure face down in the sea. Another, older child draws scenes from the bombing of his school over and over again, with the ambulance, and the teacher who loses a leg, and accurate renditions of machine guns. Another child draws a warplane with a pattern of lines on it. It is only a year later that I realize the lines are Arabic writing. A Syrian doctor translates it for me: Assad.

17 November 2016 I am in a public Greek hospital in a room with three other women. Tomorrow I will have surgery to remove my thyroid; later I will need radioactive ablation. 17th of November is also the anniversary of the Junta's attack on the Polytechnic in 1973 and is marked by an annual protest march to the US Embassy. There is something strangely comforting in hearing the slogans as the marchers pass by a street over, and the inevitable distant booms of stun grenades. In the past, my husband has usually covered the march as a journalist, and we sometimes would walk the length of it together, a sort of date night, ending up near the Embassy at the Plateia Mavili, named after a famous sonneteer who died in the Balkan Wars, where we peel off to have a drink.

29 November 2016 Activities in the yard of the squat. One Syrian girl comes out holding a rather put-upon dirty kitten her family has adopted from the street. The children are wild with it, and we try to get them to be a little more gentle. But the kitten never attempts to run away and seems to have accepted its new home and fate. It is white with blue eyes and probably deaf.

By August of 2017, the girl's family will have moved to Germany.

From the squat's page: "Our 'refugee' cat Ismael has been separated from his family due to relocation. Ismael's presence in the squat has reduced social isolation among residents, has increased well being, and has reduced symptoms of anxiety and depression. We want him to stay. The children want him to stay. In order for him to become a permanent resident though, due to the great number of pregnant women and babies, he needs to be taken to the vet."

This seems one of those projects that our group can easily take up and fundraise for; indeed the money is offered almost immediately. I deposit the money for the neutering and shots directly into the vet's account, the squat manager acknowledges, and it is done. But money keeps coming in for the cat. Even when I announce that we have made our financial goal, people keep sending it in. I tell them I will just put the money toward other things, and they don't mind, it is the idea—maybe the cat will need something else. I am struck by the fact that if I needed money toward vaccinating a child, it would be much slower coming in. Cats are uncomplicated somehow, but a child—that is someone's responsibility, someone's fault.

30 November 2016 It is raining, the autumnal rains that the olive trees in the countryside need. Here in central Athens, though, I have a poetry workshop to teach at the Melissa Network.

The sky is grey as a UNHCR blanket. It's by the blankets you recognize them, revenants wandering through the city with a backpack and one of these blankets under their arms. I see the blankets everywhere, and that particular hue of grey, a grey meant to be neutral, to show no stains. It is the identical color of despair. One day Nadina and I are sitting having coffee at Melissa Network, a community center for migrant women housed in an elegant old neoclassical house near Victoria Square. She has had it beautifully furnished with comfortable chairs and a coffee table and books and a kitchen and classrooms, a little garden patio in the back with potted flowers. Here you can charge your phone; coffee and tea are always available, and snacks and cake. It is an oasis of civilization in the middle of a neighborhood once elegant, now squalid. The walls are all painted in warm, bright colors. "I hate those grey blankets," Nadina says, and I agree. If there is one thing refugees need less of in their lives, it is one-size-fits-all bureaucratic grey.

The participants—and the class changes a bit from session to session, there are always new faces—hail from Syria and Iraq, Iran and Afghanistan, sometimes Pakistan or Congo or Somalia. They are all women, some as young as 16 or 17, some 35 or so, though they sometimes look older, aged by war and loss. Classes are unpredictable, veering from tears to laughter. Today I decide, why not just write about rain, rain that falls everywhere upon everyone. Hasti Hashemi, a slender, elegant Persian speaker from Afghanistan, produces this from my prompt:

Rain
I am like the rain
because rain is the start of deep feeling
because rain is clean sadness
because rain is filtered weather
because I am the universe
because I dance on glass.

Often, they compose in their native tongue and come up with a translation through some combination of phone apps and the resident translator, who also struggles with the subtleties of transferring poetry from one language to another; discussions sometimes end up being about translation itself. In this case, I am not sure we have understood the penultimate line. Does the writer mean rather "I am everywhere," or "I am universal"? It is only much later that I realize, or learn, that her name means "Existence" or simply "Universe" in Farsi. She is employing the ancient Persian convention of punning on her own name in the poem. *Because I am Hasti.*

Interlude:

Words I Have Learned in Persian from the Names of
  Refugee Women I Have Met in Athens

         (for Dick Davis)

      Blossom
      Lily
      Narcissus
      Beloved
      Heaven
      Dawn
      Butterfly
      Tulip
      Spring
      Swallow
      Moonlight
      Tuberose
      Peace
      Sky Blue Faience
      Existence
      Patience
      Memory
      The Evening Star

1 December 2016 We are at the squat doing art activities with the volunteers, when a 13-year-old girl from Bagdad introduces us to a new girl, 12, from Somalia. The Iraqi girl explains that her friend needs a winter coat—can we get one for her? Of course, of course, we say, moved by this friendship across race and culture, one that wouldn't exist without war and exile and upheaval, yet is also about the fellow feeling of girls the same age.

4 December 2016 Stephanie Larson, an archaeologist who has taken on fundraising for food donations and delivering them to the squat, is also a fellow mother at the American school my children attend. (Her daughter is in my son's class, and they take the same bus.) We both find the PTO exasperating, and the constant requests for baked goods for bake sales and bazaars. Today is the Christmas bazaar. We have reserved a table (at the school parents' reduced fee) for two Iranian women who make jewelry. This seems like a project with no downside, helping refugees get on their feet, and helping the school for that matter. Stephanie drives us into town to pick up the women and then to the school. There is a giddy camaraderie in it, a reminder that perhaps some of the motivation for persistence in these efforts is social. Foreign women ourselves, we understand a little about navigating a difficult new language and a new land, we have that much in common with the passengers.

13 December 2016 My FB post: "Feeling ill about Aleppo. As well as things in the US. Strange to be reminded of the American dream by a young man (26) from Syria today. He was pretty despondent about the situation here, and wanting to move on, however he could. He spoke to Adrianne Kalfopoulou and me, saying he wanted to go the US. Why? 'Because if you go to Germany, you will never be German. If you go to France, you will never be French. But in America, even if you are from Asia or Africa or Europe, you can be American.'"

He is a great reader, being a student of literature (he has read a lot of Western classics in translation) and would especially like the novels of Salim Barakat, a Kurdish-Syrian novelist and poet who is compared to South American magical realists. Well here is something we can help with, I think, and set out to track down a bookstore that will sell us Salim Barakat books. Online, I find a marvelous bookstore in Germany (alkutub.de) that specializes in Arabic books and engage in a very civilized email conversation—the bookstore not only finds me a book by the author, but it seems to be delivered almost overnight, and they are at my disposal regarding any other Arabic literature requests I might have. Yet, by the time we are back at the squat, the young man has left for Germany. I later give the book to an Iraqi teenaged girl desperate for reading material. At first, she is overwhelmed with delight and gratitude, but when I see her again, she returns the book, frowning. It is too difficult; she cannot read it.

20 December 2016 Christmas party at the squat. Or not Christmas party, of course, holiday party. (Squat management has told us it is not to be Christmassy.) In the end, though, the kids are very excited about their first Christmas in Europe and post photos of themselves on FB against the backdrop of big public Christmas trees. (Come to think of it, in Greece, St. Vasili, the Greek Santa Claus, is supposed to travel not from the North Pole, but from Turkey, as these children have.) The whole idea rather mad. We will have face-painting, and temporary glitter tattoos, and games, including an egg-spoon race. I am in charge of boiling 24 eggs. (I get the eggs very cheaply, at the farmers' market around the corner from my house, but I have to boil them in batches. My husband is, as he is often these days, bemused and/or perplexed.) There will be popcorn, and meatballs (beef), and pretzels and other snacks. We work with Narges to make a poster announcing it in English and Persian. Usually, we do activities outside, in the schoolyard; I'm not wild about the downstairs room (once a gym perhaps?), which is below street level, though with high windows, and cold. We will have pass-the-parcel with little prizes. I don't like the downstairs hallway either. Strangely, it is also one of the few times my husband is at the squat at the same time. He is outside, in the yard, filming a piece on a Syrian volunteer group (some of them refugees) who have been doing folkloric Syrian dancing with the Syrian kids. While my husband is upstairs in the wan December sunshine, I am in a narrow subterranean hallway when suddenly shouts break out (Arabic), and there is some pushing, between young men who live in the squat and young men who are running the NGO doing the dancing lessons. They are between us and the kids and the exit. Judi, the South African, often sweet and grandmotherly, but also no-nonsense, barges in and shouts at everyone in English. Evidently abashed (perhaps she reminds them of their mothers or grandmothers?), they part; the tension appears to disperse. The children seem too busy with the games to notice, and the party is reckoned a success.

I walk out into the December afternoon, through the streets of Greek shoppers trying to buy Christmas presents with whatever money austerity has left them. Tomorrow is the solstice, the darkest day of the year. But maybe after that things will look brighter.

Autumn 2018

Copyrights and Credits
☙☙
Notes on Contributors

Copyrights and Credits

Allen, Brooke. "Letter from Damascus." Reprinted by permission from *The Hudson Review* 63, no. 1 (Spring 2010). Copyright © 2010 by The Hudson Review, Inc.

Anonymous student poems in A. E. Stallings's "Letter from Athens" reprinted by permission of the Melissa Network.

Bell, Madison Smartt. "Miroir Danjere." Reprinted by permission from *The Hudson Review* 48, no. 4 (Winter 1996). Copyright © 1995 by Madison Smartt Bell.

Bennett, Joseph. "A Cambodian Diary." Reprinted by permission from *The Hudson Review* 24, no. 3 (Autumn 1971). Copyright © 1971, renewed 1999, by The Hudson Review, Inc.

Bernofsky, Susan, trans. "Homesick for Sadness: A Childhood in Incompletion," by Jenny Erpenbeck. Reprinted by permission from *The Hudson Review* 67, no. 4 (Winter 2015). Translation copyright © 2015 by Susan Bernofsky.

Bloom, Alice. "On a Greek Holiday." Reprinted by permission from *The Hudson Review* 36, no. 3 (Autumn 1983). Copyright © 1983 by Alice Bloom.

Broner, Martina, trans. "The Lighthouse at the End of the Hudson," by Antonio Muñoz Molina. Reprinted by permission from *The Hudson Review* 66, no. 1 (Spring 2013). Translation copyright © 2013 by Martina Broner.

Brown, Frederick, trans. "Alexis de Tocqueville: Letters from America." Reprinted by permission from *The Hudson Review* 62, no. 3 (Autumn 2009). Copyright © 2009 by Frederick Brown.

Brown, Jacqueline W. "The Blue Grotto." Reprinted by permission from *The Hudson Review* 53, no. 1 (Spring 2000). Copyright © 2000 by Jacqueline W. Brown.

Clark, Robert S. "Letter from Dresden." Reprinted by permission from *The Hudson Review* 38, no. 4 (Winter 1986). Copyright © 1985 by The Hudson Review, Inc.

Cox, C. B. "The British in India." Reprinted by permission from *The Hudson Review* 37, no. 3 (Autumn 1984). Copyright © 1984 by The Hudson Review, Inc.

Davenport, Guy. "Making It Uglier to the Airport." Reprinted by permission from *The Hudson Review* 30, no. 2 (Summer 1977). Copyright © 1977 by Guy Davenport.

Davis, Dick. "Iran, Twenty Years Ago." Reprinted by permission from *The Hudson Review* 51, no. 3 (Autumn 1998). Copyright © 1998 by Dick Davis.

Desrosiers, Christian N. "Letter from Indonesia." Reprinted by permission from *The Hudson Review* 64, no. 4 (Winter 2012). Copyright © 2012 by Christian N. Desrosiers.

Erpenbeck, Jenny. "Homesick for Sadness: A Childhood in Incompletion." Reprinted by permission from *The Hudson Review* 67, no. 4 (Winter 2015). Copyright © 2015 by Jenny Erpenbeck.

Giscombe, C. S. "Ontario Towns." Reprinted by permission from *The Hudson Review* 43, no. 4 (Winter 1991). Copyright © 1990 by C. S. Giscombe.

Gold, Herbert. "Tremblement de Terre! The Gods Turned Their Faces Away: Letter from Haiti." Reprinted by permission from *The Hudson Review* 63, no. 4 (Winter 2011). Copyright © 2011 by Herbert Gold.

Harwood, Gwen. "Thought Is Surrounded by a Halo," from *Selected Poems.* Poem excerpt in David Mason's "Letter from Tasmania." Text Copyright © John Harwood. First published by Penguin Books Australia 2001. Reprinted by permission of Penguin Random House Australia Pty. Ltd.

Lewis, Tess. "Introduction." Reprinted by permission from *The Hudson Review* 71, no. 3 (Autumn 2018). Copyright © 2018 by The Hudson Review, Inc.

Mason, David. "Letter from Tasmania." Reprinted by permission from *The Hudson Review* 67, no. 2 (Summer 2014). Copyright © 2014 by David Mason.

McDonnell, Lynda. "Veblen and the Mall of America." Reprinted by permission from *The Hudson Review* 47, no. 2 (Summer 1994). Copyright © 1994 by Lynda McDonnell.

Millard, Charles W. "The Gardens of Kyoto in Summer." Reprinted by permission from *The Hudson Review* 38, no. 2 (Summer 1985). Copyright © 1985 by The Hudson Review, Inc.

Moore, Paul, Jr. "Scenes from Nicaragua." Reprinted by permission from *The Hudson Review* 39, no. 2 (Summer 1986). Copyright © 1986 by Paul Moore Jr.

Muñoz Molina, Antonio. "The Lighthouse at the End of the Hudson." Reprinted by permission from *The Hudson Review* 66, no. 1 (Spring 2013). Copyright © 2013 by Antonio Muñoz Molina.

Olin, Laurie. "From Sundogs to the Midnight Sun: An Alaskan Reverie." Reprinted by permission from *The Hudson Review* 66, no. 1 (Spring 2013). Copyright © 2013 by Laurie Olin.

Seferis, George. "In the Manner of G. S." and "Last Stop." Excerpts included in A. E. Stallings's "Letter from Athens." Republished with permission of Princeton University Press, from *George Seferis: Collected Poems, 1924–1955.* Bilingual Edition. Translated, edited, and introduced by Edmund Keeley and Philip Sherrard. Copyright © 1967, renewed 1995; permission conveyed through Copyright Clearance Center, Inc.

Sisk, John P. "The Guiana Connection." Reprinted by permission from *The Hudson Review* 43, no. 1 (Spring 1990). Copyright © 1990 by John P. Sisk.

Spurling, Hilary. "Letter from Arcadia." Reprinted by permission from *The Hudson Review* 61, no. 1 (Spring 2008). Copyright © 2008 by Hilary Spurling.

Stallings, A. E. "Letter from Athens: Logbook I, Days of 2016 (and Moments Before and After)." Reprinted by permission from *The Hudson Review* 71, no. 3 (Autumn 2018). Copyright © 2018 by A. E. Stallings.

Trevor, William. "In Co. Cork." *The Hudson Review* 44, no. 3 (Autumn 1991). Reprinted by permission of SLL/Sterling Lord Literistic, Inc. Copyright © 1991 by William Trevor.

Webster, Diana. "Cannibals and Kava." Reprinted by permission from *The Hudson Review* 52, no. 2 (Summer 1999). Copyright © 1999 by Diana Webster.

Zukofsky, Louis. "A-18." Poem excerpt in Guy Davenport's "Making It Uglier to the Airport." All Louis Zukofsky materials copyright © Musical Observations, Inc. Used by permission.

Notes on Contributors

Brooke Allen (Winchester, Virginia, b. 1956) is a contributing editor of the *Hudson Review*, where she writes on literature, history, and film. She is the author of several books, including *Moral Minority: Our Skeptical Founding Fathers* (Ivan R. Dee, 2006) and *The Other Side of the Mirror: An American Travels Through Syria* (Paul Dry Books, 2011). She was on the literature faculty at Bennington College and now teaches in the Bennington Prison Education Initiative.

Madison Smartt Bell (Nashville, Tennessee, b. 1957) is the author of twelve novels, the most recent of which is *Behind the Moon* (City Lights Books, 2017). His eighth novel, *All Souls' Rising: A Novel of Haiti*, won the 1996 Anisfield-Wolf award for the best book of the year dealing with matters of race and was a finalist for the 1995 National Book Award and the 1996 PEN/Faulkner Award. He is the author of two collections of short stories, *Zero db* (1987) and *Barking Man* (1990). His *Toussaint Louverture: A Biography* appeared in 2008 from Vintage. *Forty Words for Fear*, an album of songs cowritten by Bell and Wyn Cooper and inspired by the novel *Anything Goes*, was released by Gaff Music in 2003.

Joseph Bennett (Pittsburgh, Pennsylvania, 1922–72) was one of the founding editors of the *Hudson Review* in 1947. Until 1966, he was an editor and thereafter served on the editorial board. During much of this time he worked for Wellington & Co., a New York investment banking concern, retiring as a partner in 1966. He was the author of *Baudelaire: A Criticism* (Princeton University Press), *Decembrist* (poetry), and *Luxury Cruiser* (a novel). The *Hudson Review*'s literary prize, the Bennett Award, was established in his honor.

Susan Bernofsky (Cleveland, Ohio, b. 1966) directs the program in literary translation at Columbia University. A Guggenheim fellow, she has translated classic works by Robert Walser, Franz Kafka, and Hermann Hesse. Her translation of Jenny Erpenbeck's *The End of Days* (New Directions, 2014) won the Independent Foreign Fiction Prize, the Schlegel-Tieck Translation Prize, the Ungar Award for Literary Translation, and the Oxford-Weidenfeld Translation Prize. Her translation of Erpenbeck's *Go, Went, Gone* (New Directions, 2017) won the 2019 Lois Roth

Award. She is a 2019–20 fellow at the Dorothy and Lewis B. Cullman Center for Scholars and Writers.

Alice Bloom (Collinsville, Illinois, 1935–2009) taught in the department of English at the University of Maine, Farmington. She was a noted essayist. She also operated The Corner, a craft and gift shop in Mount Vernon, Maine.

Martina Broner (Caracas, Venezuela, b. 1980) is a PhD candidate in Romance Studies at Cornell University. She is the author of *Abundancia de cielo* (Díaz Grey Editores, 2014), and her translations include Antonio Di Benedetto's *Nest in the Bones* (Archipelago Books, 2017).

Frederick Brown (New York, New York, b. 1934) is the author of *For the Soul of France: Culture Wars in the Age of Dreyfus* (Alfred A. Knopf, 2010), biographies of Emile Zola and Gustave Flaubert, and *The Embrace of Unreason: France, 1914–1940* (Alfred A. Knopf, 2014). His translation of Alexis de Tocqueville's *Letters from America* was published by Yale University Press in 2010. He is an advisory editor of the *Hudson Review*.

Jacqueline W. Brown (New York, New York, b. 1930), after retiring from a career as a certified social worker/psychotherapist, wrote memoirs of her childhood relationships and experiences growing up during the mid-1930s and early 1940s in Harlem.

Robert S. Clark (Schenectady, New York, 1934–2016) wrote music criticism for the *Hudson Review* from 1974 to 2007. He was at one time executive editor of *Stereo Review Magazine*, went on to become executive editor of *High Fidelity* magazine, then later editor of several trade publications in the field of lasers and photonics until his retirement in 2002. He loved singing as a bass in various choral groups.

C. B. Cox (Grimsby, England, 1928–2008) was a professor, editor, and activist. He had a long career at Manchester University (England), where he served as dean of the faculty of arts (1984–86) and pro-vice-chancellor (1987–91), retiring in 1993 as John Edward Taylor Professor of English Literature. His many books include *The Free Spirit* (1963), *Cox on Cox* (1991), and *The Great Betrayal: Memoirs of a Life in Education* (1992). A distinguished poet, he published four volumes of poetry, the last of which was *My Eightieth Year before Heaven* (2007). In 1990, Cox was decorated a Commander of the British Empire, at which time he was acknowledged for his dedication to the education of British youth.

Guy Davenport (Anderson, South Carolina, 1927–2005) was an essayist, short-story writer, translator, painter, teacher, and scholar. His many books include *Da Vinci's Bicycle: Ten Stories* (Johns Hopkins, 1979), *The Geography of the Imagination: Forty Essays* (David R. Godine, 1981), *The Jules Verne Steam Balloon: Nine Stories* (North Point, 1987), and *The Death of Picasso: New and Selected Writing* (Counterpoint Press,

2005). After a stint teaching at Haverford College from 1961 to 1963, he joined the University of Kentucky faculty, remaining there till his retirement in 1991. In 1990, he received a grant from the John D. and Catherine T. MacArthur Foundation (popularly known as a "genius grant").

Dick Davis (Portsmouth, England, b. 1945) is Emeritus Professor of Persian at Ohio State University. He has written scholarly works on both English and Persian literature, as well as eight volumes of his own poetry. He has published numerous book-length verse translations from Persian, most recently *The Mirror of My Heart: A Thousand Years of Persian Poetry by Women* (Mage Publishers, 2019). Penguin Classics has recently commissioned from him a verse translation of the twelfth-century romance *Layli o Majnun* by Nezami.

Christian N. Desrosiers (Washington, DC, b. 1987) is an MIT-trained artist and entrepreneur who has lived and worked in Indonesia, Somalia, and the United States. He is currently building THE REALITY INSTRUMENT, a sound project that takes real-time sensor data from around the world and applies category theory models to this data to generate a persistent, living music composition.

Jenny Erpenbeck (East Berlin, b. 1967) is the author of works of fiction including *Wörterbuch* (The Book of Words), *Geschichte vom alten Kind* (The Old Child), and *Heimsuchung* (Visitation). She won the Hans Fallada Prize and the Independent Foreign Fiction Prize for her 2012 novel *Aller Tage Abend* (The End of Days). In 2016, she was awarded the Thomas Mann Prize. She still lives in the Eastern part of Berlin.

C. S. Giscombe's (Dayton, Ohio, b. 1950) poetry books are *Here* (1994), *Giscome Road* (1998), and *Prairie Style* (2008), published by Dalkey Archive. His book of linked essays (concerning Canada, race, and family), *Into and Out of Dislocation*, was published by North Point/Farrar, Straus and Giroux. His most recent book is *Similarly* (Dalkey Archive, 2020), a volume of collected and new poetry. His recognitions include the Carl Sandburg Prize (for *Giscome Road*). He teaches at the University of California, Berkeley. He is a long-distance cyclist.

Herbert Gold's (Cleveland, Ohio, b. 1924) numerous books include *Travels in San Francisco* (Arcade Publishing, 1990), *Best Nightmare on Earth: A Life in Haiti* (Prentice Hall, 1991), *Still Alive*, memoir (reprinted as *Not Dead Yet* by Arcade), *When a Psychopath Falls in Love*, novel (Jorvik Press, 2015), and most recently *Nearing the Exit*, poetry (Omertà Publications, 2018). He has been a Fulbright fellow (1950–51), a Guggenheim fellow (1957), and a Ford Foundation grantee (1960).

Tess Lewis (Birmingham, Alabama, b. 1964) is a writer and translator from French and German. Her translations include works by Peter Handke, Walter Benjamin, Anselm Kiefer, Christine Angot, and Philippe Jaccottet. She has won multiple awards, including a Guggenheim Fellowship, the 2017 PEN Translation Award, and the Austrian Cultural Forum NY Translation Prize. She is a fellow of the New York Institute for the Humanities, co-chair of the PEN America Translation Committee, and an advisory editor of the *Hudson Review*.

David Mason (Bellingham, Washington, b. 1954) was Colorado poet laureate from 2010 to 2014. His many books include *Ludlow: A Verse Novel* (Red Hen Press, 2007), *The Sound: New and Selected Poems* (Red Hen Press, 2018), and *Voices, Places: Essays* (Paul Dry Books, 2018). He divides his time between Colorado and Tasmania, where he owns a home looking out on the Southern Ocean. He is an advisory editor of the *Hudson Review*.

Lynda McDonnell (Kansas City, Missouri, b. 1950) is a writer in Minneapolis. Her blog—*A Pilgrim's Way*—can be found at lyndamcdonnell.com.

Charles W. Millard (Elizabeth, New Jersey, 1932–2017) wrote art criticism for the *Hudson Review* from 1967 to 1985. He was a distinguished museum director and renowned expert in nineteenth-century French sculpture; his 1976 book *The Sculpture of Edgar Degas* is considered by many to be definitive. From 1971 to 1974 he was curator of nineteenth-century art at the Los Angeles County Museum, then chief curator of the Hirshhorn Museum and Sculpture Garden (1973–86). From 1986 to 1993 he was director of the Auckland Art Museum at the University of North Carolina, Chapel Hill.

Paul Moore Jr. (Morristown, New Jersey, 1919–2003) was from 1972 to 1989 the thirteenth Episcopal Bishop of the Diocese of New York. He was an outspoken liberal Christian activist. An early proponent of women's ordination, he was the first Episcopal bishop to ordain a gay woman as an Episcopal priest, in 1977. He oversaw the resumption of building of the Cathedral of St. John the Divine, the seat of the diocese, which had been interrupted by World War II.

Antonio Muñoz Molina (Úbeda, Spain, b. 1956), the Spanish novelist and essayist, lives in Madrid. In 2013, he was the recipient of both the Jerusalem Prize and the Prince of Asturias Award for Literature. In 2014, he published the novel *Como la sombra que se va*. The English translation, *Like a Fading Shadow*, was shortlisted for the Man Booker International Prize in 2018.

Laurie Olin (Marshfield, Wisconsin, b. 1938) is one of America's most distinguished landscape architects. He is Practice Professor Emeritus of Landscape Architecture in the Weitzman School of Design at the University of Pennsylvania and the designer of numerous award-winning projects that include Bryant Park in New York, the Getty Center in Los Angeles, the grounds of the Washington Monument in Washington, DC, and the Barnes Foundation in Philadelphia. He has written extensively about landscape design, history, and theory, and is the author of *Across the Open Field* (University of Pennsylvania Press, 1999), *Be Seated* (Applied Research & Design, 2017), and *France Sketchbooks* (ORO Editions, 2019). He was awarded the National Medal of Arts by President Barack Obama in 2013.

John P. Sisk (Spokane, Washington, 1914–97) was for many years a professor at Gonzaga University. Though he began teaching at that university in 1939, he left from 1942 to 1946 to serve as a captain in the Air Force during World War II. A prolific writer, he was the author of more than five hundred articles. His books of essays are *Person and Institution* (1970), *The Tyrannies of Virtue* (1990), and *Being Elsewhere* (1994).

Hilary Spurling (Metropolitan Borough of Stockport, b. 1940) has written biographies of Ivy Compton-Burnett, Paul Scott, Sonia Orwell, and Henri Matisse in two volumes, which won the Whitbread Book of the Year Award and the 2005 Los Angeles Times biography prize. *Pearl Buck in China* won the UK's oldest literary award, the James Tait Black Memorial Prize. Her latest book is *Anthony Powell: Dancing to the Music of Time* (Alfred A. Knopf, 2018).

A. E. Stallings (Decatur, Georgia, b. 1968) is an American poet who has lived in Athens since 1999. Her most recent poetry collection is *Like* (Farrar, Straus and Giroux, 2019), and her two most recent books of verse translation are Hesiod's *Works and Days* (Penguin Classics, 2018) and an illustrated version of the pseudo-Homeric *Battle of the Frogs and the Mice* (Paul Dry Books, 2019).

William Trevor (Mitchelstown, Ireland, 1928–2016) was a celebrated novelist, short-story writer, and playwright. His short-story collections include *The Day We Got Drunk on Cake* (1967), *The Ballroom of Romance* (1972), and *Beyond the Pale* (1981); his novels include *The Old Boys* (1964), *The Children of Dynmouth* (1976), and *Felicia's Journey* (1994). In 2002 he received an honorary knighthood. He was also the recipient of the *Hudson Review*'s 1990 Bennett Award.

Diana Webster (Sydney, Australia, b. 1930) was born in Australia, was educated in England, and has lived most of her life in Finland. She studied English language and literature at Oxford and went on to become a senior lecturer in both at Helsinki University. She has written a large number of books teaching English as a foreign language to young children across the world. She has also worked in radio and TV for Finland and the BBC, and written radio plays broadcast in many countries, essays on travel and English literature, and several nonfiction books published in Finland and the United Kingdom.